To a very

[handwritten signatures]

SENSORY DESIGN

University of Minnesota Press / Minneapolis London

SENSORY DESIGN

Joy Monice Malnar and Frank Vodvarka

This book is supported by a grant from the Graham Foundation for Advanced Studies in the Fine Arts.

The research on immersive virtual reality technology was funded by the National Center for Supercomputing Applications and the Office of the Vice Chancellor for Research at the University of Illinois at Urbana-Champaign under the auspices of the NCSA/UIUC Faculty Fellows Program.

Published by the University of Minnesota Press
111 Third Avenue South, Suite 290
Minneapolis, MN 55401-2520
http://www.upress.umn.edu

Library of Congress Cataloging-in-Publication Data

Malnar, Joy Monice.
    Sensory design / Joy Monice Malnar and Frank Vodvarka.
        p. cm.
Includes bibliographical references and index.
    ISBN 0-8166-3959-0 (HC : alk. paper) — ISBN 0-8166-3960-4 (PB : alk. paper)
    1. Design—Psychological aspects. 2. Senses and sensation.
I. Vodvarka, Frank. II. Title.
NK1520.M29   2004
745.4′01′9—dc22

2003018324

Printed in the United States of America on acid-free paper

The University of Minnesota is an equal-opportunity educator and employer.

12 11 10 09 08 07 06 05 04   10 9 8 7 6 5 4 3 2 1

To Frank and Blanche Vodvarka for all their support and encouragement,

and in memory of Wanda Over, whose affection we still feel.

Contents

Preface

What if we designed for all our senses? Suppose, for a moment, that sound, touch, and odor were treated as the equals of sight, and that emotion was as important as cognition. What would our built environment be like if sensory response, sentiment, and memory were critical design factors, more vital even than structure and program? In this book, we explore the nature of our sensory response to the spatial constructs that people invest with meaning. These range from buildings of various sorts and purposes to gardens to constructions of fantasy. To the degree that this response is calculable, it can serve as a typology for the design of significant spaces. We believe that such a typology would sharply contrast with the Cartesian model that dominates architecture today, resulting in a more humane design.

Architectural types are analogous to character types in literature, approximate categories that serve as context for a specific example. Seen this way, typology is a tool, a structural template for design. Rafael Moneo says that the type is thus the "frame within which change operates."[1] He underscores its importance by concluding: "The design process is a way of bringing the elements of a typology—the idea of a formal structure—into the precise state that characterizes the single work."[2] Modern architectural classification by type really originates with the work of the late-eighteenth-century French architects. Their approach paralleled the methods of the natural sciences, suggesting that architecture was a science as well as an art. The culmination of these efforts may be seen in J. N. L. Durand's *Précis des leçons d'architecture données à l'École royale polytéchnique,* published in 1805. Here he proposed that the design conditions of architecture were social need, convenience, and economy.[3] Durand also recognized that there must be provision for the development of new types in light of the expanding industrial revolution. His system was to identify the elements, or building blocks, of architecture, such as walls, doorways, and so forth. These would be combined into intermediate forms, such as rooms, porches, and the like; these forms were themselves to be joined in still larger units—the building, the street, the city.

It is arguable that one of the less desirable aspects of this "scientific" grounding for architecture has been the emphasis on formal (and, to a lesser degree, symbolic) aesthetics at the expense of the sensory. This is not surprising. Formal design principles lend themselves to being successfully taught, and thus perpetuated in the academies. Certain twentieth-century design movements have found the essentially abstract, impersonal character of formal aesthetics ideologically appropriate. But another reason concerns the perceived difficulty in verifying, much less codifying, principles of sensory response. As opposed to the formal structures of cognition, the senses seem unreliable as design parameters to the architectural community.

We hold an opposing view. We believe that the Cartesian view of typology that has existed for the past two centuries is not only fundamentally at odds with human experience but responsible for some of design's worst disasters. These are both the insidious sort, the gradual desensitizing of an entire culture to the sensuous content of design, and the rather more obvious dramatic housing failures that make the news. Thus Pruitt-Igoe, that infamous low-income housing project in Saint Louis, Missouri, which was dynamited seventeen years after construction, stands for design gone awry. Pruitt-Igoe is not unique: its counterparts can be found in virtually every major city in the world.

The primary problem, we believe, is that sensory data are rarely central to design decisions. In their preface to *Body, Memory, and Architecture,* Kent Bloomer and Charles Moore comment that in the course of their research they found that "reference was seldom made to the unique perceptual and emotional capacities of the human being."[4] On the contrary, they note that there appeared to be an assumption that "architecture is a highly specialized system with a set of prescribed goals rather than a sensual social art responsive to real human desires and feelings."[5] That architecture could appear other than "sensual" is a reflection of its reputation as a dry, calculated art best appreciated cognitively. Thus the comment by Vincent Scully: "The stuff all of us are consuming seems less and less nourishing. It is not surprising that our architecture reflects that condition."[6]

In this book, we examine the assumptions and data that underlie sensory response to spatial types, and the inferences for the future design of spaces. We concentrate on built space but also include spatial types as they occur in nature. These are often profound in character and have served as models for built form throughout history. The reader will find a strong reliance on literary descriptions, as writers depend on words to visualize scenes. If a writer can evoke a sense of place so persuasive that we can clearly envision it, that writer is necessarily aware of its essential characteristics. We also employ drawings, photographs, and illustrations to convey spatial information. Indeed, we contend that successful renditions of places in art, literature, and architectural design rely on shared sensory data, whether invoked or directly experienced. E. V. Walter points out that "a place is a location of experience. It evokes and organizes memories, images, feelings, sentiments, meanings, and the work of imagination. The feelings of a place are indeed the mental projections of individuals, but they come from collective experience and they do not happen anywhere else. They belong to the place."[7]

To repeat our earlier question: what sort of architecture will grow from this attention to our entire human awareness and sensory capacities? There are extant examples, created by designers who have been well aware of their discipline's sensori-emotional dimensions, and we have included many of these throughout our book. Some are centuries old, others are months old; all point the way to the future. Even more, they are *wonderful* in the full sense of that word. But they are, as a glance in any direction will affirm, not numerous. Thus we remain concerned about the still-operative, flawed typology that underlies mainstream architecture, and we offer some suggestions for getting somewhere.

Acknowledgments

This book was generously supported by a grant from the Graham Foundation for Advanced Studies in the Fine Arts. We thank its board of trustees, and Richard Solomon, Ben Weese, Thomas Beeby, and Sally Chapell particularly, for their affirmation of our project's worth. We take this opportunity to thank Stanley Tigerman, Cynthia Weese, Robert A. M. Stern, Carroll William Westfall, Margaret McCurry, George Ranalli, Mary Woolever, and Gary Moore; their influence has been manifested in various and critical ways.

We are grateful to our respective institutions, the University of Illinois at Urbana-Champaign and Loyola University Chicago, for a research leave in the latter case and for timely research grants in both instances. We also thank the National Center for Supercomputing Applications at the University of Illinois at Urbana-Champaign for the 2000–2001 and 2001–2002 Faculty Fellowships, which provided funds and the opportunity to begin the process of designing for sensory response in the immersive virtual reality environment known as the CAVE.

Many colleagues have supported our efforts, and we especially thank Botand Bognar for his help at a critical moment. We very much appreciated the critiques of the preliminary manuscript made by Robert B. Bechtel and Juhani Pallasmaa, which resulted in many changes for the better.

Finally, we wish to recognize each other's particular abilities and expertise in the coauthoring of yet another book. We believe that this multidisciplinary collaboration has been beneficial in producing a balanced and incisive critique of architecture's current state.

1. Spatial Constructs

The distinguished writer Henry James first visited Italy in 1869 and returned in 1872 as the Rome correspondent for *The Nation*. The result of his many years of travel is a collection of lucid impressions gathered under the title *Italian Hours*. In it he describes the garden of the Villa Medici, which he considered one of the most enchanting places in Rome:

> The part of the garden called the Boschetto has an incredible, impossible charm; an upper terrace, behind locked gates, covered with a little dusky forest of evergreen oaks. Such a dim light as of a fabled, haunted place, such a soft suffusion of tender grey-green tones, such a company of gnarled and twisted little miniature trunks . . . and such a shower of golden sparkles drifting in from the vivid west! At the end of the wood is a steep, circular mound . . . with a long mossy staircase climbing up to a belvedere. This staircase, rising suddenly out of the leafy dusk to you don't see where, is delightfully fantastic. . . . The blessing in Rome is not that this or that or the other isolated object is so very unsurpassable; but that the general air so contributes to interest, to impressions that are not as any other impressions anywhere in the world. And it is from this general air the Villa Medici has distilled an essence of its own—walled it in and made it delightfully private.[1]

James's descriptions are likewise delightful, conveying a profound sense of place through his vivid observations. But it is his underlying assumptions about the essential nature of place that interest us here (Figure 1.1).

First of all, for James, the term "place" always refers to *a* place, one whose composition is highly individual (if not unique). Second, while the composition is

Figure 1.1. Jan Frans van Bloemen (called Orizzonte), *Garden Scene with Two Statues (Garden of the Villa Medici)*, c. 1710–1720. Courtesy of Los Angeles County Museum of Art. Purchased with funds provided by Frank Ellsworth. Photograph copyright 2001 Museum Associates, Los Angeles County Museum of Art. Museum number AC1993.6.1.

individual, the elements that form it are common to the milieu. Thus the Boschetto has a special quality such that James feels compelled to comment, yet he recognizes that this quality is characteristic of Rome itself. Third, a place is always sensed. While the emphasis in this description is on the visual aspect, James makes clear throughout his work that all the senses human beings have at their disposal are required to fully comprehend the nature of a particular place. For James, sense of place meant just that—a place sensed. Fourth, it is clear that he has brought with him a particular mental set when he notes the "dim light as of a fabled, haunted place." That is, his perception is affected by some prior qualitative definition relating to the symbolic attributes of light. Finally, James is intrigued by what the garden does not reveal, by the opportunity to exercise his imagination—a quality that he calls "delightfully fantastic."

Thus, while his observation of the garden at the Villa Medici has involved the perception of a physical construct, the assessment of its individual composition has been formed in relation to a larger characteristic pattern. Memories of prior personal and cultural experiences play their part in conditioning his perception of these patterns, and delight is found in the intrigue generated by what remains unsaid. By virtue of these factors, James has experienced a sense of place so persuasive that he could happily spend all of his days there, "unpreoccupied, untormented, pensioned, satisfied."[2]

It is this totality of factors that we describe as a spatio-sensory construct, although the situation is far more complex than has so far been suggested. The constructs that we are interested in are, in the main, examples of what Gaston Bachelard refers to as felicitous space, "the sorts of space that may be grasped, that may be defended against adverse forces, the space we love. For diverse reasons, and with the differences entailed by poetic shadings, this is eulogized space."[3] And Bachelard points out that space that has been so seized upon by the human imagination can never remain indifferent space subject to physical measurement alone.[4]

Eulogized spaces need not be epic; on the contrary, the spatial constructs that we eulogize are often quite prosaic, enjoying a "special" quality in our eyes alone. In *You Can't Go Home Again*, Thomas Wolfe describes such a room as seen through the eyes of an important character, Mr. Jack:

It was a spacious chamber, twenty feet each way and twelve feet high, and in these noble proportions was written quietly a message of luxurious well-being and assurance. In the exact center of the wall that faced the door stood his bed, a chaste four-poster of the Revolutionary period, and beside it a little table holding a small clock, a few books, and a lamp. In the center of another wall was an antique chest of drawers, and tastefully arranged about the room were a gate-legged table, with a row of books and the latest magazines upon it, two fine old Windsor chairs, and a comfortable, well-padded easy chair. . . . The total effect was one of modest and almost austere simplicity, subtly combined with a sense of spaciousness, wealth, and power. The owner of this room read its message with pleasure.[5]

The response of Mr. Jack may seem somewhat odd to the distanced observer who is judging the room by its physical characteristics alone. For example, a twenty-by-twenty-by-twelve-foot room does not possess "noble proportions" in the sense of any classical proportional system. It is, however, large by urban standards, and thus significant in the eyes of its owner. And the furnishings—enjoying high social status individually—seem rather austere when placed in such a large room. But for Mr. Jack they possess a certain dignity and restraint. Even the reserved tone exuded by the multiply placed books—icons of culture—is carefully balanced by the presence of "the latest magazines." This, then, is the individual and eulogized space of someone who "liked what was solid, rich, and spacious . . . who liked order in everything."[6]

There is, of course, a significant difference between the descriptions of the two authors. James has related his depiction of a real place, one he greatly admires, for the purpose of inducing in the reader a parallel spatial experience. For Wolfe, the description is a fictional device calculated to reveal certain aspects of his character's personality. For this purpose he has omitted the very attribute that James had most delighted in, the sense of mystery. James's highly romantic point of view would be entirely foreign to Mr. Jack's personality, and so Wolfe, having no less a sense of place than James, has avoided it. It is, of course, arguable that we all arrange our rooms in the manner of Mr. Jack, that is, to impress our public (which includes ourselves).

Spatial constructs can be metaphorical; amorphous spaces customized to our particular psychic needs. Jorge Luis Borges depicts such a space, a labyrinth in the City of the Immortals, which his protagonist describes as follows:

> A labyrinth is a structure compounded to confuse men; its architecture, rich in symmetries, is subordinated to that end. In the palace I imperfectly explored, the architecture lacked any such finality. It abounded in dead-end corridors, high unattainable windows, portentous doors which led to a cell or pit, incredible inverted stairways whose steps and balustrades hung downwards. Other stairways, clinging airily to the side of the monumental wall, would die without leading anywhere, after making two or three turns in the lofty darkness of the cupolas . . . "This city" (I thought) "is so horrible that its mere existence and perdurance, though in the midst of a secret desert, contaminates the past and the future and in some way even jeopardizes the stars. As long as it lasts, no one in the world can be strong or happy." I do not want to describe it; a chaos of heterogeneous words, the body of a tiger or a bull in which teeth, organs and heads monstrously pullulate in mutual conjunction and hatred can (perhaps) be approximate images.[7]

In the first place, the reference to the labyrinth in the first sentence is not a definition but an elaboration of a definition. Borges assumes that we are already familiar with the nature of labyrinths, both from common dictionary denotation (a complicated network of paths intended to confuse) and as classical spatial paradigm. Romedi Passini notes that the oldest interpretation of its origin traces its provenance to the

Greek *Labrus,* or "double ax." As the sign of the double ax appeared both on labyrinthine caverns on Crete and the Palace of the Double Ax at Knossos *(laburinthos),* the palace is thought to be the source of the term.[8] Thus, in this latter case, Borges is making explicit reference to an architectural type, represented by the labyrinth housing the Minotaur. His negative allusion to the type's "rich symmetries" (the hallmark of classicism) being subordinated to confusion's ends raises a question of equivalent dualities, and the confusion or paralysis that can result from having to choose between them. His special situation, lacking "any such finality [of choice]," is even worse than usual (Figure 1.2).

His references to architectural elements such as corridors, windows, doors, and stairways are even more poignant. All these elements have lost their nominal function while remaining semiotically familiar. This situation is so horrifying to the protagonist, such an architectural betrayal, that he believes it to constitute a crime against history and all the humanity that has lived it. The last sentence asserts that this proliferation of nonfunctioning equivalencies makes up a "chaos of heterogeneity," such that hatred can be manifested in "approximate images." (In this, Borges suggests a deliberate assault on the protagonist's sensibilities, but the truth, as it turns out, is even more bizarre.)[9]

Of interest here is his assumption that we understand the character and implications of architectural typology. That is, Borges uses our general knowledge of types to enrich the effect of his labyrinth. Architectural types, in this sense, can serve the same literary end as character types—approximate categories that serve as context for a specific example. This is consistent with the general meaning of architectural type, which, according to Rafael Moneo, "can most simply be defined as a concept which

Figure 1.2. Frank Vodvarka, *Palace of the Immortals,* 1995.

describes a group of objects characterized by the same formal structure. . . . It is fundamentally based on the possibility of grouping objects by certain inherent structural similarities."[10] Moneo's definition of "formal structure" should not be construed as narrowly physical; as he makes clear, the notion of formal structure includes "a vast hierarchy of concerns running from social activity to building construction" (24). As this range of facts changes through time and place, the type will need to be altered accordingly. Moneo concludes that the type is thus the frame within which change operates (27). Works of architecture can not only be described by reference to type but aided in their creation as well. Thus he makes the following statement: "The design process is a way of bringing the elements of a typology—the idea of a formal structure—into the precise state that characterizes the single work" (23).

In a direct reference to Aldo Rossi, Malcolm Quantrill states: "The typology is a general design that becomes the basis for cultural action which generates a particular architectural form."[11] The implication is that while it is commonly believed that there exists a precise architectural type for a particular purpose, type should really be seen as collective memory given structural form. That is, type is ambiguous, what Terrance Goode refers to as "an abstraction, that over time becomes accepted and conventionalized."[12] And Goode notes that Quatremère de Quincy, to whom we shortly return, describes these sorts of cultural associations as "perpetuated by custom, perfected by taste, and accredited by immemorial usage" (2). Thus type is primarily concerned not with images that can be imitated but with an abstract idea that can serve as a rule; what remains vague in the type can be concretized in the model (2).

The distinction is important: a type is a general, abstract ordering of spatial elements reflecting broad cultural peculiarities; a model is a concretized image that reflects a particular spatial order responding to a specific situation. In short, the model is the type made both perceptible and acceptable within a given social context. Malcolm Quantrill points out that the typology gives only an example of the process of spatial ordering. The model provides a picture of a particular piece of this process in operation, and that model may therefore be copied.[13] The typology thus provides a design base that considers socially accepted form and its historical evolution, which are indispensable for the development of a model. Quantrill clearly refers to this when he notes the value of typology as a measuring stick for identifying persistent architectural responses to conscious rituals.[14]

Of special importance in all this is the concept of type as a creative instrument— a necessary part of the design process—as well as a passive method of historical or morphological analysis. Micha Bandini, for example, identifies three differing attitudes that have informed recent studies of typology: as a means of understanding the morphological aspects of the urban fabric; as a way of discussing architecture in stylistic and cultural terms; and as a theoretical tool for the production of architecture.[15] He maintains that the strongest emphasis has been placed on the third approach, which is dealt with either in treatise form (Quatremère) or as the concept that informs the metaproject (Rossi, the Krier brothers, et al.).[16]

In their discussion of contemporary contextual approaches to typology at the Ecole des Beaux-Arts, Ahmet Gulgonen and François Laisney define type as "characterized by a class of objects with similar and permanent peculiarities, which depend upon the criteria used."[17] This is consistent with the structure of scientific classification systems. In architecture, this takes the form of the material and cultural productions of architects within a society, whose works can stand "as intellectual instruments which permit the introduction of 'memory' into the explication, conception and production of buildings" (26). These authors rely on a demarcation they call the three conceptual poles of typology. The first regards typology as the totality of the peculiarities that characterize the architectural production of a society or social class at a given moment, the second is based on its spatial and formal characteristics, and the third classifies buildings according to their use and institutional character (26). They contend that the last view is typical of nineteenth-century French theoreticians such as J. N. L. Durand.[18]

The common theme in these approaches is the usefulness of type as a spatio-cultural benchmark. It has been pointed out that to design within a traditional context, with shared assumptions between designer and audience, is an advantage in terms of communication and the decision-making process.[19] The practice of late, however, has been to reject the nuances of traditional structure in favor of viewing types as simple geometric constructs open to adaptation. (This may be seen as an outgrowth of the second definition expressed by Gulgonen and Laisney.) Alan Colquhoun regards such latitude as illusory:

> We are *not* free from the forms of the past, and from the availability of these forms as typological models, but that, if we assume we are free, we have lost control over a very active sector of our imagination, and our power to communicate with others. It would seem that we ought to try to establish a value system which takes into account the forms and solutions of the past, if we are to gain control over concepts which will obtrude themselves into the creative process, whether we like it or not.[20]

Now, the image of typology that emerges from the preceding analysis is dissimilar from our concept of spatio-sensory construct in a major respect: it is usually used to refer to aspects of the architectural experience other than the sensory. Indeed, if sensory response is calculated at all, it is that response it is thought we ought to feel. Thus the sensuous immediacy found in the literary descriptions is avoided in favor of physical, functional, and symbolic concerns. We believe that this comparatively limited view of typology is largely due to the influence of the scientific classification systems that marked intellectual life during the late eighteenth century, as well as the industrial and mercantile mandates of the nineteenth century that found them useful. It is a view that has prevailed for two centuries, proving useful to rationalists and followers of the beaux arts alike. (Gulgonen and Laisney have, of course, based their organizational structure on the principles of scientific classification used by these French theorists.)

One of the earliest forms of architectural classification by type can be seen in the pattern books of the rococo designers. In his *Cours d'architecture* (1771), Jacques François Blondel listed the variety of building types and programs that architects should be aware of, stating that each should attain its "own manner of being, suitable for it alone, or those of its kind."[21] This system paralleled developments in the natural sciences, thus suggesting a scientific basis for architecture. (The drive toward the quantification of design theory became so imperative that Anthony Vidler states: "The search for the origins of architecture was for the Enlightenment architect tantamount to the discovery of the true principles of his art.")[22] Blondel further declared that architecture should carry the imprint of each building's intention and possess a character that determines the general form and declares the building for what it is.[23]

Perhaps the most seminal work published in the eighteenth century was Antoine Quatremère de Quincy's three-volume *Encyclopédie méthodique d'architecture,* in which he defined a wide range of theoretical interests in a dictionary format. It was to serve students and professionals and reveal "the universality of knowledge comprised by the subject."[24] Architecture, as he saw it, was "the art of characterizing, that is to say, rendering sensible by material forms the intellectual qualities and moral ideas which can be expressed in buildings; or of making known by means of the accord and suitability of all the constituent parts of a building, its nature, propriety, use, destination."[25] While this assertion reveals an impulse to definition, it by no means represents the sort of narrow view represented by Gulgonen and Laisney's third category of typology. On the contrary, what Quatremère refers to is architecture that captures the essence of its milieu, rather than mechanically relying on any overt format from the past.

Thus it is unlikely that Quatremère was responsible for either the absolute authority accorded the fixed, programmatic typology of the Ecole des Beaux-Arts or the structural priorities of the rationalists. This honor fell, rather, to Jean-Nicolas-Louis Durand, whose *Recuiel et parallèle des édifices en tout genre anciens et modernes* was published in 1801. In this work Durand organized a comparative taxonomy of types depicting all the known building types, "classified according to their kinds, arranged in order of degree of likeness and drawn to the same scale."[26] He was aided by the architect and historian J. G. Legrand, who wrote the text that accompanied Durand's illustrations.[27] Anthony Vidler notes that this "comparative method allowed Durand to arrange his specimens on the page as if in natural progression from the most primitive type to the refined versions of the present. The plans 'perfected themselves,' as it were, graphically on each page, crystallizing in ever higher forms."[28]

In the major work that followed, his *Précis des leçons d'architecture données à l'École Royale Polytéchnique*, Durand said that the design conditions of architecture were social need, convenience, and economy: "Whether one consults reason, or examines the monuments [of history] themselves, it is evident that to please has never been the object. Utility for the public and for society, such is the goal of architecture."[29] Durand realized the need to provide for the development [or evolution] of new types, especially given the new, programmatic needs of industry. His solution was to identify the basic elements of architecture—the walls, columns, windows, and doorways—which could then be combined into intermediate forms, such as stairs, rooms, porches, and the like. These intermediate forms were then joined in still larger units. This was consistent with his view of architecture as "the composition of the whole of buildings, which is nothing other than the result of the assemblage of their parts."[30] But of even greater importance was the system he employed (Figure 1.3).

His method was to divide a square into the smallest units of design. After drawing his plan on this "gridded" paper, he placed the various architectural elements on the main and subsidiary axes required to link the rooms. This process is what Durand meant by the term "composition." Composition, then, was the system of laws that regulate the final assemblage of basic elements, each to each, and to the larger architectural entity.[31] Durand compared his concept of composition to the older notion of distribution, which he defined as "the art of putting in order, according to our habits, the different parts that compose a dwelling."[32] Composition, in his view, was not only more fundamental in nature but universally applicable as well, attributes that likely reflected the methodology of scientific classification.

Anthony Vidler observes: "In one sense the division of architecture into its fundamental constructive elements, each reduced to its essential geometrical form, and the combinatory system for these elements—horizontally in plan, vertically in elevation—used to make up the rooms, circulation systems and ensembles of buildings, was a

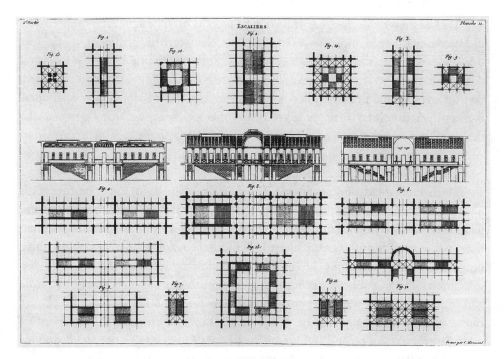

Figure 1.3. Plate from J. N. L. Durand, *Précis des leçons d'architecture données à l'École Royale Polytéchnique,* 1823. Courtesy of the Ricker Library, University of Illinois at Urbana-Champaign.

direct and logical outcome of the rational classification of the Enlightenment."[33] Durand's system proved useful to the nineteenth century for many reasons, among them the provision for a design approach responsive to the industrial mandate, and the insightful drawing of certain parallels with language patterns. It is an approach to composition that relies on a careful adjustment of parts to each other, and parts to the whole, organized on major and minor axes. He believed that this system was so flexible and adaptable that it afforded myriad solutions to any architectural problem. The move from distribution to composition, however, resulted in as least as much lost as gained.

Sergio Villari points out that this resulted in a radical redefinition of architecture as something produced by a composition of parts: "The *single, entire,* and *well-finished* Palladian body, already reeling under the blows of the baroque principle of hierarchy, is shattered now by the nearly serial composition of its elements. In particular the architectural space explodes, fracturing itself, its supposedly eternal indissolubility threatened at the core. The fragments now have need of a norm that can govern their combinatory order."[34] And what would the nature of that norm be? Part of the answer comes from Durand's own operational principles. His belief in the mission of architecture, utility for the public, was conditioned by his further belief that architectural beauty derived from economy being joined to convenience.[35] Thus Durand maintained that "the arrangement in all cases is the only thing with which the architect should be occupied, it is this arrangement that should be as proper and economic as it can be."[36]

This seems a rather modern approach to architectural design, but it was echoed in his own day. For example, Jean-Baptiste Rondelet wrote his highly influential text *Traité théorique et practique de l'art de batir* in 1802. As the title indicates, the book deals with construction techniques, but it is clear that he intended it to serve as a text for architectural practice. He wrote: "Theory is a science which directs all operations of practice. It is by the means of theory that a clever constructor arrives at the determination of the forms and just dimensions that he must give each part of an edifice, in light of its situation, and the efforts that it might support in order for it to result in perfection, solidity, and economy."[37]

Much of Durand's influence was felt through his pedagogical texts, in which he suggests a methodology—consisting of abstraction and standardization—critical to cast-iron construction. Put differently, the methodology of industrialism required that architectural form be amenable to specification by kind, an abstract, cognitive process. Durand's system provided the rationale for the forms of the marketplaces, exhibition halls, and railway stations of the nineteenth century. And if the mercantile and industrial interests of that period found it useful, twentieth-century developers found it economically convenient. What, in the hands of Quatremère, had been an open, abstract system became in Durand's textbooks a fixed catalog of parts.[38] And his emphasis on composition became largely defined by structure and program.

It can be argued that typology itself is simply a manifestation of the centuries-old "hegemony of the eye" that characterizes European cultural history. (Indeed, the root of the word "idea" is the Greek *idein*, to see, thus relating vision to intellectual under-standing.) Hans Blumenberg points out: "For Greek thought, all certainty was based on visibility. What *logoi* referred back to was a sight with form, i.e., *eidos.* . . . *Logos* is a collection of what has been seen."[39] Not that one could entirely trust any sense in comparison to reason, as Plato makes clear in his allegory of the cave. No one would argue that the Greeks denied the sensuous life; on the contrary, they lived it with great joy. But, as Anthony Synnott makes clear, "the Greek tradition insisted on drawing a clear distinction between the senses and the mind, and on the epistemo-logical and metaphysical superiority of the latter. The senses had a place, but that place was low."[40] Still, of the senses, Plato did accord primacy to sight as the founda-tion of philosophy. And Aristotle continued this line of thought, regarding sight as the most highly developed of the senses.[41] Thus sight was granted some degree of validity, primarily on the grounds that it was "enlightening." It is probably for this reason, as well as its obvious utility, that sight became the dominant sensory modal-ity in Western culture.[42]

What this also points to is the dichotomy between the value of the senses and the abiding suspicion they were held in, particularly during the early Christian era. (It is arguable that we continue to be ambivalent about the pleasures of the sensuous, much less the sensual.) Still, the "hegemony of the eye" really begins in the fifteenth century, when several inventions ensured its dominance. The first is the invention of geometric perspective, which sought to render the visible, three-dimensional world systematically comprehensible, even measurable, on a two-dimensional plane. It is a fascinating system that, in its utter regularity, suggests that it is correct despite having little basis in the facts of human perception. For the artists and architects of the Renaissance, such a system seemed a boon, although its real significance probably lay in the areas of politics and philosophy.[43] The second invention was the development of systematic drawings such as the plan, elevation, and section to render designed space intelligible. What had been the province of the master builder applying a store of knowledge in situ instead became the work of the designer communicating infor-mation to construction workers. Thus Filippo Brunelleschi's use of modular units of structure in San Spirito in Florence (1434), as well as drawn plans, was to have conse-quences for centuries to come in terms of reinforcing the visual bias.

Another major development of the fifteenth century was the invention of movable type, first demonstrated in the printing of the Gutenberg Bible. Indeed, the invention of the phonetic alphabet was itself a remarkable event. Marshall McLuhan has stated that "lineal, alphabetic inditing made possible the sudden invention of 'grammars' of thought and science by the Greeks. These grammars or explicit spellings out of per-sonal and social processes were visualizations of non-visual functions and relations."[44] McLuhan goes to great length to differentiate between ideogrammic and phonetic languages: "No pictographic or ideogrammic or hieroglyphic mode of writing has the detribalizing power of the phonetic alphabet. No other kind of writing save the phonetic has ever translated man out of the possessive world of total interdependence and interrelation that is the auditory network."[45] Nevertheless, it was not until the invention of movable type that the printed phonetic word—what McLuhan refers to as a "hot and explosive medium"—became the pervasive shaper of thought that it remains, television notwithstanding. To state the obvious, it did this through the eye.

The sixteenth and seventeenth centuries were to further exploit visual characteristics as tools of political, economic, and cultural propaganda, so profoundly that it is arguable that social classification based on visual characteristics preceded scientific classification. The epitome of this can be seen at the court of the "Sun King," Louis XIV, whose attention to the visual message was comprehensive. It is not surprising, then, that eighteenth-century typology, the stepchild of scientific classification and based on formal similarities, would be devised in relation to this ongoing visual dominance. But architectural typology is not simply an effect; its influence has become so pervasive that, in one form or another, it continues to shape the buildings we live with despite its apparent inadequacies. In contrast, we view typology as a construct that in light of particular cultural circumstances generates a concretized architectural model. We believe that such a construct—in contrast to the older definition—is fully sensory. Thus we do not fault typology as an idea, only its current assumptions and form.

But what, it can be asked, is the genesis of typology? It seems clear that the idea of type depends on even more fundamental concerns. Aldo Rossi states: "The *type* developed according to both needs and aspirations to beauty; a particular type was associated with a form and a way of life, although its specific shape varied widely from society to society. The concept of type thus became the basis of architecture"[46] The reason for the variance in response is that the type is the abstract framework of spatial ordering, while the model is the refined spatial form that derives from it. But there remains the task of defining these "needs and aspirations to beauty," and how they became expressed in a particular form.

This task is formidable. Types are usually so long established that their origins have become obscure. One position maintains, however, that they are the products of an initial impetus, the primordial archetype, which embodies the original and profound set of human circumstances. One of Carl Jung's contributions to an understanding of typology was to forward concepts such as collective unconscious, archetype, and symbol. Jung contrasted the notions of personal unconscious, earlier postulated by Sigmund Freud, with the collective unconscious, a deeper layer that does not derive from personal experience and is therefore universal: "In contrast to the personal psyche, it has contents and modes of behavior that are more or less the same everywhere and in all individuals. It is, in other words, identical in all men and thus constitutes a common psychic substrate of a suprapersonal nature which is present in every one of us."[47]

Jung theorized that the collective unconscious connected human beings to their primordial past through its contents, which he designated archetypes. He contended that certain "motives" appear to repeat themselves in almost identical form in the mythology and folklore of different peoples. This allowed him to "understand forms or images of a collective nature which occur practically all over the earth as constituents of myths and at the same time as autochthonous, individual products of unconscious origin."[48] These are the universal images that have existed for humans for as long as they have endured. Thus, the term *archetype* "designates only those psychic contents which have not yet been submitted to conscious elaboration and are therefore an immediate datum of psychic experience. . . . The archetype is essentially an unconscious content that is altered by becoming conscious and by being perceived, and it takes its color from the individual consciousness in which it happens to appear."[49] The archetype, upon entering the conscious mind, assumes an evocative and multifaceted symbolic form. Thus the archetype may be seen as the generator of the type, which in turn produces a situational model.

Jung's concept of the archetype has never found universal favor. This seems, however, to be less related to its mechanism than his insistence on its biological basis. For Jung, archetypes were not only universal in character but subject to involuntary recall. Human beings have the capacity to color these images but not substantively control them. Jung argued that archetypal ideas "have their origin in the archetype, which in itself is an irrepresentable, unconscious, pre-existent form that seems to be part of the inherited structure of the psyche."[50] He later makes reference to "its instinctual nature."[51] In even clearer support for a biological foundation, he states: "The archetypal motives presumably start from the archetypal patterns of the human mind which are not only transmitted by tradition and migration but also by heredity."[52]

As this position lacks any empirical confirmation, Jung's hypothesis does not satisfy scientific methodology. Indeed, it has been pointed out that the unconscious cannot possibly be an object of direct scientific inquiry.[53] On the contrary, it is conscious experience that provides the basis for hypotheses about the unconscious. A necessary corollary to this situation is that Jung was compelled to rely on metaphor and analogy to describe the mechanisms of the unconscious, particularly when he sought to substantiate the method of inheritance and depict their contents.[54] There is, however, no reason to reject metaphor when describing motivation, nor can mnemonic content be rejected by scientific method. Truly, the degree to which assumptions about the universality of cultural "drives" permeate the social sciences is remarkable.[55]

Jung attempted to clarify his position in "The Spirit of Psychology," written in 1946, where he says that "archetypes are typical forms of behavior which, once they become conscious, naturally present themselves as ideas and images, like everything else that becomes a content of consciousness."[56] Thus he stressed the mechanism rather than its derivation.[57] Jung's position is illuminated by Jolande Jacobi when she notes that "Jung's archetypes are a structural condition of the psyche, which in a certain constellation (of an inward and outward nature) can bring forth certain 'patterns'—and . . . this has nothing to do with the inheriting of definite images. . . . For this reason it should be stressed that the archetypes are not inherited representations, but inherited *possibilities* of representation."[58] Only, Jacobi says, "when the archetypes come into contact with the conscious mind, that is, when the light of consciousness falls on them and their contours begin to emerge from the darkness and to fill with individual content, can the conscious mind differentiate them" (66). Jung maintained that for such psychic entities to become conscious content, they had to have the quality of an image—to be *representable* (66).

It would follow that a major task of the designer is to give perceptible form to the common, elemental patterns that lie within our unconscious, so that the resultant image appears authentic. Bettina L. Knapp refers to this phenomenon:

> The creative artist—architect or writer—ushers into existence mirror images of what lies inchoate within his depths. These he develops, molds, extracts from that limit-less oceanic sphere existing dynamically and vitally within him which is referred to as the collective unconscious. As the inner eye sweeps into the hidden layers and secret folds of this world inaccessible to consciousness, it seizes universal motifs and cultural manifestations of all sorts, which have been the common heritage of all beings since time immemorial. It is the artist or architect who provides shape, line, and mass to these amorphous images that have been dredged up from subliminal spheres. . . . Whatever the path, the nothingness that existed in the void took on form and became something, definable and electrifying.[59]

Thus would the archetype be brought into its symbolic form, the type. No small thing, this. Jung said that whoever speaks with such "primordial images" speaks "with a thousand voices; he enthralls and overpowers, while at the same time he lifts the idea he is trying to express out of the occasional and the transitory into the realm of the ever-enduring."[60]

How, then, does archetype become type, a symbolic (and evocative) image with tangible characteristics? Jacobi explains that it is necessary to "distinguish the arche-types of the collective unconscious, which work upon the ego from the depths of the psyche and influence it in the direction of specific human behavior . . . from the archetypes of the *collective consciousness* as representatives of the typical norms, customs, and views prevailing in a particular environment" (110). She notes that when the archetype enters consciousness, the raw material of imagery and meaning are added, and thus the symbol is born (120). It is precisely this symbolic entity—born of primordial urge and endowed with cultural values—that we refer to as type. (The ongoing argument over heredity we will leave to others.)

While avoiding any mention of "collective unconscious," Malcolm Quantrill is referring to something very like "universal motifs and cultural manifestations" when he notes that architectural form "is capable of connecting us to the deep well of human consciousness, keeping open the channels of historical continuity by the myths, ideas, rituals, and events which it represents."[61] Type really derives much of its authenticity from its capacity to spiritually, symbolically, and sensually embody these aspects (whether called archetype or human consciousness), and its usefulness for the degree to which it inspires coherent models. And what may be most important are the ways in which these primordial drives evoke human response, such that the type carries authority. That is, what perceptible form does the type assume in order to be recognized, and in what manner does such recognition necessarily involve our senses?

If architecture is "capable of keeping open the channels of historical continuity," in no type are these properties more potently expressed than one's house. Such a concept helps explain the affection for our domiciles, and the emphasis accorded aspects of the house like entries and hearths, which are often considered sacred. In his autobiography, Jung had occasion to explain a dream in which he found himself exploring the interior of a two-story house. He began his journey on the upper floor and descended through the ground floor to the cellar, finally ending in a cave below the cellar. Each layer reached farther back in time: "It was plain to me that the house represented a kind of image of the psyche—that is to say, of my then state of consciousness, with hitherto unconscious additions. . . . The deeper I went, the more alien and the darker the scene became. In the cave, I discovered remains of a primitive culture, that is the world of the primitive man within myself."[62] He realized that his dream pointed to a cultural history consisting of successive layers of consciousness, thus suggesting an impersonal nature underlying the psyche. These layers he later recognized as forms of instinct, or archetypes (161). But of greater importance for our purposes is the fully sensory character of Jung's perception of his house.

Some question arises, for example, as to precisely how Jung identified each of these spaces as being from a certain period, thus establishing his epochs. That is, what sort of consciously evolved typology informed his perception, and how did those types appear to him? As he relates the actual dream, he notes that the upper floor appeared as "a kind of salon furnished with fine old pieces in rococo style" (159). He comments, with approbation, that the walls were covered with precious old paintings. As he descended the stairs to the first floor, he realized that this part of the house was much older, as the furnishings were medieval, and the floors were of red brick (159). It was then that he discovered a "heavy door," behind which lay a stairway leading to an ancient cellar. This cellar, he concluded, must be Roman because of the type of brickwork in the walls. Finally, he descended to the cave below the cellar, which held the remains of an ancient culture, by means of a stairway of narrow stone steps leading downward (159). Thus at each stage of his dream journey he relied on a previous knowledge of architectural types, with their objectified attributes, and a range of distinct spatial sensations. In short, he relied on a "sense of place" in his house paradigm or spatio-sensory construct.

An equally profound importance has been granted to the house by Gaston Bachelard, who states that "our house is our corner of the world . . . it is our first universe, a real cosmos in every sense of the word."[63] As such, he points out, "the house is one of the greatest powers of integration for the thoughts, memories and dreams of mankind (6). The house shelters the daydreamer and provides a site for memory.

If it is a complex house, with an attic and cellar, as well as niches and corridors, memories will be more clearly delineated than in a featureless space (Figure 1.4). Bachelard suggests a name for the study of spatial memories, topoanalysis, "the systematic psychological study of the sites of our intimate lives" (8). These memories are highly evocative because they exist outside the normal flow of measured time. Bachelard states, "In its countless alveoli space contains compressed time. That is what space is for" (8).

Two of Bachelard's ideas seem especially important. He states, "A house that has been experienced is not an inert box. Inhabited space transcends geometrical space" (47). This statement, in conjunction with an earlier comment, "all really inhabited space bears the essence of the notion of home," suggests the generative role of the habitation (5). The second comment is significant, as it clearly suggests that the critical quality of a house is its suitability as a place of dwelling. It is precisely this idea that Martin Heidegger refers to in *Poetry, Language, Thought:* "Man's relation to locations, and through locations to spaces, inheres in his dwelling. The relationship between man and space is none other than dwelling, strictly thought and spoken."[64] This points, however, to the even greater significance of the first of Bachelard's ideas, that of the vitality of "inhabited" space; to wit, how is such space experienced?

E. V. Walter observes that the moral and emotional qualities of a place grant it its familiar characteristics. He thus concludes that for a person living in a place with bad experiences, "The elegance of the 'space' or its rational appeal will hardly determine whether a person stays there or moves away. The action in the place . . . and the sense of how good or bad it is will probably be decisive."[65] This also explains the deep attachment people have for what seem, on the surface, unremarkable buildings. Such intense reactions to the perceptible attributes of buildings, coupled with the desire for spatial permanence, may account for the public's affection for older houses in established neighborhoods, as well as the obvious hostility to typical housing developments. For the most part, these developments replace a living record of human dwelling with a pure form unrelated to experience. Martin Pawley notes that neither the notion of consumer housing nor demolition recognizes "the importance of place or known objects, and neither comprehends the significance of the kind of behavioural history that accompanies and stabilizes successive generational occupations of the same dwelling."[66]

The power of place to act as a repository of memory is attested to by Thomas Wolfe in *You Can't Go Home Again:*

> He loved this old house on Twelfth Street, its red brick walls, its rooms of noble height and spaciousness, its old dark woods and floors that creaked; and in the magic of the moment it seemed to be enriched and given a profound and lonely dignity by all the human beings it had sheltered in its ninety years. The house became like a living presence. Every object seemed to have an animate vitality of its own—walls, rooms, chairs, tables, even a half-wet bath towel hanging from the shower ring above the tub.[67]

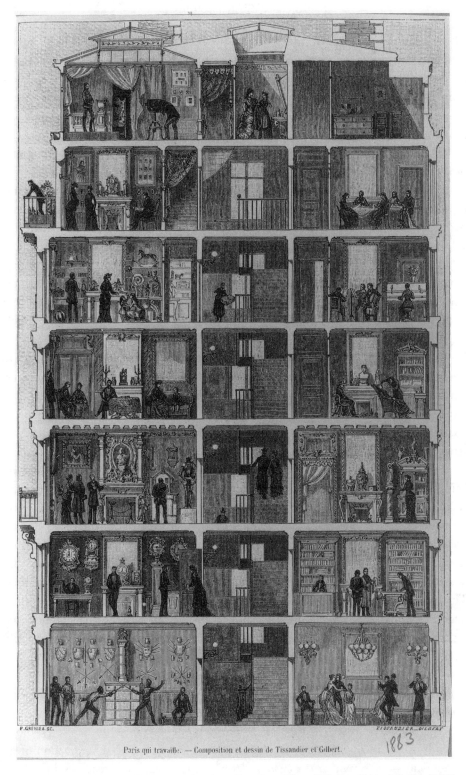

Figure 1.4. *Paris qui travaille: Composition et dessin de Tissander et Gilbert,* 1883. From Kubler Collection (2778), Cooper-Hewitt, National Design Museum, Smithsonian Institution. Courtesy of Art Resource, N.Y. Photograph by Matt Flynn.

This citation confirms that the location-spaces that result from dwelling require concrete form to be perceived. In a similar vein, Bachelard reflects on the nature of daydreaming; "faced with these periods of solitude, the topoanalyst starts to ask questions: Was the room a large one? Was the garret cluttered up? Was the nook warm? How was it lighted? How too, in these fragments of space, did the human being achieve silence?"[68]

Malcolm Quantrill describes the sensory aspects of our environment as the *genius loci,* or sense of place: "The very concept, spirit of place, depends upon the particular relationship of things to each other in a particular place."[69] Thus we may conceive environmental frameworks that conform to an underlying order of things, but we perceive those frameworks in terms of particular characteristics of form, material, color, directional emphasis, and so on, which provide a distinctive set of images to a building or place. A familiarity with places and spaces increases their mnemonic potency, so that time becomes compressed into memorable spatial images, "generating an architecture of spatial consciousness."[70] This combines with the ability of built form to provide continuity by representation of cultural myths and rituals (Figure 1.5).

We may conclude that the milieu reflects archetypal concerns—the collective unconscious—such that social amalgamations (like cities) take on a general character; but that the specific spatial construct usually takes its final form from the imperatives of the personal unconscious, the individual experience. (Thus spatial constructs are metaphorical as well as literal and rely on prior knowledge as well as immediate sensation.) An important corollary to this notion is that while the experience of archetypes is unconscious, the experience of type is conscious and sensate. Indeed, only by being sensate can type be fully comprehended and verified experientially; hence the validity of devices like topoanalysis.

Therefore spatio-sensory constructs are those types that reflect the collective unconscious in a peculiar format that is perceptible in both cognitive and sensory terms. This gives rise to the specific model, which is granted validity to the degree that it accords with the tenets of this collective conscious as perceived through the senses. The critical questions for spatial design may thus be: first, how can one elicit those unconscious patterns of the human psyche that proceed from archetypal and personal experience; second, how can they be translated into images (types) that authentically reflect their source; and third, how can these types be transposed into working models whose spatio-sensory attributes accord with our archetypal experience? We hasten to point out that these considerations do not require that Jung's theories be accepted wholesale, only that the entirely valid phenomena he addressed be accounted for in some manner. Critical to this task is the hypothesis that an authentic typology depends on sensation—both in the perception of the type and in verification of its authenticity—in a way that the current definition of type conceptually excludes.

Figure 1.5. Chicago Cultural Center, Chicago, by Shepley, Rutan and Coolidge, 1897. Photograph by Frank Vodvarka.

2. The Mind's Eye

We began this book with Henry James's description of a garden, the *boschetto*, and from it formed the definition of a spatial construct. We concluded that for James, a place is always specific, but that its elements are common, that its comprehension relies on sensory data filtered through memory, and that delight is enhanced by a degree of mystery. Thus the full comprehension of place relies not just on sensation (the flow of data received through the sense organs) but also on perception (the data after it is processed and interpreted).

We suggest that humans commonly experience three kinds of sensory response: first, an immediate physical response to stimulus; second, a response conditioned by prior knowledge of its source; and third, a response to stimulus as it has become identified in one's memory with a particular time and place. (We refer to the formation of such mnemonic sensation as sensory imprinting.) The first is an involuntary reaction of the sense organs to stimuli. The second produces a variety of reactions, depending on its character and our understanding of its source. Are we familiar with the sound? Has it in any way altered? Unfamiliar sounds and odors are likely disquieting, but potentially exciting, while those that are familiar tend to be reassuring. The third, remembered sensation, is familiar (if not always reassuring). Such sensation can invoke still other sensations, the sum of which the mind uses to reconstruct the dimensions of particular places. Indeed, imprinting can be so powerful that detailed awareness of place can occur in the presence of the stimulus alone.[1]

Frances Downing refers to this kind of mnemonic, sensory phenomenon when she says: "Memories float, waltz, and flash into our consciousness, welcome or not, infiltrating thought and powering imagination. . . . Rather than a simple repository of experience, memory is dynamic, often seeming to form and reform experience without our conscious permission."[2] And what shapes the content of this dynamic and largely involuntary recall if not the senses? Downing continues: "Mental images are an active, vital repository of information gathered through sensual experience—through sight, sound, smell, touch, and taste" (235). Such an image presents to the mind more than just an initial remembered percept; it contains multiple versions of involvement that reach into the emotional and intellectual realms (235). And so she points out that a person's memory of a pavilion in Grandmother's garden can evoke sensory experiences like the quality of shade and odor of the roses, but also emotional dimensions such as belonging and safety and cultural identity. Nor does this mental image give way in time to a more abstract, so-called mature understanding of the phenomena. On the contrary: "It continues to order the world and, within its own structure, retains meaningful detail and complexity" (235). Its mnemonic quality, moreover, especially resides in architectural configurations—old or new—that evoke a sense of cultural continuity (Figure 2.1).

Now, just how dependable is memory? Downing contends: "However powerful a mental image may seem in memory, it does not include all the environmental information contained in any particular place or event experience. Instead, the mental image presents a *version* of experience that is most important to the individual or situation at a particular moment in time" (235). This suggests that sensory memory is

Figure 2.1. Roger Ferri, Odessa Pavilion, Seaside, Florida. Photograph by Richard Sexton. Copyright 1995. All rights reserved.

selective as well as nuanced, a point that is especially apt when one is in a situation where precise definitions of time and place are not essential.

Such conditions are commonly found in literature. Marcel Proust describes a situation that sometimes arose when he only barely awoke from a deep sleep:

> For it always happened that when I awoke like this, and my mind struggled in an unsuccessful attempt to discover where I was, everything would be moving around me through the darkness: things, places, years. . . . Its memory, the composite memory of its ribs, knees, and shoulderblades offered it a whole series of rooms in which it had at one time or another slept; while the unseen walls kept changing, adapting themselves to the shape of each successive room that it remembered, whirling madly through the darkness.[3]

Of course, as he became ever more awake, his mind would finally identify the precise room that he occupied, but not before his body "would recall from each room in succession what the bed was like, where the doors were, how daylight came in at the windows, whether there was a passage outside, what I had had in my mind when I went to sleep, and had found there when I awoke."[4] Thus Proust allows the reader to experience a continuum of spatial constructs by virtue of the protagonist's memory flow. Critical to our position is the sensory nature of that memory; it is not the mind that is critical, but the mind's eye.

In the opening line of *Cannery Row*, John Steinbeck invokes a panoply of sensori-emotional dimensions: "Cannery Row in Monterey in California is a poem, a stink, a grating noise, a quality of light, a tone, a habit, a nostalgia, a dream."[5] And when the fishing boats put in with their day's catch:

> The whole street rumbles and groans and screams and rattles while the silver rivers of fish pour in out of the boats. . . . The canneries rumble and rattle and squeak until the last fish is cleaned and cut and cooked and canned and then the whistles scream again and the dripping, smelly, tired Wops and Chinamen and Polaks, men and women, straggle out and droop their ways up the hill into the town and Cannery Row becomes itself again—quiet and magical. (1)

For Steinbeck, the problem was how to capture this incredibly fragile web of sensory response and emotion in words. "How can the poem and the stink and the grating noise—the quality of light, the tone, the habit and the dream—be set down alive?" (2). In short, how does one capture the sensory dimensions of a place in a given medium?

As previously noted, our preferred term for the physical constructs that human beings find meaningful is "spatio-sensory construct." In the preface of the October 1991 issue of *The Architectural Review*, the editor states: "We appreciate a place not just by its impact on our visual cortex but by the way in which it sounds, it feels and smells. Some of these sensual experiences elide, for instance our full understanding of wood is often achieved by a perception of its smell, its texture (which can be appreciated by both looking and feeling) and by the way in which it modulates the acoustics of the space."[6] He thus postulates sensory experience as the key to understanding the essential nature of an architectural construct, in much the way that writers understand the sites they describe.

This position suggests a phenomenological view, in which direct, preconceptual experience rather than objectified quantification represents the real shape of the world. In fact, phenomenology, as formulated by Edmund Husserl after 1900, is largely concerned with the world as immediately experienced through our senses. David Abram points out that unlike the mathematics-based sciences, phenomenology seeks not to explain the world objectively but to describe the manner in which the world makes itself evident to awareness through direct, sensorial experience.[7] Indeed, Husserl's view of intersubjectivity—phenomena experienced by multiple sensing subjects—removes any clear distinction between "subjective" and "objective" realities. This apparent dichotomy is recast as the felt contrast between subjective and intersubjective phenomena, which may be thought of as a sort of consensus or agreement among a plurality of subjects.[8] Abram concludes that the world, far from being a fixed and definable "datum," is rather a matrix of sensations and perceptions—a collective field of experience. He says: "It is this informing of my perceptions by the evident perceptions and sensations of other bodily entities that establishes, for me, the relative solidity and stability of the world" (39).

Phenomenal reality is therefore the result of sensori-emotional experience, suggesting an ongoing dialogue between human beings and the entities that surround us. Abram states: "In the act of perception . . . I enter into a sympathetic relation with the perceived" (54). There is, however, evidence suggesting that perception itself is a product of cultural context, an idea we will pursue in the next chapter. Thus the world as "collective field of experience" is different for different cultures. In Husserl's conception, such differences lay in the arena of immediate experience, whereas on a more profound level there exists a deeper, more unitary life-world. And so Husserl claims that "reason is not an accidental de facto ability . . . but rather a title for an all-embracing essentially necessary structural form belonging to all transcendental subjectivity."[9] Reason refers to the possibility of verification, and verification to evidence. He concludes that all evidence "is experience in a maximally broad, and yet essentially unitary, sense."[10] (We can almost hear Jung in this hypothesis.) Of interest to us is the necessary vitality granted all things, whether the productions of nature or humankind in the phenomenological view. Abram sees that vitality within artifacts as primarily residing in the materials used: "all these still carry, like our bodies, the textures and rhythms of a pattern that we ourselves did not devise, and their quiet dynamism responds directly to our senses."[11] The content thus assigned to materials doubtless accounts for much of phenomenology's appeal to designers.

The work of Maurice Merleau-Ponty considerably advanced the phenomenological position by identifying the experiencing "self" with the bodily organism. Put differently, it is impossible to conceive of a self without the physical means of gathering information; we are, foremost, sensory beings. For Merleau-Ponty, Abram says, the "sensing body is not a programmed machine, but an active and open form, continually improvising its relation to things and to the world."[12] Thus perception is an inherently interactive and wholly participatory process, and the objects of perception are as animate as the perceiver. Merleau-Ponty himself states: "To return to things themselves is to return to that world which precedes knowledge, of which knowledge always *speaks,* and in relation to which every scientific schematization is an abstract and derivative sign-language, as is geography in relation to the countryside in which we have learnt beforehand what a forest, a prairie or a river is."[13] Facts will always appear more real than qualities, he says, "as long as the attempt is made to build up the shape of the world (life, perception, mind) instead of recognizing, as the source which stares us in the face and as the ultimate court of appeal in our knowledge of these things, our *experience* of them."[14]

Such a position contrasts sharply with traditions in Western philosophy and theology, which insist on an affirming authority outside sensation. In fact, Abram maintains that European civilization's neglect of the natural world has clearly been encouraged by a style of awareness that disparages sensorial reality on behalf of some absolute source assumed to exist outside or beyond the bodily world. He also points out that Plato's philosophical derogation of the sensible and changing forms of the world contributed to our consequent estrangement from the earthly world around us.[15] David Pearson blames both the Enlightenment and later Cartesian thought for the division of knowledge and wisdom into separate scientific specialisms, and the acceptance of reductionist thought. In the extreme, he says, "the head rules over the body and spirit leaving traditional wisdom, intuition and our sensory perceptions devalued or ignored."[16]

Indeed, this distinction may account for the differences in the human/nature interface between Western and indigenous cultures—between dominance and collaboration—and our own mind/body schism. Pearson believes that society is currently undergoing a paradigm shift from a mechanistic to a holistic, systems-based conception of reality, and he uses the terminology of traditional Eastern philosophy to describe it. He contends that a number of designers in different places—the "building biology" movement in northern Europe, the "eco-design" contributions of Christopher Alexander, and the "healing environments" of Carol Venolia in North America—are creating "an architecture that honours the senses."[17] All hopeful signs.

Nor should there be anything odd about the notion of comprehending architecture through the senses. Steven Holl points out that while a film might give us some sense of a cathedral, "only the actual building allows the eye to roam freely among inventive details; only the architecture itself offers the tactile sensations of textured stone surfaces and polished wooden pews, the experience of light changing with movement, the smell and resonant sounds of space, the bodily relations of scale and proportion. All these sensations combine within one complex experience, which becomes articulate and specific, though wordless. The building speaks through the silence of perceptual phenomena."[18]

It has been argued that the aesthetic response is primarily a function of cognition, that art and architecture are best "understood" intellectually. This has been especially true for architecture, as the physical/structural properties of buildings have usually been granted greater weight than their sensory properties. In this construct, what is aesthetically important is pure spatial form. In "A Science of Vision for Visual Art," François Molnar posits first that the aesthetic effect is an affective response, a reaction to a stimulus from the outside world, passing through the sensory channels, and second that there are no works of art without sensory input.[19] Using data obtained from a scientific examination of perceptual processes, including neurophysiological data and data derived from spatial-frequency studies, he states that there "is no doubt that the aesthetic response begins before the cognitive system gives its interpretation" (229). Thus he concludes that his results "show clearly the temporal primacy of the sensorial mechanism in aesthetic reaction" (232).

In an analysis based in philosophy, Nick Zangwill theorizes that aesthetic properties depend in part on sensory properties, such as colors and sounds.[20] He points out that architectural "functionalism," which holds that the aesthetic properties of a building depend on how well it "expresses" its function, is often fallaciously invoked. He maintains that "what generates aesthetic excellence is the *expression* or *articulation* of those functions, particularly the spatial and sensory properties.[21] Thus the vital role of sensory properties in architectural design. He concludes: "That aspect of the modernist tradition, which in ideology or practice concentrates exclusively on pure spatial structure or the appearance of spatial structure, rests on an error about the metaphysics of architecture. . . . It is sensory properties in a certain three-dimensional spatial context which have aesthetic significance in architecture."[22]

At the outset of *The House of the Seven Gables,* Nathaniel Hawthorne comments on the edifice central to the tale:

> The aspect of the venerable mansion has always affected me like a human countenance, bearing the traces not merely of outward storm and sunshine, but expressive, also, of the long lapse of mortal life, and accompanying vicissitudes that have passed within. Were these to be worthily recounted, they would form a narrative of no small interest and instruction, and possessing, moreover, a certain remarkable unity, which might almost seem the result of artistic arrangement.[23]

The house therefore enjoys a dramatic potential based, in large part, on its possessing multiple identities—some physical, others emotional.

Thus function, that often-cited quality, certainly does not lie in the realm of simple utility, of the mere physical suitability of spaces to specific tasks. It is perhaps an indication of a twentieth-century preoccupation with material needs that function is so often defined in terms of the structural and utilitarian aspects of space. As Rudolf Arnheim makes clear, all human needs are matters of the mind:

> Hunger pangs, the chills of winter, the fear of violence, and the disturbance from noise are all facts of human consciousness. It makes little sense to distinguish between them by attributing some to the body and others to the mind. The hunger, the chill, and the fear are on equal footing with the need for peace, privacy, space, harmony, order, or color. To the best of a psychologist's knowledge, the priorities are by no means self-evident. Dignity, a sense of pride, congeniality, a feeling of ease—these are primary needs, which must be seriously considered when the welfare of human beings is under discussion.[24]

Since they are requirements of the mind, he points out, they are satisfied not only by good plumbing and heating but also by light, color, visual order, well-proportioned space, and so forth.[25] If we allow this highly inclusive view of a multifaceted design comprehended through the senses to supersede the current physical view of design, Louis Sullivan's famous aphorism becomes more explicable and humane.

So why the obsession with structure and program? We referred earlier to the nineteenth-century urge to make architecture a science, resulting in a formulaic design. By the turn of the century, the parallel impulses of rationality and morality had become so intertwined that spare, structural approaches to design were seen as morally excellent. Thus the major design movements of the twentieth century—the Werkbund, the Bauhaus, and De Stijl—considered themselves universal in character, efficient in means, moral in effect, and even hygienic. (Spare designs for a humanity liberated from itself, as it were.) These movements had an influence on design out of keeping with their size, largely due to a perceived need for an intellectual and spiritual purification following World War I. They became so pervasive that we still live with their basic tenets. Of course, whether their designs actually served the largely unregenerate humanity they were ostensibly designed for is another matter.

The Werkbund began as a response to the poor quality of German production that prevailed until the 1890s, when industry began to appreciate the potential of well-designed machined products. The British had long coupled good craft to economical production, and this led Germany to send Hermann Muthesius to England in 1896 to study their methods. After eight years, he returned to Germany and reorganized education in the applied arts. In 1907 Muthesius founded Deutscher Werkbund, an organization of thirteen designers and ten craft firms, including the Wiener Werkstatten. William J. R. Curtis notes that the moral tenor of life was to be raised through the influence of good design in the marketplace, the home, and at work; in fact, in the whole human environment.[26] In 1911 Muthesius delineated the Werkbund goals in "Wo stehen wir?"

To help form to recover its rights must be the fundamental task of our era. . . .
The fortunate progress of the arts and crafts movement, which has given new shape
to the interior decoration of our rooms, breathed fresh life into handicrafts and
imparted fruitful inspiration to architecture, may be regarded as a minor prelude to
what must come. . . . Yet even this success is far from completing the Werkbund's
task. Far more important than the material aspect is the spiritual; higher than purpose, material, and technique stands form.[27]

By *form,* Muthesius had in mind form in the service of industry, design for mass
production.

Reyner Banham maintains that this speech "introduced to the Werkbund the
idea that aesthetics could be independent of material quality, it introduced the idea
of standardization as a virtue, and of abstract form as the basis of the aesthetics of
product design."[28] In short, the goal of design is the creation of form types that have
the capacity to become normative. Curtis refers to this as "an ideology in which the
artist had to function as a sort of mediator between formal invention and standardization, between personal style and the appropriate form for the *zeitgeist.*"[29] Without belaboring the point, these were form types that would soon become as bereft of
symbolic meaning as they were of familiar sensory qualities, sensitive only to the
sachlichkeit (reality) imposed by the principle of utility.

By the mid-1920s, the Werkbund was eclipsed by the highly organized Staatliche
Bauhaus. Hans Wingler notes that under the direction of Walter Gropius, the aims
of the Bauhaus were far more focused and ambitious than those of the Werkbund:
"The Bauhaus strives to bring together all creative effort into one whole, to reunify
all the disciplines of practical art—sculpture, painting, handicrafts, and the crafts—
as inseparable components of a new architecture. The ultimate, if distant, aim of the
Bauhaus is the unified work of art—the great structure—in which there is no distinction between monumental and decorative art."[30] Thus the aim of the Bauhaus
was the complete architectural entity, with arts and crafts combined under architecture. And yet architecture was not even part of the Bauhaus curriculum until the
move to Dessau in 1925. A major factor in deciding to include an architectural program at the Bauhaus may well have been the Experimental House of the Bauhaus,
designed by Georg Muche in 1923 with the support of students such as Marcel Breuer.
This house was built to showcase the design achievements of the school's first four
years, as well as its concern for cost-effectiveness. Another design concern was that
it allow for a reduction in the energy spent on household chores. Thus the surfaces
are planar, devoid of texture, and geometric; and there are, in any case, few of them.

It is no accident that Muche was a painter. In fact, almost all the design instruc-
tors were painters. Gropius felt that painting—particularly abstract painting—was
the only art form on the "cutting edge." Thus the Bauhaus employed artists such
as Wassily Kandinsky, Paul Klee, Oskar Schlemmer, and theorists Josef Albers and
Johannes Itten. One of Itten's beliefs was that there were demonstrable connections

between mental states and particular visual formats. This idea is critical to the idea of form types and suggests why the Bauhaus began to employ Gestalt psychologists in its program. After 1922 the Bauhaus took its first decisive steps toward the belief in standardized types and programs, filtered through a *Gestaltung* (shaping).[31]

At least in part this occurred because of new ideas from De Stijl as propounded through the guest lectures of Theo Van Doesburg. While there was considerable agreement between De Stijl and Bauhaus ideologies, Van Doesburg had criticized the Bauhaus for "allowing metaphysical speculation and religious sectarianism to side-track or overlay the 'real problems of *Gestaltung.*'"[32] This implied that the Bauhaus approach was less "modern" than De Stijl's. But it is arguable that another, more critical reason for the growth of a programmatic architecture was the influence of Ludwig Mies van der Rohe. Mies entered the Friedrichstrasse Skyscraper Competition in 1920 with a design for a glass skyscraper, which he further modified in 1921. The open plan in this design is really an early statement of an office aesthetic, which he explains in 1923: "The office building is a building for work, organization, lucidity and economy. Light, spacious working rooms, clearly arranged, undivided, only organized according to the pattern of the firm."[33] Nor are such arrangements for office blocks alone, as he made clear in a 1927 statement: "If one limits to developing only the kitchen and bathroom as standardized rooms because of their installation, and then also decides to arrange the remaining living area with movable walls, I believe that any justified living requirements can be met."[34]

Curiously, the house prototype that Mies describes was best fulfilled not by a Bauhaus designer but by a pillar of De Stijl, Gerrit Rietveld. The Schröder House in Utrecht was designed by Rietveld in 1924, and nowhere is De Stijl's ideology more evident than in the contrast between it and the adjacent buildings (Figure 2.2). (One

Figure 2.2. Gerrit Rietveld, Schröder House, Utrecht, 1924. Drawing by Joy Monice Malnar.

of the building's unique aspects is the sliding-wall system that divides the floor at will.) Still, the Bauhaus was the more comprehensive and influential movement, embracing the machine aesthetic for both its formal elegance and its amenability to industrial purpose. Schlemmer's statement that "we need living machines instead of cathedrals,"[35] is echoed in Gropius's belief that beauty depended on "restriction to typical basic form and color, intelligible to all,"[36] and that the "creation of standard types for everyday goods is a social necessity. It still implies the highest level of civilization."[37]

One might expect that interior spaces would fare better, allowing some provision for attributes that were symbolically reassuring and granted sensory delight. In a 1931 lecture given by Marcel Breuer, titled "The House Interior," he states:

> The deciding factors for the shaping of the interior, their basis, and their intrinsic possibilities, rest in the house itself—in its interior and total organization, in its floor plan, in its "architecture". . . we see our mission in creating a home that is simpler, lighter, more comfortable in a biological sense, and independent of exterior factors. . . . The necessity for the utmost economy in space demands a machine for living, which must actually be constructed like a machine, with engineering developments and the latest in mechanization. Practically speaking: everything is either built-in or permanent, every object is placed in a specific location . . . everything measured off in the smallest dimensions and interlocking. . . . The house, in other words, should be based on the body.[38]

In this address, he made observations about furniture (which should be modular or built-in), lighting (task and ambient), and color (which must be light, but monochromatic); in short, the office prototype adapted for living.

The last part of the quote is perhaps the most fascinating. After extolling the mechanization of this "machine for living," Breuer says that the house "should be based on the body." It is surely fair to ask what objectified view Breuer must have of the body that he sees it so disconnected from sensory response and memory. Now, Karen A. Franck points out that it *is* possible to conceive of the body as both object and self: "The body as object places the designer or writer . . . adopting this approach outside the body, looking at or into it. The body as subject positions the writer or designer within the body/self and involves not only looking but also acting and feeling."[39] She maintains that the latter view often receives far less attention from architects than the former:

> In architecture, a single objectified body can be idealised and used for deriving proportions and scale, or transformed into a metaphor for a building, or for parts of a building . . . There is no doubt that the body as object is a rich source of insight, design and invention but it is quite remote from active, organic beings with practical, everyday needs and should not be confused with them. (16)

What results, she says, are visually compelling buildings designed to be seen, but where other sources of sensory stimulation are minimized and orientation is confusing. The bodies we *are,* she concludes, "are moving, changing, permeable and fluid . . . the bodies we are require different spatial and physical conditions depending upon the task or activity at hand, depending upon characteristics of age, gender, size and culture, and depending upon the passage of time" (18). When embodiment—acceptance of our sensory, feeling selves—is embraced, sensory stimulation, movement, and activities can all become sources of design ideas.[40] Franck's position assumes, of course, that design results from considerations of human qualities, not the reverse so typical of the modernist impulse.

While the Bauhaus was more influential than De Stijl, the latter was surely the most doctrinaire source of modernist tradition. Theo Van Doesburg, in a 1922 "Report of the De Stijl Group," made clear their aim to find practical solutions to universal problems by using objective, universal, formative means.[41] By definition, these were means that should be applied to all forms of creative endeavor, including architecture. The basis for creation would be an abstract (morally neutral) series of mathematical links. Piet Mondrian defines the problem as he sees it: "As long as man is dominated by individualism, and neglects to cultivate his universal essence, he does not seek nor can he find his own person. The house too becomes the place where this fleeting individuality is cultivated, and its plastic expression reflects this trivial preoccupation."[42] To promote a healthier beauty, our environment must cease being an "outflow of our wretched personality" (24). The opposite of this lyrical expression would be a plastic expression permitting art to attain the universal: "The house will no longer be enclosed, shut in, detached. . . . The idea of a house—house dear house, home sweet home—must disappear. . . . And man? Being nothing in himself, he will be merely a part of the whole, and then, having lost the vanity of his small and trivial individuality, he will be happy in this Eden which he himself has *created!"* (26). So much for the notion of space, and the objects that fill it, acting as confirmation and expression of the individual, or for any sort of sensory delight.

It is likely that at least part of Mondrian's polemic was the result of the Great War, in which virtually all the hallmarks of culture were found wanting, even corrupt. The desire to reject the past and find a new moral high ground had resulted in an embrace of abstraction in the arts generally. But one suspects that there was also a desire to advance a design framework free of the "constraints" of human nature. It would certainly be more convenient if an abstract system, devoid of memory and universally applicable, could be developed. Central to the De Stijl vision was the proposition that in the past, relationships were confused because they were subordinated to natural form. Mondrian states, "The more neutral are the plastic means, the more possible is it to determine the immutable expression of reality. We can consider as relatively neutral those forms which show no relationship with the natural appearance of things or with some kind of 'idea'" (19). Neutral forms would encourage the expression of a universal iconographic language that would be impersonal and immediately understood, as well as reject any reliance on memory. Whatever one's opinion about these ideas as applied to the fine arts—like painting—they were startling when applied to architecture. It was a spare future, indeed, that design promised.

In 1928, delegates from many countries gathered in La Sarraz, Switzerland, and founded the Congres Internationaux d'Architecture Moderne (CIAM), which was influential for the next three decades. The La Sarraz Declaration states the organization's aims: that "building" is an elementary activity linked with the development of human life; and that the need existed for an entirely new conception of architecture that could satisfy the spiritual, intellectual, and material demands of contemporary life.[43] The congress held the following year in Frankfurt saw the first real application of their position, the question of the *Existenzminimum*, housing for the poorest sector of society. The requirements were set out by Gropius, who noted that this "is the question of the basic minimum of space, air, light, and heat which is necessary to man," who "from a biological standpoint needs improved conditions of ventilation and lighting and only a small quantity of living space, especially if this is organized in a technically correct manner."[44]

The interesting point here is not the program or the plan (which reflects its name) but the use of the phrase "technically correct manner." While the plan was consistent with modernism's program, and would have been an improvement over current living conditions for many, it surely would have been less successful in accounting for the psychological needs of humans. The *Existenzminimum* plan, contained in a proposal to CIAM in 1929, indicates a highly efficient apartment module located on two floors (with an internal stair). Such a unit type lends itself to multiplication in both dimensions, thereby permitting the standardization that would lower costs. It also suggests the rationale for the housing blocks that followed (Figure 2.3).

Thus the "functionalist" ideology that dominated the modernist movement, and continues to serve certain economic interests. We might, of course, ask whether modernism ever actually engaged in a fundamental reexamination of the basic requirements of the human organism. In a piercing series of comments, Buckminster Fuller disputed that estimation:

> The International Style "simplification". . . was but superficial. It peeled off yesterday's exterior embellishment and put on instead formalised novelties of quasi-simplicity, permitted by the same hidden structural elements of modern alloys that had permitted the discarded *Beaux-Arts* garmentation. . . . In many such illusory ways did the "International Style" gain dramatic sensory impingement on society as does a trick man gain the attention of children.[45]

In fact, the structural systems used by Mies and Le Corbusier were already long familiar to architects, and the technology was simply the newest version of extant processes. Thus Fuller criticized modernism for its failure to address the fundamental issues, settling instead for cosmetic changes. Fuller—an engineer—did tackle the fundamental issues, although, one could argue, his solution fell as short in human terms as any of modernism's. The design for the 4D House (designated the Dymaxion House in 1929) was completed in 1928. It was intended to be *un machine d'habiter,* an environment to minimize tasks and provide protection (Figure 2.4).

The Dymaxion concept represented a radical departure from conventional dwelling forms. It was a hexagonal structure with walls of variable-gauge plastic, hung by wires from the top of a duralumin mast that housed the mechanical services. The structure used the light-metal technology of aircraft construction and was spatially divided between the service core (distributed through the mast) and activity area. The advanced attributes of the house included atomizer baths, and pneumatic floors and doors. Robert Marks concludes that in this house, "the occupants were given ample space, and the logical arrangement of the equipment automatically developed the privacy appropriate to psychological grace."[46] (Perhaps, although it's doubtful.) However, the division between the service core and activity area really was revolutionary. The projected cost to the consumer, once mass production was under way, would have been $1,500 in 1928; the adjusted 1960 price would have been $4,800, occupant-ready anywhere in the United States.[47] Fuller thus envisioned an inexpensive solution to the housing crisis, structures that would be marketed via the sales methods of the automotive industry.

Fuller's comments suggest that modernism simply sacrificed cultural conviction for a shallow intellectualism, and *sensible* design for abbreviated design. It was design, moreover, that was highly ocularcentric. Juhani Pallasmaa states the problem succinctly: "Modernist design has housed the intellect and the eye, but it has left the body

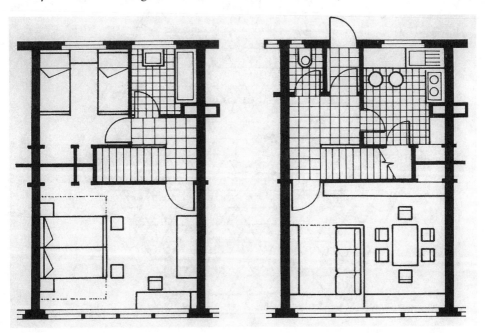

Figure 2.3. Walter Gropius, Existenzminimum plan to CIAM, 1929. Drawing by Joy Monice Malnar.

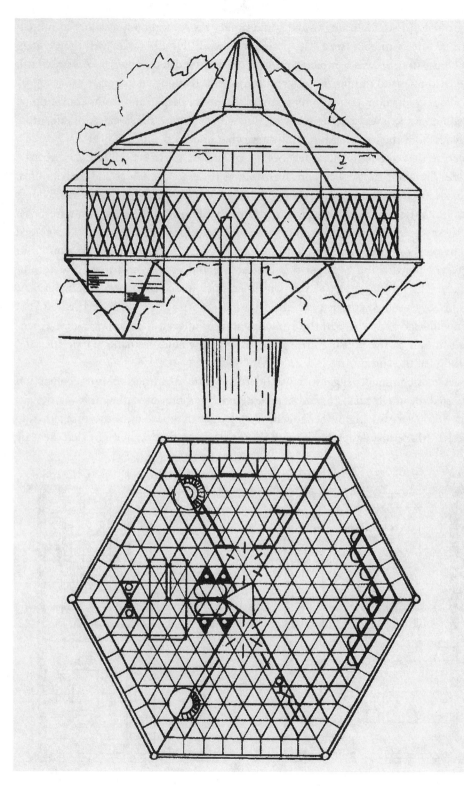

Figure 2.4. R. Buckminster Fuller, Dymaxion House, 1929. Drawing by Joy Monice Malnar.

and the other senses, as well as our memories and dreams, homeless."[48] Of course, Fuller's design failed just as spectacularly to provide a satisfactory spatio-sensory construct. Neither sensory response nor cultural memory is provided for in either case, and despite all of the Dymaxion House's advantages, only three were ever built.

One might also ask why modernism, a European movement born in a radical ideology impelled by the wholesale destruction of World War I, should have so affected the United States. There were certainly local alternatives to the modernist impulse in the early twentieth century, most obviously in the work and lasting influence of Frank Lloyd Wright. Wright's most important principle may well be his view that the architectural environment is total, consisting of enclosed space and the things that fill it. He maintained that in his organic architecture it was impossible to consider the building as one thing, its furnishings another, and its setting and environment yet a third.[49] It was his belief that the ornamental forms of the building should be designed to "wear well," by which he meant that they should not confuse one by virtue of inflexible composition or arrangement: "Good 'alive' color, soft textures, textural materials, beauty of all materials and methods revealed and utilized in the building scheme itself—these are all means of 'decoration,' so called, although not considered, as such by myself."[50]

In *An Autobiography*, he lists the nine principles that he employed in design, the eighth of which is "to incorporate as organic architecture, so far as possible, furnishings, making them all one with the building, designing the equipment in simple terms for machinework. Again straight lines and rectilinear forms. Geometrical."[51] It is in his domestic architecture of the first decade of the twentieth century that these concerns may be seen, particularly in the Robie House. In his use of materials, their patterns, colors, and textures, and concern for the relationship between the spatial form and its varied contents—furniture, lighting fixtures, glazing, and surfaces—this structure came to serve as a model for domestic design (Figure 2.5).

It was not, unfortunately, a model embraced by builders and their financial backers, despite the public's enthusiasm for most of his ideas. This is particularly evident in his design for a moderate-cost house to be known as the Usonian home. Designed during the 1930s in response to the period's socioeconomic conditions, the house served as an example of Wright's belief in human potential. In *The Living City*, he said: "Noble life demands a noble architecture for noble uses of noble men. . . . The true center (the only centralization allowable) in Usonian democracy, is the individual in his true Usonian family home."[52] This house came in kit form, with a concrete-slab foundation containing hot-water radiant heating, and a ventilation system in the roof slab. There were spatial innovations as well, particularly the use of semicontinuous cooking-dining-seating areas. And the walls took advantage of the same prefabrication methods that Fuller thought would solve the housing problem in the United States.

It is also interesting to see what attributes Wright considered essential in a house. In *The Architectural Forum* (1938), he noted, "We must have as big a living room with as much garden coming into it as we can afford, with a fireplace in it, and book shelves, dining table, benches, and living room tables built in."[53] In his Usonian house, Wright both considered and addressed the key issues in moderate-cost housing, from spatial needs to cultural symbols to the sensory attributes of materials. William J. R. Curtis comments: "It was no accident that Wright's formula should have been adopted so rapidly by building contractors and cheap home catalogues. For its free-plan interiors and exterior patios captured precisely the ethos of an emergent middle-class suburban existence."[54] He also notes that while these houses were carefully detailed and proportioned, with individual variation at each site in Wright's hands, "the insensitive imitators were all too often clumsy 'ranch-style' shoe-boxes, laid out in jerry-built monotony on the boom tracts of the 1950's."[55] Thus, while the Usonian house formed the spatial paradigm for much postwar American housing, it was a paradigm selectively emulated.

James Casey, in the *National Builder*, wrote that "the new type of home, now so popular, has utility for its fundamental principle. It aims to eliminate all that is superfluous, and to embody all modern improvements."[56] Of even greater importance than popularity, however, was the influence and policy-making power of housing agencies, government, and suburban developers. Gwendolyn Wright notes that the developers set construction standards prior to the sale of the lots, and that these rules might "specify minimum dimensions of lots and houses; placement of outbuildings, such as garages; optimal distance from house to street; even the style of architecture."[57] It is, of course, the last item that is the most problematic.

Figure 2.5. Frank Lloyd Wright, Robie House, Chicago, 1909. Photograph by Frank Vodvarka.

Both the housing agencies and developers agreed that buildings should reflect "traditional" imagery. James Ford, director of the Better Homes in America architectural committee, commented in 1931 that "the majority of small homes built in America are ugly in design and inconveniently planned."[58] This committee was founded in 1922 by U.S. secretary of commerce Herbert Hoover, to improve home design through lectures and design competitions.[59] It is worth noting that virtually all of the winners in the 1931–1932 competitions designed homes in regional styles.[60] In another civic effort to improve architecture, the nonprofit Architect's Small House Bureau was founded in 1921. This nationwide organization operated under the control of the American Institute of Architects, with Department of Commerce approval. Limited to houses of six rooms or less, the bureau supplied perspectives, complete working drawings and technical specifications, and necessary contractual documents. The costs were nominal. Some of the book's advice is intriguing: the comment, for example, that architecture is comprised of "logic, strength, and beauty,"[61] and "the fine results which may be obtained when the walls are of good proportions" (263), could appear in any design textbook. But while the bureau acknowledged that standardization would be boring, it also warned: "In considering the style of your home, remember that good design is always conservative" (271).

That position was later supported by the powerful U.S. Federal Housing Administration (FHA) when it came into existence in 1934. The FHA's loan guarantees for participating banks made possible low-interest, long-term mortgages, and by 1935, nearly 70 percent of America's commercial banking resources were part of this program. This effectively gave the FHA the power to direct U.S. domestic postwar housing. And, in fact, hundreds of thousands of prefab homes were built, all conforming to the FHA's housing norms. The power of the FHA in design decision making was immense.[62] With little incentive to individualize units, the developers built uniform structures en masse. And how would innovators like Wright fare?

> FHA evaluators were instructed to lower the rating score of houses with conspicuously modern designs because they were not considered a sound investment . . . architects like Frank Lloyd Wright had their work rejected because of a low rating in the "Adjustment for Conformity" category. In November 1955, *House Beautiful* . . . declared that his houses were the quintessence of American life, the legacy of the Declaration of Independence. But Wright's efforts to develop prefabricated "Usonian" houses for a moderate-income community did not win FHA approval.[63]

Indeed, much tract housing was spatially derived from Wright's Usonian house, and developers across the United States appropriated Wright's concepts of radiant slab heating, sliding patio windows, carports, and the open plan, usually without acknowledgment. But in the end, the "quintessence of American life" turned out to be the houses of Levitt and Sons, of Levittown fame. By 1950, their factories were producing one 650-square-foot house every sixteen minutes. Parodies of Usonian ideas abounded, especially the "built-in" features, which included televisions and refrigerators thus made eligible for inclusion in the mortgage payments (Figure 2.6). In this way did an American version of the *Existenzminimum* plan come into being in the tract housing and high-rise complexes of the postwar era, less the product of ideology than expedience.

We have so far suggested that Western architecture fell victim during the twentieth century to a string of ideological design movements on the one hand, and economic and political manipulation on the other. Those design movements, which held the first half century in thrall, left a legacy of belief that humans could be "raised" above their sensibilities. Karen A. Franck is altogether correct when she says that "in treating bodies primarily as objects and in dreaming so persistently of transcendence,

Figure 2.6. Bernard Levey and family, Levittown, New York, 1950. Courtesy of Bernard Hoffman, TimePix.

we neglect bodies as subjects and forget or disdain the bodies we are. . . . Fortunately, there is also growing recognition of the pressing need to value human embodiment, to rediscover it and to design in ways that enhance it."[64] The second problem is that of political and financial sectors that have profited—and continue to do so—from their view of "less is more" as "less is more profitable."

There are those who say that it is not modernism but the perversion of its principles that is to blame. Yet these were principles so rooted in the belief that humans were flawed, that offered so little recognition of human attributes, that such perversion must have been easy. Certainly Wright, too, was compromised; yet even the poorest knockoff of his work retains some of the original charm. Now, we do not wish to put ourselves in the position of rejecting the necessary roles played by structure, technology, and program. That would be absurd. Buildings must be constructed soundly and appropriately to site and climate, contain the technological systems necessary to human well-being, and enhance the fulfillment of human purpose that impelled their erection in the first place. All of this is necessary; none of this requires that we ignore human sensory response and attachment to memory and sentiment.

While the abstract and "timeless" aspects of reality have generally been favored by designers over the particular and transitory, not everyone has seen it this way. In her admiration for the seventeenth-century Dutch "painter of facts," George Eliot commented: "All honour and reverence to the divine beauty of form! Let us cultivate it to the utmost in men, women and children—in our gardens and in our houses. But let us love that other beauty too, which lies in no secret of proportion, but in the secret of deep human sympathy."[65]

In fact, our recollections of past houses tend to center on the intangible. In *The Poetics of Space,* Gaston Bachelard says that "if I were asked to name the chief benefit of the house, I should say: the house shelters daydreaming, the house protects the dreamer, the house allows one to dream in peace. Thought and experience are not the only things that sanction human values. The values that belong to daydreaming mark humanity in its depths."[66] This is how, he says, that "dwelling-places of the past remain in us for all time" (6). He names two more benefits. The first is the function of the house as the repository of memories, "an embodiment of dreams" (15). The second is that "a house constitutes a body of images that give mankind proofs or illusions of stability" (17). Poetry and prose, as it were.

3. Sensory Response

It is our position that a full understanding of spatial constructs depends both on perception (organized sensation) and on a mediating intelligence. In contrast to existing views of architectural typology, we believe that the former precedes the latter.[1] While the worth of sensory data in the perception of built space may seem obvious to most observers, it is nonetheless rarely central to deliberation at the inception of the design process or, for that matter, at its completion. But what constitutes sensory information?

The traditional meaning is that information collected by our five senses: sight, hearing, touch, taste, and smell. These come from Aristotle, who, like Plato, certainly did not grant them any equality, either with thought or each other. In classical opinion, the senses were inferior to cognition, and of the senses, taste and smell were the least valued. Plato was clear about this: thinking was separate from sensing, and the objects of knowledge were exclusive to the mind. This opinion was later echoed by Descartes, who stated that truth comes from ideas, not feelings. And whereas Aristotle observed that touch was the most critical sense in that it was fundamental, later philosophers (such as Hegel) lauded only the senses of sight and hearing (while still asserting the supremacy of abstract thought).[2] Sight and hearing, more abstract as senses, are more conducive to mental processes, one supposes.

In *The Architecture of Humanism,* historian Geoffrey Scott comments that because weight, pressure, and resistance are part of our habitual body experience, we unconsciously identify with these characteristics in the forms we see.[3] Scott states: "In any building *three* things may be distinguished: the bigness which it actually has (mechanical measurement), the bigness which it appears to have (visual measurement), and the feeling of bigness which it gives (bodily measurement). The last two have often been confused, but it is the feeling of bigness which alone has aesthetic value."[4] It is clear that Scott has something more complex than the classic five senses in mind.

In fact, the psychologist J. J. Gibson has taken these five senses and reformulated them into active, highly inclusive systems. This likely reflects his view that our senses, taken as a whole, are really an integrated information-seeking mechanism that functions without any mediating cognition. In place of the senses of sight, sound, smell, taste, and touch, Gibson stipulates the visual system, the auditory system, the taste-smell system, the basic-orienting system, and the haptic system.[5] It is in fact the last of these systems that most closely approximates Scott's "bodily measurement." Indeed, one could argue that the last two systems together are responsible for our understanding of three-dimensionality, the sine qua non of architectural experience (Figure 3.1).

The visual and auditory systems require little explanation, although they function in a more complex manner than traditional definition allows. Gibson regards them as active stimulus-seeking entities, enjoying a large degree of autonomy. He has combined taste and smell, as they usually function in concert and can be regarded as alternative ways to experience similar phenomena. The last two systems are crucial not only in the experience of architecture but for any spatial experience. The basic-orienting system is based on the relationship between the horizontal ground plane and our vertical posture. Gibson theorizes that the resulting orientation leads us to seek a symmetrical balance, and that our senses are always directed to that end.[6] The haptic system refers to our sense of touch extended to include temperature, pain, pressure, and kinesthesia (body sensation and muscle movement).[7] It is thus a system in which human beings are literally in contact with their environment. In *Placeways*, E. V. Walter notes: "Haptic perception reminds us that the whole self may grasp reality without seeing, hearing or thinking. It also calls attention to a primitive way of knowing that resembles mythical thought . . . a unified structure of feeling and doing."[8] These two senses in concert would go far toward explaining our sense of place, and our tactile awareness of walls and doors, compression and expansion, ascent and descent; that is, the very qualities described in Scott's comments.

There is evidence, moreover, that haptic perception is enhanced when combined with visual data. In *Town and Square*, Paul Zucker comments: "Space is perceived by the visualization of its limits and by kinesthetic experience, i.e., by the sensation of our movements. In the state of 'visual tension,' kinesthetic sensation and visual perception fuse most intensely."[9] Put differently, we understand space best when we perceive its visual aspects while moving through it. Notwithstanding, the majority of design-related research in the behavioral sciences is on visual perception.

Nor should this be thought odd. Arthur Rubin and Jacqueline Elder echo a common opinion when they say: "Man's experience with buildings is mainly visual. This view is generally supported by both architects and behavioral researchers, although for different reasons. The tradition of architecture supports the importance of visual qualities, while research findings in psychology indicate that man typically obtains

Name	Mode of Attention	Receptive Units	Anatomy of the Organ	Activity of the Organ	Stimuli Available	External Information Obtained
The basic orienting system	General orientation	Mechano-receptors	Vestibular organs	Body equilibrium	Forces of gravity and acceleration	Direction of gravity, being pushed
The auditory system	Listening	Mechano-receptors	Cochlear organs with middle ear and auricle	Orienting to sounds	Vibration in the air	Nature and location of vibratory events
The haptic system	Touching	Mechano-receptors and possibly thermo-receptors	Skin (including attachments and openings), joints (including ligaments), muscles (including tendons)	Exploration of many kinds	Deformation of tissues, configuration of joints, stretching of muscle fibers	Contact with the earth, mechanical encounters, object shapes, material states, solidity or viscosity
The taste-smell system	Smelling	Chemo-receptors	Nasal cavity (nose)	Sniffing	Composition of the medium	Nature of volatile sources
	Tasting	Chemo- and mechano-receptors	Oral cavity (mouth)	Savoring	Composition of ingested objects	Nutritive and biochemical values
The visual system	Looking	Photo-receptors	Ocular mechanism (eyes, with intrinsic and extrinsic eye muscles, as related to the vestibular organs, the head, and the whole body)	Accommodation, pupillary adjustment, fixation, convergence exploration	The variables of structures in ambient light	Everything that can be specified by the variables of optical structure (information about objects, animals, motions, events, and places)

Figure 3.1. The perceptual systems, 1966. From James J. Gibson, *The Senses Considered as Perceptual Systems* (Boston: Houghton Mifflin Company, 1966). Copyright 1966 by Houghton Mifflin Company. Reprinted with permission.

more information by visual means than by all other senses."[10] The problem is that the methodologies used by one discipline do not always translate to the other, and there is often more emphasis placed on visual anomalies than consistencies.

Probably the greatest impact on the study of visual perception in the twentieth century has come from Gestalt psychology, first developed after 1912 by Koffka, Köhler, and Wertheimer. Gestalt, meaning shape or form, is based on the idea of *pragnanz,* or "wholeness." Thus visual patterns tend to be perceived in the arrangement that optimizes structural clarity and spatial comprehension. Koffka formulated its definition: "Psychological organization will always be as good as the controlling circumstances permit."[11] The Gestaltists postulate that we organize visual data using principles such as similarity (grouping by like kind), continuity (overall structure), form constancy (the complete perception of a partially suggested shape), and the reading of figure against ground to impose visual order.

Two important conclusions reached by Gestalt are that perception is a response not to individual bits of information (sensations) but to a field of interrelated data— and that human perception actively structures its environment, rather than simply reacting to it.[12] Thus Gestalt was seen to mediate between empiricism, which maintains that the impression of the third dimension develops in the course of experience, and nativism (S-R theory), which assumes that such ability is physically innate. Gestalt theory rejects such a sharp differentiation of the mechanics of spatial perception, replacing it with a more elastic concept.[13] In his *Gestalt Psychology,* Köhler argues that "instead of reacting to local stimuli by local and mutually independent events, the organism responds to the *pattern* of stimuli to which it is exposed; and that this is a unitary process, a functional whole, which gives, in experience, a sensory scene rather than a mosaic of local sensations."[14]

Some of the more intriguing and generally useful results of Gestalt theory include the "law of good continuation," in which we tend to organize data into its clearest and most direct form, and the "law of enclosedness," the tendency to read enclosed shapes as whole figures in context. Nor is Gestalt theory entirely limited to visual phenomena. Köhler contends that the factors involved in spatial grouping are basically the same as those involved in grouping in time and movement (kinesthesia). The principle that Köhler enunciates is that of psychophysical isomorphism, which in spatial terms may be stated thus: Experienced order in space is always structurally identical with a functional order in the distribution of underlying brain processes (61). For Köhler, the correct psychological formula for perception is pattern of stimulation–organization–response to the products of organization (165). Such a broad view clearly suggests that the concept of Gestalt may be applied to aspects of human function that go far beyond sensory experience—in fact, Köhler believes that the main tenet of Gestalt is really a particular type of process, a way of viewing events as functional wholes (178).

The term Köhler uses to characterize this phenomenon is *dynamic self-distribution,* that is, a symmetrical distribution of underlying processes that, when subjected to altered conditions, will always proceed in the direction of balance (132). Nor is this limited to visual experience; all experiences—smells, sounds, weight, temperature, texture—are "localized in one perceptual space, either with precision or merely in a vague fashion."[15] Certainly the perceptual "laws" postulated by Gestalt are of vital service to design, particularly visual communication disciplines. Moreover, David Levi has pointed out that the Gestalt concern with unified experiential wholes, and the qualities of these forms as experienced, leads to the notion of those wholes having expressive qualities.[16] That is, they have latitude that can be exploited by the designer for expressive purposes.

So powerful and compelling has this approach to perception been that it almost certainly supported the move by the Bauhaus in 1922 toward a belief in standardized types and a program mediated by a *gestaltung*.[17] (Hannes Meyer, as director of the Bauhaus, reinforced this position in 1928 by sponsoring lectures by Gestalt psychologists at the school.) Gestalt is not, however, the only theory of perception extant in psychology—nor is it necessarily the most persuasive. There are several areas of weakness in the theory: its rejection of any *critical* role for learned cultural inference, its belief in its universality, and its basis in two-dimensional constructs. The third area is usually that cited as posing problems for spatial designers for an obvious reason, its difficulty in accounting for movement through space.

So problematical is this aspect that Bloomer and Moore, even while praising Gestalt for its revolutionary approach to visual phenomena, criticize the transformation of its two-dimensional findings into a new architectural aesthetic. They note that the observation of a human "will" to order through simplification has tended to support the champions of an efficient, industrialized architecture and lent credence to the thesis that coherent geometric forms are really the hallmarks of "high architecture." Thus they conclude:

> This model of perception was subsequently to buttress those notions in design which considered simplicity and the exclusion of decorative ornament a virtue and a moral necessity. It is difficult to find fault with the accomplishments of the founders of Gestalt psychology, but it is not difficult to question the direct translation of their early experimental findings in two-dimensional *visual* perception into the foundation of a new aesthetic in architecture.[18]

Again, this is not to negate Gestalt findings in human responses to two-dimensional phenomena; on the contrary, every other theory of perception needs to take those findings into consideration. Nor are two-dimensional gestalt phenomena necessarily inapplicable to architectural experience. It is rather that sound evidence is also cited for the positions taken by proponents of other perceptual theories. And in any case, the first two areas—the rejection of learning as critical and universal applicability— may really be of greater interest.

In his "Visual Perception in Architecture," Julian Hochberg describes what he considers the three major theories of visual perception: the "classical" theory (empiricism), derived from the methodology of the philosopher John Stuart Mill and the observations of the physicist Hermann von Helmholtz during the nineteenth century; the Gestalt theory; and "Direct" theories based on stimulus-response phenomena (the work of James J. Gibson in particular). Hochberg favors the first approach while noting the contributions of the other two theories. His observations have much to commend them, not the least of which is a certain sensuous authenticity.

The empiricist approach is based on the proposition that the perception of shape is a complex experience derived from an array of simpler psychological sensations, and that both sensations and the resulting experience result from *learning* about the ways in which particular physical properties are characteristically related.[19] In consequence, we form mental constructs of the world that allow us to generalize and grasp through inference. Hochberg considers three aspects of this theory significant: first, that as the world has simultaneous structure (typical patterns), so do our sensory experiences and the associations that are formed in our perceptual memories; second, that our movement through the world yields successive associations; and third, that such frequent associations become so persuasive and regular that single momentary sensations of experience are no longer discerned (37).

As a result, he says: "Our perception of an object consists of the whole complex of simultaneous associations and of our expectations—our successive associations— as to what sequence of experiences will most likely follow from any act of sensory exploration" (38). He notes that as the current view of an object is that of a structure rather than a group of sensations, this results in a sequence of sensory stimulation that allows us to perceive the arrangement of objects and events that would produce a particular pattern of stimulation most frequently (38). This habituated way of seeing could explain phenomena such as shape and size constancies, and its emphasis on successive associations would be appropriate for the continuous visual experience that typifies our passage through architectural space. It also takes culture—as the basis for any learning structure—into account.

This emphasis on learning, expectation, and habituation marks a significant difference between empiricism and Gestalt—especially as it challenges by inference Gestalt's claim to universality of response—but also important is empiricism's belief in fundamental (or nonmediated) visual sensation as the basis for perception.[20] Both theories acknowledge, and seek to explain, the visual phenomena investigated by Gestalt, and both have implications for spatial design. Hochberg's strong preference for "classical theory" derives from his view that the basis for Gestalt assumptions is not sustainable and, on a procedural level, that there are certain inconsistencies that call the entire theory into question. He does, however, acknowledge the applicability of Gestalt figure-ground concepts in design theory and later notes that "it is more difficult to achieve solutions that run counter to the Gestalt 'laws.'"[21]

The third major theory of perception, the stimulus-response approach, postulates that perception represents our direct visual response to the relationships between the objects and surfaces that fill our world. In this view, perception is an immediate response to the retinal imagery that is formed by the constant ratio of light that falls upon the retina—light that originates in the physical attributes of the reflective source. Images are thus shaped in an automatic process, without the unconscious inference postulated by Gestalt or the learned associations proposed by empiricism. In fact, James J. Gibson has held that phenomena such as distance perception and size constancy should occur without the need for visual processing on the part of the viewer.[22]

In *The Perception of the Visual World,* Gibson notes that one could describe the visual world as "extended in distance and modelled in depth; it is upright, stable, and without boundaries; it is colored, shadowed, illuminated, and textured; it is composed of surfaces, edges, shapes, and interspaces; finally . . . it is filled with things that have meaning."[23] This is a description, with the exception of the last item, of the concrete properties that inform perception. But, he says: "The accepted view of perception is still that the percept is never completely determined by the physical stimulus. Instead, the percept is something essentially subjective in that it depends on some contribution made by the observer himself. Perception goes beyond the stimuli and is superimposed on sensations" (13).

He finds this explanation unacceptable, on the grounds that the visual responses of diverse individuals are too alike for any intermediary processing to have taken place. And so he concludes: "If the total stimulation contains all that is needed to account for visual perception, the hypothesis of sensory organization is unnecessary" (25). Gibson formulated a psychophysical theory of perception, based on the assumption that there are corresponding variations in the image for the important features of the visual world (61). (What you see, is—so to speak.) Thus his theory employs a complex stimulus-response model, where the conventional definition of the term *stimulus*—a variable physical energy falling within a certain range of variation on a receptor or receptors differentially—is extended to mean a *simultaneous* variation over the set of receptors (63). He calls this the Hypothesis of Ordinal Stimulation, where "ordinal" refers to order or succession. This theory would explain variables in perception, especially distance cues and texture gradients, and has implications for the perception of movement. He concludes: "The correspondence of the visual *field* to the total retinal image is an anatomical point-for-point correspondence which is not hard to understand. The correspondence of the visual *world* to the total retinal image is an ordinal correspondence which is more difficult to analyse and specify. But the latter correspondence *is no less literal and exact,* we may believe, than the former."[24]

This approach is likely to appeal to designers, as it suggests a straightforward solution to visual perception. Gibson points out that in its reliance on constants, perception is thus not always distorted by needs, nor fated to be assimilated to social norms.[25] The difficulty, according to Hochberg, is that this approach fails to consider the Gestalt organizational phenomena (like the constancies and illusions), which are also consistent; nor does it adequately address the visual conditions that in fact occur in architectural spaces.[26] There is a body of evidence, moreover, suggesting that perceptual response *is* affected by learning and acculturation, often profoundly.[27]

The contributions of Gestalt to perceptual psychology have been enormous. Even an S-R theorist such as Gibson stated: "Perhaps the greatest contribution of the Gestalt theorists was that, having taken an unprejudiced look at the visual world they were trying to explain, they formulated problems for space-perception which were genuinely relevant. . . . They were questions about the characteristics of the visual *world*."[28] All perceptual theories, moreover, acknowledge the Gestalten and attempt to explain their process. When Köhler wrote his *Gestalt Psychology* in 1947, it was in large measure a rebuttal of empiricist theory (referred to as introspectionism) and, by extension, the S-R theory (behaviorism) that he believes serves as its basis. Now, Köhler accepts the empiricist position that (probably) few experiences remain entirely uninfluenced by learning, noting that "many psychologists do not for a moment doubt the truth of explanation in terms of acquired knowledge."[29] His criticism of this position is that, of the objective experiences around us, little is left that would be called a true sensory fact; and that therefore phases of experience so labeled will be excluded from any investigation.

> Whether the *empiristic explanation* . . . is right or wrong, in common life we are dealing almost exclusively with the first-hand objective experience which is discarded by the Introspectionist. . . . Millions of people will never transform the objects of their environments into true sensations, will always react to sizes, shapes, brightnesses and speeds as they find them, will like and dislike forms as they appear to them without recourse to introspection. (84)

Köhler is suggesting, then, that individuals still react to visual phenomena that they have never learned about, and that such an explanation is therefore artificial and contradicted, as it were, by real experience. A second criticism is based on the empiricist conviction that true sensory experiences depend only on corresponding characteristics of peripheral stimuli (92). In this view, the local stimulus is mechanical, and its import is derived from learning. The criticism of this position is that it only obtains under isolated conditions. Thus, Köhler concludes, true sensory experience depends either on local stimulation, with only the recall of previously acquired knowledge being dependent on environmental factors (empiricism), or (alternatively) on both local stimuli and stimulating conditions in the environment (Gestalt).[30] Köhler does recognize the former correlation: "We do not argue against relations between such conditions and sensory facts in general, but only against a rigid relation between *local* stimulation and *local* experience" (95). This, of course, is the crux of the matter; what precisely is the nature of that relationship?

The empiricist position, with its emphasis on learning, is highly persuasive in its explanation of that correlation. To explain, as Köhler does, that "the organism responds to the *pattern* of stimuli to which it is exposed; and that this answer is a unitary process, a functional whole," does not entirely address the question of the role of learning. Could learning not influence, for example, our definition of what constitutes a pattern and, by extension, the sort of response we are likely to experience? Does response alter in accordance with physical maturation, and what, if any, differences are likely to occur in different cultures? Finally, might culture actually affect perception itself—and not merely our reporting of it? These are all important questions for the designer.

Of interest in this regard is the process of schematization described by the child psychologist Jean Piaget. He suggests that schemata—the stereotypes we have of a thing or event that influences our reactions—are formed during the socialization process and strongly influence perception. Piaget believes that at the most basic levels, such schemata derive from elementary motor activities, while higher-order schemata are based on communication and cultural patterns, that is, they are learned. Hence the Gestalt laws (like enclosure, proximity, and the constancies) may be viewed as simple schematizations that are among the first to be acquired by children as well as being the most fundamental in nature. He acknowledges that there are difficulties in forwarding such a position. Kant, for example, considered space an a priori structure of "sensibility" whose data were then submitted to the thought process for analysis based on logical deduction; and many others (he cites Poincaré) also ascribed the formation of spatial concepts to sensory impressions as simply received and then elaborated by the intellect.

Piaget, however, rejects this sort of direct process. He acknowledges that "such a sensori-motor space begins to evolve right from the child's birth, and together with perception and motor activity it undergoes considerable development up until the appearance of speech and symbolic images."[31] He recognizes also that this space is superimposed upon preexisting spaces, but not as a simple reflection or repetition of them. On the contrary, he says, "it has its own course of development which can be traced fairly easily, and in addition, the spatial organization of sensori-motor behaviour results in new mental constructs, complete with their own laws" (3).

Complicating this process, however, is the tendency of representational thought or imagination to at first ignore metric or perspective relationships, and proportions. "Consequently," he says, "it [representational thought] is forced to reconstruct space from the most primitive notions such as the topological relationships of proximity, separation, order, enclosure, etc., applying them to the metric and projective figures yielded by perception at a level higher than that of these primitive relationships themselves."[32] By way of evidence, Piaget notes that not all of these schemata are present at the outset of life, nor do they emerge full-blown; on the contrary, "as regards size constancy, great differences still persist between an 8-year-old child and an adult" (5). And he notes that the work of others (Brunswik and Cruikshank, in particular) has demonstrated the complete absence of size constancy during the first six months of life (5).

As a result, Piaget says that "the perception of space involves a gradual construction and certainly does not exist ready made at the outset of mental development"

(33). He points out that it is not until after seven to eight years of age that measurement, conceptual coordination of perspective, understanding of proportions, and so forth result in the construction of a conceptual space marking a real advance on perceptual space.[33] He concludes that "although representational space benefits from and has its imagery enriched by forms already developed by perception, it has nevertheless to reconstruct on its own plane . . . the elementary spatial relationships, first topological then euclidean and projective" (42). Thus children progress through three stages: first, those shapes that are based on simple topological relations (like closure, proximity, and separation) are recognized; second, there is a recognition of Euclidean shapes based on the relationship of parts; and third, the connection between shapes and coordinated actions becomes apparent by virtue of a return to a fixed point of reference (43).

His conclusion, that all schemata are learned, corresponds to the position taken by empiricism.[34] Even so, Piaget praises the Gestalt organizational approach to perception. He agrees, for example, with the Gestalt position that intelligence consists only in the set of all cognitive functions whose laws can be found in the forms of equilibrium toward which the system tends when faced with problems for which an initial perceptual appraisal provides no obvious solution. In fact, there are what "amounts to an uninterrupted series of intermediate states between the most elementary perceptual structures and the most complex operational structures of intelligence."[35] Despite these states and this continuity, Piaget maintains that there is a qualitative difference between the truly operative structures of intelligence and initial perceptual structures (xxv). His position is that the Gestaltists applied the relational method inadequately, without fully exploiting the implications of their work (xxvi). And so he states: "They were right to advance the theory of Form, with its notions of field and of totality, in opposition to the atomistic ideal of the proponents of associationistic psychology, who hoped to give an account of perceptual and conceptual totalities in terms of associations between the ultimate elements or 'sensations' for which they were searching" (xxv).

Thus Piaget, in varying measure, disagrees with S-R theory, empiricism, and Gestalt: "atomism [S-R theory *and* empiricism] and Gestalt, corresponding in the final analysis to two major concepts of wholes, a geneticism without structure or a structuralism without genesis, are not the only modes of interpretation available; we claim that a third possibility exists in the relational method."[36] Piaget also objects to empiricism because of the substantial contributions (including choice) made to the process of perception by the activities of the subject. In his view, far from submitting to the constraints of the object, the subject directs perceptual activities, chooses points of centration, and relates objects to contexts. Thus Piaget offers yet a fourth theory of perception, one that is especially useful to design.

Although we cannot affirm one or another of these theories as wholly authentic, we can comment on which aspects of these positions we believe reasonably explain architectural constructs. We accept, for example, James J. Gibson's five categories of the senses, which in their entirety offer a far more profound explanation of spatial sensory information than does the more traditional view. We do not accept, however, the S-R hypothesis that sensory information is received in an automatic, unmediated form. The Gestalt position, that we read visual patterns of stimuli that optimize structural clarity and comprehension, is, we believe, amply demonstrated by the constancies and illusions that all theorists attempt to explain. We favor, as well, the sensory breadth of the principle of dynamic self-distribution, which does an admirable job of explaining the "sense of place" so commonly experienced by people. Less well handled by Gestalt is the role of learning in the development of perception. While we reject the empiristic dependence on "direct" data, we do believe that learned expectation and habituation play a role in spatial comprehension.[37] But as all learning takes place within a context, we consider Piaget's theory that the mediating structures of intelligence (derived from sensori-motor schematization) provide constant feedback into the simpler structures of perception to be quite convincing.

Thus Piaget's theory can be seen to account for the major aspects ("direct" data aside) of the other theories, but more importantly, it suggests that spatial understanding—far from being universal—will correspond to the observer's milieu. This would account for differences in definitions both within a culture and interculturally and render architectural space sensible as well. Julian Hochberg has noted that "*whether, when, and whence viewers look depends on their perceptual intentions and inquiry,* and . . . these simply cannot be reduced to matters of optics."[38] In any case, designers have always worked within the range presented by, on the one hand, the perceptual constancies (like size and shape) and, on the other, the (culturally derived) experiences of the observer. This, of course, implies that human perception is essentially "processed" sensation. Golledge and Stimson refer to this when they state that the end product of perception and cognition is a mental representation of the objective environment, in which information is filtered and effectively restructured (Figure 3.2).[39] Thus, they conclude, people do not respond directly to their real environment but respond to their mental representation or image of it.[40]

Piaget's observations are, in large measure, echoed by E. T. Hall when he says: "Everything man is and does is modified by learning and is therefore malleable. But once learned, these behavior patterns, these habitual responses, these ways of interacting gradually sink below the surface of the mind and . . . control from the depths."[41]

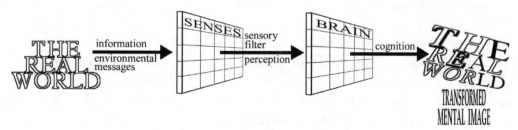

Figure 3.2. The formation of images (after Hayes). Created by Joy Monice Malnar and Frank Vodvarka.

Now, Hall is speaking of the entire structure of comprehension—sensation, perception, and mediating structures—as it manifests itself in a cultural context. But could these hidden cultural controls be so persuasive that how we perceive is influenced from the outset? This could reasonably be inferred from Piaget's position. Moreover, if all perception occurs in context, it is a context that necessarily is culturally derived through a learning process.

In *The Influence of Culture on Visual Perception,* Segall, Campbell, and Herskovits grapple with the issue of how culture influences perception: is this influence actual, or does it merely alter our reporting of perception? Segall and his coauthors discriminate between nativism and empiricism, concluding that their view "is essentially a 'moderate' empiricist position, one that hypothesizes that the pattern of visual experiences in the lifetime of the person can *modify* his perceptions of objects in space."[42] (This suggests Piaget, although he is not discussed.) They refer to studies that appear to indicate differences in "immediate perception," those steps occurring between the reception of a stimulus and an overt response to it. These studies indicate that people classify and interpret experiences in accordance with preexisting patterns that are culturally traditional. The question, they say (quoting Alfred Irving Hallowell), is whether organisms become selectively sensitized to certain arrays of stimuli rather than others owing to membership in a particular cultural group.[43] Indeed, certain studies (Bagwell, 1957) have indicated that cultural differences seem to be critical in deciding perceptual dominance (at least in conflicted viewing situations).[44] Their own study undertakes to explain cross-cultural differences in perception (using illusionary line drawings) in terms of the contrasting visual environments of cultural groups, and the corresponding visual inference habits those environments reinforce. In short, do cultural habits mediate perception? If so, to the whether, when, and whence, one could add how.

Segall and the others point out that whether perceptual mechanisms are innate, learned, or learned elaborations of the innate, "there is no doubt that learning and adaptation do influence visual perception. . . . Built into the seemingly direct process of perception are learned organizations, delineations, and interpretations" (6). Nonetheless, they state, experimental psychologists—even those associated with empiricism—have been reluctant to acknowledge that individuals or groups perceive differently. In contrast, the authors maintain that perception does vary from person to person in accord with both inhibiting and reinforcing forces provided by culturally mediated experiences (67). This has led them to formulate a series of hypotheses: (1) the visual perceptual system uses numerous cues of low and probabilistic (but still positive) validity; (2) optical illusions demonstrate the function of normally useful cues but provide atypical visual performance settings; (3) if human groups differ in their visual inference tendencies, it is because their visual environments differ; and (4) given a hereditary and a learning explanation that both fit the data, the learning (empiricist) explanation is more plausible (77–79).

Restated, psychological factors affect the probability that particular inference tendencies will be acquired, and that under certain (unusual) conditions these tendencies will lead to false (nonveridical) perceptions. These inference tendencies (or ecological cues) depend, moreover, on particular environments for their validity, and they are more likely to have been learned than biologically inherited. This is indeed a clear formulation of the basis for a "cultural perception." The authors devised their set of experiments on the assumption that as people acquire different inference habits, there will be corresponding susceptibilities to different illusions based on their respective environments. The result of their study, conducted in fifteen societies (using five geometric illusions), and relying on an empiricist approach, tended to substantiate their premise: that visual response habits do relate to cultural and ecological factors in visual environments. These habits, moreover, relate to differences in experience.[45]

David Howes has proposed an "anthropology of the senses," in which the concern is how the patterning of sense experience varies from culture to culture in relation to the meaning and emphasis accorded each modality of perception.[46] He continues: "It is also concerned with tracing the influence such variations have on forms of social organization, conceptions of self and cosmos, the regulation of the emotions, and other domains of cultural expression" (3). To state the obvious, these are all design concerns. Howes underscores the need to experiment with other ways of sensing the world in Western culture by saying: "Indeed, if we do not 'come to our senses' soon, we will have permanently forfeited the chance of constructing any meaningful alternatives to the pseudo-existence which passes for life in our current 'Civilization of the Image'" (4). Here he refers to the altered—and highly ocularcentric—relationship that has developed between the observer and the observed, largely as a result of the systems of perspective developed in the fifteenth century: "In effect, Alberti's grid screens out all the smells and sounds, tastes and textures, of the artist's environment. It 'steps up' the natural power of the eye to survey things from afar, while at the same time de-emphasizing the other senses as ways of knowing and communicating" (5).

Howes offers, as an alternative paradigm, a design created by the Shipibo-Conibo Indians of eastern Peru for their healing ceremonies. These sorts of designs are perceived floating downward by a shaman, who is in a hallucinogenic trance. As the designs reach the shaman's lips, he sings them into songs that, upon making contact with the patient, turn once again into designs that enter the patient's body and heal the sickness. These design songs even have an olfactory dimension, as their "fragrance" is believed to account for their efficacy. Howes concludes: "The essence of aesthetic experience by Shipibo-Conibo standards is, therefore, *pluri-sensorial*, whereas the contemporary Western aesthetic is almost exclusively visual. The former integrates the senses while the latter dissociates them" (6). And he wonders what the world must seem like to cultures that "take actuality" in sensory terms that have less of a visual bias than we are accustomed to. The result here is a design that is multireferential and pulsates with life (Figure 3.3). Corollaries in architectural design do exist, but only rarely are they found in current Euro-American paradigms.

The concern in Howes's text is the failure among anthropologists to carefully observe the manner in which sensations present themselves to human consciousness, and the cultural structure that is formed by virtue of institutionalizing the importance of one sensorial grouping over another. Thus a culture might base its cosmology on a taste-olfaction or acoustic structure rather than the typical visual-spatial structure of the West and value certain interplays of sensory data over others. Even more critically, Howes wonders, "What if there exist different forms of reasoning, memory, and attention for each of the modalities of faculties of consciousness (seeing, smelling, speaking, hearing, etc.) instead of reasoning, memory and attention being general

Figure 3.3. Shipibo-Conibo dream design. Drawn by a woman from Caimito, 1981. Courtesy of Angelika Gebhart-Sayer, Germany.

mental powers?" (10). While we have long assumed the latter, recent research in cognitive psychology has indicated that there may indeed be specific intelligences connected to sensory modalities, and that knowledge of the world is coded in a modality-specific rather than unitary fashion.[47] Howes concludes that insofar as different cultures emphasize the development of different modalities, their ways of thinking will also differ.[48]

In support of this thesis, he cites the work of Marsella and Quijano, who investigated ethnocultural differences in memory imagery (the capacity to imagine an object in its absence and to evaluate the vividness of the image) between Filipinos and Caucasian Americans. The authors speculated that differences in sensory modalities would be related to variations in patterns of socialization.[49] It was found that Filipinos scored higher on the kinesthetic, gustatory, cutaneous, and olfactory modalities, and the rank order of preferences and capabilities across different sensory modalities indeed differed between the two groups. They concluded that Filipino socialization processes encourage imagistic modes of thought representation, as well as different patterns of sensory use that subsequently affect the preferences and capability for vividness of imagery in different sensory modalities.[50]

This provides an interesting argument for an acculturated sensory response that is not confined to the possible, or even useful. That is, practical dominance does not ensure cultural dominance. Walter J. Ong points out that "cultures vary greatly in their exploitation of the various senses and in the way in which they relate their conceptual apparatus to the various senses."[51] Ong describes the sensorium and the entire sensory apparatus as an operational complex and contends that differences in culture can be thought of as differences in the sensorium.[52] Mallory Wober echoes this position when he defines the sensotype as the prevailing pattern of childhood intake and proliferation of information from the various sense modalities that differ according to culture.[53] And Constance Classen points out: "As our habits of eating, dress, language, and so on are determined by our culture, so are our habits of perception, and as the former express cultural codes, so do the latter."[54]

The clear implication is that not only is sensory response critical to any cultural outcome (like design), but the specific societal context (the sensory ratio of that culture) will need to be addressed if it is to resonate with its users. In the conclusion to *Varieties of Sensory Experience,* Howes and Classen offer five valuable considerations for the anthropologist: first, other cultures do not necessarily divide the sensorium as we do; second, the first step is to discover what sorts of relations between the senses a culture considers proper; third, senses that are important for practical purposes may not be important culturally or symbolically; fourth, sensory orders are not static but develop and change over time, just as cultures do; and fifth, there may be different sensory orders for different groups within a society.[55] That every culture develops its own sensory formula must surely provide a warning for the architect as well.

In light of these studies, we have postulated the following formula, not as a truism but as an operational device (Figure 3.4). This formula, PS / CM = CP, obtains where PS represents Piaget's view of perception as sensation mediated by learning structures, and CM represents the enviro-cultural factors that influence what, when, whence, and how we look. Put differently, we regard perception as an integrated system (sensation plus interpretation) of tendencies whose outline, shape, and meaning are the product of learned cultural inference. Thus the fundamental sensations—as seen in Gibson's five categories—provide the raw materials for a response influenced by context.

$$\frac{\text{Perceptual systems}}{\text{Cultural modifiers}} = \text{Contextual percept}$$

Figure 3.4. Contextual percept diagram. Created by Joy Monice Malnar and Frank Vodvarka.

The discussion of how we perceive our spatial environment has so far centered on visual phenomena, but as the principle of dynamic self-distribution maintains, perception taken as a whole is what is crucial to spatial experience. Of course, perception/response factors, insofar as they have meaning for design, exist to serve some expressive (and predictive) end. Rudolf Arnheim points out that "it is necessary to distinguish between the balancing of forces in the perceptual field itself and the 'outside' control exerted by the artist's motives, plans, and preferences. He can be said to impose his structural theme upon the perceptual organization."[56] Thus psychological theory can provide organized principles of perception (as well as other information) that can be used to reconcile complex design relationships (Figure 3.5).

Now, form follows function, we are told, which has often been taken to mean that the form proceeds directly from the purpose; discover the purpose, and the form will be obvious. But Arnheim maintains that form is not simply function made visible; "rather, it *translates* an object's function into the language of perceptual expression."[57] Thus Arnheim sees form as the particular way in which order is expressed, its visual symbolic manifestation. Because form always deals with this dual aspect of order, that of function and its image, it is critical that the two be in concert. Arnheim notes that outer order often represents an inner order and must therefore not be evaluated on its own; and that a lack of correspondence between outer and inner order will produce an element of disorder.[58] This disorder may be experienced when the visible order is perceived as fundamentally at odds with known reality, when the chosen elements of form seem inappropriate for the message, and when the cultural format is alien. Arnheim suggests that such a consonance between function and image results in true order, "a prerequisite of survival."[59] It is that order that we experience when the arrangement of a structure accords with a sense of place, and when our perception of the spatial construct agrees with that construct's ostensible purpose.

This clearly points to the multiple aspects of our comprehension of space, and the difficulty in obtaining this agreement. We believe that it is precisely these concerns

Sensory System	Stairs
Visual system	Color, material pattern, size of staircase, location of staircase in space, and whether in an enclosed or open space
Auditory system	Treads made of materials that emit tone when stepped on or tapped with a cane
	Space echoes or absorbs the sound of footsteps
	Mechanical sound introduced into enclosed stairwell
Taste-smell system	Venting to include whiff of fragrance to indicate stair room or beginning and end of stair run
Basic orienting system	Continuous run or changes in direction
	Rectangular or spiral
Haptic system Touch	Treads—material texture gradient, and change in degree of hardness; selection of material for its thermal conductivity to facilitate temperature transfer when walking barefoot
	Railings—material texture gradient (rough vs. smooth), change in degree of hardness (rubber vs. steel), thermal conductivity (copper vs. wood), drag (leather vs. marble)
	Vibration transfer between treads and railing or mechanical system and railings
Kinesthesia	Change in tread-to-riser ratio to decrease or increase exertion and speed of person (take into consideration stairs typically thought of as going below ground level or up into attic or loft space)
	Landings located to provide moments of rest
Temperature and Humidity	Heating and air-conditioning vents located at ankle, hand, or head height to indicate first and last stair treads
	Air vents located at top or bottom of stair to coincide with direction of main movement on stair
	Distinct air velocity, temperature, and/or humidity change at top and bottom of stair

Figure 3.5. Sensorially designed stairs. Created by Joy Monice Malnar and Frank Vodvarka.

that inform the relatively new discipline of environmental psychology. For example, it is the position of David Canter and Stephen Tagg that a starting point for an architectural classification system might be the implications that manipulations of form have for the architect, and the (hopefully) parallel implications for the building's users.[60] In this formulation, *form* refers not to a set of relatively rigid structural principles but to a kind of spatio-sensory calculation. They say, "If we are to classify buildings (and thus inevitably their parts) from a semiological viewpoint that has its roots in recordable human responses then it is of value, initially, to consider the different ways in which buildings can act as signs or symbols."[61]

Canter and Tagg divide these aspects into three contiguous areas: first, the physical attributes of buildings; second, the (affective) evaluations we make of them; and third, the type of activities we expect to occur within them. The inclusion of the second category, in our opinion, is highly significant. In fact, the authors conducted a series of studies based on connections between the physical characteristics of rooms and people's evaluations of them based on adjective pairs. Specifically, these attributes included window size, ceiling shape, and furniture layout, all of which were systematically varied and evaluated by the test subjects. They found, for example, that the building type has a direct effect on the way people classify aspects of that building (both as a whole and for the interior), and that furniture types related both to room scale and activities. The second conclusion should be seen in light of existing data showing that furniture is the most important determinant of room friendliness.[62]

We regard these studies as significant for three reasons: first, that their subject's sense of place and its relation to function seemed to be well structured and clear; second, that two of these categories are concerned with "human-response" aspects of the building rather than its structure; and third, that the real determinants of spatial satisfaction lie at least as much in what is communicated as in what is physically permitted. Critical in this regard is the willingness to consider sensory data (whatever the perceptual system and mediating structures) as an authentic response of people to the environment in which they are placed. Accordingly, in the next chapter we will pursue the idea of space, designed and natural, as a sensory cultural construct.

4. The Meaning of Meaning

We thus maintain that it is sensation—mediated by experience and culture—that shapes our response to spaces. But what is the precise nature of that reaction? Certain theorists have held that our most immediate reaction to sensation lies in the realm of emotion, with cognition following at a later point. William James makes this clear when he says that "the emotional brain-processes not only resemble the ordinary sensorial brain-processes, but in very truth *are* nothing but such processes variously combined."[1] Now, the extent to which James's observations are applicable to perception is questionable in that the emotions under consideration are those having a "distinct bodily expression" (12). More precisely, it is James's thesis that the bodily changes follow directly the perception of the exciting fact, and that our feeling of the same changes as they occur is the emotion (13).

Thus Köhler, while noting the theory with interest, avoided its direct invocation: "The James-Lange theory of emotional life claims that emotional experiences *are* sensory facts, namely, vague impressions which originate in our muscles, viscera, and so forth. There may be some truth in this theory. But it seems inadvisable to connect our present argument with this or any other theory."[2] Köhler points out, for example, that perceptual and emotional facts might simply resemble each other; and, more importantly, that the sort of visual and auditory phenomena he is interested in are not really addressed by the theory.[3]

It should be noted, moreover, that James acknowledges the possibility that feelings of pleasure and displeasure, interest and excitement, may occur in mental operations without any obvious bodily expression. He recognizes that arrangements of sounds and colors may be found agreeable, and that sequences of ideas may delight us. The first example—sounds, lines, colors—he regards as bodily sensations (or their image); the second he views as depending on processes in the ideational centers. James states that "together, they appear to prove that there are pleasures and pains inherent in certain forms of nerve-action as such, wherever that action occur."[4]

Common sense, he says, suggests that after an event occurs, we react—first emotionally and then physically. But James believes this order of sequence (common sense notwithstanding) is incorrect, that a more rational statement would be that we react physically to an event, which in turn induces the emotion.[5] He recognizes that this hypothesis appears somewhat unusual, but he argues: "Without the bodily states following on the perception, the latter would be purely cognitive in form, pale, colourless, destitute of emotional warmth" (13). And James reminds the reader that "the nervous system of every living thing is but a bundle of predispositions to react in particular ways upon the contact of particular features of the environment."[6] The more closely he scrutinizes his states, he says, the more he is persuaded that his moods, affections, and passions are actually constituted by the very bodily changes ordinarily thought to be their expression or consequence. Thus, were he to become corporeally anesthetized, he would be "excluded from the life of the affections, harsh and tender alike, and drag out an existence of merely cognitive or intellectual form" (18).

Now, this may not be so revolutionary an idea if we continue to hold that perception is conditioned by an experience, which has been, in a sense, codified.[7] This would, in broader terms, produce an emotional response conditioned by experience, and this likely represents our primary (and most profound) reaction to spatial constructs. It is this response, moreover, that underlies the formulation of nonrational, or mythic, space. E. V. Walter points out that the criteria used to form rational space are sometimes used to condemn mythic space, while to the mythic formation of consciousness, rational space is intangible and meaningless. "Modern 'space' is universal and abstract, whereas a 'place' is concrete and particular. People do not experience abstract space; they experience places."[8] Walter considers the subjective dimension of located experience as an expressive reality, in the same way that there are physical, perceptual, and cognitive realities. He notes: "A place is a concrete milieu and an expressive universe within specific social and physical boundaries. . . . 'Expressive' means laden with emotional and symbolic features of experience."[9]

Walter is mainly concerned with the features of outdoor, public spaces—but we will later argue that this might also include the expressive details of the interior. Moore, Allen, and Lyndon note that "a good house . . . speaks not just of the materials from which it is made, but of the intangible rhythms, spirits, and dreams of people's lives. . . . In its parts it accommodates important human activities, yet in sum it expresses an attitude toward life."[10] As we will argue throughout this chapter, those "intangible" aspects of buildings are largely responsible for the consequent responses of their inhabitants. We hasten to point out, however, that "intangible" is not the same as "unknowable," nor is affective response necessarily more obscure as a design parameter than the need for certain physical affordances. These designers go on to say, "Rooms are *unspecific spaces,* empty stages for human action, where we perform the rituals and improvisations of living. They provide generalized opportunities for things to happen, and they allow us to do and be what we will. . . . The empty stage of a room is fixed in space by boundaries; it is animated by light, organized by focus, and then liberated by outlook" (82).

Moore, Allen, and Lyndon define focus as the point—the center of interest—that acts to organize the space, such as a fireplace, piece of furniture, or collection of special objects. They later develop this idea by pointing out that there are a series of acts that add to the "livability" of a house, which they call inflections. The first of these inflections is "mapping," an essentially architectural process involving the actual elements of the house, which we discuss at length (as cognitive mapping) in a later chapter. The second inflection they call "collecting," which includes the display of personal and meaningful possessions. "By surrounding yourself with things that have special meaning for you, which you have chosen from among other similar things . . . you can add dimension to the place you inhabit and to its capacity to nurture your imagination."[11]

This statement in large measure recalls another of James's observations: "An emotional temperament on the one hand, and a lively imagination for objects and circumstances on the other, are . . . the conditions, necessary and sufficient, for an abundant emotional life."[12] But no matter how emotionally lively the temperament, he says, without a lively imagination for objects and circumstances, one's life will be cold and dry.[13] Writers have, of course, long known this and consequently exploited buildings for their expressive value. In a reference to literature, Phillipa Tristam remarks that the beginning of the nineteenth century witnessed a marked alteration in attitude to the domestic environment:

> For most historians of architecture and decor this transition is regrettable, since it is marked by the collapse of taste; but for the novelist it opens up many new territories for exploration. It is not only that the social range of fiction becomes much more inclusive, allowing the writer to explore interiors that make no claim to architecture, but that living space itself develops individual character . . . a true home, in the eyes of the novelists, is not defined by its likeness to other houses of similar or superior social standing, but rather by its individuality expressed in unpretentious honesty; its contents, that are determined by the affections, not by conformity to an agreed standard of "taste."[14]

Thus the dwelling is quite special, and the architect Martin Pawley has devised both a theory to account for spatial meaning and a method to authenticate it. In his essay "The Time House, or Argument for an Existential Dwelling," Pawley argues for a definition of spatial design that takes into account (among other things) the intimate identification of individuals with objects: "design is the arrangement and metamorphosis of objects to correspond to the ambiguous demands of human consciousness."[15]

He suggests that our possessions represent the "object-evidence" of our lives by offering tangible evidence of the past, and our place in it.[16]

Such evidence is vital, Pawley contends, because people have in large measure lost control of continuity in time and place in the public realm, as evidenced in the destruction wrought by both "development" and "redevelopment." That sense of permanence desired by human beings generally has been, in the interest of "progress" and economics, excised from the environment.[17] The result, he says, has been an ingrowing privatization, a tendency to withdraw into our homes as a place of refuge. If change is to become an acceptable fact of life (much less a desirable one), it will be necessary to outfit dwellings with mechanisms capable of absorbing the evidence of time—and its constituent change—so that the horror of that change might be mitigated (138). This would result, he says, "in the concretization of the evidence of human association with place within the dwelling itself" (138). The problem in designing thus is that "it is impossible to functionally define the act of dwelling, which is a continuously evolving drama, not a pattern established once and retained forever."[18]

Pawley has devised an interesting dwelling, the Time House, to solve this problem. Its concept rests on five interrelated axioms: first, that the public realm is inauthentic, as it cannot acknowledge the simultaneous presence of subject and object in the individual; second, that subjective and individual aspects of design can only be expressed in the authentic world of individual experience; third, that individuals authenticate an environment through the process of dwelling, thus making the

Figure 4.1. Martin Pawley, the Time House, 1968. Photograph courtesy of Martin Pawley, Oxford, United Kingdom.

private realm that of authentic experience; fourth, that places and objects are proof of individual experience; and fifth, that a continuous record of individual object relations could clarify the significance of place and object, as well as enable individuals to come to terms with environmental change (143). The Time House is designed to record that person/object interface and later play it back for the occupant. This process, argues Pawley, will allow us access to continuous information about the way we actually live, thus enhancing self-perception. We could thereby become clinically aware of our behavior in space and time and develop a greater appreciation for the characteristics of place (Figure 4.1).

This is an intriguing proposition, obviously more fantastic than serious, but with potential significance for the course of design in the future. That is, it combines two areas that seem promising for developments in spatial design: semiotics and environmental psychology. Indeed, insofar as all cultural phenomena constitute sign systems, architecture may be seen as a form of communication as well as the embodiment of spatio-functional paradigms. Umberto Eco speculates whether this idea might be "applicable to any type of design producing three-dimensional constructions destined to permit the fulfillment of some function connected with life in society."[19] (Thus his definition includes articles of practical design but excludes objects designed with purely aesthetic intent.) Eco concludes that we do experience architecture as communication, while still recognizing its functional aspect (12). That is, while architecture permits events to occur, it also actively suggests those events that are appropriate and assists in their formation.

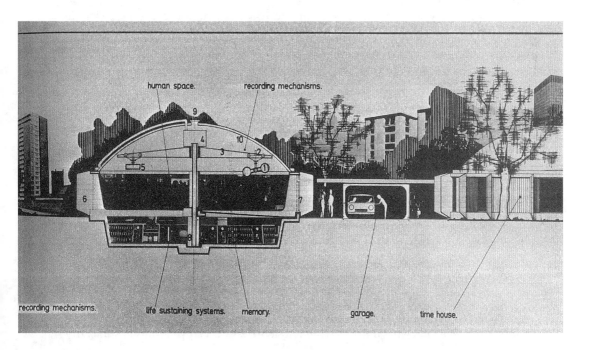

Eco therefore restates the "form follows function" principle as "the form of the object must, besides making the function possible, denote that function clearly enough to make it practicable as well as desirable" (22). This denotation should be sufficiently clear that it aids in the fulfillment of that function. He concludes that the tie between form and function needs to be explicitly communicated, and that the function should be denoted on the basis of habits and expectations, or code systems (22). There are two inferences that can be drawn from this: first, that all design draws on past codes for meaning; and second, that the meaning of *function* must include all possible uses of design, including the symbolic.

Geoffrey Broadbent notes these two approaches to architectural meaning—semiotics and environmental psychology—and states, "it seems to me that neither, alone, throws sufficient light on the subject but the two together offer some of the most exciting developments in the whole of architectural research."[20] And if these approaches seem too abstract to be of use, they represent a vast improvement over the built abstractions that surround us, which "convey blank alienation and contempt for humanity."[21] Now, it is surely appropriate to ask in what manner building forms—whether already constructed or still on the planner's table—"convey alienation and contempt," and what assumptions underlie such a self-defeating process.

It is not our position that designers have, during this past century, been purposefully attempting to produce oppressive housing paradigms. On the contrary, most housing—and we are thinking of that built in the public sector particularly—has been constructed with the best of intentions and a clearly articulated theoretical base. For example, the plan for "A City of Towers," Le Corbusier's 1920–1923 design for Paris, is often cited as the model for the American high-rise complex (Figure 4.2). But that may be less than fair. While he does refer to them as "apartments or flats," it is unlikely that he saw them as actual living units. In fact, he states: "It is evident that such buildings would necessarily be devoted exclusively to business offices and that their proper place would be in the centre of great cities. . . . Family life would hardly be at home in them, with their prodigious mechanism of lifts."[22] The structures that he conceived as living units (in 1920) were far more sympathetic to human scale:

> Vast airy and sunlit spaces on which all windows would open. Gardens and playgrounds around the buildings. Simple façades with immense bays. The successive projections give play of light and shade, and a feeling of richness is achieved by the scale of the main lines of the design and by the vegetation seen against the geometrical background of the façades. . . . A street such as this would be designed by a single architect to obtain unity, grandeur, dignity and economy. (60)

While the precise physical relationship between the high-rises and the residential housing remains somewhat unclear, we are nonetheless struck by Corbusier's sincerity of purpose.

We are less sanguine, however, about the assumptions that underlie that purpose. Whose vision of unity and grandeur is under discussion, for example, and who profits from the economy? When we consider Corbusier's view of what constitutes a proper way of life—and hence appropriate building characteristics—we are also struck by his elitism. He states, for example, that "what we need is towns laid out in a useful manner whose general mass shall be noble. . . . We have need of streets in which cleanliness, suitability to the necessities of dwellings, the application of the spirit of mass-production and industrial organization, the grandeur of the idea, the serenity of the whole effect, shall ravish the spirit and bring with them the charm that a happy conception can give" (40). It is, of course, his own "happy conception" that is meant.

In the chapter of *Towards a New Architecture* titled "Mass-Production Houses," Corbusier presents a series of housing concepts for varying circumstances, many of which are thoughtful and humane. Once again, the underlying ideology is not. He opens with this polemic:

> If we eliminate from our hearts and minds all dead concepts in regard to the houses and look at the question from a critical and objective point of view, we shall arrive at the "House-Machine," the mass-production house, healthy (and morally so too) and beautiful in the same way that the working tools and instruments which accompany our existence are beautiful. Beautiful also with all the animation that the artist's sensibility can add to severe and pure functioning elements. (210)

Figure 4.2. Le Corbusier, *A City of Towers,* 1923. Copyright 2002 Artists Rights Society (ARS), New York/ADAGP, Paris/FLC.

Thus the house is to be healthy, moral, functional, and (most important, one suspects) designed with an individual artistic sensibility. As we have pointed out, this has been the attitude of modernism generally; to the degree that modernism persists, so too does this viewpoint.

Rob Krier comments on Corbusier's Paris scheme: "For us, with the hindsight granted by fifty years of planning experience, this plan bears almost tragic significance. . . . The strikingly abstract design underlying this scheme, realised under the direction of a major architect, unfortunately generated an unforgivable epidemic of 'urban blight.'"[23] This is surely no exaggeration; so persuasive was this design that other such plans have surfaced with regularity in its wake.[24] Most of these "utopian" designs have, almost certainly for the better, never been built. But when they have, it has generally occurred in the area of public housing where the laws of supply and demand are suspended. Corbusier's statements echo in the words of Minoru Yamasaki, design architect for the now-notorious Pruitt-Igoe housing project in Saint Louis, built from 1952 to 1955. (In fact, Yamasaki claims to have been influenced not by Le Corbusier but by Mies van der Rohe.)[25]

At the outset of his autobiography, Yamasaki states: "Each building should enhance the lives of the people who enter or see it . . . for the individual person, a structure should communicate a sense of security and be so arranged that one never feels lost inside it."[26] In another place, he says that "it seems to me that the architect, by bringing order to people's lives, can make a significant contribution to a contemporary society that is too often fragmented and discordant."[27] (It does not require a great imagination to sense the presence of Corbusier in the phrase "bringing order to people's lives.") Now, Corbusier's Paris project was never built, and its viability was therefore never tested; were a socially intact population to voluntarily become occupants, it might have prospered. Pruitt-Igoe, with few stores or social service agencies nearby, a surfeit of deferred maintenance, long corridors, vulnerable elevators, and lack of controlled semiprivate space, was a disaster waiting to happen. And so Yamasaki's project profoundly failed and was dynamited less than twenty years after its completion.

Nor does Pruitt-Igoe represent a rare case; its counterparts appear with amazing consistency in most major American cities. In Chicago, the Robert Taylor Homes serve as reminder of Pruitt-Igoe both in building type and poverty of surroundings. A study of such social paradigms found that neighborhood social ties are inhibited by crowded, dangerous, and noisy settings, especially when there is strong possibility (or fear) of crime.[28] On the other hand, neighborhood social ties are promoted by environmental features that enhance the quantity and quality of informal social contact among neighbors (826). At the Robert Taylor Homes, to state the obvious, the former characteristics outweigh the latter. An interesting finding—to which we will return—is that trees and grass play an important role in attracting people to common spaces in inner-city neighborhoods, where such social contact can occur. The authors point out that the Robert Taylor Homes had originally been planted with trees and grass, but these elements were systematically removed or ignored over the years to keep maintenance costs low, resulting in a barren landscape (829). We find it significant that the residents are not involved in such decisions, for which there is little funding in any case. In any event, a substantial part of the Robert Taylor Homes was leveled in 2001 and 2002 as unsalvageable. It is a remarkable tribute to the human need for place that such a brutal environment could nonetheless serve as subject for personal decoration (Figure 4.3).

One might ask why these experiments failed. One answer lies in the form of the high-rise itself. In his influential book *Defensible Space,* Oscar Newman concludes that "the new physical form of the urban environment is possibly the most cogent ally the criminal has in his victimization of society. The concentration of population in large metropolitan areas has produced an urban form that makes hapless victims of its occupants."[29] Notably, Newman is making an argument not against population density per se but against the particular form of structure that we typically use to house that population. While he believes it possible to design such structures with "the range of mechanisms—real and symbolic barriers, strongly defined areas of influence, and improved opportunities for surveillance—that combine to bring an environment under the control of its residents," such tends not to be the case (3). The rationale for these structures lies, he points out, in the realm of economics alone, and once built they seldom satisfy even this limited criterion (7).

Figure 4.3. Young man with Robert Taylor Homes tattoo, Chicago, 1998. *Chicago Tribune* photograph by Ovie Carter.

Newman offers a broad range of solutions to the problem of lower-income housing, including the notion of low-rise construction that seems to have finally taken hold of the political imagination.[30] These also include the territorial definition of space, circulation and entry elements that provide security, and recreational zones that are actually usable. (As these elements are conspicuously absent, small wonder present housing becomes a center for crime.) We especially note his comment that the form of such buildings "evolved in response to pressures for higher densities, with no reference to previous traditions and no attempt at understanding the range of need to be answered in human habitat."[31]

Another answer is that it is the nature of "idealized" housing—built to serve ideological and sociopolitical ends—to be doomed to failure when occupied by those who do not share the designer's ideology, and cannot mitigate it. It was certainly the case with certain of Corbusier's other designs, like his worker's houses in Pessac, near Bordeaux (Figure 4.4). Over time these houses have been personalized by their inhabitants nearly to the point of architectural (though surely not symbolic) incoherence. The inhabitants of these abstract structures had license to alter the buildings in accordance with local custom and took full advantage of it (Figure 4.5). Moore, Allen, and Lyndon point out that "the carefully constructed dreams that Le Corbusier had forged were either not recognized or not accepted by those who came to live there. These people looked instead for confirmation of their own image of a house."[32] And indeed, why should they not?

Such housing, moreover, is usually conceived in near-total ignorance of the sensory attributes of the space, and how its occupants will respond. The relatively featureless quality of Corbusier's designs seems to have been particularly distressing. In fact, the inhabitants were so dissatisfied with, and alienated by, the designer's intent that when Philippe Boudon revisited Pessac some forty years later, he found it incredibly changed: "It seems that everybody has now converted his 'machine to live in' into a 'chez soi.' . . . This impression is sufficiently pronounced for the visitor to feel that, in addition to the normal processes of aging, there has also been a real conflict between what the architect intended and what the occupants wanted."[33]

Boudon goes on to say: "In this conflict the architect considered himself to be in the wrong: 'You know, it is always life that is right and the architect who is wrong . . . ,' Le Corbusier once said when speaking of Pessac. . . . But to speak of failure in this sense would be to assume that architecture is immutable and that architects are capable of satisfying their client's deepest habitational need."[34] We see two major problems in this assessment. In the first place, Corbusier, despite his entirely correct misgivings about Pessac (whose proposed inhabitants he knew little about), continued to support such a demonstrably inadequate design methodology in the years to come. In the second place—contrary to Boudon's assertion—we believe that architects have a profound responsibility to be sufficiently aware of their client's "deepest habitational needs" such that their clients need not resort to extraordinary measures to make buildings habitable.

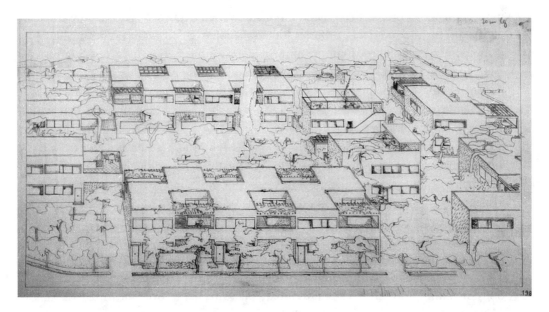

Figure 4.4. Le Corbusier, workers' houses, *Cité Fruge—Bordeaux-Pessac,* 1924. Copyright 2002 Artists Rights Society (ARS), New York/ADAGP, Paris. Copyright Fondation Le Corbusier.

Figure 4.5. Le Corbusier, workers' houses, Bordeaux-Pessac, 1924 (with owner's alterations, 1967). Courtesy of Philippe Boudon.

We will, a bit later, more thoroughly examine E. T. Hall's concept of "contexting," but it will suffice at this juncture to say that the designers of low-income complexes (or, for that matter, Corbusier himself) projected "low-context" codes onto the relatively "high-context" culture of the tenants. In this framework, "low-context" refers to fairly abstract, "socially constructive" codes being used to determine design parameters for a set of prospective inhabitants with a relatively high-context set of expectations and living modalities.[35] Here we might refer to the formula that we advanced in the previous chapter: PS / CM = CP. Our notion of "contextual percept" is like, and partially derived from, Segall's "cultural perceptions," where our view of the artifacts of existence—architecture included—is colored by our cultural experience. And low-context design, not to belabor the point, seldom considers such perceptions.

Previously, sensation was considered as a basis for expression, but expression in turn occurs within a structure we refer to as culture. And as E. T. Hall makes clear, there isn't a single aspect of human life untouched or unaltered by culture, even self-expression and our very modes of thinking.[36] Hall points out that one of the functions of culture is to screen the mass of data that threaten to overwhelm individuals with what has been called "information overload." One way of increasing our capacity to cope with this increase of complex information is through preprogramming, or "contexting." In communication between human beings, contexting compensates for the relative inaccuracy of language, as language is really an abstraction of an event (and written language a further abstraction of the spoken system). Thus an event is usually far richer in nuance than the language used to describe it.[37]

Hall maintains, however, that selective attention and emphasis—contexting—are characteristic not of language alone but of culture in its entirety. In fact, "in real life the code, the context, and the meaning can only be seen as different aspects of a single event."[38] The "rules" of selective perception comprise at least five categories: the subject or activity, the particular situation, one's social status, past experience, and culture (87). These collectively give meaning and structure to one's world, as well as permit us to more fully comprehend partial information. Thus Hall comments: "Internal contexting makes it possible for human beings to perform the exceedingly important function of automatically correcting for distortions or omissions of information in messages" (117). Hall further maintains that contexting is embedded in the processes that govern the evolution of both the nervous system and the sensory receptors, and that one of the chief consequences of the evolution of the neocortex has been the ability of humans to work with patterns to a greater degree (118).

It is these very tendencies that lead to an idiosyncratic view of the world around us. Hall says that his "studies of space—how people experience it and create a model of the spatial world in the central nervous system—forced me to acknowledge the perceptual clichés of my culture. These studies revealed the multisensory character of man's existence. . . . My world became round and deep and real. Full of smells, tastes, textures, heats, sounds, and muscular sensations . . . man, like all organisms, must not only respond with each of his senses but must be able to store and retrieve multisensory information as well" (177). The question, then, concerns the nature of the context that we understand this information in, since meaning and context are intertwined. And while it is possible to intellectually analyze linguistic codes as abstract entities, such is not possible in the arena of "real life."

Hall distinguishes between high-context (HC) messages, in which most of the information lies within the physical conditions themselves or is internalized in the person (while comparatively little is contained in the explicit part of the message), and low-context (LC) messages, where the mass of information is fixed within the explicit code.[39] While no culture, he maintains, strictly occupies one end or the other of this scale, complex multi-institutional cultures tend to be low context.[40] In cultures where LC communication is the norm, codes attempt to account for every exigency by being very explicit; in the process, incongruity between those codes and the individuals who must live them out often occurs.[41] Hall points out that this is not an entirely odd state of affairs; it is in fact difficult for someone to appreciate an informal, unstated need in another when that need is not shared. And these needs, often fugitive and indirect, are almost always seen as "less real" than the physical aspects of the building.

Thus low-context cultures place great emphasis on structural characteristics of buildings, the square footage and amenities, instead of (for example) opportunities for social intercourse and role-playing. These cultures express all this in complex specifications and building codes, as well as detailed listings of facilities. A high-context group, on the other hand, needs no such specifications; people agree about how a building should appear and function. In the United States, we are placed in the unenviable position of serving the needs of various high-context subgroups via the procedures of the larger low-context society. This raises an interesting question: might low-context design succeed if, as was the case at Pessac, the future inhabitants are given license to alter the buildings? (Individual alteration of living units represents a part of the solution for certain designers, as will become clear in our later discussion of Hundertwasser's project in Vienna.) Another problem, Hall notes, is that architects tend to consider (largely as a function of their education) spatial experiences as primarily visual.[42]

Bill Hillier and Julienne Hanson state: "Insofar as they are purposeful, buildings are not just objects, but transformations of space through objects."[43] They point out that space creates a special relationship between function and social meaning, and they conclude that the ordering of space in buildings is really concerned with the ordering of relations between people (2). Their theory is based neither on proxemic assumptions derived from territoriality nor on semiotic models (which are faulted for treating architecture as merely another type of artifact). They contend, rather, that the designed physical world "is already a social behaviour. It constitutes (not merely represents) a form of order in itself; one which is created for social purposes, whether by design or accumulatively, and through which society is both constrained and recognisable" (9). Thus spatial form results from a system of largely involuntary rules of behavior.

These authors make a further distinction that we find interesting. They note that in contrast to exterior spaces, interiors characteristically have more categorical differences between spaces (and thus spatial relationships), as well as a greater definition of what and where things can happen. "Interior space organization might, in short, have a rather well-defined relation to social categories and roles" (19). They conclude that the differences between interior and exterior represent differences in the ways that societies generate and control encounters: "interiors tend to define more of an ideological space, in the sense of a fixed system of categories and relations that is continually reaffirmed by use, whereas exteriors define a transactional or even a political space" (20). This duality is, then, "a function of different forms of social solidarity" (20). This description suggests that interior space is a form of high-context environment, while the exterior of a building is more likely to reflect low-context concerns. Of interest here is the obvious suggestion that, in either case, the appearance of the structure is of little concern—what counts is the manner in which it acts as a reflection of its culture.

In the prologue to their *Dwellings, Settlements, and Traditions,* Bourdier and Alsayyad point out: "The way one constructs meaning and understands semantically how a house is conceived, like the way one builds a house, is often indicative of either an ideology or a world view."[44] Now, the authors are speaking of "traditional" houses in particular, houses that are the result of a process of transmission and have cultural origins involving common people.[45] Although isolated studies from the eighteenth and nineteenth centuries certainly exist, it is only since the 1960s that the traditional building styles of non-Western peoples have been examined with such critical interest and, more importantly, an interest that is architectural as well as anthropological. Put differently, there is a new appreciation for the manner in which non-Western architecture functions socially, sensuously, and constructively in its own right, and not merely in contrast to Euro-American paradigms.

One would expect, therefore, to find an architecture that most profoundly reflects cultural imperatives in high-context cultures. And indeed, it is in indigenous cultures that we most frequently encounter spatial constructs that clearly represent concretized values. The sociologist Emile Durkheim, in his study of Native American tribal groups, has affirmed that their social organization has served as a model for their spatial organization, in fact reproducing it.[46] The anthropologist James W. Fernandez used Durkheim's social organization theories, as well as his notion of integral contradiction, to analyze the aesthetic principles employed by the Fang of equatorial Africa. This analysis, particularly as it pertains to the notion of cultural vitality as represented by contradictory elements in Fang art objects, is fascinating.[47] We shall, however, consider his arguments only insofar as they pertain to spatial constructs.

Fernandez notes, for example, that the Fang village is laid out with two long rows of houses facing each other across a narrow, barren court, thus giving an immediate impression of opposition, and that this is in fact quite deliberate.[48] This opposition may be found, moreover, not only among distantly related members of a clan *(mvogabot)* but within the family itself, as well as in the very important men's council house. The opposition that exists within the minor segment of the village—whose relationships are distant and tenuous—is spatially expressed by buildings placed opposite one another. Those families feeling strong allegiance to each other *(ndebot),* on the other hand, build their houses side by side, but only for as long as that allegiance remains solid. When those close bonds are no longer felt, spatial adjustments take place in the village. Thus the spatial configuration of the village is dynamic and reflects the constantly changing nature of relationships. Fernandez says that far from being adverse, this is necessary:

> One row of houses without its opposite does not constitute a village; such a village cannot be good, pleasing, or functional. Two opposite rows of houses, it is said, stand off the forest and in the old days of internecine strife provided a closed, fortified rectangle against surprise attack. Moreover, the social antagonisms of lineage members living on opposite sides of the court are one important source, it is admitted, of the animation *(elulua)* and vitality *(enin*—the word is actually used) that is one of the desired features of village life.[49]

Thus what is aesthetically appropriate is also that which is socially necessary; the spatial scheme both reflects and ensures social viability. It is in that permanent tension between opposites—expressed in spatial paradigms—that vitality is to be found in Fang life.

Much the same phenomenon has been described by Suzanne Preston Blier in her study of the aesthetic criteria identified with the building traditions of the Batammaliba people of northern Togo and Benin. Batammaliba domiciles, two-story earthen structures notable for their integrated design and monumental form, are, the author points out, studies in duality. In fact, she uses the term *oppositions* to describe their visual aspect; that is, balanced and dynamic, austere and lively, straight and curved, et cetera. But the essential meaning of these buildings is, she contends, "grounded in ethical canons and social mores."[50] Blier points out that this accounts for the orientation of Batammaliba houses to the west, where lies the abode of Kuiye, the deity of ethics, morality, life, and death. The house is, moreover, typically built on the foundation of an ancient house, thus incorporating "the corporate identity of the past family and community members" (339). So intimate is the connection between family and house (the same word, *takienta,* is used for both) that their strengths and weaknesses are seen as corollary. Hence a house may be rebuilt at important occasions (such as initiations and marriages) so as to remain ever young and beautiful (Figure 4.6).

The Batammaliba house is made of earth, and the drying process itself is seen as representing Kuiye, the solar deity. Blier notes: "A building which is made durable and strong through the heat of the sun is beautiful not only because it is better able to fulfill its function as a house but because it encourages one to see in oneself those qualities given by Kuiye, qualities which are essential both to one's well-being and the well-being of society" (342). Indeed, the whole of the architectural canon—evenness and balance *(yala)*, straightness and smoothness *(kunanku)*, and unity and containedness *(tamkumutabe)*—makes clear the close relationship between beauty, structure, and social mores in this society. Even the design of the house itself—its division between front (the positive, public social statement) and back (antisocialism and disorder)—speaks to that notion of oppositions pointed out by Fernandez. There are other fascinating aspects to Blier's article; for our purpose, however, her statement that "each beautiful building visually reaffirms the social mores and ethical values that help to bind the community together" should suffice (353). What is also clear is that such meaning can only occur in high-context societies with clear definitions of the social good.

China is somewhat of an anomaly in that it is a high-context but technologically advanced culture. It is perhaps because of this unusual combination of aspects that the Chinese have developed one of the most sophisticated systems of spatial definitions and attributes in history: feng shui. Sarah Rossbach says that "feng shui evolved from the simple observation that people are affected, for good or ill, by surroundings: the layout and orientation of workplaces and homes. In addition . . . some surroundings are better, luckier, or more blessed than others. Every hill, building, wall, window, and corner and the ways in which they face wind and water have an effect. . . . The aim of feng shui, then, is to change and harmonize the environment—cosmic currents known as *ch'i*—to improve fortunes."[51] For inspiration, feng shui

Figure 4.6. Batammaliba houses, Africa. Drawing by Joy Monice Malnar.

draws on sources such as Buddhism, Taoism, and animist magic, as well as simple observation. It is applied both to the siting and construction of a building and to its interior amenities (walls, openings, and furniture) with a view to mitigating the relationship between humankind and the environment. What is especially intriguing about feng shui is that in its emphasis on precise attributes of building character, it is low context; in its shared assumptions, it is decidedly high context.

Of particular importance is the connection between feng shui and Taoism, a philosophy based on the patterns of nature. Taoism, in turn, relies heavily on a pre-Taoist text, the *I Ching*, for inspiration. Rossbach remarks that the symbols of the *I Ching* "conjure up cosmic power and energy and . . . its trigrams provide feng shui men with eight bearings to properly align desks, doors, and buildings, setting man along a correct course in life."[52] But beyond such advice, much of which is quite practical, a feng shui expert seeks to divine and mitigate the spirit of the house, and the consequent sensations of its occupants. This notion of clarifying the nature of a particular place vis-à-vis a larger pattern should be familiar; it is in fact the essence of Henry James's experience described in chapter 1. Nor is it far removed from our own concept of contextual percept. On the contrary, it is a topoanalytic methodology that seeks to put the contents of the collective unconscious (postulated by Jung) to practical advantage. And much like Jung's hypothesis, it relies on metaphor.

Certainly Jung must have seen the parallels between his own theory and that of feng shui. He in fact wrote the foreword to the Richard Wilhelm translation of the *I Ching* in 1949. Jung was obviously fascinated by it, noting that it "is more closely connected with the unconscious than with the rational attitude of consciousness."[53] In any case, he points out, Western science is based on the laws of causality, and the "axioms of causality are being shaken to their foundations: we know now that what we term natural laws are merely statistical truths and thus must necessarily allow for exceptions."[54] Now, we do not wish to make a case for the absolute validity of feng shui or, for that matter, the *I Ching*.[55] It is rather the case that spatial paradigms, quite aside from their aspects of utility, can—and regularly do—serve as microcosms of culture. And it is this aspect of architecture that is a primary contributor to a sense of place.

Malcolm Quantrill has described the sensory aspects of the environment as the *genius loci,* or "sense of place." This tendency (as is true of feng shui) often takes the form of ascribing a spiritual persona to particular aspects of a building. E. V. Walter comments: "The *genius loci* . . . stood for the independent reality of a place. Above all, it symbolized the place's generative energy, and it pictured a specific, personal, spiritual presence who animated and protected a place."[56] This explains, for example, the Roman custom of placing various locations in the house under the stewardship of particular spirits, and granting certain points in the house more weight than others. Walter defines place as a location of experience: "It evokes and organizes memories, images, sentiments, meanings, and the work of imagination. The feelings of a place are indeed the mental projections of individuals, but they come from collective experience and they do not happen anywhere else."[57]

But "collective experience" is not the same thing as "universal experience"; rather, it refers to the experience of particular cultures. Thus the *genius loci* is always tied to the cultural reality of particular groups of human beings. This means that high-context building traditions tend to remain local, while low-context design may in fact be quite portable, at least in the mind of the designer so working.[58] Of course, the difference between the (usually novel) designs of a professional architect and the traditional practice of a village artificer appear quite striking. In Western culture, the separation is somewhat narrower, usually expressed as the distinction between architecture and the vernacular. The former has been thought to be responsive to theory, with an attendant concern for "beauty." Domestic buildings usually belonged in the category of the vernacular, "architecture without architects," which tends to be influenced by nearby models.

Thus the vernacular is cast as a simple regional building style, variable only within parameters such as climate, materials availability, personal finances, and social acceptability. Indeed, the term *vernacular* appears to derive from *vernaculi* (those born within the house), in reference to the importance of the owner's ideas in the design process. Alan Colquhoun notes: "Within the context of European history, then, the word *vernacular* can be taken to apply to practices of *making* (linguistic, constructional, etc.) that are either anterior to or untouched by classical theory and practice."[59] Thus it has been held that architecture, in the sense of design that responds to classical theory, aspires to a higher purpose than the vernacular. But is classical theory the pinnacle of design sensibility, or simply a reflection of a Eurocentric bias? Need theory be formally articulated to be present? And perhaps most important, should the formal-cognitive aspects of design take precedence over the sensory-affective features?

Amos Rapoport, for example, argues for a more inclusive definition of architecture, one that includes primitive, vernacular, and high-style environments. He points out that built environments have various purposes, such as sheltering people and their possessions from the climate, their enemies, and the supernatural, with a view to establishing a humanized, socially reinforcing space in a dangerous world. He concludes, "Socio-cultural factors in the broadest sense are thus more important than climate, technology, materials, and economics in influencing built form."[60] Both the primitive and the vernacular perform these cultural tasks with a high degree of congruence and redundancy that results from the users themselves creating built form through a system of shared (high-context) assumptions. For Rapoport, cultures design environments that a particular group sees as normative and for the lifestyle that it regards as significant. Thus an order is expressed; "a particular set of cognitive schemata or 'templates' representing some vision of an ideal is given form—however imperfectly" (287). The difference between the primitive and vernacular is that the vernacular has more latitude in its choice of culturally acceptable solutions—in part because of its awareness of high-style design. For Rapoport, these solutions reflect a characteristic way of looking at the world and, more importantly, of *shaping* the world.[61]

High-style design (low-context) implicitly is less congruent with cultural values, and hence less effective at transmitting similar schemata, or information. And yet high-style design, Rapoport argues, can only be understood in the context of the vernacular, from which it derives much of its imagery and ideological content. This begs a question: What is it that has been lost, if not cultural conviction, as a result of an effort to form a universal thesis? Of real interest is Rapoport's inclusive definition of architecture, which holds that all artificial environments are necessarily designed in that they embody human decisions and modify the world in a purposeful way (291). Such a view suggests that the hallmark of architecture ought to be the degree to which the environment has been successfully manipulated to provide physical and psychic comfort for its inhabitants, regardless of the degree to which the design has been personalized or draws on the codes of "high culture."

The success of vernacular housing is, in large measure, due to its ability to project a high-context image, and thus evoke appropriate responses. It is arguable that people subscribe to such imagery even when it is inappropriate to their heritage, in the comforting belief that the image will aid in their local integration. Moore, Allen, and Lyndon point out that as publications (especially pattern books) became common in the middle of the nineteenth century, people began to realize the wealth of choices open to them. They comment: "Western architecture became a catalogue to be rummaged through. . . . The impulse to recall the architecture of the past, though, was not silly. On the whole, people who made their houses recall far-flung historical precedents must have done so because these precedents meant something to them."[62] We are not, of course, any more defending the products of blind emulation than are Moore, Allen, and Lyndon. Rather, we are pointing out that in such evocations of the past are to be found the kind of sensuous and symbolic comforts usually lacking in our built environment.

5. The Talking Spring

Rome of the fourth century A.D. had never been in greater need of oracular prophecy to guide its uncertain future. And so Emperor Julian (the Apostate) sent his envoy Oreibasios to consult the aged Pythia at Delphi. Her response, however, was less than satisfying:

> Tell ye the King: the carven hall is fallen in decay;
> Apollo hath no chapel left, no prophesying bay,
> No talking spring. The stream is dry and had so much say.[1]

Thus did the oracle, more than a millennium old, cease to cast the future. But the power of Delphi to awe its many visitors has not ceased.

Delphi has, from mythic times, been a site of divination. The first such diviner was the mother of the gods, Gaia, followed by her two daughters, Themis and Phoebe. In *The Eumenides*, classical playwright Aeschylus has the Pythia pronounce this succession in the opening lines:

> I give first place of honor in my prayer to her
> who of the gods first prophesied, the Earth; and next
> to Themis, who succeeded to her mother's place
> of prophecy; so runs the legend; and in third
> succession, given by free consent, not won by force,
> another Titan daughter of Earth was seated her.
> This was Phoebe.[2]

The guardian of this sacred place in pre-Olympian times was Python, a female serpent who was slain by Phoebus Apollo after a great struggle (graphically recounted in the Homeric Hymn to Apollo). Apollo then founded his own oracle at this site, speaking through a priestess, the Pythia, whose incomprehensible cries were translated by some elders, or *prophetai* (Figure 5.1).[3]

The site of Apollo's *temenos* (sacred district) at Delphi is spectacular. It is said that when Zeus wished to locate the center of the Earth, he loosed eagles from the two ends of the world; they met at Delphi, the "navel" of the Earth. This place is marked by the *omphalos,* or navel stone, where pilgrims left offerings. The sacred precinct at Delphi lies high on the slope of Mount Parnassos, where there is a cleft in the rock; from this gorge flows the Kastalian Spring, where both priests and pilgrims purified themselves before entering the sacred precinct. The effect of the site may again be gauged from the Sacred Hymn to Apollo, which, addressed to the young god, records his first sight of Delphi: "You climbed rapidly, running across the hill-tops and you reached the regions of Krisa below Mount Parnassos which is covered with much snow . . . while below a wild valley stretches out; this was the spot the Lord Phoibos Apollo decided to have a beautiful temple."[4]

Before entering the sacred precinct, the pilgrim passed between a *gymnasion* and the *palaistra* with a central court. These areas served as venues for multiple forms of physical exercise and cultural activity. The path then passed the sacred Kastalian Spring, whose waters are so clear and musical. Upon entering the precinct through the main entrance in the southeast corner of the site, the visitor was regaled with a political litany in stone and bronze, statues that were placed there by the various cities to celebrate their victories (usually over each other). The path—a sacred way—then leads to the west and upward past the "treasuries" that held the offerings of the city-states to the shrine, until it reaches the huge temple of Apollo built in 369 B.C. This is the third temple to occupy the site in historical times, and the sixth if one counts the quasi-mythical first three. On the path one passed the *omphalos,* center of the earth, but also the tomb of Python. Above the temple is a theater in good condition, where musical contests were held, and still further up the mountain is a *stadion* for athletic events (Figure 5.2).

There are many fine texts that deal with the architecture, religious rites, and political aspects of Delphi. We are interested here in the qualities—sensory and other-wise—that early on convinced the Greeks that Delphi was a sacred place. Malcolm Quantrill described these sensory aspects of our environment as the *genius loci,* or sense of place, noting that we perceive frameworks of order in terms of particular characteristics of form, material, color, and directional emphasis.[5] It is, in fact, a familiarity with the details of places and spaces that increases their mnemonic vitality. Time thereby becomes compressed into memorable spatial images, "generating an architecture of spatial consciousness."[6] And we noted E. V. Walter's position that the *genius loci* represented the independent reality of a place, its generative energy.[7] Places, says Walter, are the locations of experience; a place evokes and organizes memories,

Figure 5.1. *Pythia of Delphi,* artist and date unknown. From Paul Christian, *Histoire de la magie* (Paris, n.d.).

images, sentiments, and meanings.[8] Thus do spaces come to be regarded as sacred or profane. Now, what combination of spatial images convinced the Greeks that this site was a *sacred* place?

For the Greeks, a sacred place always appeared so; that is, its distinction was evident in the physical and sensory aspects of its situation. Apollo looked at a number of sites before settling on Delphi, but found none "that did not yet thy minde's contentment yeeld / To raise a Phane [sacred district] on, and a sacred Grove."[9] Thebes had a suitable woods but was isolated and somewhat inaccessible to travelers. This was clearly inappropriate for what was to be a "public" oracle. While Delphi was similarly free from human settlement (a desirable thing), it could only be entered by humans on foot; that is, without coaches drawn by horses, which would be "quite exempt from awe" (535). Delphi, then, was a wild (but narrowly accessible) location overlooking a beautiful valley never broken by plow.

The place had still other attributes, having in part to do with human alterations and events. The temple raised on the spot, for example, was meant to endure: "Being all of stone, built for eternall date" (537). And, of course, it was home to Python, that representative of a matriarchal tradition cast and supported by Hera, wife of Zeus. All the necessary elements seem present at Delphi: a wild place high on the slope of a special peak; accessible but not easily so; a site where a cosmic drama is free to play out. In the comprehension of such a place, all the senses become involved, as well as knowledge of the symbolic context.

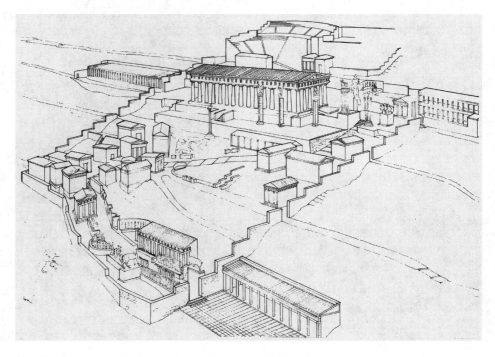

Figure 5.2. General view of Delphi, Greece, c. 1400 B.C. Drawing by Joy Monice Malnar.

In his *Space and Place,* Yi-Fu Tuan asks in what ways people attach meaning to and organize space and place.[10] In answer, he sees three consistent themes. First, he says, there are the "biological facts" of human comprehension of space, which includes notions such as front/back, upright/prone, and so forth. Second, there is the relationship between space and place, the manner in which the former gradually—through experience—becomes the latter. (Thus does the *spot* where Zeus's eagles meet become the *place* of the *omphalos.*) Third, there is the effect of experience and knowledge on our perception of space—an experience that can be direct and sensory or indirect and conceptual, mediated by symbols.[11] Thus there was an early, immediate experience, or perception, of Delphi such that the space itself was memorable; that space gradually became a special place by virtue of its extraordinary appropriateness to what occurred there, that is, the oracle; and third—most certainly at Olympian Delphi—its experience became very rich intimately and symbolically through the attention lavished by the various city-states and rulers. This also raises the question of distinctions—as expressed in the descriptions of Delphi—between sacred and profane space, at least as seen in forms of landscape.

Oedipus at Colonus was written by Sophocles just prior to his death and produced posthumously. The story concerns the royal house of Thebes, a topic he had explored twice before. These were the plays *Oedipus the King* and *Antigone.* The former tells the tragic story of Oedipus's murder of his father and subsequent marriage to his mother, events that had been foretold and which Oedipus had tried to avoid. In his anguish and self-loathing, he blinded himself and wandered into exile. It is this play that sets the stage for *Oedipus at Colonus. Antigone* tells the story of the civil war between Oedipus's sons that followed, and his daughter Antigone's death. Although written much earlier, this play really serves as the temporal sequel to *Oedipus at Colonus.*[12] What is of interest to us is Sophocles' evocation of two very different sorts of spaces at the outset of the play.

Oedipus and Antigone make their way along a path, he blind and old, she lending her support. He asks: "Where have we come, Antigone, my daughter?"[13] Antigone replies that they are coming to a city, but that where they now stand "is surely sacred ground, where vines and laurels and olive trees grow wild; a haunt of birds, where nightingales make music in the coverts."[14] In the ensuing conversation, it becomes clear that although Antigone knows that they are somewhere near Athens, she does not know the precise location. She asks if she should find that information out. Oedipus answers in the affirmative, if indeed there are any people in the vicinity to ask. What is clear from the exchange is that the place where they stand has two identities, one sacred (immediately noted by Antigone) and the other profane (and yet to be ascertained).

E. V. Walter points out that when Antigone says that this is a holy place (sacred ground), she uses the older Greek word for place, *choros,* rather than the more prosaic term, *topos.* Oedipus again asks where they are, and she replies that she does not know whom the *choros* honors, nor what *topos* they stand in, but she will find out. In fact, the goddesses of this spot are the Eumenides, the Gentle All-Seeing Ones. (Thus the *topos,* a spot near Colonus, quickly becomes an entirely secondary concern in comparison to the *choros.*) Somewhat later in the play, Oedipus tells Theseus that he will reveal the *choros* where he must die, but asks that Theseus not reveal its *topos.* Walter notes: "Here, *topos* stands for the mere location of the container of the sacred *choros,* the grave."[15] Thus the place distinctions that Oedipus makes at the outset of the play and later are important, confirming that places have physical and spiritual characteristics.

Now, the point was made earlier that for the Greeks, a sacred place always appeared so. Thus Antigone knew immediately that wherever she and her father were, it was surely sacred ground. How can she know this, unless she is responding to a landscape archetype? Here Sophocles is using a rhetorical *topos (ecphrasis),* one already well established by the fifth century B.C. in the description of vines, laurels, olive trees, birdsong, and the like. It is clear that while a *topos* might have one or another of these qualities, the presence of all of them indicated a special place. These elements are again present in the first *stasimon,* or choral interlude, of the play:

> You have come, friend, to the finest
> Land on earth, that breeds fine horses;
> Colonus, where the meadows
> Sparkle in the sun, where choirs
> Of nightingales, on leaf and branch,
> Make a green world of music,
> Nesting where the ivy hangs
> Dark as wine, and in the bushes
> Bursting with berries, here
> In god's own private garden, safe
> From sun and wind and weather,
> Favored haunt of Dionysus
> And the nymphs that wait upon him.[16]

Sophocles goes on for another three stanzas to describe the morning dew, flowing waters, golden flowers, and above all that "gray nurse of youth, the olive tree."[17] Nor does he neglect to praise the gods responsible for all this.

In his commentary on the works of Sophocles, James Hogan points out that "the first stasimon . . . praises Colonus, the olive tree, Athens, and, obliquely, Athena and Poseidon, whose gifts have made the country great. In the first two stanzas (668–94) we have a common rhetorical topos on the theme of the *pleasance* (Latin *locus amoenus*)."[18] He notes that Ernst Robert Curtius has offered a description of such a pleasance, at least as it was formulated in the Roman period, that closely parallels that postulated by Sophocles. In fact, Curtius says that the pleasance is "a beautiful, shaded natural site. Its minimum ingredients comprise a tree (or several trees), a meadow, and a spring or brook. Birdsong and flowers may be added. The most elaborate examples also add a breeze."[19] Curtius observes that this rhetorical device can be found in the works of Homer, with whom "the Western transfiguration of the universe, the earth, and man begins. Everything is pervaded by divine forces. . . . Nature shares in the divine . . . a cluster of trees, a grove with springs and lush meadows."[20] In fact, both the *Iliad* and the *Odyssey* abound with descriptions of places that the reader knows are special by virtue of their spatial inventories.

While the *locus amoenus,* or pleasance, may have had its origins in the Greek world, Curtius obviously believes that it flowered during the Roman Empire. Thus he cites a poem by the fourth-century poet Tiberianus:

> Through the fields there went a river; down the airy glen it wound,
> Smiling mid its radiant pebbles, decked with flowery plants around.
> Dark-hued laurels waved above it close by myrtle greeneries,
> Gently swaying to the whispers and caresses of the breeze.
> Underneath grew velvet greensward with a wealth of bloom for dower,
> And the ground, agleam with lilies, coloured 'neath the saffron-flower,
> While the grove was full of fragrance and of breath from violets.
> Mid such guerdons of the spring-time, mid its jewelled coronets,
> Shone the queen of all the perfumes, Star that loveliest colours shows,
> Golden flame of fair Dione, passing every flower—the rose.
> Dewsprent trees rose firmly upright with the lush grass at their feet:
> Here, as yonder, streamlets murmured tumbling from each well-spring fleet.
> Grottoes had an inner binding made of moss and ivy green,
> Where soft-flowing runlets glided with their drops of crystal sheen.
> Through those shades each bird, more tuneful than belief could entertain,
> Warbled loud her chant of spring-tide, warbled low her sweet refrain.
> Here the prattling river's murmur to the leaves made harmony,
> As the Zephyr's airy music stirred them into melody.
> To a wanderer through the coppice, fair and filled with song and scent,
> Bird and river, breeze and woodland, flower and shade brought ravishment.[21]

Curtius contends that this highly sensuous poem is based on a rather strict structure that relies on the "six charms of landscape" enjoined by another fourth-century writer, Libanius; these are the now-familiar springs, tree groves, gardens, flowers, birdsong, and soft breezes.[22] Indeed, in the last line alone, all six charms are alluded to. Also significant, in our view, are the references to whispers (of the breeze), murmurs (of the river), caresses, colors, and perfume; in short, all of our senses are appealed to. Tiberianus thus relies on landscape archetypes that combine sensory pleasure with a sense of the sacred, all found through "fortunate happenstance."

This rhetorical device—the *locus amoenus*—thus served as a means of denoting certain physical spaces as special. And as the Greco-Roman tradition intertwined landscape with divine presence, that "special" quality had profound overtones. Curtius notes that this device was considered a "poetical requisite" by writers on style well into the Middle Ages.[23] In this way, the characteristics that made Delphi or the Vale of Tempe immediately recognizable to the ancients as significant places were made available to writers of the Middle Ages such as Walter of Châtillon and Dante.[24] Thus Dante's description in his *Purgatorio,* canto 28:

> Eager now to explore inside and around
> The heavenly woodland, thick with living green,
> That made the new day gentle to my eyes,
> Without waiting any longer, I left the slope
> And slowly started out across the field.
> The ground was breathing fragrance everywhere.
> A sweet breath of air, which had no change of
> Motion in it, was brushing my forehead
> With as little violence as a soft wind.[25]

Dante goes on to include a sacred hill, birdsong, and streamlets in his description of the ancient wood. Curtius believes that a study of romance poetry would yield many other connections with the Latin/Medieval traditions as well. Of interest to us, however, are the parallels between the pleasance as literary device and landscape construct. After all, the meaning of the pleasance in literature depends upon our awareness of its physical embodiment, of how such described spaces are sensorily experienced. We know the place because of the archetype, a fact relied upon by authors well into our own century (Plate 1).

What is clear is that the definition of "pleasance" had greatly altered by the eighteenth century. This can be seen explicitly in the five Oxford English Dictionary definitions of the term. The first four deal with pleasure, delight, the condition or feeling of being pleased, enjoyment, joy, a pleasing manner or behavior, that which awakens or causes pleasure, that in which one delights, and so forth. Number five— the most elaborate and precise—is a place of delight, a pleasure ground, usually attached to a mansion; sometimes a secluded part of a garden, but more often a separate enclosure laid out with shady walks, trees and shrubs, statuary, and ornamental water, sometimes surviving as the name of a street or place.[26]

Specifically, the notion of pleasance has changed from the Greco-Roman notion of a place of symbolic aspects (trees, water, meadow, breeze, etc.) arranged by divine manipulation and chanced upon by a fortunate humanity—a place whose features were highly sensory in nature—to that of a designed space, a garden, usually attached to a residence. Nicolas Le Camus de Mézières, in his lively *The Genius of Architecture* (1780), says: "Gardens are a great enhancement to buildings when well related; when the esplanade in front is well proportioned; when the parterres are in proportion, maintaining always the happy disarray, the piquant oddity, that marks the productions of nature; when Art, while seeming neglected, contrives to show us agreeable and charming vistas terminated by delightful points of view that excite the liveliest curiosity."[27] A few lines later, he comments on the *Essai sur les jardins* (Essay on gardens) by Claude-Henri Watelet: "In it, all is sensed, all is foreseen, all is reasoned and dictated by delicacy."[28] In short, gardens are opportunities for displays of design sensibility and taste in which divine presence is denoted by "the piquant oddity."

Now, the basic premise of *The Genius of Architecture,* that sensation can be predicted and guided, is one that we have little problem with. But what does the author mean by sensations? And from whence are they derived? It seems clear that, far from the symbolic yet immediate and highly visceral impressions that characterized the pleasance in prior centuries, we now have a calculated and cognitive sort of venture. This is, in large degree, unavoidable: gardens are designed by humans, the classical pleasance by divinities. Nonetheless, in this new conception, the pleasance seems already destined to evolve into the intensely ordered, ocular-centric pathway (parterre, esplanade, and, by extension, avenue) that is so central to nineteenth-century design, especially in France.

In this paradigmatic shift, the topistic aspects of ordered space—the control of elements and symbol—have replaced the spiritual attributes that marked a *choros.* Such gardens still have spatial character, of course, but it is in celebration of the human ability to manipulate data—usually geometric—to specific ends, usually involving axis, proportion, and symmetry. Other designers of the late eighteenth century will take this approach further, and more absolutely, an approach in which it is clear that *topos* has replaced *choros,* and the built the natural. But how does design make such spaces memorable in the way that ancient spaces were?

In the case of nature, at least, it would appear that the process of isolating and identifying special spaces was already a literary convention by the classical age. These aspects have further been codified into garden elements and organized into a more or less regulated system of design. Landscapes, to state the obvious, are not gardens. Indeed, "it is only through the selection and composition of their elements and materials that gardens are made."[29] The debate, by the eighteenth century, really concerned the degree of regularity thus imposed on the garden. In this sense, it echoes the great debate over the relative merits of neoclassicism and romanticism generally. While France of the seventeenth century and early eighteenth witnessed an increased devotion to the notion of a semidivine autocracy revealed in the wonders of engineering, England saw (particularly in the eighteenth century) a remarkable attempt to evoke those older Greco-Roman values in romantic countryside estates.

The epitome of neoclassical garden design in France is likely the garden complex at Versailles, designed by André Le Nôtre in the seventeenth century. Its assertion of an ordered nature set in a geometrically derived structure seems fitting tribute to Louis XIV, a sun king with attributes both human and divine (at least in his mind). But an equally ordered, slightly less grandiose design by Le Nôtre can be seen at Vaux-le-Vicomte. The château, designed by Le Vau, stood in a 170-acre estate, with a fine view of the gardens in all directions. Le Nôtre's design at Vaux (1656–1661) in fact precedes Versailles and marks a departure from the more cloistered gardens of the Middle Ages.

> Here, for the first time, the pattern garden, previously cut off from a hostile world by a clear and definite edge, plunges through that edge and invades nature, while it eludes containment. At Vaux the canal is placed *across* the axis, so it vanishes out of the manicured garden into wild and uncontrolled nature, which had for so long seemed too hostile to penetrate but which seemed at last, in the confident seventeenth century, ready for human engagement.[30]

This statement is interesting for several reasons: first, that this garden is the product of axial symmetry; second, that it is seen as invading a "hostile world," comprising a "wild and uncontrolled nature"; and third, that until the "confident seventeenth century," it was a nature unready for "human engagement." The authors are of course indicating not how they necessarily see the situation but how the seventeenth century likely saw it. Still, it is an apt description of how distinct the garden had become from landscape in general.

An examination of Vaux reveals that it comprises a large, roughly rectangular area marked, at one end of the longitudinal axis, by the château fronted by elaborate parterres (Figure 5.3). At the other end is a domed fountain with semicircular plantings to its rear, fronted by a grotto. In fact, the château is marked by such plantings

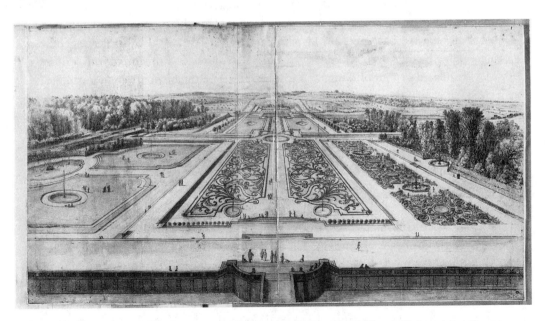

Figure 5.3. Israel the Younger Silvestre, *View in Perspective of the Garden at Vaux-le-Vicomte.* Photograph by J. G. Berizzi, Louvre, Paris, France. Copyright Réunion des Musées Nationaux, Art Resource, N.Y.

to its rear as well, resulting in a figural containment of the "château to fountain" axis.[31] The minor axis, set at a right angle to this development, is represented by the canal. The effect of this elaborate garden is that of "a pattern that speaks of power, over nature and over men. It uses finite formal geometries to bring us to the brink of infinity."[32] Above all, as Louis XIV must certainly have noted when he visited it, the garden had the power to awe its audience.[33]

At a somewhat later date, Le Nôtre designed still another garden on a smaller scale than either Vaux or Versailles. Marly-le-Roi (1679–1686) is located just outside Paris and relies on an elegant combination of parterres and water features contained within a jewel-like, enclosed setting for effect. Within, all is ordered and serene; outside the wall is the chaos of life, including the sorts of creatures excluded from Delphi (Figure 5.4). The "extensions" into nature that Le Nôtre had provided at Vaux, as well as the complex axial planning, are eschewed in favor of a single axis from château to grotto, all carefully controlled and centralized.

In stark contrast to the gardens at Vaux-le-Vicomte—and certainly Marly-le-Roi—are the estate gardens at Rousham in England, designed by the architect, painter, and landscape designer William Kent. In his *History of the Modern Taste in*

Figure 5.4. Pierre Denis Martin, *View of Castle and Pavilion at Marly,* 1723. Courtesy of Chateaux de Versailles et de Trianon, Versailles, France. Copyright Giraudon, Art Resource, N.Y.

Gardening, Horace Walpole said that Kent was "born with a genius to strike out a great system from the twilight of imperfect essays. He leaped the fence, and saw that all nature was a garden."[34] Critical to his approach, of course, is the notion of a nature that simply required a few nudges (and corrections of prior designs) to be improved. Here Kent has used the rather picturesque turning of the river to advantage, balancing its asymmetrical movement with a series of symmetrical fishponds and some "classical" garden structures. This last item is crucial, as it suggests both a divine presence and the passing of time. J. Douglas Porteous comments that the chief tenets of romanticism were idealist and religious. As nature is divine, it was necessary to conduct a metaphysical quest to discover the divine essence manifested in natural forms.[35] This precluded, however, neither formal development of landscape elements nor the use of classical reference.

Thus the meandering river is hinged to a minor axis formed by the ponds. The result is a larger composition that is figurally asymmetrical—quite unlike Vaux—that can be discovered only through a gradual process of unfolding, also unlike Vaux. Kent accomplishes his ends through the massing of plantings, creation of water features, and the enhancement of vales and terraces. Even the necessary fences are hidden, using a device called the ha-ha.[36] That he seeks to invoke—through spatial inventories and constructions—a Greco-Roman world is clear enough. And while one can argue that his approach is no less calculated than that of Le Nôtre, his intention is certainly distinct from French gardens "characterized by their uniformity and rectangularity, with endless vistas punctuated by statuary."[37]

Of special note are the designs of Lancelot Capability Brown, whose name has become synonymous with eighteenth-century English landscape design. He earned the sobriquet "Capability" by virtue of his regard for the existing pattern of elements at the site, which became a starting point for his improvements. He typically designed extensive open areas that carried up to and around the manor house, in sharp contrast to the older notion of surrounding the house with smaller, defined garden areas. The effect was one of increased connection between structures and landscape in a strikingly modern conception. As always, water was used as a major element, as were temples and, perhaps most surprising, farm animals.[38] Brown's redesign of the park at Blenheim in Oxfordshire is instructive; here he altered a landscape design as rigidly arranged as the palace—designed by Sir John Vanbrugh for the Duke of Marlborough—itself.

The result is a pastoral park that gently contrasts with the palace and softens its effect, as the altered plan illustrates (Figure 5.5). William Mavor, in *A New Description of Blenheim* (1789), affirms the effects: "The Water, the Palace, the Gardens, the Pillar, Woodstock, and other near and remote objects, open and shut upon the eye like enchantment; and at one point, every change of a few paces furnishes a new scene, each of which would form a subject worthy of the sublimest pencil."[39] But even Brown's creations were subject to change. The sweeping lawns at Bowood House in Wiltshire, once reaching the house, are now interrupted by an extensive parterre

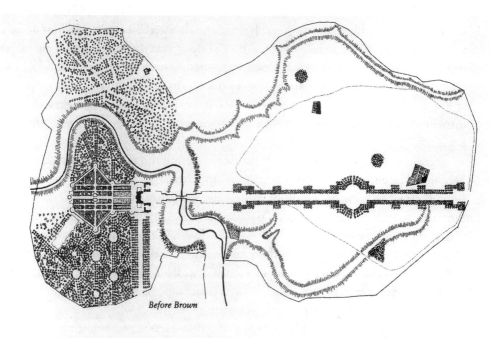

Before Brown

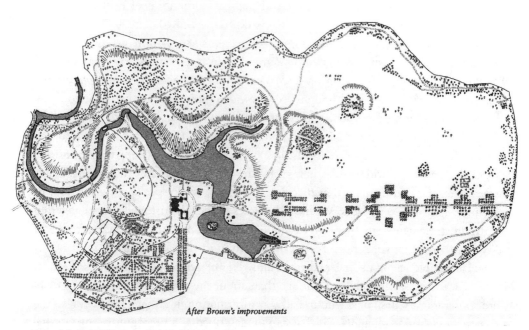

After Brown's improvements

Figure 5.5. Plan of Blenheim Park, Oxfordshire: *above,* pre-1764 plan; *below,* design of Capability Brown, 1764. Drawings by Maya Reiner for Charles W. Moore, William J. Mitchell, and William Turnbull Jr., *The Poetics of Gardens* (Cambridge: MIT Press, 1988). Copyright 1988 Massachusetts Institute of Technology.

emplaced during the nineteenth century. Even at Blenheim Palace, formal gardens were reintroduced early in this century. In both cases, the influence of French design can be seen, something Brown would have found disagreeable. In the draft of a letter written in 1775, he states: "In France they do not exactly comprehend our ideas on Gardening and Place-making which when rightly understood will supply all the elegance and all the comforts which Mankind wants in the Country. . . . Placemaking, and a good English Garden, depend intirely upon Principle and have very little to do with Fashion; for it is a work that in my opinion disgraces Science wherever it is found."[40]

Brown notwithstanding, English landscape during the nineteenth century often became as dependent on formal structure as any French garden. And both were compromised by the miniaturization of garden elements made necessary by the shrinking space allotted them. In England, the decline in the landscape movement after 1815 was noted (and deplored) by the last of the "grand" garden designers, Humphry Repton, indicating how early in the nineteenth century the movement effectively ended.[41] The young United States, of course, had land aplenty. And, in fact, there has always been a marked preference for wild landscape (certainly in art), in perhaps the most direct evocation of the Greco-Roman pleasance of all.

This search for divinity in the forms of nature can be seen most clearly in the paintings of such Hudson River school artists as Thomas Cole and Asher B. Durand, particularly Durand's *Kindred Spirits*. And popular admiration of primitive nature is attested by the establishment of national parks in the United States—the first being Yellowstone in 1871—and the still impressive percentage of land reserved for natural evolution. Gardens, when designed on a grand scale at all, tended to follow the lead of European counterparts. And on a smaller, more familiar scale, they have usually served pragmatic purposes, although recent research indicates that their function may be broader and more far-reaching than previously imagined.

What becomes increasingly clear is that we in the twentieth century have inherited a fairly ritualized set of landscape archetypes. A pleasance, we have learned from the classical world, can be known by the presence of water (talking or otherwise), tree groves, birdsong, flower scent, and so on, while special rocks (such as at Delphi) signify special places. We have examples of these landscape factors converted into garden elements, whether formally (as in France) or picturesquely (as in England). We know how to invoke memory, as can be seen in the use, especially in England, of classical temple elements or "medieval ruins." If the references seem at times a bit strained, it may say more about our age than about the past. And, in any case, there are contemporary designers who use all this information in rather creative ways.

In an elaborate reference to what can be described as a precognitive, primordial state, Charles Jencks has designed a garden based on symbol and chaos theory:

In a garden without flowers, exotic ideas flourish. Amid the rolling borderlands of Scotland, this 300-acre "theme park" bursts from the fertile mind not of a gardener but of an architectural theorist. Over the past five years the erudite and glamorous Charles Jencks . . . has transformed the staid country estate of his mother-in-law, Lady Keswick, from a charming bosk-and-dell affair into a landscaped folly of bizarre originality. In place of herbaceous borders and seasonal plantings, there are folds and fractals, solitons, snakes and snails. . . . Jencks's intent was to demonstrate the rich design potential to be mined from chaos and complexity theories.[42]

The water elements were the idea of Maggie Keswick, a scholar of Chinese land-scape design, which in turn reflected a long-standing interest in feng shui. The two mounds, however, were Jencks's idea. The "snail" is constructed of earth piled to the point of collapse ("phase transition" in chaos theory), and the snake form is based on the concept of "enfolding," or combining two disparate elements into one. Thus the snail and snake mounds represent the garden's cardinal metaphors (Figure 5.6). Other elements in the garden depict various events in the history of the universe. All in all, it is a garden ordered by principles of disorganization, a representation of clarity revealed by mystery.

The shape of the snake mound is particularly evocative, recalling the Great Serpent Mound in Adams County, Ohio. The largest ritual object of the Adena peoples, it is one of perhaps five such mounds in Ohio.[43] E. G. Squier and E. H. Davis, in their

Figure 5.6. Charles Jencks, Snail Mound, seen from Snake Landform, 1994. Lakes designed by Maggie Keswick. Courtesy of Charles Jencks, London.

remarkable survey of 1846, drew a splendid diagram of the mound (Figure 5.7). It is sited on a hill that sharply rises 150 feet above Bush Creek; on the side away from the creek, the slope is far gentler. Squier and Davis describe the serpent as having a body (five feet high in places) made up of graceful undulations that span about seven hundred feet and end in a triple coil at the tail.[44] They continue: "The neck of the serpent is stretched out and slightly curved, and its mouth is opened wide as if in the act of swallowing or ejecting an oval figure, which rests partially within the distended jaws" (97). They also point out that serpent forms—with or without such accompanying oval or egg shapes—are common features in many societies, in both the Old and New Worlds (97). This perhaps accounts for the oddly familiar, primordial quality of the mound, an attribute often found in early North American effigy mound structures. It is, moreover, a quality that suggests a larger, more significant content is present.

Another evocative design, one that combines architectural information with a symbolic park setting, is *Emilio's Folly: Man Is an Island* (1984), a projected weekend retreat by Emilio Ambasz (Plate 2.). The design, he says, came to him as an image, "full-fledged, clear and irreducible, like a vision."[45] The design comprises a wide, flat, green field with a sunken area—half lake, half steps—that contains a hollow mountain. The entrance to this area, located at the apex of the steps, is through a baldachin upheld by three columns and crowned with a lemon tree. Access to the mountain is by a log barge covered with a thatch roof, on which Ambasz could travel from the bottom of the steps to an opening in the side of the mountain—or, alternatively, to an L-shaped cloister at its base, where he could meditate or engage in creative activity.

The cloister—obviously of prime importance to Ambasz—contained a series of alcoves that he began (in his vision) to fill with meaningful objects from his life. He started with the things of his childhood and progressed with the storage as his life progressed, creating a repository of significant objects: "Not all the things I stored in these alcoves were there because they had given me pleasure, but I could not rid myself of them."[46] Thus this represented neither the collector's passion nor a romantic self-indulgence; on the contrary, it was powerfully autobiographical and self-revelatory. One of the alcoves formed an entrance to an underground tunnel from the mountain to an irregular pit, in which a dense mist provides an endless rainbow. In this case the landscape and the architecture are conflated and guide our response through metaphor and symbol. Some further insight into the design's meaning—indeed, any design—may be gained by Ambasz's statement "Architecture is not the answer to the pragmatic needs of man . . . but . . . giving poetic form to the pragmatic."[47]

For a final example of a garden that deeply partakes of the symbolic, we might consider Carl Jung's country home at Bollingen. A house that grew by accretion, each addition representing a central event in his life, it became a tribute to memory. Nor is the garden neglected in Jung's view of spatial paradigms. Of special interest here is the stone that Jung covered with inscriptions and placed in his garden. In a letter

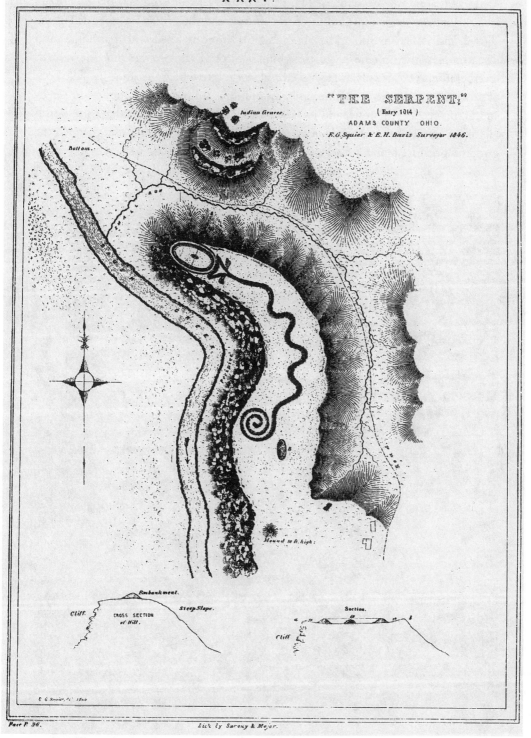

Figure 5.7. E. G. Squier and E. H. Davis, Serpent Mound, Ohio, 1846. Courtesy of the Rare Book and Special Collections Library, University of Illinois at Urbana-Champaign.

of 11 February 1956, he wrote: "The stone belongs to its secluded place between lake and hill, where it expresses the *beata solitudo* and the *genius loci*, the spell of the chosen and walled-in spot. The air round the stone is filled with harmonies and disharmonies, with memories of time long ago, of vistas into the dim future with reverberations of a faraway, yet so-called real world into which the stone has fallen out of nowhere. A strange revelation and admonition."[48] Jung's inscriptions—in Greek and Latin—cover the stone, and included is a drawing of a man's image corresponding to the pupil of the eye. It is in every sense an offering, a pivot around which the garden is organized, and a place of memory as well (Figure 5.8).

Figure 5.8. Carl G. Jung, garden stone, Bollingen, Switzerland. Courtesy of Fritz Bernhard, Uster, Switzerland.

We have now, for the better part of a chapter, been tracing and cataloging aspects of the natural landscape (in the case of the *choros*) and the manner in which those aspects have been distilled and deployed (in the case of the garden *topos*). But the question must be asked: do any of these characterizations of landscape, literary or real, have a basis in our modes of perception? Do human beings distinguish between one kind of landscape and another? And if we do, is a consistent preference demonstrated? Finally, does access to aspects of nature have any demonstrative effect on human beings? These are likely the questions that designers need to have the answers to if design methods and outcomes are to be affected. As it turns out, research indicates that the answer to all these questions is affirmative.

In their remarkable book *The Experience of Nature*, Rachel and Stephen Kaplan maintain that human beings are far more likely to prefer settings in which they can function more effectively. "Aesthetic reactions thus reflect neither a casual nor a trivial aspect of the human makeup. Rather, they appear to constitute a guide to human behavior that is both ancient and far-reaching. Underlying such reactions is an assessment of the environment in terms of its compatibility with human needs and purposes."[49] An aesthetic reaction is thus a sign of an environment favorable to effective human functioning. This position is reminiscent of Appleton's (1975) general "habitat theory," which suggests that human beings experience satisfaction with landscapes insofar as they are perceived to aid in the realization of biological needs.[50] The environments that grant us the greatest opportunity tend to be most valued. And, in fact, Kaplan and Kaplan go on to provide examples that indicate that nature is vital in terms of human function.[51] Not surprisingly, the salutary effects of nature transcend ethnicity, class, and culture, but preference for settings does not.

We might also return to the Robert Taylor Homes study that we made reference to in the previous chapter. We may remember that while vegetation—in the form of trees and grass—was once present at this site, maintenance costs had gradually diminished its presence. It was hypothesized that there was a positive correlation between the "greenness" of the surroundings and the strength of neighborhood social ties among people living nearby.[52] In fact, the study found:

> The more vegetation in a common space, the stronger the neighborhood social ties near that space—compared to residents living adjacent to relatively barren spaces, individuals living adjacent to greener common spaces had more social activities and more visitors, knew more of their neighbors, reported their neighbors were more concerned with helping and supporting one another, and had stronger feelings of belonging.[53]

While virtually all the physical characteristics of inner-city neighborhoods—crime rate, noise levels, crowding, and so on—work against social ties, the presence of green space acts to strengthen them. In fact, the implications of the "greening" of spaces contiguous to large housing projects include improved sense of safety and adjustment, and the possibility of lowered crime levels. The authors go on to note that while the Chicago Housing Authority has a commendable policy of involving residents in policy decisions, the question of landscaping falls outside the purview of that practice. But it is, in fact, unlikely that any urban housing authority places a high priority on green elements, resident involvement or not.

We are interested here in what factors influence perception, and whether humans demonstrate *preference* for particular landscape elements. Certain preferences seem intuitively obvious, such as water. Residential water views command high rents, and homes actually situated on a lake or river exorbitant prices. Curiously, this prestigious landscape element need not actually be used to be prized; its mere view suffices.[54] But such preference for water is by no means solely American, or even Western; Byoung-E Yang's 1988 study of non-Western landscape preference using native Koreans and Western tourists indicated that both groups preferred the group of scenes dominated by water features.[55]

The basis for the work of Kaplan and Kaplan rests on several assumptions: first, that perception and preference are closely related, and that perception is strongly influenced by prior experience; second, that the factors that account for the preference for natural settings include both contents (kinds of settings) and the patterns of organization of the setting; and third, that variations in preference are the result of cultural and ethnic patterns, as well as people's personal experiences (11). The authors' method, the second assumption noted, uses two type categories: first, content, the specific elements of a scene; and second, spatial configuration, the way in which elements of a scene are arranged, or how we might visualize ourselves moving around in a scene.[56]

In the content-based category, there appears to be a concern for the balance between human influences (the built area) and the natural (landscape). Put differently, the demonstrated degree of human influence is an important factor in spatial perception. A housing study by R. Kaplan identified three types of areas: building dominated; open residential; and natural spaces free of structures (29). Miller's 1984 study used five categories, ranging from "Man-Dominated Nature" to "Man in Harmony with Nature," and it indicated the underlying sensitivity of the participants to the balance between the natural environment and human influence.[57] Kaplan and Kaplan note that the balance between built and natural elements is a consistently dominant theme in the experience of the environment.[58] It is worth noting, for example, that roads, though distinct, were rarely a perceptual category. Thus in the study by S. Kaplan, Kaplan, and Wendt roads sometimes appeared in "nature" scenes despite the apparent contradiction (30).

The spatial configuration category may include, as an underlying criterion, the degrees of usefulness and limitation the scene seems to permit. This, say the authors, is similar to Gibson's 1979 notion of affordances, the possibilities that are offered the observer. Two themes seem prominent in forming separate nature groupings: the degree of openness, and spatial definition (32). These categories are not mutually exclusive. *How* they are precisely seen may in fact reflect their content. Relatively open forests that enjoy a high degree of spatial definition (by virtue of unmassed trees) suggest to people that they could function more easily in that space; such "transparency" also seems favorable to human entry, or at least visual access. And so forth. The authors conclude:

> People are extremely sensitive to the spatial properties of the environment. It is apparent that in the rapidly made and largely unconscious decision regarding preference, there is an assessment of the glimpsed space and its qualities. This rapid assessment appears to be heavily influenced by the potential for functioning in the setting. Thus indications of the possibility of entering the setting, of acquiring information, and of maintaining one's orientation emerge as consistently vital attributes.[59]

What this points to is that accurate environmental perception is vital to survival, and that apt preference emerges as a life mechanism.[60] An exception to the rule of preference for natural settings over buildings occurs when the structure under consideration is a Small Structure in a Natural Setting.[61] Small wonder that the cabin in the woods, or on the lake, paradigm is so popular in Western imagination![62]

Kaplan and Kaplan note that while their discussion of preference has been concerned with two basic informational needs, understanding and exploration, the combination of these two domains results in four distinct patterns. Complexity refers to the preference people have for patterns that are neither high nor low in information; in a scene, the intricacy of the elements. Coherence refers to the sense of order and the degree to which one's attention is directed. Legibility is a notion to which we will return in the next chapter; it basically refers to our ability to form a clear mental image of a space and later recall it. (Thus both complexity and coherence play a role in legibility.) Mystery is perhaps the most intriguing factor, as it describes not what is there but the degree to which it is suggested that more information is available if we pursue it. Thus the space beyond the screen of trees, or beyond the bend in the path, holds promise of as yet unknown delight.[63]

We find the last pattern—mystery—is as close as Kaplan and Kaplan come to a consideration of the choristic aspect of landscape. In a study (based on the Kaplans' work) by Gimblett, Itami, and Fitzgibbon, mystery as a factor in landscape preference was examined; specifically, whether observers perceive this dimension as an independent attribute of landscape scenery, and the physical factors that contribute to this perception. Mystery was defined as the degree to which you can gain more information by proceeding further into the scene.[64] There was in fact a high degree of agreement among observers, but of greater interest to us is the character of the five attributes agreed on. These were screening, the degree to which the larger view is obstructed; distance of view, the distance from the observer to the nearest elements; spatial definition, the degree to which the elements enclose the viewer; physical accessibility, the apparent means of moving through the scene; and radiant forest, the sunlit areas we see beyond the darkened foreground.

In terms of the study, vegetative screening consistently appears in scenes rated highly for mystery, although the ratings decrease when the screening lacks definition. In general, the farther the elements of view, the lower the mystery rating. As spatial definition increases, the rating for mystery does as well. Interestingly, as physical accessibility is seen to increase, so do mystery ratings. Apparently, mystery only exists when possibilities for interaction do also. Thus the eternal fascination—in the visual arts and poetry—with paths that are "less seen" or that wind away from view. Wooded scenes (especially) are rated highly for mystery when the foreground lies in shade but the area beyond is flooded with light. (The result of this study is an affirmation of the Kaplans' research framework and a theoretical approach to perception and preference generally.) The authors of this study conclude that "the results of this research indicate that the promise of information and locomotion are two components of mystery that aid the observer in developing a mental image of the landscape."[65]

There are alternative theories of environment to consider. One critique of Appleton's theory is that it fares less well with urban environments. (And, in fact, the built landscape is only marginally dealt with in the Kaplans' studies.) In *The Syntax of Cities* (1977), P. F. Smith pursues a theory based on the needs of the neocortex and the two lateral hemispheres of the brain.[66] This theory does explain some of the delight people take in urban environments, which are usually noted for sensory overload. Rapoport and Kantor suggest that humans prefer complexity and ambiguity in their everyday environments, and Porteous suggests that although humans seek to optimize input, they prefer overload to deprivation.[67]

Now, it is our intent that this information be instrumental in answering our four earlier questions: Do the characteristics we give to landscape have any basis in perceptual modes? Do we distinguish clearly between categories of landscape? Is there a consistent preference exhibited? And is there any demonstrable salutary effect of landscape on human beings? The research indicates that for human beings, preference is clearly tied to perception, and perception, in turn, is largely the result of experience—although ethnic origin and culture play a role. People not only categorize spaces but do so on the basis of contents and spatial configuration. In the first instance, there is a marked sensitivity for the balance between the human (as indicated by structures) and the natural, resulting in an implicit valuation. In terms of spatial configuration, there is an awareness of the properties of usefulness and limitations in scenes. In fact, landscape is usually judged on the basis of affordances—the degree to which scenes allow physical and visual access. Finally, people make allowance for a well-defined set of mystery factors, confirming that everything need not be obvious at first glance. Thus there is research that affirms the first three questions. The fourth, the usefulness of landscape on human functioning, we have already discussed and will have occasion to do so again.

There is also the question of corollaries between the "six beauties" of Greco-Roman literature, Capability Brown, and the studies just referenced. At least three of those beauties are part of these studies: the open meadow punctuated with groves of trees, the value of the presence of water, and the ability to move through the scene. But these qualities also mark a landscape park by Capability Brown, who was known for his development of large meadow areas with tree groves situated so as to afford definition. And his placement of water features would meet with approbation as much now as in the eighteenth century. The research we have cited is, of course, ocularcentric, asking that its subjects make decisions based on visual data. But as will become apparent in subsequent chapters, two features of the pleasance—odor and sound—are likely as archetypal as sight when it comes to such preferences as flower scent and birdsong. Finally, it is our position that if these aspects of *choros* have lasted as long as they have, it is because the information they convey is as sensorily persuasive now as then.

6. There . . . and Back

The research on landscape preference that we referred to in the previous chapter depends on vision, although the Greco-Roman literature alludes to sound, odor, and touch, as well. Implicit in both the research (as in access affordances) and the literary descriptions, however, is the possibility of human movement in space. Indeed, these sensory phenomena have always been regarded in the context of continuously experienced environments. By the Middle Ages, the literary reference to spatial movement had become explicit.[1] Put differently, haptic perception has long been integral to spatial experience.

Earlier, we quoted E. V. Walter's comment that "haptic perception reminds us that the whole self may grasp reality without seeing, hearing or thinking."[2] (James J. Gibson, we may remember, defines haptic perception as a sense of touch that includes temperature, pain, pressure, and kinesthesia, encompassing both body sensation and muscle movement.)[3] Thus Thomas Thiis-Evensen's reference to bodily experiences:

> Such experiences are common to all people and are gained through confrontations with the phenomena which surround us. These things are givens, such as gravity and the forces of nature. Experiences with these phenomena can be described in terms of motion, weight and substance. As acting individuals, we move in relation to a dynamic reference which is defined by gravity and which therefore represents a vast range of characteristics for us. . . . Tactile experiences teach us about the differences between soft and hard, coarse and fine, wet and dry. These experiences form a complex net of references which are the basis for our reactions when we move in relationship to objects in space.[4]

He concludes that how we experience our movements in space—ascent and descent, over things or through them—is not only universal but also significant.[5]

Forrest Wilson comments that when we walk around or through a building, we are concerned with the diagrams of perpetual forces that usually "are intuitively felt to be present in the changing sequences of movement."[6] (Thus the Futurists, by drawing parts of the significant phases of that movement, created a new, synthetic image comprised of fragments of retained information.) Wilson contends that our ability to see the three-dimensionality of form is really our ability to combine the succession of many views (fragments) into a coherent whole.[7] Following the argument of Thiis-Evensen, we maintain that this succession is multisensory and temporal.

In their analysis of landscape, Moore, Mitchell, and Turnbull note that "some great gardens unfold like a narrative or a piece of music as we move through them and view their carefully choreographed wonders. . . . The journey in a garden is often around a lake or pond, the memory of it sequential, like a movie."[8] Moreover, this narrative can, in a manner analogous to music, establish a physical cadence in the viewing modes. In their description of the magnificent gardens at the Katsura Imperial Villa in Japan, the authors say:

> The garden is generally visited by moving clockwise around its central pond. The imposition of a definite sequence on the collection of scenes imparts extra meaning to the garden and allows the development and amplification of a composition in time—with rhythms, fast and slow, regular and irregular, and pauses, syncopations, diminuendos, and fortissimos. Attention shifts from one amazing object to the next, sometimes viewed up close and sometimes seen in long vistas across the water.[9]

The gardens at Katsura encircle a lake that is deceptively small, relying on sensory restatements set up through the clever use of pathway intricacies, angle of view, and time passage, as well as subtle alterations in haptic information (Figure 6.1).

The last point refers to variations in the level, position, and surface of the path, all of which compel us to pay attention as we walk it. Curiously, this concern may result in an increased biological sensitivity to the qualities of the path generally. Hermann Schöne notes that utricles (statoliths, or stabilizing organs in the brain) in a "normal" upright head position tilt backward at approximately thirty degrees off horizontal, thereby reducing effectiveness. Thus "a man walking on an uneven surface tips his head forward about 30° so that he can take in the ground ahead of him at a glance. This tilt brings the utricles into their most sensitive position."[10] This suggests that uneven pathways heighten our awareness of surfaces by obliging us to bring our sensory organs into the best alignment to perceive them (Figure 6.2).

Movement through space also involves its corollary, the passing of time. Moore, Mitchell, and Turnbull conclude: "A garden you walk through . . . must be composed in time as well as space."[11] One assumes that time, in this context, enjoys several layers of meaning: the amount of time in the act of movement itself; the interval

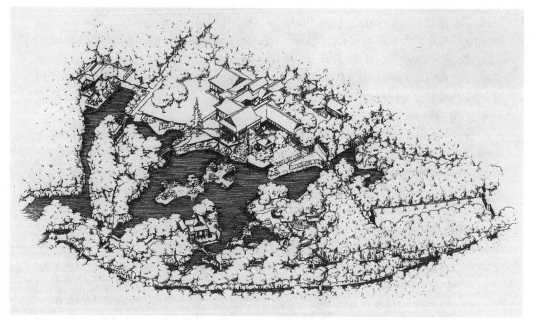

Figure 6.1. Schematic of gardens at Katsura Imperial Villa, c. 1640. Drawn by Maya Reiner for Charles W. Moore, William J. Mitchell, and William Turnbull Jr., *The Poetics of Gardens* (Cambridge: MIT Press, 1988). Copyright 1988 Massachusetts Institute of Technology.

spent at any one site; and references to some quasi-historic point of interest, such as "classical ruins" or Jencks's primordial snake.

Another example of haptic experience—albeit on a far smaller scale than the gardens at Katsura—may be seen in the typical entrance garden at a Japanese teahouse. The tea garden's *rōji* (dewy path) is really an extended entryway composed of gravel and stepping stones passing through a simple maze of mosses and other woodland plantings. It replicates, on a small scale, the long journey from the city to a

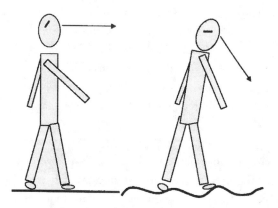

Figure 6.2. Statolith theory of head tilt, after Hermann Schöne, 1980. Drawing by Joy Monice Malnar.

teahouse in the mountains. This "journey" takes place in a diminutive space and is distinguished by the several focal points that are encountered en route. Thus the *rōji* consists of a series of landmarks, at which the visitor "is encouraged to release the concerns of daily life and progressively enter a 'tea' state of mind."[12] The object of this garden is a spiritual cleansing, a preparation for arrival at the tearoom and its ceremony (Figure 6.3).

Teiji Itoh distinguishes between the courtyard garden, the *tsubonouchi*, which is seen from the tearoom, and the *rōji*, which serves as a path to the tearoom. He says that the *tsubonouchi* "gave importance to a tranquil scenic or spatial composition to be viewed from a static position, while the roji . . . laid major stress on providing the guests with a series of spatial experiences as they walked through it. To put this even more simply, the tsubonouchi functioned on the premise that the guests would be sitting still, the roji on the premise that they would be in motion."[13] He concludes that the tea garden, "finding support in a new aesthetic philosophy, taught a new concept of design that relied on a sequence of spatial experiences to create its own special effects."[14] These "spatial experiences," not to belabor the point, involve vision, time, and kinesthesia. They also involve touch, as the rich textures that characterize both path and garden elements clearly suggest.

We earlier made reference to Paul Zucker's observation that space is perceived through visual and kinesthetic experience, and that in a state of "visual tension," the two fuse with the greatest intensity. The power of such a fusion (and time passage as well) can be experienced on the Spanish Steps at Santa Trinità dei Monti in Rome, designed by Francesco De Sanctis and Alessandro Specchi in 1721. A. C. Sewter states: "Their light rising rhythms, punctuated by the oval fountain at the bottom and the obelisk at the top, are a perfect expression of the Rococo delight in spatial flow."[15] The steps in fact connect these two points—which suggest still further depth and height, respectively—in a kind of structured elasticity, relying for effect both on sight and on the kinesthetic acts of ascent and descent. Vincent Scully comments:

> They are spacious and swelling and present an open invitation to the drama of movement. At the same time, their spaces, which seem so free, are in fact symmetrically focused by the solid shaft of the obelisk above them. . . . All movement is around fixed points. It is a union of the opposites of order and freedom. . . . It is therefore an architecture that is intended to enclose and shelter human beings in a psychic sense, to order them absolutely so that they can always find a known conclusion at the end of any journey, but finally to let them play at freedom and action all the while.[16]

In this structure, vision, movement, and time combine; even balance (Gibson's basic-orienting system) is required to navigate the steps, which are timeworn.

It is difficult to illustrate such a complex program in a single image, and virtually all attempts to date have been lacking in one respect or another. In an understandable

Figure 6.3. Path in Jōan teahouse garden *(rōji)*, 1618. Photograph by Botand Bognar; copyright 2002.

if misguided effort to project a *visually* unified sense of the Spanish Steps, aerial photographs—usually without human presence—have been used. This results in a view of the steps in quasi plan; not only is it experientially unlikely, but it denies the pronounced vertical character of the structure as well. The other major mode of representation, used extensively by earlier chroniclers, is that of the drawn elevation. Indeed, one of our illustrations—a quasi elevation—is taken from Guadet's *Éléments et théorie de l'architecture,* a late-nineteenth-century text. While it suggests the verticality of the steps, it fails (in common with all elevations) to adequately depict the recessive quality that results in a series of contained perspectives (Figure 6.4). Nor is any human presence depicted. We have tried to suggest both of these qualities in a companion image (Figure 6.5). Of course, it is arguable that our photograph is only a partial view and is thus just as lacking. We therefore offer another illustration, one that combines aspects based not on any single view but on the sequence of perspectives one would experience while ascending the steps. We believe this heterogeneous construction is more representative of the structure's complex nature than the preceding views (Figure 6.6).

In fact, the Spanish Steps combine the rather more expected attributes of stairways, ascent and descent, with the piazza's people-gathering properties. This is attested by the crowds that are constantly assembled on the steps, day and night. Indeed, at any given moment, there are far more people occupying the stairs than are at the top or the bottom; nor are they going anywhere. The undulations of the steps, obviously designed to direct the flow of movement, in fact provide excellent resting places for people to socialize (and watch other people). Finally, the piazza aspect is enhanced by the very openness of the steps in such a dense quarter of Rome. Thiis-Evensen states: "Stairs are a path dramatized. Their diagonal direction suggests the same tension as does their function, which is to connect two different levels, up and down. Herein lies their content as well. . . . The stair-motif, therefore, is particularly emphasized in monumental architecture."[17] Here, of course, the stair *is* the architecture.

In another example, more somber in nature, we again find the kinesthetic attributes of movement and touch. This remarkable structure is the Vietnam Veterans Memorial in Washington, D.C., designed in 1982 by Maya Lin. The aerial photograph that we use suggests the deep cut in the earth reminiscent of Jencks's fractured landscape, or the entrance into hell depicted by Dante (Figure 6.7). And yet the monument also refers to our historic past, with its arms on axis with the Washington and Lincoln memorials. The sloped ramp makes use of our basic-orienting sense, and people's constant touching of the 58,000 names inscribed on the two black granite walls attests to our haptic sense. Karen A. Franck says:

> Visitors look for particular names as they move along the wall: they touch or trace
> the names of those they have come to remember; they stand and reflect; they cry;
> they embrace; and they leave flowers, flags, and mementos. . . . In her design Maya
> Lin envisioned a new and different purpose for a memorial: to acknowledge loss and

Figure 6.4. Francesco de Sanctis and Allesandro Specchi, Spanish Steps, Rome, 1721–1725. From Julien Guadet, *Éléments et théorie de l'architecture.* Courtesy of University of Illinois at Urbana-Champaign.

Figure 6.5. Spanish Steps, Rome. Photograph by Frank Vodvarka.

Figure 6.6. Photographic analysis of Spanish Steps. Photographic construction by Frank Vodvarka.

Figure 6.7. Maya Lin, Vietnam Veterans Memorial, Washington, D.C., 1982. Reproduced from the Collections of the Library of Congress 306668, Washington, D.C.

to bring about healing; the subjectivity and the movements and feelings are central to such a purpose.[18]

In fact, haptic sensibility is likely more central to this monument than to any in Washington, and the offerings so numerous that the National Park Service has a warehouse to store them.

Time itself is evoked by virtue of the chronological order used in recording the names of the dead. The inscription on the first panel reads: "In honor of the men and women of the armed forces of the United States who served in the Vietnam War, the names of those who gave their lives and of those who remain missing are inscribed in the order they were taken from us." And there are the occasional additions of names in the open spaces left for that purpose. It was Lin herself who proposed that the names be listed by date of death: "Chronological listing was essential to her design. War veterans would find their story told, and their friends remembered, in the panel that corresponded with their tour of duty in Vietnam. Locating specific names with the aid of a directory would be like finding bodies on a battlefield."[19]

There is also a significant difference between the symbolism of first descending (as the war quickened) and then ascending (back to the surface, at war's end). That the wall widens in the middle is a function of the rising body count, but also, we presume, Lin's way of illustrating the war's "progress." Yet this could have been accomplished by raising the wall *up,* and maintaining a level path. That she chose not to was brilliant not only for the symbolic value but for the way in which it involves our senses. Finally, that the memorial involves us all is made clear as we view our reflections in the wall while reading the names of the fallen. Few monuments have been as successful at suggesting the choristic elements of landscape as this one, or as effective at controlling movement. The moving photograph published in the *National Geographic* magazine is a tribute to the monument's power (Figure 6.8).

What factors are actually involved in spatial movement? We might recall Arnheim's description of architecture as a temporal construct formed out of a complete perceptual image. He argues that such images are not precisely like frames of film for the reasons already discussed: that the viewer becomes an active part of architecture; appearances alter as a result of particular sequence; and that "frames" are read as part of a larger whole. Yet the film-frame analogy is not without merit. Harry Heft and Joachim F. Wohlwill, for example, refer to these momentarily discrete views as "retinal snapshots" and observe that the apparent temporal continuity and spatial

Figure 6.8. Reflections in wall of Vietnam Veterans Memorial. Photograph by Medford Taylor, National Geographic Image Collection.

extension of our environmental experience implies that cognitive procedures are used to compile and integrate this information.[20] Environmental perception, in this paradigm, is indirect and mediated, which accords with the Gestalt view.

If we combine Heft and Wohlwill's concept of "retinal snapshots" with the ideas of Hillier and Hanson on the nature of human interaction with buildings, our view of structured space might be very different. Earlier we quoted Hillier and Hanson as saying that buildings are transformations of space through objects, and that the ordering of space in buildings is really concerned with the ordering of relations between people. Seen this way, one might construct an illustration of an architectural design—like the Spanish Steps—that considered the sequential nature of our interaction with the physical facts of the design, as well as the limitations imposed by arbitrarily limited sight lines and personal preferences as indicated by viewing frequency. In this formulation, people are at least as significant a factor as stone and mortar (Figure 6.9).

James J. Gibson has offered an alternative view of perception as the result of direct stimulus information. These stimuli provide data that are changing (perspective structure) and static (invariant structure), which together provide temporal information about movement and the pathway. But Heft and Wohlwill maintain that the two views are not necessarily mutually exclusive, as environmental conditions (contextual factors) and personal goals may ultimately determine whether perceptual or cognitive processes are required: "In this light, way-finding may be viewed as a form of environmental *perception,* considering perception as involving the pickup of information over time. . . . On the other hand, tasks such as constructing maps or models of an environment . . . may draw directly on *conceptual knowledge.*"[21] Thus the "film" discussed earlier is in constant perceptual adjustment, with the correspondence between reality and its appearance the result of individual interpretation. The designer, then, organizes transitions that are direct or ambiguous, and points of entry that are static or dramatic. Bloomer and Moore point out that "the choreography of arrival at the house (the *path* to it) can send out messages and induce experiences which heighten its importance as a place."[22] But it seems clear that interior paths function in like manner.

This of course implies that as spaces can be denoted by type, so too can pathways. Reginald G. Golledge maintains that paths consist of two elements, origin and destination. These are connected by procedural rules that are transposed into spatial components, including distance, direction, and orientation.[23] While design may influence the choices, it cannot completely control them. Direct experience and individual memory, moreover, exercise influence, as does the clarity of the linked landmarks (or nodes). Golledge states that "there is a commonsense reason to expect that a minimal set of primary nodes or landmarks that define the end points of any given path system not only anchor a cognitive configuration but also precede path learning, and that they similarly define a given path segment."[24] And Quantrill points out: "The path, the way forward and backward, is a basic property of consciousness. A path gives us continuity in space and time."[25] From this it is clear that places and paths together form a coherent system. From this to the cognitive map, which may be thought of as the sum of the schematic knowledge we have of our environment, or, for that matter, environments in general, is a short step.

In their seminal text *Cognition and Environment,* Stephen and Rachel Kaplan comment that mental models or cognitive maps seem intuitively promising in understanding how humans experience the environment. They conclude that such a map would have to meet three criteria to be useful: the model must be able to extract generalities if it is to cope with dissimilarities in environmental configurations; the coding process must function economically in order to make access to information speedy and reliable; and the map must function as if continuous despite large gaps

Figure 6.9. Interactive analysis of Spanish Steps. Photographic construction by Frank Vodvarka.

in information.[26] They refer to these factors as generality, economy, and connectedness. (We assume that prior experience plays a role in all three.) The authors point out that perception itself is a complex process, involving (notwithstanding our emphasis on sight) all the senses as well as locational accuracy. "Thus the *whatness* (object) and *whereness* (space) aspects are essential to perception regardless of which sense is involved" (18).

The Kaplans have developed an intriguing and elegant model for cognitive mapping. It rests on two premises: first, that representation stands for an internal summary of a class of stimulus patterns, that is, it represents an object in the world; and second, that the stimulus patterns are organized in a network model using contiguity as the operative principle. The change from incoming information to representation in turn has four aspects: simplicity, the discarding of unnecessary information; essence, the maintenance of the stereotypical aspects; discreteness, the arrangement of experience into categories; and unity, the clear organization of data against its background (34). The forming of a representation is, of itself, insufficient. Comprehending spatial patterns requires that there be some form of continuity between representations if there is to be an internal model of the environment, a cognitive map. It is the Kaplans' position that this need not be a strict form of functional continuity, but simply connectedness—the possibility, for example, of going from one place to another.[27]

The authors point out that as there is such a great emphasis on discrete points of representation, it is necessarily so for the landmarks that the representations stand for. This, they say, suggests a number of hypotheses: first, that we attach a landmark to a key directional point even if it is only nearby; second, that we recall landmarks as being more prominent or distinctive than is actually so; third, that we postulate line of sight for necessary landmarks; and fourth, that landmarks provide distance cues—the more there are, the greater the distance seems (47). They conclude that such a map fills the expectations postulated as necessary, it expedites decision making even when insufficient information exists, it provides a basis for innovation, and it constitutes a basis for anticipation. The authors also postulate the existence of hierarchical mapping, which describes the maps we form at different scales and complexities. And they theorize the existence of generic maps, the general image we carry with us of typical situations, for example, small town, highway interchange, and so on. Such generic maps allow us to generalize about one situation from what we know of another.

Out of all this emerges their version of cognitive mapping. "Cognitive maps code proximity and distance, order and sequence. There are paths between some things and not others. There are regions and levels, allowing one to deal with the same domain at different scales. In other words, cognitive maps have a set of relational spatial properties that constitute what we call structure" (51). And so, reasonably enough, simple and clear structural patterns—in public buildings, for example—cause the least disorientation in people finding their way.[28] The second major aspect of cognitive mapping concerns our ability to visualize spatial locations. That is, as part of the mapping process, we can not only specify location by proximity and distance but also "picture" our own position within such a space as well as its contents (54). Thus the two aspects—schematic mapping and locational visualization—fashion our view of "whereness."

Now, the perceptual mapping model proposed by the Kaplans is both direct and convincing. Its main drawback is in the area of design usefulness. That is, the mapping process, as they describe it, is essentially passive. It is a likely explanation of what happens when human beings attempt to locate themselves spatially. But it offers little—except implicitly—information about how to design spaces that may easily and fruitfully be mapped by the people destined to inhabit them. Hence our continued admiration for the (also seminal) work of Kevin Lynch.

In Lynch's major work, *The Image of the City,* he too uses the term *cognitive mapping* to define the mnemonic representation of the spatial information we have stored about our physical and sociocultural environments. His studies examined what people knew of their environments in three cities, and the resultant maps and descriptions indicated that they thought of those spaces in fairly discrete terms. Lynch found that environmental images could, in fact, be divided into three parts: identity, an object enjoying recognition as a distinct entity; structure, the spatial or pattern relation between the object and other objects, and between the object and the observer; and meaning, the utilitarian meaning of the object to the observer.[29] "Thus an image useful for making an exit requires the recognition of a door as a distinct entity, of its spatial relation to the observer, and its meaning as a hole for getting out" (8). He uses this system to determine what makes cities *imageable,* referring to "that shape, color or arrangement which facilitates the making of vividly identified, powerfully structured, highly useful mental images of the environment."[30] Jon Lang similarly notes that a highly imageable city, building, or interior is one that is perceived as a structured system of related components.[31]

It is, however, Lynch's categories of the elements used to form cognitive images that most interest us: he refers to these as Paths, Edges, Districts, Nodes, and Landmarks. Paths are the passages (streets, alleys, and corridors) of our environment; Edges represent the more or less permeable boundaries that separate areas; Districts are areas with fairly definable characteristics (like theater districts or reception areas); Nodes are strategic focal points (like traffic circles or central staircases); and Landmarks are easily identified, dominant physical elements (representations in the Kaplans' model). It seems clear that Lynch intended these categories to be used in an urban analysis; they are, however, useful generally for both exterior and interior spatial configurations. They have, moreover, appeared in some form in the theories of others. Christian Norberg-Schulz, for example, speaks of Places, Paths, and Domains; and Bloomer and Moore employ terms such as Place, Path, Pattern, and Edge.

The Kaplans find Lynch's model interesting as well, noting that while they find the nodes and landmarks he describes important parts of wayfinding, they are less sure that such elements are actually differentiated by people. They find both edges and districts (regions, in Kaplans' model) more abstract than the simple points and connections they postulate. And, most significantly, they view their definition of paths as different from Lynch's in several respects. Specifically, Lynch's paths are highly active and composed of whole sequences of representations.[32] By contrast, their model conceives of paths as relatively simple, contentless connections between representations, or landmarks. Another important issue concerns whether landmarks precede paths in the learning process; the Kaplans cite a 1975 study by Siegel and White that supports this idea, and a later study by Evans that tends to also agree.

They conclude: "From a network point of view, then, it would seem that the notion of points (representations that correspond to places or objects or events) and connections (associations linking the points) is sufficient to form the building blocks of cognitive maps. The addition of a hierarchical structure that permits 'points' to designate increasingly abstract representations provides the basis for discussing both the features of the environment and our constructions of these features into shared concepts."[33] It is the second notion that characterizes Lynch's model. These, then, are the ways in which the two mapping systems are dissimilar and similar. If we find Lynch's the more useful of the two, it is because of three factors: first, in its precise descriptions of spatial elements, it is prescriptive rather than passive; second, as it posits a hierarchy of structural elements, it aids in a progressive design strategy; and third, we are in fundamental agreement with the more active, even profound, view that Lynch has of pathways. We also believe that paths are generative elements of spatial design, as evidenced by various models.

The Spanish Steps provide an excellent example of why we find Lynch's analysis so convincing. The steps are both dynamic pathway (in that they provide a method of reaching a part of the city on a different level) and piazza (a place of gathering in which ascent and descent are unimportant). The roles of thoroughfare and final destination do not always peacefully coexist, as people are often forced to acknowledge the opposed aspects of movement and relative stasis by making appropriate concessions. Even the visual aspect changes from one that both observes (albeit briefly) and searches for route cues to one that scrutinizes but is content to remain in place. The result lends an uneasy, even dynamic, character to the steps. Thiis-Evensen aptly remarks that "the path-motif is a visualization of one's own action radius. The path leads but at the same time expresses an independent action . . . the path is active and purposeful as well as goal-orientated."[34]

There is a wonderful little song in the first chapter of *The Fellowship of the Ring*, the first book of Tolkien's epic *The Lord of the Rings*. The song is a recurring ditty attributed in the tale to a certain Bilbo Baggins:

The Road goes ever on and on
Down from the door where it began.
Now far ahead the Road is gone,
And I must follow, if I can,

Pursuing it with eager feet,
Until it joins some larger way
Where many paths and errands meet.
And whither then? I cannot say.[35]

Finishing his song, Bilbo "trotted down the long sloping path. He jumped over a low place in the hedge at the bottom, and took to the meadows, passing into the night like a rustle of wind in the grass."[36] Thus was the stage set for an adventure with a modified cast of characters.

The epic journey that Tolkien describes depends for effect on the fascination people have always had for pathways. They have always had an adventurous, even perilous, air about them. We know, almost instinctively, that pathways are often more exciting and physical than points of departure or, for that matter, arrival. Now, transition through a structured space is surely familiar to all human beings. And yet the generative role of the path, and its sensory character, has seldom been given much consideration by architectural theorists. In *The Environmental Memory*, Malcolm Quantrill makes the point that architecture has traditionally concerned itself with spatial ordering, formal expression, and construction techniques; as a result, the role of pathways has received little attention. That is, while architectural history and theory have focused on points of arrival such as the room, the atrium, and the piazza, "the means of getting there—the street, the alley, the stairs—in some cases the very anatomy of the house or city, is often ignored both in the planning process and in the discussion of spatial and formal order."[37]

Quantrill's point is that transitional elements tend not to fare well in design analysis, seldom being regarded as other than functional components that connect significant spaces. And yet they are critical in forming a sensory experience of space generally, and (following Lynch) essential to movement through space. Rudolf Arnheim points out that psychologists, unlike architectural theorists, assume that as objects (such as buildings) are available to us only as perceptual experiences, they must be considered as sensory objects.[38] That is, human percepts typically turn around the autonomous existence of objects as they are formed from innumerable individual impressions. Thus the image that we form is the result of our spontaneous integration of these visual projections into a total perceptual image (13).

Three aspects of this theory are crucial: first, that a comprehensive mental image of spatial phenomena, in this case buildings, develops as a perceptual process; second, that this image incorporates the sensations generated in the viewer by sequential experience; and third, that such spatial phenomena exist both outside time and as a measured event. Arnheim is not negating the importance of our knowledge of a building's intended use, only that its perception is as real an aspect of it. Thus the first two aspects are concerned with the visual attributes of spatial phenomena that form an appropriate objective percept. He concludes, "All is well when particular views of aspects display essential structural properties of the design as a whole."[39]

But does the third point not imply far more than is stated? Most structures are stationary; the only way in which we can temporally experience them is by moving through them. Arnheim later refers to three temporal "particularities" of architecture: first, that the viewer's experience of architecture is participatory; second, that an intended sequence of views can result in a building's components having varied appearances; and third, that the sequence only makes sense as an aspect of the building's enduring nature. He concludes: "Beyond utility, it is aesthetically indispensable that viewers become aware of the interplay between timeless spatial structure and the time-bound avenues through the building" (17). Here he implies that certain spaces may be static and eternal in nature, but that pathways through structures are active, participatory, and temporal. This is not very far removed from Thiis-Evensen's interesting depiction of human behavior, that "we wish to 'be' what a volume does. Therefore we walk swiftly in a corridor and slowly and ceremoniously in a broad space."[40] Of course, such anticipation can be negated by prior experience and immediate perception. We do not walk swiftly in the corridors surrounding courtrooms (where much court business takes place), nor do we linger to savor hospital waiting rooms. And we are all familiar with the experience of prolonging a journey because it is more pleasurable than the point of arrival is likely to be.

Indeed, what is a labyrinth but an extended pathway system, the experience of which promises to variously bring us revelation, enjoyment, and stimulation? Thus labyrinthine patterns were designed into the floors of cathedrals at Rheims and Chartres to serve as metaphor for the Christian spiritual journey, made into hedge mazes in England (such as that at Hampton Court) for public amusement, and developed into complex architectural motifs as intellectual pursuit. And their use as highly irregular street configurations by the builders of medieval cities attests to their ability to cause confusion among invaders, and perhaps some solidarity among the city's citizens (Figure 6.10). One can argue that the diversion prompted by a limited path uncertainty is welcome even in more conventional settings. (Indeed, studies demonstrate that people prefer a fairly high degree of spatial complexity in their environment.)

But is it possible, as Arnheim suggests, to really be aware of both corridors and the rooms they serve? Romedi Passini points out that "unlike a drawing, no overall view is offered when a person walks along a corridor. Not only is it impossible to see what is happening on the other side of the wall, but the conditions are repeated on other visually inaccessible levels."[41] Thus our journey down the corridors of large institutions is visually constrained. When such a labyrinth is projected into the third dimension, the possibilities of becoming "lost" increase exponentially. This is especially true in buildings like hospitals that tend, as Passini points out, to have grown in piecemeal fashion and rely on signage, usually ineffectively.

This is no small issue; spatial disorientation can be not only life threatening (as in detaining emergency personnel such as medical technicians and firefighters) but psychologically painful and extremely expensive as well. Passini references a 1979

Figure 6.10. Medieval Tivoli, Italy. Photograph by Frank Vodvarka.

study by Stea and his collaborators that used cost-factored efficiency criteria to assess a hospital complex in Los Angeles. These included the direct disorientation cost (time lost in finding one's way, giving directions to others, and learning new routes) and indirect disorientation (stress and its effects on turnover and absenteeism). The inefficiency costs were judged high.[42] The desire to avoid the wayfinding difficulties so common to architectural mazes leads to other odd behavior as well. A study carried out in Montreal found that people refused to frequent certain shopping centers for fear of becoming lost. Crowding, too, can be a factor. A study of conditions affecting environmental cognition found that while high-density conditions did not affect focal information about products, significant deficits in accuracy and detail of cognitive maps were noted.[43] Still others refused to use parking complexes or, if given no choice, would seek familiar spots to park.[44] It is ironic that spaces, the usual goal of path development, can be sensorially and operatively so ill served by such prevalent failures in development.

This raises the question of how one defines a space. One view is that space simply exists, a void that may or may not be occupied by material things. Implicit in this view is the notion of space as a matrix in which objects can be located precisely by virtue of three coordinates (measuring height, width, and depth). This Cartesian system suggests a mathematical model underlying nature. One consequence of postulating such a space is that it is necessarily finite. Cartesian grids are useful for urban planning generally, and for the dull, mechanical order that has characterized modernist structures. But one might also see space as the rather elastic distance between objects. In this conception, a single object occupies its own spatial center, until a second object interactively creates a spatial dialogue. Additional objects further complicate relationships in this object space, particularly when some of them assume greater significance than others. This may be seen as the difference between absolute space and object space (Figure 6.11).

 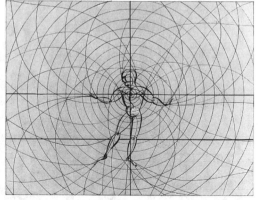

Figure 6.11. Oskar Schlemmer, delineation of space by human figures (theoretical drawing), 1924. Photograph courtesy of the Museum of Modern Art, New York; copyright 2002.

As object space assumes no preexisting matrix, it is dynamic in nature. Furthermore, the spaces between objects become active and vital. And, of real interest, this physical definition closely corresponds to a psycho-physiological perception of space in which how objects are rated likely depends on personal valuation. Object space is essentially what is meant by the term "proxemics." Whereas Cartesian relationships are based on symmetry and axis, proxemic relationships are based on the distance and direction of objects (animate and inanimate) from each other and the viewer. Edward T. Hall says that human perception of space "is dynamic because it is related to action—what can be done in a given space—rather than what is seen by passive viewing."[45] It is thus arguable that cognitive maps—unlike conventional maps—are proxemic in nature.

It is also a good idea to move from the Cartesian axis to the proxemic path, at least conceptually. The axis is really a particular path type, whose assigned function goes beyond that of circulation or the connecting of landmarks. In fact, the axis has traditionally been regarded as the essential skeleton of the structure, its primary organizing element. The ability to design an unambiguous axis, arranged symmetrically, has always been regarded as the high point of an Ecole des Beaux-Arts education. David Van Zanten notes that a student at the Ecole arranged spaces and volumes symmetrically and pyramidally along axes that intersected at right angles (often at a major central space).[46] The result was a ritualized axial planning that remained cogent long after other aspects of beaux-arts education fell into disuse. Le Corbusier says: "Architecture is based on axes. The axes of the schools are an architectural calamity. The axis is a line of direction leading to an end. In architecture, you must have a destination for your axis."[47] Thus his view, while still affirming axial planning, is an improvement in that the axis is seen as generative rather than static.

Axes have often been seen as different in kind; types, if you will. They can be undeviatingly linear, leading single-mindedly from departure point to destination. An excellent example of this sort of monolithic axis is that at the Temple of Khonsu in Egypt. Paul Zucker notes that "the aesthetically decisive element is not the individual spatial unit of the courts themselves, but the succession of courts following each other. . . . It is the axis as such which dictates the movement."[48] Such a pathway was perfect for the depiction of the absolute, an ideal mirror for the cultural beliefs of the ruling class.[49] In his *Culture of Cities,* Lewis Mumford perceptively observes, "The more shaky the institution, the more solid the monument."[50] One might add, the more ceremonial the function, the more pronounced the axis.

While it is thus possible for a pathway to serve as such an easily comprehensible totality, it is rather more usual that it is experienced in sequence, with distinct focal points. (Here Lynch's view of landmarks and nodes seems particularly relevant, especially when they link up so closely as to make their division from pathways moot.)[51] One way of viewing such sequences has been proposed by Bernard Tschumi. He suggests that architectural sequences are composed of at least three relations: first, the transformational sequence (design methodology); second, the spatial sequence (alignment along a common axis); and third, the programmatic sequence (the social and symbolic factors that characterize those spaces).[52]

Tschumi notes that spatial sequences have historically emphasized pathways with fixed focal points linked by continuous movement, but that as architecture is inhabited, it is the programmatic factors that are crucial. He states that "sequences of use, of perception and meaning are always superimposed on those fixed spatial sequences. These are the programmatic sequences that suggest secret maps and impossible fictions, rambling collections of events all strung along a collection of spaces, frame after frame, room after room, episode after episode."[53] He concludes that the spatial sequences may be structural, in that they may be viewed independently of assigned meaning, but that the programmatic sequences are inferential, drawn from the appearance and arrangement of the spaces. This suggests a continuous state of tension between space and its habitation; dualities—path and space, form and program—that are never quite resolved. A far cry from the conventional view of axis, to say the least.

In its most liberal definition, *wayfinding* refers to our ability to locate ourselves spatially, despite the difficulties imposed by "unachieved resolution." We may recall that Heft and Wohlwill referred to wayfinding as a form of environmental perception based on the pickup of spatial information over time, and that maps or models thus formed might draw on conceptual knowledge as well as experience. In this, they combine spatial experience over time with the formal attributes of maps, resulting in cognitive maps shaped by individual interpretation. Such maps should have a high degree of legibility, which (following the Kaplans) refers to our ability to form a clear mental image of a space and later recall it so that we can locationally visualize ourselves. This view of wayfinding not only seems authentic but also explains why people find it difficult to understand the spatial instructions of others, or, for that matter, give them.

Passini's initial definition of spatial orientation goes far in meeting these criteria. He says it can be described as a "person's ability to mentally determine his position within a representation of the environment made possible by cognitive maps."[54] But, he points out, even as important as the concept of cognitive maps is, it is nonetheless inadequate as a vehicle to understand spatial orientation. The definition must be extended, he maintains, to include the ability to determine "what to do in order to reach a place."[55] He refers to the first definition as static in nature, while the second is dynamic. And only in situations where both are absent will people have the sensation of being lost or disoriented (44).

In Passini's conception, mental representations and behaviors together form a complementary system of wayfinding. Thus his final definition of wayfinding as "cognitive processes comprising three distinct abilities: a cognitive mapping or information-generating ability that allows us to understand the world around us; a decision-making ability that allows us to plan actions and to structure them into an overall plan; and a decision-executing ability that transforms decisions into behavioral actions."[56] This way of looking at wayfinding, he believes, includes both perceptual and cognitive phenomena as well as ways people can relate to the spatial environment and destinations, involves memory and learning, and is suited to design and planning (46).

After such splendid analyses of wayfinding by others, it is likely an act of hubris to attempt our own; but we do so anyway. It appears likely to us that there are at least four dimensions to wayfinding: first, active sensory perception, in which kinesthetic and visual experience are most instrumental in forming a net of references that provide the basis for our reactions to objects in space; second, the formation of cognitive maps, which code proximity, distance, order and sequence, and connectedness/paths, as well as locational visualization; third, identity, structure, and meaning, which result in an entity being "imageable," and the correlated concept of object space, where sequences of use, perception, and meaning are superimposed on fixed spatial sequences; and fourth, the desirability of the objective, our motivation to employ the spatial information at our disposal. Taken together, these factors imply that haptic information is vital to navigating our environment, as is a legible cognitive map. That map, furthermore, must be an "imageable" one, composed of objects/landmarks that are sensorially and emotionally meaningful. Finally, we must actually wish to avail ourselves of all these dimensions.

Studies tend to bear this hypothesis out. In a limited example, Peponis, Zimring, and Choi found that search patterns are strongly shaped according to the degree of integration of each space and each choice node of the circulation system that marks the layout. They thus formulated the idea of a search structure where intelligible properties of layouts interact with navigation rules to produce characteristic patterns of exploration.[57] In short, the discernible attributes of particular structural patterns (of buildings, for example) interact with specific "rules" of maneuvering to produce a typical exploration methodology. Again, Passini points out that routes appear longer when they contain many intersections and barriers; the more cluttered the route, the greater the cognitive distance. He notes as well that positive valence (the liking of a place) results in a shortening of estimated distance.[58] We would assume that a low valence or high "clutter" appraisal would both result in a disinclination to explore that spatial environment.

A study by Carpman, Grant, and Simmons conducted at the University of Michigan Medical Center examined wayfinding in hospitals. They concluded that "the form and organization of a building probably have the greatest impact on finding one's way."[59] Nonetheless their research into the placement and content of signage, consistency in numerical designation, and use of comprehensible visual cues suggested a number of strategies for lessening the problem of institutional mazes. The authors offer a number of conclusions, of which four are particularly interesting to us: first, that related functions should be located close to each other; second, that interior landmarks be developed using light, color, texture, and plants; third, that architectural elements and landmarks be incorporated into the map design; and fourth, that a "birds-eye" perspective view of the building layout be used for interior maps.[60]

The last item—the birds-eye perspective—is especially interesting, as it is entirely typical of older maps. In fact, such map types yield not only spatial information but also detailed information about the objects that occupy those spaces. In reference to a more modern version of the historical map, Edward R. Tufte notes that "this fine texture of exquisite detail leads to personal micro-readings, individual stories about the data: shops visited, hotels stayed at, walks taken, office windows at a floor worked on—all in the extended context of an entire building, street and neighborhood."[61] In fact, this kind of map enjoys an unusually high degree of "whereness," or legibility (Figure 6.12).

What gives this type of map its character is a combining of symbolic data with visual characteristics that allows us to locate ourselves in what would otherwise be a blank abstraction. In a series of observations, Tufte comments that although we travel through a perceptual world of three spatial dimensions on a daily basis, the world portrayed on our informational displays is two-dimensional in nature. Thus communication takes place on a flat surface. He concludes: "Escaping this flatland is the essential task of envisioning information—for all the interesting worlds (physical, biological, imaginary, human) that we seek to understand are inevitably and happily multivariate in nature. Not flatlands."[62] Indeed, the first illustration in his book is a map from the *Guide for Visitors to Ise Shrine,* which, he points out, is a hybrid of design technique combining abstract route information with concrete visual imagery.

There is still other research about the numerous factors that influence wayfinding. Carol S. Holding has studied the roles of hierarchical clusters and reference points in individuals' mental representations of their environment. She found that two of the results supported the role of reference points in drawing together categories.[63] Also of interest was the finding that sex differences in accuracy on the spatial judgments suggested that females were more dependent on clustering and reference points than were males.[64] This of course raises the intriguing question of gender differentiation in wayfinding.

Carol A. Lawton examined wayfinding strategies and found, among other things, that women were more likely to report the use of a route strategy (following instructions to move from place to place), whereas men reported an orientation strategy (sustaining a sense of position in relation to reference points in the environment). As the orientation strategy was found to be positively correlated with spatial perception ability and negatively correlated with spatial anxiety, it comes as no surprise that women reported a higher level of spatial anxiety than men did.[65] Lawton points out that route knowledge involves learning a sequence of instructions about how to go from one location to the next, while survey knowledge (orientation strategy) involves a cognitive map that integrates routes into a gestaltlike network of relationships between locations. While both types of knowledge permit successful navigation of the environment, route knowledge is relatively rigid in contrast to survey knowledge, which makes allowance for new information (766). Lawton also notes that the items in her study involving map use were differentially associated with the two strategies:

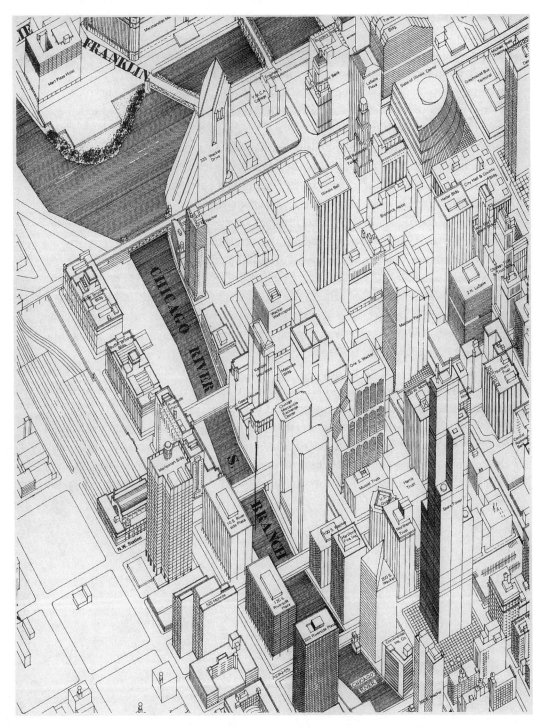

Figure 6.12. David A. Fox, axonometric map of Chicago, 1982. Courtesy of David A. Fox, Narberth, Pennsylvania. Copyright 1982.

the orientation strategy favored published road maps; the route strategy favored hand-drawn maps, presumably because they omitted all but essential information. Women were also more likely to report navigation anxiety than men were; a possible reason for this is that the relative absence of sense of position in the environment leads to anxiety should the intended route be missed. As an alternative answer, anxiety about becoming lost may reduce the ability to focus on spatial cues. And she mentions related studies that found that stress resulting from noise or crowding reduces memory of spatial locations (777).

Nor are these strategies temporally constant. Lawton found that higher levels of orientation strategy were reported by both genders with age (and hence lower levels of spatial anxiety). Of real interest is the finding that there remains a substantial difference in strategy between older men and women, but less between younger subjects of both genders. She conjectures that this may be the result of changing gender roles in society that afford greater wayfinding opportunities for women (777). There are still other studies that tend to support the notion that stress has a negative effect on wayfinding ability. The study that we cited in regard to crowded conditions also found that while noise stress actually increased the speed in which information was processed when it involved sequential order, it resulted in poorer memory for materials that required more time and capacity to encode.[66] The researchers also found that stress dramatically reduced relocation accuracy.[67]

Now, it should strike no one as odd that movement through space, and the character of the pathways, should be sensory in nature. And yet such phenomena are usually discussed as though not a muscle had been exercised, nor things seen, smelled, heard, and felt. (Nor, for that matter, that individual goals and motivations should be determinant.) This may be the legacy of our ocularcentric education, or perhaps the constraints imposed by a belief in the superiority of cognition over sense. As that may be, it is nonetheless the sensory aspects of such transit that grant pathways and spaces their enduring nature, and much of their reason for being as well.

7. Sensory Cues

Space, we have argued, is not the same as place. Yi-Fu Tuan points out that space is a more abstract concept than place: "What begins as undifferentiated space becomes place as we get to know it better and endow it with value."[1] The way in which we "get to know it," he makes clear, is through our senses, whose procedures may be difficult to express. Thus he concludes: "In the large literature on environmental quality, relatively few works attempt to understand how people feel about space and place, to take into account the different modes of experience (sensorimotor, tactile, visual, conceptual), and to interpret space and place as images of complex—often ambivalent—feelings" (7). The author further explores those "ways of knowing" with an emphasis on the nonvisual senses. "Taste, smell, and touch are capable of exquisite refinement. They discriminate among the wealth of sensations and articulate gustatory, olfactory, and textural worlds" (10). Humans, however, tend to be ocularcentric. Accordingly, the designed environment little acknowledges touch and sound—and routinely lacks the "pungent personality that varied and pleasant odors can give" (11). This is unfortunate, he says, as "odors lend character to objects and places, making them distinctive, easier to identify and remember" (11).

The power of odor to endow spaces with special character has long been noted by poets. Hence the depiction by the twelfth-century poet Chu Shu-chên in her "Plum Blossoms":

The snow dances and the frost flies.
Through the bamboo blinds I see vaguely
The sparse shadows of slanting plum branches.
Unexpectedly a cold perfume

Borne with the sound of a Tartar flute,
Is blown to our bed curtains.
Enveloped in this puzzling scented wind,
Who can appreciate such a subtle joy?[2]

Here the experience of place is enhanced by an inexplicable but enjoyable odor.[3] But might there be more involved than the mere oddness of the scent's origin?

In a study investigating the potential effects of pleasant fragrances on task performance, Robert Baron and Jill Thomley found that such fragrances can indeed enhance performance by serving as a source of environmentally generated positive affect.[4] In their study, they cite the research on the impact of ambient fragrance completed by others.[5] The findings, they say, "indicate that pleasant fragrances . . . can sometimes (a) increase alertness and performance on vigilance and cognivite tasks . . . (b) facilitate recall of pleasant memories . . . and (c) reduce reported preferences for resolving interpersonal conflicts through relatively ineffective means (e.g., avoidance and direct confrontation)."[6] While the first and third points likely have commercial implications, the second—recall of pleasant memories—may have an effect on human behavior generally.

The authors point to another study by Baron indicating that persons exposed to pleasant fragrances report more positive current moods than those not so exposed (769). And there are still other studies supporting the thesis that pleasant fragrances have salutary effects on mood and memory. Thus Baron and Thomley state: "Together, these findings suggest that pleasant fragrances may induce increments in positive affect and that these shifts in affective state, in turn, may play a role in the impact of such environmental stimuli on behavior."[7] In short, Chu Shu-chên may have been persuaded by more than the unusual circumstances of the scent, which, it is arguable, is really a cognitive assessment of the situation. Is it not possible that the scent, of itself and without mediation, inclined her to a positive evaluation of the situation?

Thus can an otherwise unremarkable space be transformed into a place of significance by the introduction of an odor. Rooms can, of course, already possess an odorific presence—one so strong, in fact, that it grants the room its primary character. Such are the rooms described by Charlotte Mew in her poem of that name:

I remember rooms that have had their part
    In the steady slowing down of the heart.
The room in Paris, the room at Geneva,
The little damp room with the seaweed smell,
And that ceaseless maddening sound of the tide—
    Rooms where for good or for ill—things died.[8]

Both poems contain additional element: sound. The sound of the flute in Chu Shu-chên's poem and the sound of the tide in Charlotte Mew's both play a complementary role to the odors. The two sounds do not, however, elicit the same response. Chu Shu-chên finds the sound of the flute delightful; Charlotte Mew refers to the "ceaseless" tide as "maddening."

Here, as with odors, there may be underlying considerations that lead to these two conclusions. In his study on the nature of sound in urban environments, Michael Southworth found that the blind—who tend to be more than usually sensitive to sound—preferred low to middle frequency and intensity sounds, and that delight increased when sounds were novel, informative, responsive to personal action, and culturally approved. In contrast, sounds with a "a rush and roar" were considered annoying, especially when their masking effects were high.[9] Also clear from South-worth's study is that there is nothing inherently irritating about sounds like that of the tide; they only become so when they are unrelenting and loud like Charlotte Mew's tide. In either case, however, the odors and sounds have granted those spaces their sense of place.

Few authors have been as masterful at such place evocation as Joseph Conrad. When his protagonist Marlow describes his upriver journey to find the legendary Mr. Kurtz in *Heart of Darkness,* he says: "Going up that river was like traveling back to the earliest beginnings of the world. . . . An empty stream, a great silence, an impenetrable forest. The air was warm, thick, heavy, sluggish. There was no joy in the brilliance of sunshine. The long stretches of the waterway ran on, deserted, into the gloom of overshadowed distances."[10] And a short time later: "We penetrated deeper and deeper into the heart of darkness. It was very quiet there."[11]

What Conrad is describing is familiar to travelers who have gone to places completely outside their experience. The silence, to Marlow, is unexpected and frightening. And to his dismay, such sounds as occasionally do erupt in the stillness are, in their alien quality, not reassuring at all. He has no memory of such phenomena, no past experience to give them a context. Conrad's riveting stories derive their power, their uncanny ability to project a sense of place, from the careful attention he pays to every sensory detail, as well as to the character's emotional response to them. This, of course, presents some difficulty in proposing a viable sensory typology. After all, many of the atmospheric characteristics of Venice—so passionately described by numerous authors throughout history—are similar to those noted by Marlow on his East African journey. Clearly, no characteristic inherently produces a given reaction. Rather, we react to *patterns* of characteristics in a larger, more comprehensive experience.

Yi-Fu Tuan observes: "A city such as San Francisco is recognized by its unique setting, topography, skyline, odors, and street noises. An object or place achieves concrete reality when our experience of it is total, that is, through all the senses as well as with the active and reflective mind."[12] It is recognized, of course, only if it was previously experienced—at least in the case of topography, odors, and street noises. The skyline and local scenery may be familiar from travel brochures, but sensory data such as odor and sound must be experienced. To really know why San Francisco is not Paris, you must *sense* it.

The Notebooks of Malte Laurids Brigge, by Rainer Maria Rilke, is particularly rich in this regard. Rilke begins by having the protagonist describe his walk in the streets of Paris: "The street began to smell from all sides. A smell, so far as one could distinguish, of iodoform, of the grease of pommes frites, of fear. All cities smell in summer."[13] But, of course, all cities don't smell the same. On the contrary, the particular odors of a place mark it in depth and invoke still other sensory memories. For all that, our sense of smell tends not to be highly valued, nor is odor given any acknowledgment as a design parameter.[14] This despite a growing body of evidence that odor may well be the most persuasive motivational factor in human behavior. Piet Vroon points out that smell plays a significant part in many of our psychic processes and behavior patterns.[15] He also notes that the ultimate interpretation of smell impressions takes place mainly in—and mainly affects—those areas of the brain connected with emotions, feelings, and motivation; thus the sensation of a smell usually leads to a direct behavioral response (116).

Western philosophy has consistently undervalued our senses. Vroon notes: "During the 'scientific revolution,' the Enlightenment and the Industrial Revolution, great emphasis was placed on the intellect. Human rationality was seen as *the* engine of progress. This meant that a certain contempt arose for emotions and for the body as a whole" (5). Smell, especially as it related to bodily odors, was particularly contemptible in the tradition of Plato and Kant, based as it is on an adherence to "rationality." He goes on to describe smell as an old sense in evolutionary terms, with relatively few connections to the left neocortex, the area that houses our "language centers." It has many connections, on the other hand, with older brain structures that regulate emotions and motivation, including the limbic system, the brain stem, and the pituitary gland (through which smell influences bodily function via hormone production) (13). Thus "we do not in the first instance rationalize and verbalize what we smell, but have an immediate *reaction* to a smell and a tendency to act in accordance with it. In other words . . . smelling something generally leads to emotionally colored and sometimes even instinctive actions."[16]

S. Van Toller similarly describes the link between emotion and olfaction by noting that the limbic system is an important and complex set of structures (and their pathways) in the brain relating to emotion, and that a major function of this system is to combine the many parts of the brain.[17] He demonstrates this integrated relationship in an intriguing diagram (Figure 7.1). This thesis is further supported by J. R. King, who notes that the limbic system is the area of the brain that controls emotions and mood states and is closely integrated with the olfactory paths.[18] He further speculates that the connection between smell and emotion may be reciprocal; that is, smells influence mood states, which in turn modify the experience of a smell. He states: "In the olfactory system a kind of 'autonomic tuning' . . . may operate via the trigeminal nerve, in which varying degrees of emotional colouring may be imparted to incoming odours."[19]

The position that humans may instinctively react to specific odors is not universally subscribed to. Trygg Engen, in his analysis of the relationship between odor and memory, tends to discount any purely reactive response. He finds, for example, that there are few odors, even unpleasant ones, that inherently produce a given response, although odors whose nature and source are unknown will keep one aroused, and continual arousal is a key factor in stress.[20] "Odor per se does not motivate behavior; rather, the relationship between odor and behavior is context determined" (10). He uses the term *sensory memory*, by which he means the comparison of a remembered sensation to one currently experienced. He uses it, he says, "to distinguish this kind of memory from the more familiar notion of long-term odor memory that brings back 'remembrances of things past'" (29). Thus sensory memory—unlike associative memory—serves to monitor an odor in an environmental context within a brief time frame (29).

There are other ways of characterizing odor. Rubin and Elder, for example, place odor (in common with other sensory stimuli) into two categories: source (odors at their point of origin) and ambient (odors in the general atmosphere).[21] They further distinguish between sources that are confined (such as smokestacks or vents) or unconfined (such as sewage treatment plants), where sheer size precludes any containment. Confined sources can further be characterized in terms of volumetric rate of discharge, temperature, moisture content, location, elevation, and area (198). (These are the sources that tend to command design interest, as they are usually seen as

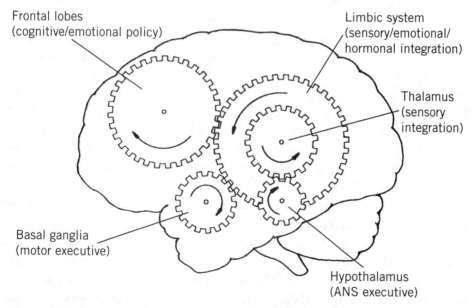

Frontal lobes
(cognitive/emotional policy)

Limbic system
(sensory/emotional/
hormonal integration)

Thalamus
(sensory
integration)

Basal ganglia
(motor executive)

Hypothalamus
(ANS executive)

Figure 7.1. Integrative nature of the brain, 1988. From S. Van Toller, "Emotion and the Brain," in *Perfumery: The Psychology and Biology of Fragrance,* edited by S. Van Toller and G. H. Dodd (Dordrecht: Kluwer Academic Publishers, 1988), 125. Copyright 1988 Chapman and Hall. Reprinted with kind permission of Kluwer Academic Publishers and S. Van Toller.

controllable.) Finally, the authors maintain that odors can be characterized by intensity (the numerical or verbal indication of strength), quality (a verbal description based on vocabulary capability and common benchmarks), acceptability (the acceptance or rejection of an odor based on intensity or quality), and pervasiveness (the ability of an odor to spread through a large volume of air and persist) (198).

There are some cautionary factors involved in making these assessments. Forrest Wilson points out that odor sensitivity varies over the course of the day, our sense of smell rapidly fatigues, and generally sensitivity diminishes with age.[22] Even more important, from our point of view, is that responses to odors are not totally objective because psychological responses vary among observers.[23] Thus, while we find these categories useful in the assessment of potential design sites, we place more emphasis on odor's mnemonic function. We therefore distinguish between immediate (a confined source, if you will) and ambient odors—as in a figure/ground relationship—and involuntary (a physical reaction) and episodic (memory-related association). Such association might include other senses and have spatial dimensions as well.

Indeed, our sense of smell excels in its ability to invoke place awareness. Studies demonstrate that our short-term recognition of smells can sometimes be faulty.[24] However, our long-term memory of particular smells is excellent.[25] Smells remembered after a day tend still to be remembered after a month, and even a year.[26] The corollary to this is that the simpler in character and more familiar the smell, the more efficiently it is retained in memory.[27] Engen and Ross conclude that "a considerable degree of uniqueness must be attributed to the odor-coding process since it is less accurate but far more enduring than coding of the major sense modalities."[28] They attribute this to the idea that odors produce a much more unitary perceptual experience than is true with other sense modalities, even sight.[29] In fact, Engen has demonstrated that odor memory, which he defines as the relative permanence of our ability to recognize specific odors, is far stronger than recognition memory for pictures. Recognition of episodic odor remains quite close to the original strength over time, while recognition of laboratory pictures—initially as strong—decreases rapidly.[30] Laboratory odors are not as well recognized in the first place, and that recognition further diminishes after a small interval of time; however, like episodic odors, it shows little long-term loss (Figure 7.2).[31]

As we have noted, smells have the capacity to evoke other memories—sensory and cognitive—of a particular time. Thus Vroon says: "Sometimes the sense of smell can function as a kind of 'starter motor' that evokes all kinds of apparently forgotten experiences and events from the past."[32] Vroon concludes that smells can therefore serve as memory aids or as means of conditioning our reactions and performance, and that a smell can be given specific meaning by virtue of the context in which it is perceived.[33] Trygg Engen points out that odor memory "involves significant episodes . . . and odors of foods (including those to which one has an aversion because of their association with illness), persons and places."[34] In this context, Charles Baudelaire's *A Phantom,* is particularly poignant:

Hast thou inhaled—O reader, say!—
With zest and lazy greed, the old
Incense that chapel arches hold
Or the stale musk of a sachet?

O magic spell, O ecstasy!
—To make the present yield the past!—[35]

Juhani Pallasmaa praises the "space of scent" when he says: "The strongest memory of a space is often its odor. . . . A particular smell may make us secretly re-enter a space that has been completely erased from the retinal memory; the nostrils project a forgotten image and we are enticed to enter a vivid daydream."[36] Like us, Pallasmaa succumbed to the sensorially rich passages in Rilke's *Notebooks of Malte Laurids Brigge,* and we find little fault with his conclusion: "Contemporary images of architecture appear sterile and lifeless as compared to the emotional and associative power of Rilke's olfactory imagery."[37] Just so.

Of course, one might ask Baudelaire whose past he has in mind—or Pallasmaa the vintage of the nostrils in question. In a 1991 study conducted by Dr. Alan Hirsch

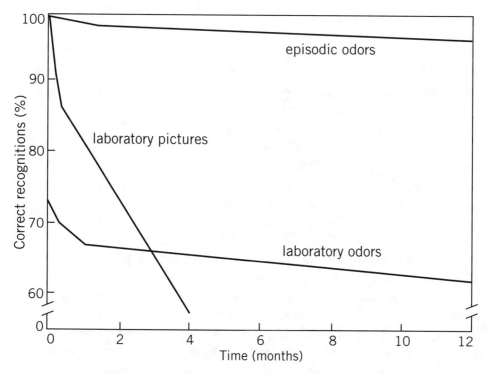

Figure 7.2. Special strength of odor memory, 1987. From Trygg Engen, "Remembering Odors and Their Names," *American Scientist* 75 (1987): 498. Reprinted by permission of *American Scientist,* magazine of Sigma Xi, the Scientist Research Society.

and presented to the October 1991 conference of the Association for Consumer Research, respondents in a Chicago shopping mall were asked the question "What odor causes you to become nostalgic?" The answers from people born between 1920 and 1950 stood in sharp contrast to those born between 1960 and 1980. The first set (1920–1950) included odors such as pine, roses, hot chocolate, violets, baking bread, cut grass, ocean air, cinnamon, hay, fresh air, manure, and burning leaves. All pleasant odors, excepting perhaps the manure. The change in the second set of odors (1960–1980) was startling, including Play-Doh, chlorine, marijuana, smoke, airplane fuel, disinfectant, urine, garbage, plastic, dog waste, exhaust, factories, scented magic markers, and burning tires.[38] Dr. Hirsch comments: "If society's concern is to preserve species and the natural environment depends in large measure upon our nostalgic feelings for an unspoiled green world of childhood, then its importance may be greatly eroded when a new generation, most of whom will have grown up in an urban environment, only experience olfactory-evoked recall of childhood in response to the stimuli of manufactured odors."[39] And not merely "manufactured odors" but odors that a previous generation would have thought little of.

In what seems a bridge across generations, writers have generally used olfactory imagery to vivid effect despite the age of the reader. As Ratty and Mole, Kenneth Grahame's two protagonists in *The Wind in the Willows,* return to Ratty's home on the riverbank, Mole suddenly catches the familiar scent of home: "He stopped dead in his tracks, his nose searching hither and thither in its efforts to recapture the fine filament, the telegraphic current, that had so strongly moved him. A moment, and he had caught it again; and with it this time came recollection in fullest flood. Home!"[40] The smell of it called to Mole "telling him . . . through his nose, sorrowfully, reproachfully, but with no bitterness or anger; only with plaintive reminder" (72). He called out to Ratty to stop, but Ratty was far ahead and could not hear him. And night was falling.

When Mole finally caught up to Ratty, he was distraught: "'I know it's a—shabby, dingy little place,' he sobbed forth at last, brokenly . . . 'but it was my own little home—and I was fond of it—and I went away and forgot all about it—and then I smelt it suddenly—on the road, when I called and you wouldn't listen, Rat—and everything came back to me with a rush—and I *wanted* it!'" (74). In the event, the two of them returned to find Mole's humble abode, which Mole's "unerring nose" detected in due course. The extent of its shabbiness had been quite underestimated; clearly olfactory memory had won out over visual memory.

Other studies have made clear that smells do not usually have a direct effect—positive or negative—on performance but tend to work through associations and learning processes.[41] Even so, smell does sometimes directly influence human behavior in reasonably predictable ways; thus the various efforts by commercial interests to use scents. Lavender appears to help students study mathematics more efficiently (and reduces stress in general), "new car" smells help sell old cars, and home owners are advised to bake cookies or brew coffee when showing their houses to prospective buyers.[42] The notion, therefore, that particular odors can endow otherwise neutral spaces with specific character—a sense of place—is hardly strange.[43] Nor is it strange that it should be exploited.

Baron and Thomley point out that several large companies (notably, Shimizu of Japan) make equipment for introducing fragrances into the heating and air-conditioning systems of office buildings.[44] The claim is that scents such as lemon and peppermint increase alertness and energy, and scents like lavender and cedar reduce tension.[45] These systems have in fact been installed in buildings in various cities. One study supports the idea that pleasant fragrances enhance performance on cognitive tasks such as word construction and decoding.[46] Baron and Thomley's own study concludes that exposure to pleasant fragrances can enhance task performance even under conditions of moderate stress, suggesting that such exposure might be useful in countering the reductions in task performance brought about by stress.[47] Another, more cautionary finding suggests that the affective reactions to fragrances may be more important in determining behavior than specific olfactory qualities.[48]

The question remains whether odors—and our sensing of them—can act as primary determinants of spatial judgments. If by this we mean affective spatial judgments, the answer must surely be affirmative. C. Clifford's 1985 study indicates that in a comparison of otherwise identical rooms, subjects indicated that the room containing a low level of fragrance was brighter, cleaner, and fresher. These are, of course, all evaluative judgments.[49] Of equal interest is the fact that not one of the test subjects actually noted the fragrance, which was present in sufficient quantity to be sensed, but not consciously noted. Schleidt, Neumann, and Morishita found that odor memories reflect the whole of the environment and everyday life, and that such odors are judged quite uniformly.[50] The researchers also noted a possible relationship between territoriality and odor preference: "the sleeping place and other intimate rooms where one feels 'at home' and secure was mentioned by the subjects in connection with pleasant odour memories."[51]

Such spatial judgments will necessarily be different from the visual appraisals we are accustomed to. In his description of the "sensuous worlds" of smell and sound, J. Douglas Porteous points out that "any conceptualization of smellscape must recognize that the perceived smellscape will be non-continuous, fragmentary in space and episodic in time, and limited by the height of our noses from the ground."[52] And he notes: "The smellscape is an emotive environment, not an intellectual one, and as such, should be cherished."[53] Thus the "smellscape" has long been exploited by writers. The observations of Thomas Wolfe's character Mr. Jack continue as he stands in front of an open window of the same room described in chapter 1:

With fingers pressed against his swelling breast, he breathed in a deep draft of the fresh, living air of morning. It was laden with the thrilling compost of the city, a fragrance delicately blended of many things. There was, strangely, the smell of earth, moist and somehow flowerful, tinged faintly with the salt reek of tidal waters and the fresh river smell, rank and a little rotten, and spiced among these odors was the sultry aroma of strong boiling coffee. This incense-laden air carried a tonic threat of conflict and of danger, and a leaping wine-like prophecy of power, wealth, and love. Mr. Jack breathed in this vital ether slowly, and with heady joy.[54]

Of course, not just odor is involved in our characterization of places. Rilke's protagonist, who earlier commented on the smells that characterize Paris, continues:

To think that I cannot give up sleeping with the window open. Electric street-cars rage ringing through my room. Automobiles run their way over me. A door slams. Somewhere a window-pane falls clattering; I hear its big splinters laugh, its little ones snicker. Then suddenly a dull, muffled noise from the other side, within the house. Someone is climbing the stairs. Coming, coming incessantly.[55]

These are typical sounds of the city. In his call for sensitivity to sonic qualities in the designed environment, Michael Southworth points out that the contemporary city dweller is bombarded by a stream of attention-demanding sounds, smells, and microclimates. His experience of the city is like a crazy quilt of sense impressions, each contributing to the total picture.[56] "A place which seems pleasing must do much more than appeal to the eye, a fact which designers often ignore" (52).

Just how important are sonic conditions to people in their assessment of the city? Southworth's study indicates that sound seems "to provide an important link to reality and has a protective and enriching function. Without sound, visual perception is different: less contrastful, less attention-demanding, and less informative."[57] As previously indicated, subjects (both auditory and visual-auditory in his study) tended to prefer clear and informative sounds rather than generalized background sounds that yield little information. The ratio between the two is, of course, variable depending on time of day (Figure 7.3). All subjects liked quiet but informative places, and constantly varying soft personal sounds like footfalls and fragments of conversation or whistling. Moreover, quiet spaces fostered a sense of independence. Sirens, jack-hammers, and airplanes—to no one's surprise—fared the worst in the study, as they were stressful and distracting.

Southworth concludes that the visual experience of cities is closely related to the accompanying sounds; if further research confirms this, he says, it would be significant for the design of cities. He thus points out that "visible form conceived as an isolate can never be experienced as intended by the designer when the sonic form, or even other nonvisual factors such as the microclimate or olfactory environments are not designed in correlation" (65). His study further suggests that sound also has important emotional and social consequences. The geographer Douglas Pocock states, "Sound not only surrounds but can penetrate to the very core of the sentient. This primitive power, which bypasses the cerebral and directly addresses the heart, elicits an emotional response."[58] And, Pocock makes clear, just a few notes can "trigger" an

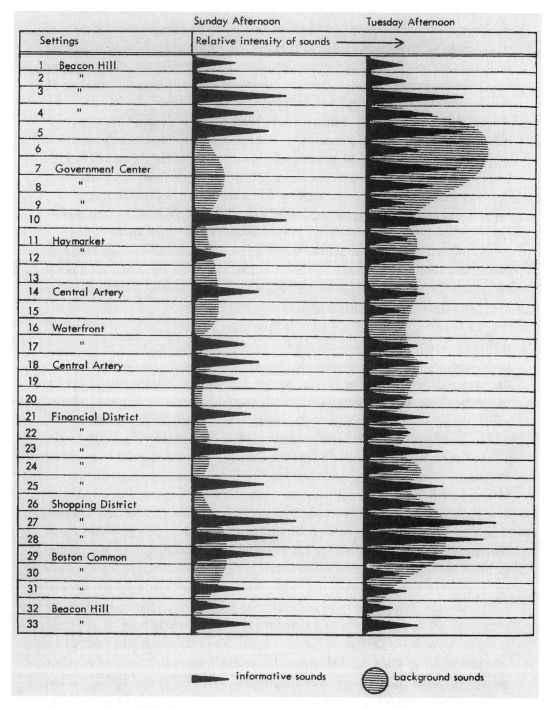

Figure 7.3. Temporal change in sounds, 1969. From Michael Southworth, "The Sonic Environment of Cities," *Environment and Behavior* 1, no. 1 (1969). Copyright Michael Southworth and *Environment and Behavior*.

entire world of memory. In this he is implicitly making a connection between the senses of smell and hearing, both of which function through the limbic system.

Southworth makes several concrete proposals to improve the sonic quality of cities, which we shall return to in chapter 12. Of interest to us here is his assertion that such measures would "develop the sensory awareness of city residents and would provide an environment more responsive to human action and purpose."[59] R. Murray Schafer notes the early use of the term "acoustic space" by Marshall McLuhan, who characterized it as "boundless, directionless, horizonless, the dark of the mind, the world of emotion."[60] Schafer reminds us that there is a distinction between visual space, which we look into, and auditory space, which we stand in the middle of (94). This sort of differentiation has appeared in the design of the built environment, if not always understood by critics. Schafer comments: "When architectural historians begin to realize that most ancient buildings were constructed not so much to enclose space as to enshrine sound, a new era in the subject will open out" (93).

At this point in his text, Schafer has in mind the medieval buildings—such as cathedrals—brought to his attention by McLuhan, buildings whose acoustical properties are at least as remarkable as their visual ones. But ongoing research indicates that many other designed environments may have been constructed primarily on the basis of acoustics. Devereux and Jahn, for example, question whether ancient ritual structures—in this case prehistoric chambered structures in England and Ireland—could have arrived at their proportions as the result of the empirical recognition of the acoustical properties of the kinds of singing or musical sounds they were intended to accommodate. The initial research indicates that the range of resonant frequencies within the structures were neither wide ranging nor random, but rather fell precisely within the range of the male voice, suggesting a ritual function for the spaces.[61]

Still other research exists. Watson and Keating examined megalithic structures in Scotland—one a recumbent stone circle, the other a passage grave—and found elemental acoustic properties suggesting the ritual use of sound. They went on to compare the range of the lower resonant frequencies for a total of eight passage-grave chambers and found that the range demonstrated remarkable consistency in sound characteristics. The authors say: "In combination, the results from these studies suggest that the acoustic properties of these sites should be considered alongside visual and spatial analyses."[62] They emphasize that while it cannot be conclusively demonstrated that the architecture of monuments was deliberately configured to enhance acoustic performance, sound would have been an unavoidable factor.[63]

Pocock points out that "sound plays a crucial role in the anticipation, experience and remembering of places."[64] He notes that sound is a dynamic world of activities rather than artifacts, sensations rather than reflections, and is temporal in nature. Sound, he says, contributes to the process whereby environments become places; an environment without sound is lifeless and unreal, without flow or rhythm, and frightening.[65] Thus even more threatening to Rilke's protagonist than the sounds of the city is the lack of them: "But there is something here that is more terrible: the stillness."[66]

(How oddly similar this is to Marlow's comment in *Heart of Darkness*.) What makes the quiet so frightening is that it is atypical.

Sounds can certainly produce sensory overload, but in the general run of things, they are normal, and thus reassuring.[67] In a moving tribute to such aspects of normalcy, Carl Sandburg wrote "A Teamster's Farewell, Sobs en Route to a Penitentiary":

> GOOD-BY now to the streets and the clash of wheels and
>   locking hubs,
> The sun coming on the brass buckles and harness knobs.
> The muscles of the horses sliding under their heavy
>   haunches,
> Good-by now to the traffic policeman and his whistle,
> The smash of the iron hoof on the stones,
> All the crazy wonderful slamming roar of the street—
> O God, there's noises I'm going to be hungry for.[68]

In this case, it is the ordinary that will be missed, the sorts of sounds that make cities comforting to those who dwell in them. There is also reference to the mechanisms— muscles of the horses, smash of the hoof—that make the sound. It is notable that, with the possible exception of the "roar of the street," these are sounds that the auditory subjects in Southworth's study noted with approval. (They are all sounds, as well, that can be plotted onto a distinctive "sonic map" that profiles a particular place at a specific time.)

Sounds can be incredibly subtle, with an effect that depends on their being strange and recognizable at the same time. Keith Waldrop describes this in "A Door Opening."

> lesser noises
> penetrate
>
> wind in a subtle
> bluster
>
> along deserted
> corridors and up
> the stairs
>
> strange, and strangely
> familiar[69]

Here a minor event—the wind blowing through a hallway—can assume an evocative character. This is consistent with Southworth's study, in which all of his subjects appreciated "quiet but informative places," and his auditory subjects especially noted factors such as wind. Indeed, sound is so commonly a part of the environment, both natural and built, that one might assume that its characteristics have been extensively studied. Not so.

J. Douglas Porteous comments that "with the rapid urbanization of the world's population, far more attention is being given to noise than to environmental sound. . . . Research has concentrated almost entirely upon a single aspect of sound, the concept of noise or 'unwanted sound.'"[70] In this definition, the relationship between noise and sound is much the same as that of weed to rose. Schafer has constructed a more specific definition of noise: (1) unwanted sound, (2) unmusical sound, (3) any loud sound, and (4) disturbance in any signaling system. Studies have indicated that the origin of the sound matters; even when a sound has two or more "annoying" aspects, it will tend not to be noted if it is self-generated.[71]

Porteous goes on to describe the study of the true "soundscape" as the examination of the entire continuum of sound, including both its positive and negative qualities, an analysis not wholly reducible to simple physical measurement.[72] While two conclusions have been reached of general interest—that of the injurious effects of noise on performance levels and the salutary effects of music on mood and life enhancement—empirical soundscape research has been quite limited. This is odd, as sound is a major factor in human evaluation of spatial paradigms, and this has vital economic implications. Porteous points out that a detailed analysis of real estate values in Victoria, British Columbia, revealed that the higher the real estate value, the lower the average sound level, and that a sliding scale of sounds from pleasant to unpleasant followed a distribution of real estate values from high to low (62). And so forth. The ironic result, he says, of noise proliferation is that we, as a people, are really in a state of privation, as we settle for massive quantities of low-grade sounds, sights, and odors.[73]

It is perhaps to be expected, absent a high scientific priority, that some of the most significant research on sound has been done by R. Murray Schafer, a composer. In *The Tuning of the World,* Schafer offers a dynamic (and unforgiving) critique of our aural existence. In so doing, he establishes a vocabulary to discuss the soundscape. The main themes of a soundscape, he says, are keynote sounds, signals, and soundmarks. Keynote refers to the fundamental tonality of the composition, sometimes unconsciously heard, and signal refers to the clear foreground sound consciously listened to. A signal/keynote relationship is much like the figure/ground relationship in the visual arts. A soundmark refers to a characteristic community sound (like church bells) and is thus related to the notion of landmark. Finally, he uses the term *archetypal* to describe sounds that are primordial in nature, and usually symbolic.[74]

Schafer provides two other terms that are helpful: hi-fi soundscape, which enjoys a high signal-to-noise ratio; and lo-fi soundscape, which provides a low ratio that effectively masks any aural distinctions (43). He points out that as lo-fi soundscapes obscure individual sounds, perspective is lost: "On a downtown street corner of the modern city there is no distance; there is only presence" (43). He thus describes a transition from a hi-fi to a lo-fi soundscape, one that has taken place over many centuries to our detriment. One of the contributors to a decidedly lo-fi, uninformative environment has been Muzak (and similar systems), which has reduced music from figure to ground.[75] Another has been the development of the sound wall. Schafer maintains that walls used to delimit physical and acoustic space, but that the latter function has been unstressed in modern buildings. The result has been the development of audioanalgesia—the use of sound as distraction. "Walls used to exist to isolate sounds. Today sound walls exist to isolate."[76]

And what of the architect in all this? Schafer pointedly says: "Architects of the past knew a great deal about the effects of sound and worked with them positively, while their modern descendents know little about the effects of sound and are thus reduced to contending with them negatively, (220). He points out that the designer of the Greek theater at Epidaurus (c. 330 B.C.) paid such careful attention to acoustics that a dropped pin can be heard distinctly in each of the fourteen thousand seats.[77] (This effect would presumably have been enhanced when the theater's resonators— large bronze vessels filled with water—were in place.) And he notes that the visually stunning Shah Abbas Mosque in Isfahan, completed in 1640, enables the visitor who stands directly under the apex of the main cupola to hear the echo of a spoken word seven times perfectly, while hearing nothing when standing to either side of the apex.[78]

Precisely how well were such acoustic principles known in the ancient world? In his *De Architectura*, Vitruvius delineated the principles for employing these bronze sounding vases in theaters. In book 5, he discusses the mathematical concepts underlying "harmonics" and follows immediately with a section that deals with the use of sounding vessels. Here he states:

> In accordance with the foregoing investigations on mathematical principles, let bronze vessels be made, proportionate to the size of the theatre, and let them be so fashioned that, when touched, they may produce with one another the notes of the fourth, the fifth, and so on up to the double octave. Then having constructed niches in between the seats of the theatre, let the vessels be arranged in them, in accordance with musical laws.[79]

In short, musical principles must take precedence over the architectural principles Vitruvius usually pays great attention to. But in fact acoustic concerns appear— and sometimes dominate—in six of the twelve sections now organized into book 5.[80] Significantly, in the section preceding the discussion of harmonics, Vitruvius warns: "Particular pains must be taken that the site be not a 'deaf' one, but one through which the voice can range with the greatest clearness."[81] In short, he suggests doing one's homework first, so that acoustic-mitigating measures can be minimized. One may wonder, as Schafer does, how such fundamental principles became lost to design.

Surely it was relatively recently. Steen Eiler Rasmussen points out that cathedrals, for example, were designed with great attention to acoustics. In large churches with marked reverberation, there is often a region of pitch that is reinforced, a "sympathetic note." A Latin prayer or psalm from the Old Testament, he says, "could be intoned in a slow and solemn rhythm, carefully adjusted to the time of reverberation."[82] Vaulting in general and domes in particular can have strong reverberation characteristics. And so Rasmussen points out that when Giovanni Gabrieli composed for Saint Mark's in Venice, he took advantage of the cathedral's two music galleries, each with its own dome as resonator. Thus the music was heard from the two sides, "one answering the other in a *Sonata Pian e Forte*" (230). Even residential architecture was given acoustic consideration well into the late eighteenth century. Rasmussen describes rococo rooms with

> intimate and musical tones—a large dining room acoustically adapted for table music, a salon with silk- or damask-paneled walls which absorbed sound and shortened reverberations, and wooden dadoes which gave the right resonance for chamber music. Next came a smaller room in which the fragile tones of a spinet might be enjoyed and finally, madame's boudoir . . . where intimate friends could converse together, whispering the latest scandals to each other. (234)

Schafer points out: "Old buildings were thus acoustic as well as visual spectacles . . . but when such buildings . . . became merely functional spaces for silent labor, architecture ceased to be the art of positive acoustic design."[83] A tough critique, but not fundamentally unfair, as attested by the multiple acoustic retrofits of buildings actually designed for the hearing of sound. Thus Schafer says that the study of sound in architectural schools only comprises sound reduction, isolation, and absorption.[84] Surely architecture can do better, if only because it has.

Unfortunately, contemporary architecture's record with the haptic—touch, extended touch, temperature, and kinesthesia—is not much better. In *The Hidden Dimension*, Edward T. Hall comments on the significance of active touch, which he believes is largely lost on designers in Western culture. That is, the texture of surfaces on and within buildings seldom reflects conscious decisions; thus our urban environment provides few opportunities to "build a kinesthetic repertoire of spatial experiences."[85] This need is an important one, Hall says, as human beings tend to synthesize experience at certain points, and learn while they see; and what they learn in turn influences what they see.[86]

He believes that this early exposure to textural nuance may account for the notable spatial sensitivity in certain cultures, especially those of Asia. He even extends this evaluation to architects practicing in Asia, or influenced by Asian design principles.[87] Thus he considers Frank Lloyd Wright's success with his 1921 design for the Imperial Hotel in Tokyo to be a result of his (and presumably his client's) sensitivity to the textures of surfaces. To create continuity, the brick and native lava stone were carried from exterior to interior, and as guests moved from the public to semiprivate to private areas, the textures became progressively smoother. This had the secondary effect of relating textural scale to building scale.

Rasmussen similarly praises Wright for his sensitivity to various structural materials in the design for Fallingwater at Bear Run, even while criticizing him in virtually everything else. Rasmussen also approves the Bauhaus method of teaching textural sensitivity, which involved learning through (hands-on) experience: "By recording their impressions of the various materials they worked with, the students gathered a compendium of valuable information for future use. The tactile sense was trained in experiments with textures systematically arranged according to degree of coarseness. By running their fingers over the materials again and again, the students were finally able to sense a sort of musical scale of textural values."[88] Two other aspects of such study are a consideration of the suitability of exterior materials for use in the interior (a sad practice we have grown habituated to), and the effect of light sources on our visual perception of texture. The latter aspect is particularly striking. In the past, the value change produced by light manipulation was prized for its dramatic capacity and used when spiritual or meditative qualities were sought.

Juhani Pallasmaa poetically describes what he refers to as "the shape of touch": "The skin reads the texture, weight, density and temperature of matter. . . . The tactile sense connects us with time and tradition; through marks of touch we shake the hands of countless generations."[89] This implies that the felt and visible textures that mark surfaces are content laden. So too with temperature. The warmth of the fireplace, he says, forms a space "of ultimate intimacy and comfort."[90] And, in fact, at least one study has demonstrated that sight and touch are considered equally dependable in the determination of texture.[91] This is somewhat startling given the usual weight accorded vision in a wide variety of tasks. The authors conclude that "the modality superiority and ecological validity presented in this article argue for consideration of relative dominance in terms of the *appropriateness* of the task for the modalities in question."[92] Thus macrospatial tasks—form, size, and location—are suited to vision, while texture-related tasks are more equally appropriate to both modalities.[93] And still another study has indicated that haptic feedback affects visual surface perception.[94]

Some of the more intriguing experiments with tactile qualities have occurred in the arts. Ann Hamilton, for example, has long been interested in combining the full range of human senses in a wide variety of media. Sarah J. Rogers notes that "to Hamilton, the body is the locus for empirical knowledge: it is through our bodily senses—tactual, aural, visual, olfactory, and cognitive—that we find experience and knowledge."[95] Hamilton designed a series of three rooms at the Museum of Contemporary Art in Los Angeles that explore "the capacity of absorption" by combining all the senses. In the middle room, Hamilton took a conventional, entirely familiar object—the table—and transformed it into a multisensory experience. The table has as its top a layer of water that appears solid. A figure stands at the table's end with his fingers placed in ten holes in the tabletop, and another series of holes is available for viewer participation (Figure 7.4). Rogers comments: "The table's surface appears highly polished and reflective; only by the accident of touch do we comprehend it as covered with water. Standing at the table, with our fingers in the holes, we begin to apprehend a nexus of associations: life, labor, nourishment, and nurturing."[96] Indeed, even the algae-covered walls and floor and the presence of crickets contribute to the highly sensory experience.

So far we have considered only one aspect of the haptic: active touch. While it is an important one, we would like to consider two other aspects of the haptic here. Those are kinesthesia, or kinesthetic perception, and spatial extension, our ability to expand our sense of touch beyond our physical limits. Kinesthetic perception more specifically refers to the information that we derive from the movement of muscles. Such movement could be the product of focusing eye muscles, muscles in the fingers as we squeeze something, or our leg muscles as we walk. The important aspect of kinesthesia is that the muscle response is highly informative; it tells us how far away objects are, the composition of materials, and the distance we have traveled. When kinesthesia is coupled with active touch, the information is increased, allowing us to become aware of the surface qualities of the path we are on.

Figure 7.4. Ann Hamilton, *The Capacity of Absorption*, 1988. Photograph by Wayne McCall, Santa Barbara. Photograph courtesy of Ann Hamilton and Sean Kelly Gallery, New York.

But kinesthesia also provides physical information about the sociocultural expectations of others. In his discussion of staircases, Jonathan Miller says: "Apart from their practical function, staircases are often theatrical in their nature. They enable human beings to stage their preoccupations, choreograph their politics, and dramatize their religions. For that reason they are often designed with hyperbolic redundancy."[97] In this view, symmetry and size are really functions of social intent, not any "functional" need. Miller points out that stairs also act as metaphors for psychological states, and thus they "symbolize all that is fugitive in human life."[98] What concretizes their meaning at any given point is their context. For the successful, he says, the staircase symbolizes achievement even as it epitomizes failure and frustration for the powerless. It is surely no accident that the "grand staircase" has so often graced the reception area of mansions.

It is also interesting to examine the haptic space that accompanies the individual who traverses the staircase. John Templar believes that "stairs engage the user's motions and their senses to a remarkable degree—perhaps more so than any other architectural element."[99] He points out that the elements of the staircase guide movement through the space, and the dimensions of the risers and treads govern the cadence of the gait.[100] Small wonder that the riser-to-tread ratio is one of the most regulated items in the building code. In fact, the garden of the château of Vaux-le-Vicomte designed by André Le Nôtre (discussed earlier) contains an unusual staircase. The steps are located at the end of a path from the château and lead to a water feature below. What makes them unusual is their constantly increasing tread size from top to bottom, which has the effect of forcing a gait of ever-increasing stateliness (Figure 7.5).

Figure 7.5. Garden stair at Vaux-le-Vicomte, France. Drawing by Joy Monice Malnar.

In the more practical companion to his first book, Templar provides interesting schematics that graphically describe the "zones" that human beings need for locomotion, both in level walking and on stairs. He maintains: "All of the perceptual systems acting synchronously are involved in stair cognition, approach and traverse."[101] He points out that the auditory system informs us about others who are approaching (but out of sight); the haptic system informs us about the floor, tread, and handrail surfaces; the taste-smell system is active in conditions of human proximity; and the basic orienting system monitors our body equilibrium. He maintains, however, that the visual system—locomotor vision particularly—supplies most of the information for mapping, directing, and locomotion processes, as witnessed by the care with which poorly sighted individuals negotiate stairs.[102] It is arguable, however, that time-worn stairs—in their irregularity—may similarly produce caution (Figure 7.6).

Because there is an element of risk in any disruption of our basic-orienting sense, irregular surfaces tend to be the product of one of two circumstances: the passage of time or purposeful disorientation. The Spanish Steps represent the former; amusement park devices that provide uneven floor surfaces, often in motion, represent the latter. Seldom is such treatment common in architecture; Friedensreich Hundertwasser not only provides such a floor but offers a justification for it as well. He says: "A lively, uneven floor in the public area means a regaining of the human dignity which man is deprived of by the levelling tendencies of urbanism. A crucial experience has been taken away from him."[103] People not only have eyes and ears and noses; "people also have a sense of touch in their hands and feet" (282). If human beings have to walk on flat surfaces, "the way they are thoughtlessly conceived with the ruler in the designer offices, alienated from his natural relationship with the earth which goes back to the dawn of time, from contact with the earth, a crucial part of man is blunted, with catastrophic consequences for his psyche, his emotional balance, his well-being and health" (282).

Thus Hundertwasser has placed irregular, uneven tiled floors in the lobby and restaurant areas of the KunstHausWien, designed in 1989 (Figure 7.7). But he says

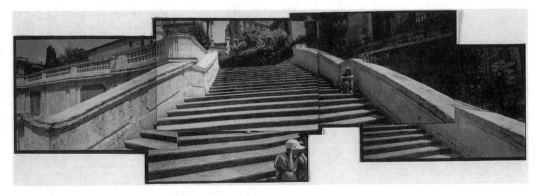

Figure 7.6. Spanish Steps. Photographic construction by Frank Vodvarka.

that such an approach would be appropriate for other venues as well. For example, it would be particularly effective for "the customarily barren, smooth, anonymous corridors" that typify public-sector residential construction where human dignity is often in short supply. Thus the passageway "should be a source of humaneness, warmth, beauty, familiarity and 'non-regulated irregularities' for all the senses when you walk through it, including the sense of touch in the feet."[104] A fascinating, if eccentric, concept.

We return to Templar's spatial premise for just a moment. "Using the perceptual systems to perceive, evaluate, and react to potential hazards, pedestrians maintain a bubble of space between themselves and other objects in the environment. . . . This bubble of space is called the *sensory zone* because its magnitude is maintained through the monitoring performed by the sensory systems."[105] He also points out that this "spatial bubble" is somewhat elastic, depending on velocity of movement and crowd conditions. This idea corresponds quite closely to the theories of Edward T. Hall *(The Hidden Dimension)* and Robert Sommers *(Personal Space),* both of whom are critical to our current view of proxemics. Proxemics is the term invented by Hall for "the interrelated observations and theories of man's use of space as a specialized elaboration of culture."[106] Hall divides his model into three parts: the *infracultural,*

Figure 7.7. Friedensreich Hundertwasser, KunstHausWien restaurant, Vienna, 1989–1991. Photograph by Peter Strobl, Vienna. Copyright 2002.

which he defines as the basic behavioral patterns, rooted in our biological past, that underlie culture (like territoriality); the precultural, which he defines as a physiological basis for perception that nonetheless relies on culture for structure and meaning; and the microcultural, the spatial organization of individual and group activities.[107]

As a manifestation of microculture, proxemics is divided into three spatial types: fixed-feature, semifixed-feature, and informal. Fixed-feature space is probably the most fundamental way of organizing human activities. Hall notes that it includes both the physical and the hidden, internalized aspects that govern human behavior. "Buildings are one expression of fixed-feature patterns, but buildings are also grouped together in characteristic ways as well as being divided internally according to culturally determined designs" (103). Semifixed-feature space is space regulated by features such as furniture. In his study of a Canadian hospital, Sommer found that furniture arrangements were influential in determining whether people experienced spaces as sociofugal (tending to keep people apart) or sociopetal (tending to bring them together).[108]

The third spatial type Hall refers to is informal space, the space that exists around and between people. As is clear from numerous sources—Templar included—human beings rely on spacing mechanisms to maintain an appropriate distance from others, a distance highly dependent on culture and emotion. Hall identifies four sets of interpersonal ranges of distance based on voice level and sensory awareness (skin odor, warmth, focus of vision, etc.). These are intimate distance (0–18 inches), from lovemaking to physical immediacy; personal distance (18–48 inches), from intimacy to casualness; social distance (4–12 feet), from informal business to formal business; and public distance (12–25 feet or more), public speaking to celebrity status.[109] In each case, the individual's sensory input reflects the physical distance from other persons. "The specific distance chosen depends on the transaction; the relationship of the interacting individuals, how they feel, and what they are doing."[110]

Hall's personal distance is often associated with another idea, personal space, although the two are not congruent. Sommer describes this as "an area surrounding a person's body into which intruders may not come. . . . It has been likened to a snail shell, a soap bubble, an aura, and 'breathing room.'"[111] He maintains that a connection exists between individual distance (the normal spacing of humans) and personal space, which may be thought of "as a portable territory, since the individual carries it with him wherever he goes, although it disappears under certain conditions, such as crowding."[112] It is the sort of space that W. H. Auden refers to in his "Prologue: The Birth of Architecture":

Some thirty inches from my nose
The frontier of my Person goes . . .[113]

This raises the question of just how far our "frontiers" actually do go, and the degree to which each sense is responsible for understanding distance. Golledge and Stimson point out that because the real world is complex, sending out millions of

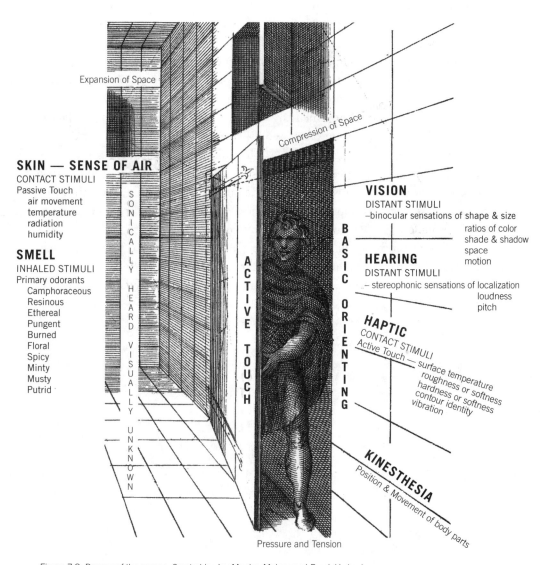

SKIN — SENSE OF AIR
CONTACT STIMULI
Passive Touch
    air movement
    temperature
    radiation
    humidity

SMELL
INHALED STIMULI
Primary odorants
    Camphoraceous
    Resinous
    Ethereal
    Pungent
    Burned
    Floral
    Spicy
    Minty
    Musty
    Putrid

Expansion of Space

Compression of Space

SONICALLY HEARD VISUALLY UNKNOWN

ACTIVE TOUCH

BASIC ORIENTING

VISION
DISTANT STIMULI
–binocular sensations of shape & size
    ratios of color
    shade & shadow
    space
    motion

HEARING
DISTANT STIMULI
– stereophonic sensations of localization
    loudness
    pitch

HAPTIC
CONTACT STIMULI
Active Touch — surface temperature
    roughness or softness
    hardness or softness
    contour identity
    vibration

KINESTHESIA
Position & Movement of body parts

Pressure and Tension

Figure 7.8. Ranges of the senses. Created by Joy Monice Malnar and Frank Vodvarka.

information signals, we can only be aware of a small portion of them. This information is experienced and recorded as differentials of color, heat, motion, sound, pressure, direction, and whatever else is present and within the range of the senses.[114] Because we record only those stimuli that have a bearing on our particular needs, perceptions may differ. In fact, the authors maintain that "the perceptions of two individuals vary as a function of differences in the content of the information presented and the differences in the ability of individuals to pick up the information messages" (190).

Of course, the senses themselves are equal neither in kind nor in range. However, as the authors point out, much information is secondary. And so they conclude that the "meaning of perception can be expanded to include the *immediate apprehension of information* about the environment by one or more of the senses" (190). Helen Keller said: "In my classification of the senses, smell is a little the ear's inferior, and touch is a great deal the eye's superior."[115] She rather dryly notes that great artists and philosophers seem to agree with her assessment, quoting Diderot: "I found that of the senses, the eye is the most superficial, the ear the most arrogant, smell the most voluptuous, taste the most superstitious and fickle, touch the most profound and the most philosophical."[116] We have tried to illustrate the range of each sense by maintaining Gibson's categories of senses (Figure 7.8). There is much overlap in their range, suggesting that which one takes precedence is unclear, and that even the ranges of the senses depend on the type of information being examined. What is clear is that an entire spatial structure can be constructed out of the envelope formed by our senses.

8. No Mere Ornament

The literary glorification of doorways, and the paths that lead to them, appears in yet another song attributed to Bilbo Baggins of Hobbiton fame:

> Still round the corner there may wait
> A new road or a secret gate,
> And though we pass them by today,
> Tomorrow we may come this way
> And take the hidden paths that run
> Towards the Moon or to the Sun.[1]

We have explored aspects of paths at some length. We are interested here in doors and gates, as they are part of the more complex and sensuous (even sensual) entry paradigm through which passage is always significant.

Put differently, there is always a meaning or content invested in transitional elements. Thus doors have long been valued by writers and artists alike as metaphors. The door marks the point of passage from public to private, from exterior to interior, and from known to unknown. In *The Door in the Wall*, H. G. Wells describes the approach to, and entry through, a special door that at its first sight had caused his protagonist to "experience a peculiar emotion, an attraction, a desire to get to the door and open it and walk in."[2] Although he did experience anxiety about actually entering it,

> he had a gust of emotion. He made a run for it, lest hesitation should grip him again,
> he went plump with outstretched hand through the green door and let it slam behind

him. And so, in a trice, he came into the garden that has haunted all his life. . . .
There was something in the sight of it that made all its colour clean and perfect and
subtly luminous. In the instant of coming into it one was exquisitely glad—as only
in rare moments and when one is young and joyful one can be glad in this world.
And everything was beautiful there. (9)

Wells proceeds to inform us about the contents of the garden behind the green door,
which taken together suggests that it was enchanted. We can nonetheless recognize its
attributes as typical of the classical pleasance.

The garden is described, for example, as having a wide path lined with flowers
and lit with a warm and mellow light. Under the blue skies was an avenue of old,
shady trees, white doves, and two spotted panthers. The avenue led "to a spacious
cool palace, full of pleasant fountains, full of beautiful things" (10). And he notes that
"it stretched far and wide, this way and that . . . with . . . hills far away" (9). He thus
describes that shaded meadow with water and birds that Curtius maintains is characteristic of the pleasance. Wells even includes marble statuary, and an image of an
old man, perhaps a philosopher, musing amid the laurel trees (Figure 8.1).

Of equal interest, however, is the nature of the door itself. After all, Wells's
character had entered the garden that so haunted him only once. Although he had
seen the door several times subsequently, each time he found a reason not to enter
it. Thus the door served not only as a vivid reminder of a most remarkable event but
as an expression of desire. In short, the door represented the garden. Accordingly, it
was the door—a green door with a crimson Virginia creeper on it against a white
wall—that Wells goes to great pains to describe in his later, unfulfilled encounters.

It has long been assumed that a door prepares us for that which lies on its other
side, at least in part because it is the initial element encountered by the visitor. It
is an expectation, moreover, with both social and physical dimensions. In the first
instance, the particular door we are to enter—its location, sequential position, scale,
and detail—informs us of the current state of our relationship with the structure's
proprietor, who is welcome and who is merely suffered. The Roman villa of antiquity,
for example, comprised a series of entries through which one successively passed only
by possessing the proper social credentials. As the Roman home was site to a broad
range of relationships, it was a structure composed of areas both public and private.
The degree to which individuals could pass through the progressively private entries
depended on the intimacy of their relationship to the owners and business at hand.
Vestiges of this arrangement remain even in our relatively informal age.

Scale and detail have likewise been used to mark status. For example, social
importance is granted entries that are larger than usual. That is, large entries do not
necessarily indicate actual need but rather are used to grant social and political distinction. A grand entry suggests grandeur waits on its other side. Intricate detail is
likewise used to signify status, display wealth, and prolong the visitor's passage. Arthur
Drexler has described Charles Garnier's approach to the interior design of the Paris

Figure 8.1. Alvin Langdon Coburn, *The Enchanted Garden,* London, 1911. Courtesy of George Eastman House, Rochester, N.Y.

Opéra as one in which detail is used to signal the appropriate rate of movement; the slower the intended rate, the more copious the detail.[3] It was common in the past to use a system of differential scale and detail to indicate which doorways were for the owners and guests, and which for the servants. And not only doorways; this applied to the design of stairs and corridors as well. While luxuriant detail—in the form of carved or applied ornament—was seen as appropriate for the owners, a spare and expedient design sufficed for the servants.

In his "Figures, Doors, and Passages," Robin Evans notes that the plan above all describes the nature of human relationships, since elements such as doors and walls are first used to divide inhabited space and then selectively recombine it.[4] Comparing architectural plans and representations of the human figure, he concludes that in the time between the Renaissance and the nineteenth century, the definition of convenience radically altered.[5] "In 16th century Italy a convenient room had many doors: in 19th century England a convenient room had but one. The change was important not only because the entire house would need to be rearranged, but also because it radically recast the pattern of domestic life."[6] From this sprang the notion of the terminal room, that is, a room with only one entry.

He points out that as a corollary, the corridor was developed to minimize interaction between family members of the household, and between the family and the servants. Thus in the sixteenth century, circulation occurs in and through the rooms themselves, while in the nineteenth century the circulatory elements consist of corridors and passages servicing the rooms. And the overscaled, ornamented doors between rooms are used, rather like picture frames, to provide generous vistas through the length of the house. Evans concludes that "the integration of household space was now for the sake of beauty: its separation was for convenience—an opposition which has since become deeply engraved into theory."[7] In this way, two opposing ideas have been accommodated: extended vistas to "flatter the eye" and the "isolation of individual compartments" for the sake of privacy. The evolution of single-access rooms and corridors is thus seen as a result of both familial reticence and class awareness.

When one compares the plan of Andrea Palladio's design for the Palazzo Valmarana with that of John Webb's Amesbury Abbey, the similarities are striking (Figure 8.2). Webb's design, however, makes use of a central corridor. This ensured privacy for the family without sacrificing servant access, perhaps reflecting the change from the earlier habit of employing distant relatives in service to that of employing professional servants. In his analysis of Amesbury Abbey, John Bold comments: "The disposition of the stairs appears to have been Webb's starting-point in his planning of the house. The neatness of the contrivance, allied with the provision of the corridors, enabled him to make the rear rooms especially usable as self-contained apartments."[8] The implication in Evans's analysis is that social factors historically impelled design decisions, whose results then shaped society.[9]

Entries also prepare us for the physical realities of the space within by virtue of their materials, decoration, and scale. There is, of course, an experiential distinction

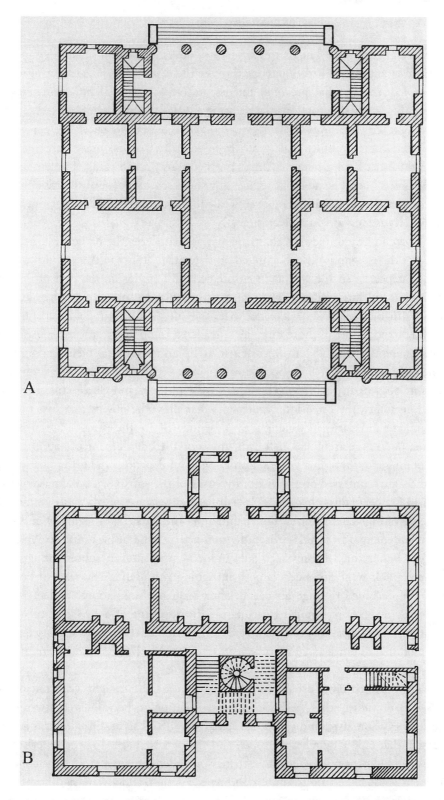

Figure 8.2. (A) Andrea Palladio, Palazzo Valmarana, Lisiera, 1563–1564. (B) John Webb, Amesbury Abbey, Wiltshire, c. 1661. Drawings by Joy Monice Malnar.

between *entry* and *door*. The first experience of doors is visual, while entries are haptically experienced by virtue of passage through them. The door suggests or promises; the entry discharges that promise. Entries are often expanded into porticoes, increasing their sensual nature. In a larger sense, entries can offer symbolic reassurance, overawe, protect, and project status. And most of us have experienced the perceptual, even visceral, discontinuity that results from an entry that has misrepresented what lies on the other side. Of course, this is not necessarily a bad thing. The protagonist in *The Green Door* was, after all, seduced by the disparity between the modest door and the garden of enchantment it concealed. It would seem that you can always promise less as long as you deliver more.

The architectural question that usually arises concerns the design of a *successful* entry. For the Roman house, it centered on the entry's ability to communicate social appropriateness in such a way as to ensure certain behavior on the part of the visitor. A successful entry for multipurpose structures may be something quite different. Brodie Ann Bain expresses her belief that "the entry's inherent characteristics may actually provide some of those qualities considered to be important in a pleasurable environment as a whole."[10] By way of setting up an operational preliminary model of the "successful entry," Bain postulates five issues. These are first, a sense of place, which involves clear distinctions between inside and out, and clear paths and goals; second, legibility, the provision of elements that allow the observer to structure the environment and clarify its function; third, sequential art, the effective use of successive, temporal aspects of space; fourth, mystery, the engagement of the observer's sense of inference through a gradual unfolding of information; and fifth, sense of dignity, the status conferred on the visitor by virtue of the entry's symbolic placement.[11]

Bain further refines this model by conflating the sense of place, sequential art, and sense of dignity categories, but maintaining the integrity of legibility and mystery. What emerges from this revised division is that sense of place and legibility are the most important, with mystery only indirectly valued as a "subset" of legibility. The methodology of this study is both intriguing and useful. The reactions of students were recorded through a series of entry-sequence simulations. Sufficient consistency of reaction occurred to permit the development of a hypothetical model that affirms the critical role of the entry.[12] And it is a model that uses sensory enquiry and emotional response as primary aspects of judgment. Both of these attributes are related to ornament.

Now, the question of ornament is both fascinating and fraught with controversy. We stated previously that we believe time estimation to be influenced by sensory data such as odor, taste, and touch, as well as sound and sight. Ornament is an area of design that especially relies on touch and sight, as well as being the repository of intense symbolic meaning. Therefore there is no "mere ornament." On the contrary, ornament is usually an aid to understanding the design, and always significant. And such controversy as has swirled around it has usually involved some ideological issue, not its value as a linguistic form or its perceptual effectiveness.

Any analysis of ornament involves a discussion of materials—their sensory characteristics (color, texture, temperature) and associative and symbolic character. Vitruvius devoted all of book 2 of *De architectura* to a discussion of construction materials. Similarly, Leon Battista Alberti relegates all of book 2 in his *De re aedificatoria* to the subject, asserting "that no man ought to begin a building hastily but should first take a good deal of time to consider, and resolve in his mind all the qualities and requisites for such a work."[13] From Alberti's text, it is clear that such material qualities will include both strength and beauty. But materials also actively contribute to the determination of form. Henri Focillon points out that "form does not behave as some superior principle modeling a passive mass, for it is plainly observable how matter imposes its own form upon form."[14]

Focillon draws two conclusions: first, that certain materials have intrinsic formal vocations, and their inherent qualities can "call forth, limit or develop the life of the forms of art"; and second, that these suggestive and individual materials "which demand so much from form and which exert so powerful an attraction on the forms of art, are, in their own turn, profoundly modified by these forms."[15] Thus knowledge of materials is critical to design intention because a dialogue always occurs between that intention and the materials used to realize it. Materials, moreover, have inherent qualities, their physical nature, and associational qualities, their ascribed nature. The irony is that inherent qualities are usually transformed into associational qualities by virtue of the material's manipulation, ensuring that every material has a sociocultural aspect. (Indeed, if we reconsider Amos Rapoport's thesis that primitive and vernacular buildings enjoy a high degree of cultural congruence, we might conclude that part of that agreement is due to the use of culturally agreed upon materials.)[16]

What are the inherent qualities of materials? One could analyze the compressive, tensile, and density characteristics of a particular material (a cognitive-structural concern), or examine the material's sensory qualities, such as texture, color, pattern, and temperature. Plastic, for example, can be described as smooth, nonporous, and poor for detailing; wood is warm, easily joined, texturally varied, and a good insulator; concrete has high compressive strength and crude surfaces and is damp; steel is hard, structurally strong, cold, and reflective when polished. While the qualities in these depictions that refer to structural attributes are well known and codified in building standards, the sensory qualities are seldom referred to, perhaps because they are seen as ornamental—and thus inessential.

Yet as Juhani Pallasmaa notes: "Every touching experience of architecture is multi-sensory; qualities of matter, space, and scale are measured equally by the eye, ear, nose, skin, tongue, skeleton and muscle."[17] Moreover, the qualities of materials carry much of the design content. Steven Holl implies this when he says: "Architecture, more fully than other art forms, engages the immediacy of our sensory perceptions. The passage of time; light, shadow and transparency; color phenomena, texture, material and detail all participate in the complete experience of architecture."[18] And again: "The total perception of architectural spaces depends as much on the material and detail of the haptic realm as the taste of a meal depends on the flavors of authentic ingredients."[19] Clearly, the sensory presence of the materials used is critical to both an understanding and an assessment of the architectural construct.

Another way of considering inherent qualities is to examine their responsiveness to particular needs or intentions. Indeed, the real importance of inherent qualities might be seen as their relative appropriateness to design intention, rather than their innate qualities as such. Of course, this implies an actual control over the shaping of architectural materials by either the designer or craftsworkers who understand the design. But this sort of "hands-on" direction seldom occurs now. Consequently designers have resorted to ever more precise drawings. There are alternative approaches. Frank Gehry uses processes and materials that reflect current reality, and he notes that workers (carpenters and sheet metal workers in particular) often become involved with his projects by virtue of his incorporating them at their craft level. The result of this approach can be seen in the 1979 addition to his own house in Santa Monica, California. The materials that Gehry used are corrugated siding, wire mesh fencing, plywood, asphalt, and gypsum board, all commonly found on any construction site, but not commonly used in this manner.

This approach, the use of local materials and building skills, presaged Gehry's design for a far more ambitious project, the Guggenheim Museum (1998) in Bilbao, Spain. Here he uses steel plate for the building's skin, and local shipbuilding workers to apply it. Thus he exploits a local resource familiar to his workers and provides jobs for an economically depressed industry in the bargain. The museum's extraordinary design has also resulted in a radical increase in tourism for Bilbao, an economic boon that has surely been noted by civic leaders around the world. The result is a striking building whose significance goes far beyond its ostensible purpose (Figure 8.3).

The capacity of unusual materials in an unusual design to have an economic impact, combined with a "progressive" cultural content, likely played a part in the choice of Gehry to design the new stage in Chicago's multimillion-dollar Lakefront Millennium Park.[20] The steel latticework that covers a listening area for eleven thousand people (four thousand in permanent seating) not only unifies the space but provides the structure for an extensive speaker system to ensure good acoustics. In fact, the latticework will be 600 feet long, 300 feet wide, and 60 feet high. But the stage itself is most striking, with steel ribbons that rise 90 feet, at least in the preliminary design (Figure 8.4). Blair Kamin, architecture critic for the *Chicago Tribune,* notes that the design's being preliminary "should stop no one from appreciating the extraordinary merits of Gehry's plan, both urban and architectural, and what they mean for Chicago's design scene. The band shell seems destined to become an instant landmark."[21]

But the larger question may well be, what is the purpose of ornament? One answer is that ornament can inform us of the purpose of an otherwise obscure spatial paradigm. Now, we may be tempted to deny the value of ornament. We have,

Figure 8.3. Frank O. Gehry, Guggenheim Museum Bilbao, Bilbao, Spain, 1997. Photograph by Jeff Goldberg; copyright Jeff Goldberg/Esto.

after all, been indoctrinated in our contentless age to believe that ornament is, at best, a superfluous addition to structure and, at worst, an affront to sensibility. John Summerson contends that this view of ornament arose with the Victorians. His position is interesting. He maintains that a certain amount of "ornament"—detail that is not structural—may be necessary to make a thing what it is, "a grammatical form of communication."[22] He concludes that it is necessary to distinguish between uneconomical elements that are linguistic and those that are ornamental.[23] Summerson is thus maintaining that if the so-called ornament is critical to an object's message qua object, as when a capital and base denote a particular sort of column, then it is not merely ornament but an essential part of architecture.

At what point, then, does ornament become a linguistic form? The roots of this sort of role can already be seen in Vitruvius's *De architectura,* where he lists the fundamental principles of architecture. These are order, arrangement, eurythmy, symmetry, economy, and propriety. Order is an attention to elements so that their scale and proportion will correspond to that of the larger work. Arrangement refers to the way in which elements are adjusted to actually shape the work using formats such as plan, elevation, and perspective. Eurythmy refers to the beauty that comes from harmonious proportions. Vitruvius defines symmetry as an agreement among elements, and between elements and the total work, in accordance with a standard. Economy refers to "the proper management of materials and site, as well as a thrifty balancing of cost and common sense in the construction of works."[24] This includes

Figure 8.4. Frank O. Gehry, Millennium Park Stage, Chicago, 1999. Photograph by Whit Preston. Courtesy of Gehry Partners.

choices of materials based on availability and suitability, the client's social position, and the intended use of the structure.

It is Vitruvius's sixth principle, that of propriety, that especially interests us here. Propriety can be thought of as appropriateness to a situation that comes from prescription (a determination of what is "correct" based on social or moral principles), usage (a consistent approach to design and materials), or nature (those factors occurring naturally and affecting siting). The first of these definitions suggests that certain building formats are appropriate for certain buildings:

> The temples of Minerva, Mars, and Hercules will be Doric, since the virile strength of these gods makes daintiness entirely inappropriate to their houses. In temples to Venus, Flora, Proserpine, Spring-Water, and the Nymphs, the Corinthian order will have peculiar significance, because these are delicate divinities, and so its rather slender outlines, its flowers, leaves, and ornamental volutes will lend propriety where it is due. (15)

And Vitruvius goes on, in similar fashion, to describe the appropriate use of the Ionic order.

Clearly, Vitruvius has in mind some historical derivation of these orders, as well as an attention to their appearance. In fact, in book 4 he discusses the origins of the three orders, stating that the ratio of width to height for each column type originated in the ratio of a human foot to human height. Thus the Doric column has a ratio of six to one and as used in buildings exhibited "the proportions, strength, and beauty of the body of a man" (103). But later, when a temple to Diana was to be built, these footprints were translated "into terms characteristic of the slenderness of women" (103). In this way the Ionic order (7:1) was devised. Vitruvius concludes: "Thus in the invention of the two different kinds of columns, they borrowed manly beauty, naked and unadorned, for the one, and for the other the delicacy, adornment, and proportions characteristic of women."[25] Vitruvius's interest is not merely historical; he clearly believes that the orders signal a priori the structure's nature. A change in the order may really indicate a change in the disposition of the building, how we are meant to perceive it. An alteration in the ornament results in a redefinition of the institution, and the more ingrained the sign, the more significant any departure from the usual.

In *The Sense of Order,* E. H. Gombrich notes the power and pervasiveness of habit that derives from a sense of order. Habit establishes the "frame of reference against which we can plot the variety of experience."[26] He says that although *art* and *artifice* have the same psychological roots, "It is artifice first of all which is called upon in human culture to resist change and to perpetuate the present."[27] Thus Thomas Wolfe has Mr. Jack's wife, in a manner not unlike the husband, look lovingly at the contents of her room, "which she had assembled in a crowded lifetime of work, travel, and living. Indeed, all these objects . . . had been brought together at different times and places and fused into a miracle of harmony by the instinctive touch of this woman's hand . . . 'Ah, here it is,' she thought. 'It is living like a part of me. And God! How beautiful it is!' she thought. 'How warm—how true!'"[28] Artifice (ornament and decoration) is therefore essentially conservative in nature, whereas art is free to be radical. This in turn implies that ornament possesses the symbolic content of the age in which it was first produced.

Now, it has been argued that in an age of electronic media, the meaning of social space (and the ornament that characterizes it) is, in any case, largely academic. Joshua Meyrowitz points out that if people wished to experience each other in the past, "they had to travel through space, stay through time, and be admitted through the entrances of rooms and buildings."[29] He contends that although the change from oral to print culture did little to alter the facts of information flow to and from places, the rise of electronic media has led "to a nearly total dissociation of physical place and social 'place.' When we communicate through telephone, radio, television, or computer, where we are physically no longer determines where and who we are socially."[30] Well, perhaps—but only if you believe that people have ceased to place valuation on the mode in which information is presented.[31]

Meyrowitz nonetheless makes a strong argument for the importance of recognizing the impact of electronic media on social situations and identities. We are especially interested in his insight into the importance of entries in the social process, and their violation by these new media. "Entrances and the rites associated with them, whether formal . . . or informal . . . traditionally allowed for orderly transitions from situation to situation and from behavior pattern to behavior pattern."[32] He argues that boundaries such as walls and doors are now effective only to the degree that they restrict information.[33] Also apparent in his argument is the connection between entries and walls as elements of control.

In fact, walls, like entries, have various characteristics. They can divide physical entities while connecting the idea of them, separate homogeneous groups while uniting the larger milieu, and serve as symbol of both division and reconciliation. They are at once social, physical, perceptual, metaphorical, and symbolic. This becomes clear when one considers that the Vietnam Memorial wall, the Berlin Wall, the Great Wall of China, and the Wailing Wall in Jerusalem—while all *walls*—have radically different contexts and meanings, both from each other and over time. Thus no wall lacks controversy.

In his "Mending Wall," Robert Frost raises one of the great questions about the fundamental nature of walls:

> Before I built a wall I'd ask to know
> What I was walling in or walling out,
> And to whom I was like to give offense.[34]

This is the question he would like to ask of his neighbor but doesn't. In any case, his neighbor—unasked, and twice—offers up his pat answer: Good fences make good neighbors.[35] What he is saying is that if neighbors keep the demarcation between their respective spaces—in this case a stone wall—in good repair, so will their relationship be in good repair.

We are reminded of Hillier and Hanson's position that differences in spaces reflect differences in the way societies generate and control encounters.[36] But it seems clear that walls that divide the internal domain of an individual are vitally different from walls separating unrelated individuals. Jill Stoner points out that the party wall is different from other walls in that it is an aspect of enclosure for two separate groups.[37] "While other walls separate domains that can be defined as interior or exterior independently of one's own position, the space on either side of the party wall is either 'interior' or 'exterior' relative to one's own position."[38] She concludes that the geometry of the party wall is therefore socially symmetrical. The definitions of wall types within enclosures are complex, especially when they separate unrelated parties with equal claim, as in apartment blocks.[39] Stoner notes, however, that the party wall can also mediate between adjacent units, thereby encouraging us "to focus on the potential for social relationships to act as generators of dwelling form."[40]

Studies have demonstrated that there are few, if any, decisions that are based on pure cognition; on the contrary, people's feelings exercise powerful effects on cognitive processes.[41] And since emotion colors perception, it affects all our decisions—as does context. One of the better-known studies involving subjective evaluation of planar surfaces was made by Thiel, Harrison, and Alden. Two studies were conducted to test the hypothesis that the perceived differential enclosing effect of architectural surfaces depends on their position, with the horizontal-over surface having the greatest effect, the vertical side surfaces less, and the horizontal-under surface the least of all.[42] The study used one-point perspectives of a room with, in the case of the second study, representations of a person and furnishings. The room's proportions were length equal to 1.6 times width, which in turn was 1.6 times height (roughly the dimensions of a golden room).

The hypothesis was essentially borne out, with both males and females perceiving the same differences in the relative contribution of each surface to a sense of enclosure.[43] Now, how dependable are the conclusions of the study? Pedersen and Topham repeated the study and found that in general, the Thiel group's findings held true— but only for certain sizes of rooms. This second study suggests that as space gets larger, the correlation between the theoretical ranking and the way people actually perceive the space becomes lower. They therefore call for more studies to determine if in fact the theoretical values themselves are less accurate for spaces of increasing volume.[44] And there are other questions, most of which are raised by Thiel, Harrison, and Alden in their earlier study.

Suppose, for example, the rooms under consideration were not quasi golden rooms? (The value of lesser to greater size, .6, is very close to our cone of optimum vision, approximately 65 degrees with an emphasis on the horizontal.) How many spatial paradigms have we experienced of such a visually fortuitous nature? What happens when we are forced to seek visual definitions that lie beyond our field of optimum view? And the authors state that they would want to check the effect of varied shapes and sizes of openings in the planes, as well as "surface color, texture, illumination, temperature and humidity, odors, acoustic qualities, and the number and activity of human occupants."[45] Finally, they note that "ideally all these studies in simulation should be checked with full-scale real-world conditions."[46]

There are two points that we consider important here, and even applaud. The first is that there is a clear recognition on the part of the investigators that any sense of architectural enclosure is the product of many sensory data beyond that of sight; the second is that no simulation takes the place of a real encounter with spatio-sensory constructs. Most studies of this kind do rely on photographic representations. In a study conducted by Shafer and Richards, both the actual scenes and photographs of them were presented to test subjects. Their research suggests that when pictorial representations adequately depict the variation of natural and built environments, the tested response to the pictures corresponds to the on-site responses to the same scenes. If, however, the pictures include only a portion of the total variation, the recorded responses differ significantly from on-site responses.[47]

In short, the amount of information had a significant effect on the subject's responses. The authors note that "a photograph that shows only part of a scene can change, not only one's word description of the scene, but may also change one's reaction to resource or landscape-management procedures [the author's concern] involving the total environment where the photograph was taken."[48] Well, sure. But it is not merely that the viewer has more opportunity to view a scene in situ, but that a far greater array of sensory data is available to base judgments on. In fact, virtually all the items cited by Thiel's group for further study require fully sensory contact to be experienced. This is especially true for those factors that rely on the haptic sense, such as texture, temperature, and humidity.[49]

Now, architectural enclosure relies on the delineation of detail, whose definition is complex. It can refer to process, drawing, or thing. As a practical matter, the term is often used to refer to the joining of two building elements. In fact, detailed notations are used to describe construction procedures, either because they are not obvious to the workers or for legal reasons. Designers have really been fascinated, however, by the detail revealed and exalted. And as it is visible, such detail is essentially ornamental. Put differently, it isn't the joint that constitutes the detail, but what visually and tactilely occurs at that joint. What is significant is the visual transition from one element to another, a transition that relies on sensory and symbolic factors. Thus ornamental detail is the meaningful, sensory event that occurs where design elements join.

In "The Tell-the-Tale Detail," Marco Frascari notes that possibilities of innovation and invention lie in the details, and designers can use these to give harmony to the most difficult or disorderly environment that can be generated by a culture.[50] "The art of detailing is really the joining of materials, elements, components, and building parts in a functional and aesthetic manner" (23). Frascari describes two kinds of details: material joints, such as the capital that connects column shaft and archi-trave; and formal joints, such as a porch that connects the interior to the exterior (24). The detail is always a joint, or junction. As the smallest unit of signification in architectural meaning, it is also the expression of structure and utility. This unusual view of detail stresses its active, sensory role rather than its capacity for structural delineation.

What qualities does the detail—the joint—have that might promote such an active, sensory role? G. T. Buswell engaged in a series of studies in 1935 at the University of Chicago, published under the title *How People Look at Pictures: A Study of the Psychology of Perception in Art.* As the title shows, Buswell's primary interest was whether the representations advanced in the literature on the psychology of art, which he felt were based on introspective and subjective evidence, were also sup-ported by objective data. "It will be interesting," he says, "to find the extent to which the objective evidence obtained from photographs of eye movements corroborates the hypotheses that have been built up subjectively relating to the general patterns of perception in looking at pictures."[51] His objective data were obtained through the use of an eye-movement apparatus built at the University of Chicago to measure such movement in terms of direction and duration.

In fact, the observations made by the art experts fared reasonably well on average, though not always for the reasons thought to be operative. Some of the conclusions that he reached, beyond their applicability to art viewing, are of interest to us. He found, for example, that certain areas of the surface commanded more interest than others, and that the initial pattern of perception differed from later examinations. The period of visual fixation tended to increase with time and, in any case, was influenced much more by the individual characteristics of the viewer than by the nature of the observed picture.[52] A more recent study was designed to determine the possibility of establishing some kind of relation between landscape preferences and those parts of the landscape the subjects fixate with their eyes. Paired sets of photographed land-scape slides were shown to subjects, and their ocular fixation points were recorded.[53] The authors conclude: "Results showed that, on average, there were more eye fixations in the preferred than in the non-preferred landscape, and, what is more interesting, the subjects who preferred humanised landscape had fixed their eyes specifically on houses and other human constructions, while the subjects who chose the unchanged landscape seemed not to notice those parts."[54] Thus preference on the part of the subject controls what will be seen as well as how.

Buswell found that some interesting characteristics of perception emerged when the subjects analyzed an architectural picture: "In general, the pattern of percep-tion . . . started with the lower part of the picture, swung up the column to the upper part, where great interest was evidenced in the details of decoration."[55] And in still another picture, "a considerable amount of detailed examination was given to the decoration at the top" (102). It is also interesting that the decoration, or ornament—much of it consisting of spirals—was not observed in a linear fashion, that is, the eye did not follow the linear path of the shape. On the contrary, such detail tended to be read as pattern. Nor are particular types of design necessarily more effective than others in moving the eye from one place to another. Buswell concludes: "It is evident that the movements of the eyes are adjusted in some manner to produce the most effective pattern of perception, but the inner interpretation from these patterns of perception are in all probability derived from ideational and emotional experiences" (115). (Thus his conclusions are consistent with both Gestalt and classical principles.) In general, however, the two aspects of pictorial representation that most successfully commanded attention were contrast and detail. He notes that in general, the addition of detail to an area where there was very little attracted eye fixations more often for longer periods. Hence the compositional value of ornament is that it supplies symbolic information that is almost certain to be read by the viewer.

The details that Buswell notes consisted, in the main, of complex interactions between shape units. Gombrich maintains that the implication of Buswell's study is that humans tended to look at the point where two elements met rather more than other areas. Thus the transition points, or joints, are significant, as can be seen in a diagram of eye fixations (Figure 8.5). Gombrich notes that these "photographs of eye movements and fixation points show that continuous contours appear to have been less thoroughly inspected than those parts of the design which cannot simply be 'taken as read.'"[56]

Another study of similar phenomena—without the intent to test artistic principles—confirmed many of Buswell's basic conclusions. While most of the material in Alfred L. Yarbus's *Eye Movements and Vision* is concerned with principles of physiological optics, he does note that knowledge of the principles governing eye movements and the perception of images that are stationary relative to the retina is useful to motion pictures and television and for evaluating possibilities of perception in complex situations.[57] Yarbus relied on a miniature optical system that used a plane mirror to activate a device that writes a continuous record of eye position on film. This device offered a striking improvement over the instrument used by Buswell thirty years earlier. Yarbus maintains that analysis of eye-movement records shows that the elements attracting attention may contain information useful and essential for perception, but those elements on which the eye does not fixate, do not (171). He thus concludes that neither detail nor contrast per se attracts the eye; it is rather when these elements contain essential and useful information.

Before continuing with conclusions, it is important to note a curious fact of human perception. Yarbus points out that as his subjects examined the pictures he provided, change in fixation points was accomplished by high-speed eye movements. These consisted of identical and simultaneous rapid rotations of the eyes termed "saccades" (103). The function of saccades is to change the fixation points by bringing the fovea, which covers a limited area of the field, into position to view a particular element of the thing being perceived. We are not aware of this movement, nor do we actually see during it; rather, we see during the static fixation stage that occurs

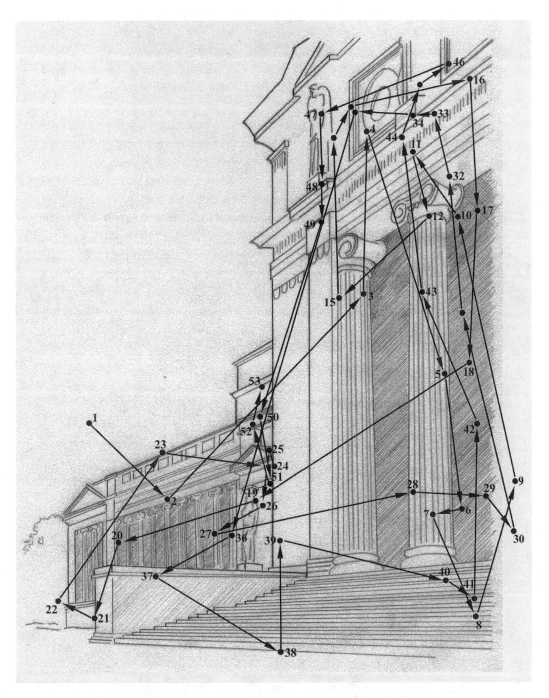

Figure 8.5. Records of eye fixations, after G. T. Buswell, 1935. Drawing by Joy Monice Malnar.

between saccades. Yarbus illustrates this phenomenon with an interesting diagram (Figure 8.6). Here *a* represents a series of geometrical figures presented to the subject, *b* the record of eye movements while the subject attempted to trace the lines as smoothly as possible, *c* eye movements during a twenty-second examination of the figures without instruction, and *d* eye movements during a twenty-second period after instruction was given to "look at the figures and count the number of straight lines" (105).

These alternating saccades and fixation points provide the "objective evidence" that eye movement studies rely on. One of Yarbus's simpler illustrations of how we see is based on a photograph of a girl's face, where the subject's examination occurs over one minute with both eyes (Figure 8.7). Clearly the eyes, nose, and mouth received most of the attention, especially the eyes, with a fairly cursory attention paid to the shape of the face. Yarbus points out that the eyes—the most expressive part of the photograph—receive such attention "that the examination of the portrait was in fact reduced to the repeated alternate fixation on first one and then the other of the girl's eyes" (193). Of course, the areas so intensely examined also happen to be the most detailed (in the case of the eyes) and high contrast (in the case of the face).

Yarbus agrees with Buswell that "individual observers differ in the way they think and, therefore, differ also to some extent in the way they look at things" (192). He makes the following series of observations:

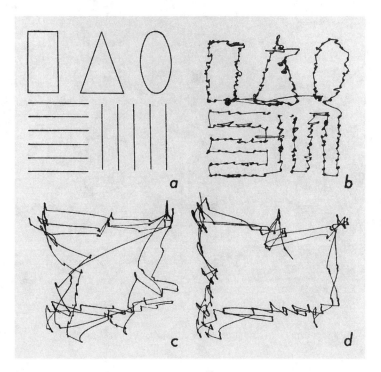

Figure 8.6. Alfred Yarbus, eye fixation charts, 1965. From Alfred L. Yarbus, *Eye Movements and Vision* (New York: Plenum Press, 1967). Reprinted with permission of Kluwer Academic Publishers and Plenum Publishers, New York.

The human eyes voluntarily and involuntarily fixate on those elements of an object which carry or may carry essential and useful information. The more information is contained in an element, the longer the eyes stay on it. The distribution of points of fixation on the object changes depending on the purpose of the observer. . . . The order and duration of the fixations on elements of an object are determined by the thought process accompanying the analysis of the information obtained. (211)

He thus concludes that people who think differently to some degree see differently.[58]

Both propositions—that form complexity and association value influence visual memory—have been confirmed by other studies, although the evidence is somewhat conflicted for the latter. Clark's 1965 study found that subjects probably stored an uncoded image of the entire shape of simple, but not of complex, forms, and that complex forms were presumably remembered by making associations to them.[59] In a series of studies by Goldstein and Chance, evidence was not found to support the notion that association value aided in the recognition of random shapes, but neither was it excluded as a possibility in certain instances. What the authors did conclude was that familiarity with a class of pictorial stimuli improves recognizability of new members of that class; that familiarity might not be the only factor involved; and that some pictorial material may not be facilitated for memory by natural-language mediation.[60] It may, however, be significant that Clark used randomly constructed shapes in his study, whereas Goldstein and Chance used three sets of recognizable forms for which language identifiers were superfluous. And it is significant that there were statistical differences in both studies based on whether the forms to be identified were simple or complex.

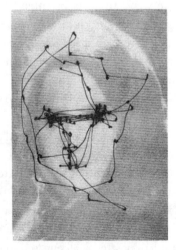

Figure 8.7. Alfred Yarbus, portrait with fixation points, 1965. From Alfred L. Yarbus, *Eye Movements and Vision* (New York: Plenum Press, 1967). Reprinted with permission of Kluwer Academic Publishers and Plenum Publishers, New York.

In fact, it has been demonstrated by Davis (1977) and Lawless (1978) that "feature-impoverished" visually presented shapes can behave like odors in paired-associate learning and in recognition memory.[61] We find the study by Lawless particularly interesting. He theorizes that the memory of simple shapes and odors is encoded in a similar fashion, as they are unitary images with few features, with subjects reporting coding the simple figures in a holistic fashion as with odor.[62] He also points out that neither verbal coding nor time had significant effect on the recognition memory of either odors or simple shapes (494). And Lawless refers to the earlier study by Clark, in which Clark reports that his subjects relied on remembering images of the whole contour of simple forms, as opposed to complex stimuli where associations were often employed.[63] Thus the conclusion that, while our memory of complex free-form figures is good in short-term memory, we begin to rely on association in the longer term; that such association is directed by familiarity and valuation; and that simple figures are more accurately remembered in the long term than are complex ones.[64]

All this would go far toward explaining why the pyramids at Giza are memorable, if uneventful, and Victorian rooms are a continuing perceptual delight despite their visual confusion and the fact that we have seen them before. These studies, moreover, tend to confirm the conclusions of Buswell and Yarbus, and even more particularly Gombrich's hypothesis. We are fascinated by ornamental detail, not only because it marks transition points but because we do not long remember it. It is thus ever new and interesting, and we are willing to devote our information-seeking attention to it.

But architects have, of course, long known this. An extraordinary example of a building that uses our fixation patterns to advantage is the previously discussed Paris Opéra, designed by Charles Garnier in 1861. While the building is organized in an axial manner, the facade and interior spaces are highly plastic, and lavishly ornamented (Figure 8.8). In 1871, Garnier published *Le theatre,* in which he explains his design approach. He views the acts of entering the structure, circulating and socializing, and arriving in the auditorium as a sequence experienced both psychologically and physically. Thus the plan reflects a division of the circulation requirement into two activities, processional and functional. An analysis of the resulting spaces is revealing, especially the Grand Stair. Garnier remarks that in the past, no one believed that the crowded staircases could be as much a spectacle of pomp and elegance as the plays, "but today, luxury is spreading, comfort is demanded everywhere, and there are those who love to see the movement of a varied and elegant crowd."[65]

Garnier's treatment of the foyer and central stairs of the Opéra, which were to allow people to move through the theater "gracefully and comfortably," is a fine example of ornamental detail being used to control the character of that movement. Arthur Drexler describes Garnier's approach to circulation: "The more commodious the space in which to linger, the more elaborate the detail. Thus the stair hall is like a plaza surrounded by streets, all encased in ornament signaling the appropriate rate of movement. Only when Garnier wants movement to be quick does he eliminate ornament entirely."[66] He points out that the ornament is supplemented by other control

Figure 8.8. Charles Garnier, Grand Stair, Paris Opéra, 1861–1875. Engraving by Piquois and Sulpis for Charles Garnier, *Le Nouvel Opéra*. Courtesy of the Rare Book and Special Collections Library, University of Illinois at Urbana-Champaign.

devices, such as the compound curves of the stairway, the curved and projecting balconies, the ceiling arches in the Grand Foyer, and the use of color to integrate various elements. Thus Garnier relies on our fixation patterns and short memory for complexity.

The point here is that ornament, far from being an embellishment of inherently deficient design or simple visual excess, serves a vital function. It serves to precisely identify a thing for what it is—its social and cultural function—and transmit that identity to an audience. It also controls our response to that which it ornaments through the sensory faculties of the observer. A splendid example of this phenomenon can be seen in the lobby of the Chicago Board of Trade, designed by the firm Holabird and Root in 1930. The building was conceived in a fundamentally art deco style, as evidenced by its use of setbacks and pyramidal roof design. The three-story lobby alternates flowing, highly sculptural cream marble surfaces with massive black marble piers. Theatrical lighting extends from the ceiling plane down the walls, and the liberal use of linear elements suggests energy and activity. In all, it is a space clearly meant to suggest the vitality of trade in a modern world (Figure 8.9).

While seventy years of modernism have taken their toll on the celebration of ornament, the situation is not without hope. A fine contemporary example of ornamental purpose may be seen in the acroteria, palmettes, and owls that embellish the Harold Washington Library Center in Chicago, designed by Thomas Beeby of Hammond, Beeby and Babka Architects (Figure 8.10). The elaborate ornamental program represents the joint effort of Beeby, Kent Bloomer, and Ray Kaskey and goes far toward marking the building for what it is—a repository of culture. Paul Goldberger of the *New York Times* stated:

> It is grand, it is noble, it is a temple of urban glory . . . no building erected in our time has demonstrated more clearly a total commitment to the notion of the public realm. This building is of the city and for the city; every brick, every piece of carved granite, every metal gargoyle, proclaims a respect for the street, a love of the city, and a deep belief in the idea that architecture can ennoble everyday life.[67]

Beeby's interest in the capacity of ornament to project civic and cultural identity extends to every aspect of the structure. The rusticated texture of the granite blocks contrasts with the smooth, slanted brick wall above it, as well as being juxtaposed against the refined cast-stone ornament. A chainlike pattern called a *guilloche* visually ties the building together. In short, the entire structure relies on an ornamental program to mark its identity as a public building, and to pay homage to the specific architectural tradition of Chicago. And there are other examples.

In 1991 an extensive restoration program was undertaken for Saint Patrick's Roman Catholic Church, Chicago's oldest public building and survivor of the 1871 fire. The stained-glass windows and ornate stenciling of "Old St. Pat's"—representative of the Celtic Revival—were originally designed by artist Thomas O'Shaughnessy and

Figure 8.9. Chicago Board of Trade Building, Chicago, by Holabird and Root, 1930. Photograph by Frank Vodvarka.

Figure 8.10. Harold Washington Library Center, Chicago, by Hammond, Beeby and Babka, 1992. Ornament conceived by Thomas Beeby, Kent Bloomer, and Ray Kaskey. Photograph by Frank Vodvarka.

Figure 8.11. Interior of Old Saint Patrick's Roman Catholic Church, Chicago, by Booth Hansen Associates, 1999. Photograph by Nick Merrick; copyright Hedrich Blessing.

served as cultural affirmation to the many thousands of Irish immigrants who came to Chicago. Laurence Booth of Booth Hansen Associates chose to remain faithful to the original ornamentation of the interior, which was based on the eighth-century *Book of Kells*. These included windows in greens, reds, and golds celebrating Irish kings, saints, and martyrs, and elaborate stencil patterns based on a fifty-six-color palette. Fortunately, enough survived of these designs that they could serve as a guide for the manufacture of new stencils.

Even more remarkable, from our point of view, was Booth's creative additions to the church that remained true to the original spirit. These consisted of a reconfiguration of the main floor, in which the pews have been redesigned so that they are, as critic Blair Kamin notes, "humanistic in image as well as reality."[68] The additions also included a new altar, altar screen, and baptismal font. The altar screen uses the same tripartite division that characterizes the main doors, and cleverly continues the stenciled ornament on to its modeled surface (Figure 8.11). Thus the original ornament of the structure, visually rich and symbolically reassuring, also served as an example for the creative efforts of a contemporary architect. Kamin comments that "Booth merged past and present in a lyrical whole that is architecturally rigorous even as it enriches human experience. . . . The project's significance transcends architecture."[69] This project also offers evidence that craftsmanship is perhaps not as passé as has often been assumed; nor is technology antithetical to decorative purpose.

9. Objects of Our Lives

Objects are, by usual agreement, those things perceptible to our senses—particularly touch and sight. But the definition of *object* is far richer than this. The *Oxford English Dictionary* notes the word's derivation from the Latin *objectum* (thing thrown before or presented to the mind or thought): thus its definition as something placed before the eyes or presented to the sight or other senses; a material thing seen or perceived; that to which action, thought, or feeling is directed; and something that on being seen excites a particular emotion.[1] From this it is clear that objects are the tangible, sensory repositories of experience. It can in fact be argued that they are human experience incarnate. This explains the dual aspect or role of objects, self-confirmation and social communication—the latter aspect being more commonly assumed in the social sciences.

Russell W. Belk points out that the underlying premise of many disciplines—that the property relationship between people and their possessions is essentially Cartesian—fails to account for the power and mystery inherent in many of these relationships. Cartesian rationality, he says, has sought to demystify the role of possessions in our lives, leading us to believe that they are devoid of magical powers and blinding us to their mystery, beauty, and power.[2] In his conception, the rational and measurable benefits of material goods are secondary to their magical function; the myth of rational possession fails because "it denies the inescapable and essential mysteriousness of our existence."[3]

Belk identifies five cases in which possessions transcend their utility and become "special" in the sense that they acquire intense symbolic meaning. He refers to these as parts of self (bodies and body parts, jewelry and clothing, foods, and transitional objects); extensions of self (home, vehicle, burial and grave goods, and pets); objects of magic, science, and religion (including icons and relics, amulets and fetishes, and medicines); memory-laden objects (gifts, souvenirs, family photographs, heirlooms, and antiques); and rare and mysterious possessions (treasure and money, collections, stars and their relics, art, corporate icons, sexual fetishes, and pornography). All these things, he argues, far from being mere commodities, are invested with special meanings (35). Belk has even evolved a series of benchmarks by which we can measure whether that "specialness" is in fact present.

Since these "tests for non-rational relations with objects," as Belk refers to them, are related to our thesis, we include them here: (1) unwillingness to sell for market value, or perhaps for any price; (2) willingness to buy with little regard for price, the counterpart of the first test; (3) nonsubstitutibility, when something similar in kind is unacceptable; (4) unwillingness to discard, the retention of no longer used items; (5) feelings of elation or depression due to object, when sense of self is enlarged or diminished by objects; and (6) personification, the anthropomorphizing of objects (35–36). All of these—which need not be present in their entirety—indicate the presence of objects of unusual and nonrational status. The existence of such objects, particularly as they are represented in tests three, four, and five, argues for their role in self-confirmation.[4] (Thus Werner Muensterberger comments that the source of the collecting habit is "the emotional state leading to a more or less perpetual attempt to surround oneself with magically potent objects.")[5] We will return to Belk's position later in our treatise, as it has implications for the direction of design in the future.

In his *Meaning and Modernity,* Eugene Rochberg-Halton makes a persuasive argument for the temporal significance of objects:

> A present from one person to another involves more than the temporal present. It involves the past context of relationships and future consequences symbolized by the gift. Similarly, the domestic environment of cherished possessions is more than a simple, perceptual present. It is personal time embodied, a storehouse of signs of treasured people, events, and achievements that communicate one's personal and cultural identity and that serve as contexts for further cultivation.[6]

It is in this sense, he says, that he proposes a view that might be termed "critical animism."[7] Rochberg-Halton is not necessarily making a case for animism per se; rather, he is proposing that "objects are not merely inert matter but are living signs whose meanings are realized in the transactions we have with them and that need to be critically cultivated in the context of the consequences they bring about."[8]

This also suggests a basis for the second argument—social communication—which occurs more commonly in the literature of the social sciences. For example, using a "self-presentational analysis," Burroughs, Drews, and Hallman studied the relationship between the information contained in personal possessions and personal identity. The results indicated that the subjects involved considered possession information useful, and that personality inferences made by others (based on possessions) agreed with those the owners made about themselves.[9] The theoretical basis for the research lies in a dramaturgical model of self derived from role theory and symbolic interactionism, where it is assumed that individuals commonly engage in "performances" to convey a consistent set of social impressions. "The possessions that surround individuals, such as clothing or home furnishings, are critical components of the fronts presented to an audience and are integral parts of performances. By manipulating the possessions around them, performers exert control over the information audiences receive."[10] This position is echoed by Wallendorf and Arnould: "Objects serve as the set and props on the theatrical stage of our lives. They situate an individual's character or personality in a context. We use markers as objects to remind ourselves of who we are. In this sense we derive our self-concept from objects."[11]

Collectively, these findings are in accordance with numerous studies indicating that individuals can in fact make reliable inferences about people's personal characteristics from possession cues, thus implying general agreement that information is not only present in possessions but also readily accessible.[12] That their inferences do in fact correspond to the images that the owners believe they are expressing is borne out by still other studies.[13] A corollary to this notion is the necessity that possessor and observer share a common symbol system for this communication to occur. One study carried out by Burroughs, Drews, and Hallman for their analysis sought to determine whether (common-culture) subjects preferred to draw social conclusions from information cues that were artifactual or behavioral in nature. The study found that the former were preferred to the latter, suggesting that the information gained from artifact (possession) cues was considered superior to that obtained from behavioral inferences.[14]

This thesis is confirmed by studies that demonstrate that individuals prefer products whose images correspond to their self-image, including automobiles, food products, and clothing, as well as home furnishings.[15] The corollary to this—in an equally broad range of areas—is that the information associated with possessions is reliable and influences the perceptions of others. This includes clothing, cosmetics, and automobiles. Of special interest are the studies that confirm that home residence style may serve as the basis for reliable inferences, and when the furnishings are included in studies, additional consistent information is generated.[16]

That such information, shared within a common-symbol culture, should be regarded as socially dependable lies at the heart of the social constructionist framework. This position maintains that the ways in which people relate to their possessions are reflections of their self-image and how they relate to their environment. Helga Dittmar argues that "socially shared meaning-systems may be viewed as organising principles of identity as well as of the meanings of possessions as self-extensions . . . as embodiments of cultural meanings."[17] She points out that the meanings and functions of possessions for identity can in fact be arranged schematically (Figure 9.1). (It will be noticed that Dittmar in this instance also uses the notion of duality, here called "instrumental" and "symbolic," but to a social-communication end.)

The two aspects of identity that Dittmar investigates are gender role stereotypes and socioeconomic stratification. Her findings have significant implications for both areas. Given the type of responses obtained, she says that "it can be argued that gender identity–related meanings of possessions range from a 'male' self-oriented, activity-related functional extreme to a 'female' relational, symbolic pole."[18] (N. Laura Kamptner makes a similar point in her study when she notes that males prefer objects that emphasize activity and instrumental qualities, and females prefer objects that are less physically interactive and more symbolic and expressive in nature.)[19]

Dittmar's study also revealed a variety of responses to possessions depending on whether one is employed or unemployed, male or female. She concludes that "meanings of personal possessions related to a social-material position range from a symbolic, long-term extreme (strongly endorsed by people from a high social-material position) to a functional, short-term pole (predominantly used by people from a lower social-materialist position)."[20] The implications of her approach, however, are the most important to our argument: first, that as meanings of material symbols are socially constituted and shared, they will be historically and socioculturally varied; and second, that material symbols have profound significance for the social and psychological reality of our daily lives.[21]

Of special interest in this regard is the second of Belk's categories of items, particularly those aspects relating to the home. He points out that homes have strong emotional meanings to those who live in them, and that other people believe that our homes express our identities. Homes, in this sense, are complex affairs; not only

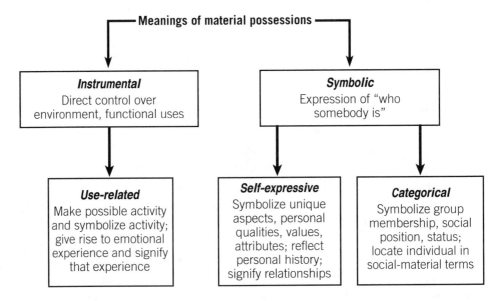

Figure 9.1. Meanings of material possessions for identity, 1992. From Helga Dittmar, *The Social Psychology of Material Possessions: To Have Is to Be* (New York: St. Martin's Press, 1992). Copyright 1992 Helga Dittmar and St. Martin's Press. Reproduced with permission from Helga Dittmar, Brighton, United Kingdom.

are there divisions between exterior (the facade we present to others) and interior (the intimate world we show to a select few), but differences between interior spaces themselves. Thus while the "public" areas represent our social selves, the "private" areas represent our true selves.[22] Indeed, Clare Cooper suggests that "the house might be viewed as both an avowal of the self . . . and as a revelation of the nature of self."[23] Thus to the aphorism, "I have, therefore I am" can be added the notion that "things speak louder than actions."[24]

It is in this way that the home acts as both repository of and testimonial to our life experience. Belk notes that "besides representing personality, history, and feelings of belonging, the home provides us with a 'place identity.'"[25] Now the question really is this: what are the precise material aspects of the home that impel this reaction? The inescapable conclusion is that much of that "place identity" occurs because one's home is filled with objects "invested with special meanings"—from family portraits to antiques—that serve not only a mnemonic function but as a form of "self-extension." Belk describes this as involving feelings of competence or mastery, individuation, connection to others, connection to the past, and connection to the future.[26] In a similar vein, Muensterberger notes that a collector "combines his own re-created past consoling experiences with the fantasied past of his objects in an almost mystical union."[27]

These findings are in fundamental agreement with the widely disseminated study undertaken by Csikszentmihalyi and Rochberg-Halton, *The Meaning of Things: Domestic Symbols and the Self*. In fact, in the preface to their work, the authors comment that "the transactions between people and the things they create constitute a central aspect of the human condition. Past memories, present experiences, and future dreams of each person are inextricably linked to the objects that comprise his or her environment."[28] (This speaks to our essential role as *homo faber*.) Thus objects are not only expressions of self but, perhaps more importantly, parts of self. And so one of the authors says that his "old living-room chair with its worn velvet fabric, musty smell, creaking springs, and warm support has often shaped signs in my consciousness, and because my self is inseparable from the sign process that constitutes consciousness, that chair is as much a part of myself as anything can be" (15). There are two important ideas expressed here: that objects exist in a sensory matrix (touch, smell, sound, and haptic, in this case); and that they are part of a semiotic.

It is in this latter capacity that the author points to the chair's vital role in conveying the possessor's persona—as is the case of a throne to a king, a bench to a judge, or a chair to a distinguished professor (15). This is an apparent reference to a position taken by Ananda Coomaraswamy, who has said that "if, for example, the judge is only a judge in act when wearing his robes, if the mayor is empowered by his chain, and the king by his crown, if the pope is only infallible and verily pontiff when he speaks *ex cathedra*, 'from the throne,' none of these things are mere ornaments."[29] Nor, by extension, is the sensory character of these items unimportant. It is not the chair per se that the author feels to be part of him, but the *sensed* chair—the chair in its sensory detail. It is critical, moreover, that the sensory character of the signifier be in keeping with its purported significance if its authority is to be maintained.

In any case, there is little disagreement with the authors' conclusion that "the home contains the most special objects: those that were selected by the person to attend to regularly or to have close at hand, that create permanence in the intimate life of the person, and therefore are most involved in making up his or her identity."[30] Their rather extensive study pursues these issues: what the theoretical links between persons and things are; why these person/object interactions occur; and the relationship between these patterns and people's goals. (Interestingly, they conclude with a discussion of the viability of such goals in today's state of the environment, a question with ethical dimensions.)[31] Before examining their findings in detail, we want to consider some of the ways in which objects, articles of furniture, for example, have been used to convey meaning in literature.

The role ascribed to the settle, that ubiquitous hearthside bench that is at the ideological heart of the English home, has traditionally been one of comfort and security. In *The Return of the Native,* Thomas Hardy writes: "Outside the settle candles gutter, locks of hair wave, young women shiver, and old men sneeze. Inside is Paradise. Not a symptom of a draught disturbs the air; the sitter's backs are as warm as their faces, and songs and old tales are drawn from the occupants by the comfortable heat, like fruit from melon plants in a frame."[32] Such is Hardy's description of the front sitting room at Bloom's End, a quaint old house "encrusted with heavy thatchings."[33] Brief but highly evocative descriptions of this house abound in his work, such that one is not surprised to learn that Hardy's first profession was that of architect.

A similar view of the settle was held by Kenneth Grahame, as his description of Badger's home in *The Wind in the Willows* attests. As conceived by Grahame, it is a warm place with a well-worn brick floor and a wide hearth, and high-backed settles to provide seating for the sociably disposed: "It seemed a place where heroes could fitly feast after victory, where weary harvesters could line up in scores along the table and keep their Harvest Home with mirth and song, or where two or three friends of simple tastes could sit about as they pleased and eat and smoke and talk in comfort and contentment."[34]

In fact, the hearth itself, with or without settles, has historically served as the ideological heart of the home. Carl Jung's house at Bollingen had, from the very beginning, a large hearth that served in precisely this role. Jung notes, "In practical matters, especially in the kitchen where one really should have an open fire, there are to be found mysterious ecstasies of which the purely functionally-minded never dream."[35] Bollingen is, of course, a structure built of archetypal form, expanded by accretion, and serving as a repository of significant objects. As Jung comments: "There is nothing in the Tower that has not grown into its own form over the decades, nothing with which I am not linked. Here everything has its history, and mine."[36]

A reference was made previously to E. V. Walter's position that to the mythic formation of consciousness, rational space is intangible and meaningless. He accordingly refers to a *place* as an "expressive universe" with specific social and physical boundaries, a space filled with the emotional and symbolic features of experience.[37] In this we are reminded of Philippa Tristram's comment that a true home is defined by individuality expressed in unpretentious honesty, and its contents by the affections. And since experience provides the framework within which this occurs, it may be regarded as constituent to the object's reality.

Sigmund Freud's study in Vienna was devoted to the display of objects. Not only were there paintings and photos, and walls of books, but also a wide range of archaeological artifacts. These included Roman glassware, Sumerian seals and statuettes, and Chinese jades. In all, there were over 2,300 pieces of work. While these were objects of aesthetic interest, they also offered Freud insights into the human condition and thus served a professional function. And their acquisition provided emotional gratification. Indeed, Freud once characterized his passion for collecting as an addiction second only to his nicotine addiction.[38] In an article for *Smithsonian,* Helen Dudar comments: "Freud bought steadily the way collectors often buy: for the joy of buying, for the pleasure and for the childlike, almost primitive sense of power that ownership of valuables evokes."[39] So critical was this function to Freud's sense of structure that he made certain all of his objects were arranged in his new study in London exactly as in Vienna (Figure 9.2).

Figure 9.2. Freud's study, Berggasse 19, Vienna, 1938. Photograph by Edmund Engelman; copyright Edmund Engelman.

Few people seem to have quite the mania for collecting that Freud did; yet on balance, most of us have vastly more artifacts than we might casually suppose—and we collect them for reasons much like Freud's. Thus to the functions of self-confirmation and social communication we may add the pleasure that is seemingly inherent in acquisition. This complex combination is potent, providing the object possessor with a sense of security and mastery.[40] Dittmar accordingly argues that possessions symbolize both the personal qualities of individuals and their social standing within the larger group.[41] This, in turn, means that those material possessions serve to express such individual qualities to others (11). The implication of her schematic is that possessions in fact act as mediators between ourselves and those we interact with (Figure 9.3).

Dittmar further develops this line of reasoning, noting that while objects often serve purposes that can be viewed as instrumental (the ostensible function), they can at the same time be serving as symbols of certain emotional states and experiences. She states that in fact, "material objects serve as *symbolic expressions of who we are.*"[42] It is precisely this quality that Csikszentmihalyi and Rochberg-Halton refer to when they state: "The home is a shelter for those persons and objects that define the self; thus it becomes, for most people, an indispensable symbolic environment."[43] In so saying, the authors are careful to point out that the ultimate value of the home and its contents is bound up not with their material presence per se but with such aid as is rendered to enable us to find meaning in our lives. "The battle for the value of life is fought in the arena of meaning."[44] Quite right.

During the 1930s, the usual living room sofa came to be accompanied by a coffee table whose function was to expedite the practical aspects of social gatherings. It is arguable, however, that the secondary aspect of the table—a place for the gathering of artifacts—was more vital. In *The Place of Houses,* Moore, Allen, and Lyndon comment on the social function of this item: "We require that the clues to our host's concerns be combined and multiplied and personalized. A coffee table laden with the objects its owner derives pleasure from and which reflect his current concerns serves a useful role, enhancing verbal intercourse instead of killing it as the television does."[45] The authors continue: "By surrounding yourself with things that have special meaning . . . you can add dimension to the place you inhabit and to its capacity

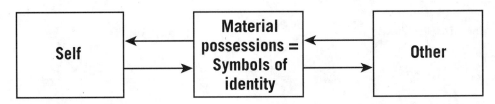

Figure 9.3. Material possessions as symbols of identity, 1992. From Helga Dittmar, *The Social Psychology of Material Possessions: To Have Is to Be* (New York: St. Martin's Press, 1992). Copyright 1992 Helga Dittmar and St. Martin's Press. Reproduced with permission of Helga Dittmar, Brighton, United Kingdom.

to nurture your imagination."[46] There can be little doubt that Charles Moore's own house served in precisely this capacity, especially given his own mania for collecting (Figure 9.4).

Philippa Tristram argues: "Every new-built house or freshly furnished room is a fiction of the life intended to be lived there. Every inhabited building or interior tells a different story, of how life is or was . . . a house, like a novel, is a small world defined against, but also reflecting, a larger one."[47] In this sense, she points out, houses are like stories, and vice versa. And so it is not surprising that the titles of so many nineteenth-century novels reflect the houses they are structured around. Most of life, she notes, "is spent within four walls, and the space they define, the objects that fill them, the prospects on which they open, inevitably influence and express our consciousness" (2). Nor should it be surprising that our houses and their contents are regarded as opportunities to visually communicate that consciousness to our personal public.

The tendency to exhibit our possessions has varied in accordance with social acceptability and architectural fashion. During the nineteenth century, the quantity and types of furnishings to be displayed had so grown in number that descriptions of living space abound in literature. In the novels of Charles Dickens, for example, descriptions of interior contents often serve to define the essential nature of his fictional characters. Tristam points out that Little Nell, in *The Old Curiosity Shop* (1840), owes her interest to "the 'heaps of fantastic things' in the old curiosity shop which, by making her exist in a kind of allegory, suggest her story" as a solitary individual in a world of odd companions (17). The contents of the shop, filled with character in their own right, consequently cast an individual light on one of the characters. In this way, rooms—and their contents—serve individuals in varied and idiosyncratic ways.

Nowhere can be seen a more solitary individual in possession of more varied and idiosyncratic rooms and contents than Sir John Soane. In fact, Moore, Allen, and Lyndon describe at considerable length Soane's house at 13 Lincoln's Inn Fields in London. "His was a collector's passion, delighting in the juxtaposition and aggregation of meaning, as in the mysterious effects of light and shadow; it was a passion too strong to be constrained by conventional precedent or regular arrangements of space."[48] Indeed not; before Soane was finished in 1833, his collections had spread through three houses in spaces precisely constructed to display and enhance them. These interesting exhibition spaces contained ingenious hinged panel systems to hang layers of paintings on, recessed openings for sculpture, and special rooms to hold all the urns, architectural fragments, and classical artifacts. There was even a mummy case procured by the infamous Belzoni. Just a brief glance of the plan gives some indication of the extent to which the central space expanded (Figure 9.5).

This is one of the two points we want to make—that the spaces were shaped in accordance with the scope and nature of Soane's collections, so that the collections were spatially generative as well as intellectually reflective. The second point concerns the way he saw these spaces, aside from the articles that filled them. In their use of

Figure 9.4. Charles Moore, Richard Dodge, and Arthur Andersson, Moore House, Austin, Texas, 1985. Photograph by Timothy Hursley.

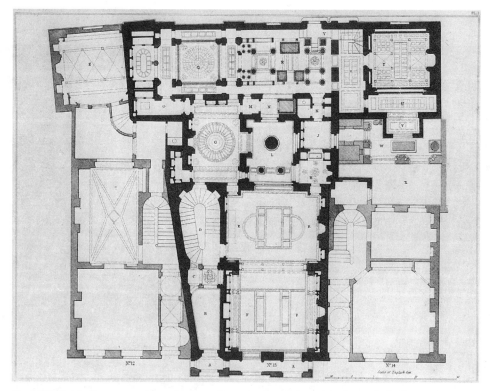

Figure 9.5. Sir John Soane, ground floor plan, Soane House, London. Photograph by Geremy Butler Photography, London. Reprinted by permission of the Trustees of Sir John Soane's Museum.

shape, color, materials, and mirrors, they not only are startlingly original but refer constantly to ideas larger and more complex than themselves. To sit in the Library is not only to be aware of the paintings, sculptures, and other artifacts that surround you but—by virtue of the convex and flat mirrors set between rooms—to enjoy a sense of transparency and continuity (Plate 4). Quite possibly the most intriguing room of all is the Breakfast Room, with its shallow pendentive dome and use of convex mirrors (Figure 9.6). Soane himself notes that "the mirrors in the ceiling, and the looking-glasses, combined with the variety of outline and general arrangement and the design and decoration of this limited space, present a succession of those fanciful effects which constitute the poetry of architecture."[49]

In his text for the Soane Museum catalog, Stefan Buzas comments that Soane's preoccupation with death—a theme that Sir John Summerson had alluded to— seemed evident throughout the house. One had only to look at the vast collection of funerary objects "to realize his feelings for the transience of life."[50] And it seems undeniable that this repository of cultural artifacts—primarily from the classical world— was collected and organized with a view to ever-present mortality. But it was also a monument to Soane's life, its tragedies and successes, and to his obsessions. This

Figure 9.6. Sir John Soane, breakfast parlor, Soane House, London, 1784. Photograph by Richard Bryant, Arcaid.

building had many purposes and was therefore incredibly complex in its attributes, perhaps a product of designer and client being one and the same.

The situation is far more complex when designer and client are not one. As we have seen, spaces not only have multiple aspects but have little necessary agreement about the meaning of them. Thus difficulty in communication between designer and end user may stem from the use of differing definitions of the space's essential meaning, rendering conventional design vocabulary ineffective. But how, then, are we to know what objects are absolutely meaningful to us, the precise manner in which we interact with them, and their ability to communicate?

Here one might recall Martin Pawley's Time House, which—among other things—provides for the intimate identification of individuals with objects. To repeat Pawley's view, "design is the arrangement and metamorphosis of objects to correspond to the ambiguous demands of human consciousness."[51] He offers us a persuasive example, that of an elderly pensioner sitting amid of his years of furniture, bric-a-brac, and photographs. As the "object-evidence" of his life, they sustain him against a hostile world by offering tangible evidence of former times, "evidence that he once existed beyond his present fate" (126). This image argues for the power of objectified space, and against any plan devoid of memory and detail.

In an earlier chapter, we noted Pawley's five axioms, the fifth of which is that a continuous record of object relations would enable the individual to cope with environmental change as a necessary life condition.[52] The Time House is designed to absorb the "object-evidence of experience," to be a "neutral memory" that will observe and record the person/object interface. Pawley contends that this would not only enhance self-perception but increase awareness of our spatial behavior as it involves the objects in that space. This is important, he believes, because individuals populate their dwellings with objects having both iconic and functional value. But, he says, "the *subjective* value of these objects resides not in themselves but in their inter-relation, their sequence and their significance as extensions of the personality of the owner" (141).

Such an examination would not be easy, at least not in its initial stages. In an especially poignant paragraph, Pawley notes the fragmented character of the objects that occupy our lives, such as photographs and letters, clothes, and home movies:

> Incomplete information constitutes a "hot" medium. . . . Hot with tears and the receding and distorting effort of the empathetic pursuit of fugitive images. The act of completion is an act of distortion. We end up filling the gaps in the object evidence of the past with the energy of the present. And this is true of the memories of our own actions as well as those of the dead.
>
> The partial Time House will be painful. More painful than its totality (146).

Nonetheless he maintains that when complete, his mechanism would be desirable and even dictate the development of dwelling forms. At the least, it would be amenable to incorporation into current design formation (like a heating unit). But how will we live with revealed memory?

The power that inheres in memory of place was attested to by Thomas Hardy on the occasion of his refusal of an invitation to the United States—at least in part, he said, because the "prints of perished hands" detained him in the Old World:

> I trace the lives such scenes enshrine,
> Give past exemplars present room,
> And their experience count as mine.[53]

It must be said that his reason for not going seems somewhat disingenuous in light of another of his comments, "The worst of taking a furnished house is that the articles in the rooms are saturated with the thoughts and glances of others."[54] So adversely taken was he with this notion that he built an entirely new house for himself, Max Gate, to avoid such a fate.[55] Inherent in this statement—and in basic conflict with the premise of the verse—is the shift of emphasis from human interaction to the power of objects to influence the present.

In any case, what's so bad about the historical aspect of articles? In another place—Mole End—Grahame has his weary proprietor prepare for bed. But before Mole, away from his home too long, finally fell asleep that night, he looked around at his familiar possessions: "He saw clearly how plain and simple—how narrow even—it all was; but clearly, too, how much it all meant to him, and the special value of some such anchorage in one's existence . . . it was good to think he had this to come back to, this place which was all his own."[56] For Mole, those possessions—with their warm and welcoming history—are agents of sustenance, confirmation of a personal existence.

In her study of personal possessions and their meanings, N. Laura Kamptner comments that in our late adulthood there "appears to be a tendency of possessions to function as reminders of the past, and as markers of personal history and the relationships that comprise one's lifelong sense of self. These functions of possessions may be interpreted as assisting in the maintenance and assessment of older adult's lifelong sense of self."[57] Dittmar similarly notes studies by Goffman (1961, 1968) that affirm the identity-maintaining aspects of personal possessions in institutional settings such as prisons and mental hospitals, as well as the vital role of possessions for elderly, mentally retarded, and psychiatric patients.[58] Of particular interest are the studies of the elderly by Kalymum, McCracken, and Sherman and Newman that stress the importance of allowing treasured personal possessions into homes for the elderly because they symbolize people's lives and thus the continuity of persona.[59]

The 1977 study by Sherman and Newman is especially persuasive in this regard. They note that "the valued possession of the aged person, with its symbolic meanings and associations, may assist him in coming to terms with his past."[60] This tends to confirm the importance of cherished possessions in the transition from independent living to institutional care. The results are illuminating: first, a majority (81 percent) of respondents were able to identify a most cherished possession; second, the ability to do so correlated with age; third, different possessions enjoyed different referents and meanings; and fourth, there existed a positive correlation between cherished possessions and life satisfaction among the elderly. The researchers conclude that this last item "raises the possibility that at least some kinds of cherished possessions might indeed serve as adaptive objects of reminiscence . . . allowing elderly persons to make a positive adjustment to and come to terms with old age."[61]

Dittmar concludes: "This kind of literature carries obvious implications for institutional policies, but it also highlights the symbolic aspects of possessions: they help people to maintain a general sense of identity and integrity, they can serve as locatory markers for status, and they provide a symbolic record of one's personal history."[62] Butler and Lewis have made the observation that cherished possessions provide a sense of continuity, aid the memory, and provide comfort, security, and satisfaction; and that fear of their loss at death is a frequent preoccupation among older persons.[63] Such possessions include pets, familiar objects, photo albums, heirlooms, scrapbooks, and old letters. And they too note that some institutions are now encouraging people to bring some familiar possessions with them.[64]

Simone de Beauvoir has said that habit "provides the old person with a kind of ontological security."[65] We know who we are because of our habits, and we derive security by knowing that tomorrow, to some degree, will be very much like today. And, she continues, "Clinging to one's habits implies an attachment to one's possessions: the things that belong to us are as it were solidified habits—the mark of certain repetitive forms of appropriate behaviour" (469). It is because of these possessions that the elderly person can be assured of his identity "against those who claim to see him as nothing but an object" (470). (As it were.) This is a recurring theme for many writers. One of Virginia Woolf's most interesting essays concludes with the observation that "street haunting" in winter is the greatest of adventures: "Still as we approach our own doorstep again, it is comforting to feel the old possessions, the old prejudices, fold us round; and the self, which has been blown about at so many street corners, which has battered like a moth at the flame of so many inaccessible lanterns, sheltered and enclosed."[66]

Csikszentmihalyi and Rochberg-Halton point out that people build homes out of their fundamental essence, to shelter their personalities, but that simultaneously they are shaped by that very construction.[67] "The home is an empirical and normative entity, constituted through time by the objective patterns of psychic activity that people invest in different areas of the house, in different objects, and in different activities. Thus the home is a goal or intention that becomes realized through the attention the inhabitants give to it" (138). And one of the most important purposes of the home is that of repository for the objects that have shaped one's personality and are needed to concretely express those aspects that are valued (139). This study suggests, moreover, that people who enjoy close ties to other people tend to represent them in concrete objects. The authors conclude that the emotional integration of the home is concretely embodied in the objects of the household (165).

More precisely, "the meaning of cherished possessions is realized in the transaction between person and object" (175). And as was the case with the issue of gender-related viewing, there is a gender-based object sensitivity. Earlier we mentioned the meanings of possessions ranging from a "male" self-oriented, activity-related pole to a "female" relational, symbolic pole. In the study by Csikszentmihalyi and Rochberg-Halton, the category of objects most often mentioned as special was that of furniture, whose possession assumes a settled lifestyle (Table 9.1). The reasons (638) given for this by individuals in the study were numerous, with the largest categories relating to memories (15 percent), stylistic reasons (12 percent), and experiences (11 percent); only 5 percent of the meanings were utilitarian in nature (62). While furniture ranked first for both men (32.6 percent) and women (35.5 percent), the remaining preferences indicated a strong female bias toward objects of contemplation rather than action. The authors note that these differences confirm, at the level of symbolic household objects, the common distinction between instrumental male roles and expressive female roles, and that the objects that women choose in the home environment relate highly to domesticity itself (111). Perhaps of equal interest is the coherent matrix or context that both men and women develop for their interests.

The accumulation of material goods is often referred to as consumption, which tends not to occur haphazardly or, for that matter, individually. On the contrary, both acquisition and consumption are increasingly social activities. Lunt and Livingstone note that the shopping mall or center thus creates a fantasy world in which desires and identities are created.[68] The choices that consumers make are "not to be understood as the individual shopper satisfying a need but as a mode of involvement with, and celebration of, the organization of goods."[69] This point also lies at the heart of Jean Baudrillard's critique: "Few objects today are offered alone, without a context of objects to speak for them. And the relation of the consumer to the object is consequently changed: the object is no longer referred to in relation to a specific utility, but as a collection of objects in their total meaning . . . a calculus of objects."[70] The conclusion he reaches is that the shopping mall succeeds in creating a venue "where all activities are summarized, systematically combined and centered around the fundamental concept of 'ambience.'"[71]

Continuing his post-Marxist polemic, Baudrillard says: "In the phenomenology of consumption, the general climatization of life, of goods, objects, services, behaviors, and social relations represents the perfected, 'consumated,' stage of evolution" (33). Thus while Baudrillard might well agree with Csikszentmihalyi and Rochberg-Halton about the vitality of possessions in people's lives, he finds their accumulation—for the most part—socially repugnant. He regards it as a sad substitute for real human relationships, a manipulation of sign systems to the ends of self-identity and status. Baudrillard may have a peculiar definition of possessions in mind here; the evidence, as we have noted, is that possessions tend to be associated with strong ties

Table 9.1 Frequency of special objects

Number	Type of object	Number of objects mentioned as special in each category	Percentage of total sample mentioning at least one special object in each category ($N = 315$)
1.	Furniture	187	35.9
2.	Bed	43	13.7
3.	Visual art	136	25.7
4.	Sculpture	108	19.0
5.	Collections	49	13.3
6.	Musical instrument	77	21.6
7.	Television	68	20.9
8.	Stereo (record player)	74	21.6
9.	Radio	24	7.6
10.	Books	79	22.2
11.	Photographs	93	23.2
12.	Plants	48	14.9
13.	Plates	68	14.6
14.	Silverware	17	5.1
15.	Glass	36	8.3
16.	Pets	29	8.3
17.	Aquariums	11	3.5
18.	Appliances	56	13.7
19.	Refrigerator	16	5.1
20.	Lamps	31	8.9
21.	Clocks	30	7.2
22.	Tools	12	2.8
23.	Sports equipment	33	8.3
24.	Trophies	21	4.8
25.	Camera	8	2.2
26.	Toys	15	4.1
27.	Stuffed animals	18	3.8
28.	Clothes	21	5.4
29.	Jewelry	31	8.5
30.	Quilts, textiles	31	7.9
31.	Carpets	20	5.1
32.	Fireplace	15	3.8
33.	Bath	11	3.5
34.	Whole room	26	6.7
35.	Miscellaneous	67	17.1
36.	Whole house	9	2.9
37.	Scrapbooks	23	5.4
38.	Vehicles	20	6.3
39.	Telephone	9	2.9
40.	Yard	15	3.5
41.	Candlesticks	9	2.9

Source: Mihaly Csikszentmihalyi and Eugene Rochberg-Halton, *The Meaning of Things* (New York: Cambridge University Press, 1981). Reprinted with the permission of Cambridge University Press.

to, and interaction with, others. Thus Wallendorf and Arnould note: "Rather than serving as substitutes for a social network, favorite objects serve to solidify and represent one's connections to and differences from others."[72] In fact, favorite object attachment expresses connections to others.[73]

Of particular interest to us in this discussion is not the socioethical implications of acquisition but its organized nature. If material objects, whether aesthetic, utilitarian, or status granting, are purchased in matrix fashion—and articles for the home surely represent the largest such category—these same articles will logically be displayed in like manner. This tendency has been called the "ensemble effect." Tristram quotes Henry James, who once commented that "objects and places, coherently grouped, disposed for human use and addressed to it, must have a sense of their own, a mystic meaning proper to themselves, to give out."[74] This, she says, accounts for the helpless quality of household furniture when it is dispersed after the death of its owner.[75] Goods acquired in an organized manner by a human sensibility—an ensemble—have become strewn and lack any raison d'être for their existence beyond intrinsic interest.

That an individual sensibility can act as the unifying element of any ensemble is attested by 13 Lincoln's Inn Fields, a place dedicated to Soane's *horror vacui* (fear of empty space). Thus are objects assembled in both space and time and as such form a material, illustrated history of who we are, ordered in such a way as to provide a sense of continuity in time. It has in fact been pointed out that objects arranged thus do not merely remind us of the past but actually *shape* memory construction through material settings.[76] Dittmar explains: "Possessions can be memories in a direct sense, as are literal documents and records (family trees, photograph albums), but others can serve similar functions as symbols and triggers for memories."[77]

This represents, we believe, a persuasive argument for a spatial and temporal fabric of objects, whose stability is directly related to its extent. That is, the greater the number of object referents, the more complex the fabric and the richer the possibilities of memory. We can thus conceive a situation in which an individual—like Soane or Freud—stands at the center of an "object matrix" with profound, interrelated functions: self-confirmation, social communication, acquisition pleasure, image maintenance, defense against age, and mnemonic aid. None of these things is trivial, and if we indeed cannot environmentally afford the continued manufacture and consumption of objects, a meaningful substitute will be needed. Madame Merle, in Henry James's *Portrait of a Lady*, observes: "Every human being has his shell and you must take that shell into account . . . I've a great respect for *things!* One's self—for other people—is one's expression of oneself; and one's house, one's furniture . . . these things are all expressive."[78]

The reference to the human shell is interesting. It is arguable that our domiciles, insofar as they act as the repositories of significant objects, are shells also. That is, the primary purpose of the home—whether house or apartment—is to serve as receptacle for the life-confirming and socially communicative objects of our lives. In this construction, our personal possessions constitute the essential meaning of spatial constructs, with the architectural form of the paradigm being entirely secondary in nature. Certainly the studies of Canter and Tagg support this thesis, as do those of Belk, Kamptner, and Goffman. But this argument is supported by common observation of human behavior as well. (We are reminded that Charles Moore, when designing his own home in New Haven, Connecticut, made extensive provision for his toy collection.)

Possessions, moreover, are endowed with multiple sensory attributes, an aspect that is also not trivial. While we have, for most of a chapter, been commenting on the symbolic, expressive, and self-confirming aspects of possessions, we should not forget that they are also objects that grant sensory pleasure. In his introduction to *Excavations and Their Objects: Freud's Collection of Antiquity*, Stephen Barker contends that "Freud was so greatly drawn to and charmed by the objects he had gathered around him that, sitting at his desk with that array of tiny friends before him, he posited in them the collective psyche of aesthetic culture."[79] No small thing. But we find at least as interesting Lynn Gamwell's comment that Freud's household maid recalled his habit of affectionately stroking his Egyptian marble statue of the Baboon of Thoth, as he did his pet chows.[80] She goes on to say that "Freud understood the origin of collecting in childhood sensual pleasures, which explains the intensity of the passion."[81]

There are two major moving days in Chicago. On these days the streets are lined with moving vans, as a substantial part of Chicago's population moves from one dwelling to another. This movement is facilitated by the degree of psychological investment people have in their personal possessions, such that they will "feel at home" as long as those possessions accompany them. The character of the building one is moving to is clearly of lesser importance, save in one significant respect: it usually involves obtaining more square footage. More space to put more things, as it were. This is not to suggest that the nature of a building will be overlooked, only that the essential aspect of our existence is the collection of meaningful sensory objects that we fill the building with. Seen this way, spatial design may really be about providing flexible receptacles for our possessions. It is also clear that the objects of our lives need to be considered as an aspect of our connectedness to a larger sensory milieu. As such, their accommodation is a design issue.

10. The Light Fantastic

In *The Innocents Abroad,* a delightful series of travel accounts, Mark Twain describes his night on the Athenian Acropolis:

> We crossed a large court, entered a great door, and stood upon a pavement of purest white marble, deeply worn by footprints. Before us in the flooding moonlight rose the noblest ruins we had ever looked upon—the Propylae, a small Temple of Minerva; the Temple of Hercules; and the grand Parthenon . . . one of the most graceful and beautiful edifices ever erected. . . . Here and there in lavish profusion were gleaming white statues of men and women, propped against blocks of marble, some of them armless, some without legs, others headless—but all looking mournful in the moonlight and startlingly human! . . . and through the roofless temple the moon looked down and banded the floor and darkened the scattered fragments and broken statues with the slanting shadows of the columns. . . . The place seemed alive with ghosts.[1]

The approaching dawn caused Twain and his companions to hasten back to their ship. As they did so, they had a last view of the Parthenon with the moonlight streaming through colonnades whose capitals seemed to be made of silver. "As it looked then—solemn, grand, and beautiful—it will always remain in our memories" (251).

Of interest here is that while this secret visit was prompted by the monument's architectural fame, Twain's sense of the Acropolis is almost entirely picturesque. He notes "that these edifices were all built of the whitest Pentelik marble, but have a pinkish stain upon them now," and that "most of the Parthenon's imposing columns are still standing, but the roof is gone" (248–49). Thus he has considered the marble's

199

color shift at least as noteworthy as its origin, and what he finds interesting about the Parthenon (as he proceeds to explain) is that it had remained intact until the Venetian powder magazine stored there exploded. Above all, Twain is fascinated by the mood created by the moonlight; it has made the statuary seem alive, and the structures dramatic and grand. And so the Acropolis lives in his memory as a sensory experience highly dependent on the dramatic qualities of light.

It is surely this aspect that ensures for the great cathedrals of the Middle Ages their lasting power to excite the imagination. Indeed, we have every reason to assume that their sensory aspects are precisely what inspired their builders to construct such incredibly expensive and unnecessarily complex buildings in the first place. Henri Focillon points out:

> Nothing could have determined the astonishing height of the naves of those cathedrals save the activity of the life of forms: the insistent theorem of an articulated structure, the need to create a new space. Light is treated not so much as an inert factor as a living element, fully capable of entering into and of assisting the cycle of metamorphoses. Light not only illuminates the internal mass, but collaborates with the architecture to give it its needed form. Light itself is form.[2]

Nowhere is this clearer than at Chartres Cathedral, whose soaring nave is filled with dramatic colored light. Henry Adams describes the overpowering feeling that the glass and the figures it represents have on the viewer: "No words and no wine could revive their emotions so vividly as they glow in the purity of the colours; the limpidity of the blues; the depth of the red; the intensity of the green; the complicated harmonies; the sparkle and splendour of the light; and the quiet and certain strength of the mass."[3] In his *Poetics of Light,* Henry Plummer expands on this observation: "Miniature spectacles appear deep within layerings and laminations, forming a lightscape of interflowing mists and colored atmospheres. . . . We feel that we can visually sink into, almost step into, these crystal depths."[4] And in the next paragraph, he cites Paul Scheerbart's *Glasarchitektur* and Bruno Taut's *Alpine Architecture* as manifestos of a culture expressed by crystalline form. These two designers were members of the "expressive" wing of the Werkbund. In his *Glasarchitektur,* Scheerbart had used phrases such as "Light wants crystal" and "Colored glass destroys hatred." He called for nothing less than the liberation of enclosed space, stating that "only glass architecture, which will inevitably transform our whole lives and the environment in which we live, is going to help us."[5]

His words served as inspiration for the Glass Pavilion in Cologne, designed by Bruno Taut in 1914 in what Taut referred to as the "spirit of a Gothic cathedral." This structure, designed by a creative architect who imagined a world built of crystal, marked a lively (albeit unrealized) alternative for contemporary architecture. The tiered chamber was lit by sunlight passing through glass-block walls and stained-glass panels. The ceiling was made of red and gilded glass tiles and marked by an oculus

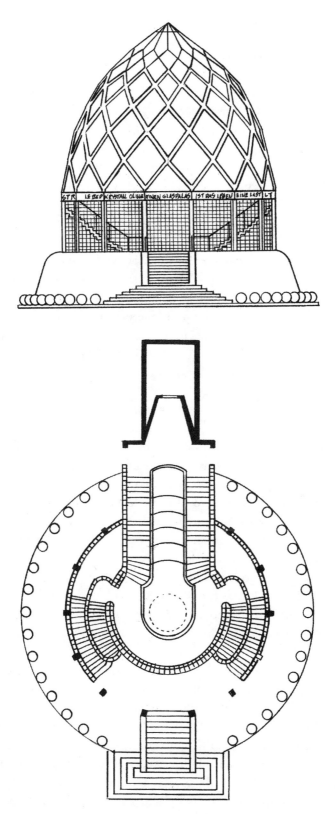

Figure 10.1. Bruno Taut, the Glass Pavilion, Werkbund Exhibition, Cologne, 1914. Drawings by Joy Monice Malnar.

whose light fell on a waterfall cascading over glass pearls. Even the metal stairs contained translucent luxfer prisms. The net effect is that of a timeless, prismatic structure outside conventional experience (Figure 10.1).

The power of light to transcend the exigencies of temporal reality has always ensured its place in religious architecture. The Madonna della Strada chapel, located on the campus of Loyola University Chicago, was designed in 1929 in the art deco style.[6] It is surely one of Andrew Rebori's finest buildings and represents the future as expressed by the concept of "streamlining." Its carefully considered massing is combined with exquisite detailing and a stunning site. Set on an east-west axis, the east facade faces Lake Michigan, over which the morning sun rises. The light floods not only the eastern portals and rose window but also the apse, by virtue of an unusual series of east-facing apsidal openings. Set within the folds of the five stone arches—each representing one of the five human senses—are continuous bands of glass blocks (Figure 10.2). The halos of light thus created draw attention to the altar and the mural behind it. From the nave, the origin of this light is undetectable, and hence mysterious (Figure 10.3). The series of slit windows in the apse visible in the photograph capture the intensity of the western light later in the afternoon. In this way Rebori has accounted for the dramatic passage of light over the course of the day.

Light alters our perception in remarkable ways. Henry Plummer writes that "there are deep emotive reverberations between light atmospheres and our feelings—in the cheery invigorative light of a sparkling day, the soft dreamy light of fog and snow, and the depressing light that is flat and dreary. . . . Changing emotive qualities endow places with a kind of soul, an image of our own existence that permeates yet is apart from matter, allowing us to feel related personally to our surroundings."[7] Thus there are both affective and physical dimensions to light that are unrelated to simple sight thresholds. Plummer points out that over the millennia in which human beings observed their environment, they must have gained an appreciation for the association between luminosity and living energy, "a causal reality that our senses perceive and which directly affects our bodies."[8]

This is surely no exaggeration. There is ample evidence that energy levels in human beings fluctuate with light levels, both daily and seasonally. Indeed, parts of our bodies, such as the pineal gland (located at the top of the head), are apparently sensitive to light. Marietta S. Millet points out that as this gland controls our hormones, it determines our reactions in response to daylight patterns, even in the absence of sight. The research is so abundant that there has been a new recognition of Seasonal Affective Disorder (SAD) in the last decade.[9] Hence the importance of artificial lighting as an adjunct to natural light. Judith H. Heerwagen refers to this when she says: "Given the broad range of biological and psychological effects of light that are beginning to surface, lighting decisions must begin to encompass a full range of human needs, not just task visibility and visual comfort."[10] This is especially important due to the increasing evidence that the influence of light on mood, energy,

Figure 10.2. Andrew Rebori, Madonna della Strada Chapel, Chicago, 1929. Photograph by Frank Vodvarka.

Figure 10.3. Andrew Rebori, apse, Madonna della Strada Chapel, Chicago, 1929. Photograph by Frank Vodvarka.

sleep, and weight change is much more pervasive than previously thought, especially in northern latitudes and places with customarily gray weather.[11]

Heerwagen's call for more knowledgeable lighting decisions at this late date is ironic. One of the first influential works dealing with light and color was by Faber Birren: *Color Psychology and Color Therapy.* This work was published in 1950, with a revised version appearing in 1961, and yet another edition in 1982. Birren had, from the early 1940s, been employed by industry and government to manipulate interior color and light to the end of increased production, improved efficiency, and enhanced worker safety and welfare. The first edition consisted of a combination of psychological data, general observation, and qualified mysticism, but Birren was clearly interested in physiological response as well. Unlike many in the lighting profession, Birren did not believe that high light intensity invariably led to good visibility. On the contrary, he maintained that ocular fatigue was more likely the result of strong brightness contrasts and task difficulty than low levels of ambient lighting. Mahnke and Mahnke support Birren's position: "Glare, constant adjustment to extreme brightness differences, prolonged fixation of the eyes, and constant shifts in accommodation will tire eyes quickly, causing headaches, tension, nausea, and other disturbances."[12]

In fact, the effects of SAD are enhanced by the typical work environment that has depended, since the late 1940s, on fluorescent lighting, whose spectral composition differs markedly from natural light. Norman Rosenthal and Associates found, however, that the use of full-spectrum light, in conjunction with time alterations, tended to alleviate this condition.[13] A 1974 study by Maas, Jayson, and Kleiber found that when lighting approximates the spectral quality of natural sunlight, there is less perceptual fatigue and improved acuity.[14] (Full-spectrum lamps, by definition, have a high CRI, or color rendition index, and high-CRI lamps achieve a higher subjective clarity than ordinary bulbs.) Fritz Hollwich studied the effect of strong artificial (fluorescent) light and concluded that the unpleasant effect of high-intensity artificial light comes from the stressful reaction elicited by increased metabolic activity—even though the human organism can adapt to high levels of intense outdoor light without difficulty.[15] He goes on to point out that while the threshold for physiological stimulation by means of artificial light and for the pathological stress effect of light varies individually, "an increase in the intensity of light to 2,000 and 3,000 lux—sometimes called for by architects and lighting experts—can trigger a stress reaction in a relatively large number of people."[16] It has been demonstrated, on the other hand, that the use of full-spectrum lighting decreased hyperactive behavior in school children.[17] It is time, in Hollwich's opinion, to direct attention to the medical aspects of light: "Above all in the case of children who attend schools without windows, we must be prepared for the eventual appearance of pathological consequences."[18]

As though echoing this warning, even newer evidence suggests that full-spectrum light may be more vital than so far suggested. Küller and Lindsten conducted a study designed to assess the effects of light on the production of stress hormones, classroom performance, body growth, and sick leave of schoolchildren. They found that "work in classrooms without daylight may upset the basic hormone pattern, and this in turn may influence the children's ability to concentrate or cooperate, and also eventually have an impact on annual body growth and sick leave."[19] Mahnke and Mahnke conclude that full-spectrum lighting should be used in classrooms, libraries, and gymnasiums, but not necessarily in short-occupancy places such as corridors. And there is general agreement that artificial lighting should never be thought of as other than adjunct to daylight. All this, to be sure, sounds like progress.

Heerwagen is, however, less than completely optimistic about the future. She points out that interior lighting typically accounts for 30 to 50 percent of commercial buildings' total annual energy costs. Thus current strategies to reduce lighting costs call for lower ambient light levels with focused task lighting. This may, she says, produce psychologically gloomy environments, despite there being sufficient light for tasks. "Furthermore, energy efficient glazing greatly reduces the amount of daylight entering the interior of a building, thereby relegating most building inhabitants to light exposure far below that needed for alleviation of mood and energy disturbances."[20] The correct formula would seem to be a generous provision for daylight with any deficits made up by full-spectrum artificial light.

Color is an important dimension of light. Red light has been shown by R. Gerard (1957) to enhance functions of the autonomic nervous system, evoking more tension, excitement, and hostility than the color blue. For that matter, red light seems to produce anger and anxiety in infants and the mentally ill, and tests at Yale University indicated that the color red tended to detrimentally affect mental activities such as problem solving, decision making, and social conversation.[21] Red light has also been shown to increase bodily activity and extreme emotion, while blue light is physically calming.[22] As males and females experience ambient temperatures differently, such studies may have a gender component. Two experiments conducted by Igor Knez showed that, in the first instance, the color temperature that induced the least negative mood enhanced performance in long-term memory and problem-solving tasks in both genders. In the second experiment, the combination of color temperature and illuminance that best preserved the positive mood in one gender enhanced that gender's performance in problem solving and free recall tasks. Thus the subjects' cognitive performances varied with their different emotional reactions.[23] Some of the data on warm and cool light sources are interesting. Knez found that "an interaction between colour temperature and gender showed that the 'cool' room light induced least negative mood in males, and that the 'warm' room light accounted for the same effect in females."[24] And he notes that the problem-solving, long-term recall and recognition results yielded a similar interaction between color temperature and gender.[25] The physiological and psychological effects of light qualities are obviously considerable.

Millet points out that lighting is often considered at one end or the other of its capability: either solely as an aesthetic medium or solely for providing task visibility. As she maintains, both aspects are always present.[26] It is nonetheless the simple question of minimally necessary sight thresholds that tends to dominate the discussion of light within architectural settings. This is certainly the view held by Ettore Sottsass, who points out that much of today's architecture tends to be designed for electric light that is installed as an afterthought.[27] And he notes the difficulty with the term *illumination:* "Light does not illuminate, it tells a story. *Light gives meanings,* draws metaphors and sets the stage for the comedy of life."[28] Nowhere is this clearer than in those places designed to exploit this drama to some emotional end, as is made clear in a photograph of the Kirin Plaza Osaka (Japan), located on the Dotonborigawa Canal (Plate 5).

When the great Russian writer Maxim Gorky first saw New York's Coney Island in 1906, he found it debased and tawdry, "a slimy marsh of boredom."[29] Even so, when he saw the same place at night, his description was that of a glittering apparition born of imagination and electricity:

> Thousands of ruddy sparks glimmer in the darkness, limning in fine, sensitive outline on the black background of the sky, shapely towers of miraculous castles, palaces and temples. Golden gossamer threads tremble in the air. They intertwine in transparent, flaming patterns, which flutter and melt away in love with their own beauty mirrored in the waters. Fabulous and beyond conceiving, ineffably beautiful, is this fiery scintillation.[30]

The American critic James Huneker referred to Coney Island's Luna Park as a "cemetery of fire" with "mortuary shafts of flame," and to Dreamland as a "dazzling apparition . . . fretted with fire."[31] Such was the power of Coney Island's light fantastic.

Henry Plummer makes an interesting point about the nature of "optical vitality": "Radiant things are tensed with dynamic patterns of light against darkness, their bodies turned tremulous and vigorous, so that they stand forth and rise into more active states of being than when dull."[32] And he observes that light tends to advance and expand. Of course, light quality is relative to the ambient darkness it occupies. Thus even low light levels in very dark settings can create a surface vitality, or luminosity. Millet confirms that the luminous effect depends on four factors: the source of its intensity; the geometry or relationship between the source and receiving surface; the (reflective) surfaces that receive and modify light; and the person who views both the source and the illuminated surfaces. She concludes: "By observing how light behaves, we can work with it to reveal architecture."[33]

The work of James Turrell is instructive in light of these criteria. In early 1981, Turrell was invited to install four pieces of work at Seattle's Center on Contemporary Art, all of which depended on the vitality of light at low perceptual levels. Sigrid Asmus describes one of the works, *Iltar,* as a vibrant field of color in which "corners can seem to project forward, planes appear to slant back directly from the aperture's edge, and fine vertical-line patterns may appear on the lighter, nimbus-like area at the center . . . it seems natural . . . to gaze at the soft, grainy field that inhabits the other side of the aperture, and which at once seems to 'sit out' from the wall three or four inches, and to extend away an unfathomable distance."[34] The result is an optical reality that shifts in accordance with certain perceptual principles and our own cultural experience (Figure 10.4). Turrell says that to come to terms with it, one will need to assemble a picture of reality that can accommodate these contradictions. "I'm interested in playing with not only the physical limits of how we perceive, but the learned limits."[35]

Turrell also makes the point that this piece is somewhat similar to a camera, "in that there is a space that you are using as a 'sensing space,' and that space has nothing of itself, and it looks out onto another space, as with a camera."[36] And in a later interview, he says that those "sensing spaces" draw all their energy from the spaces just outside themselves, that is, the space the viewer is standing in.[37] Thus light is used not to illuminate (much less light) but to construct a unique visual reality (Figure 10.5). Millet says: "By revealing our reactions at the limit of our perceptual capabilities, he makes us aware both of the enormous power of our perceptual abilities, as well as the thin line of their limitations."[38]

Figure 10.4. James Turrell, *Iltar,* as installed at Center on Contemporary Art, Seattle, Washington, 1982. Photograph by Mark Sullo. Reprinted by permission of James Turrell.

Using much the same methodology—to an even more striking effect—Turrell designed *Amba*. Asmus notes that "pink/blue cloudlight floods into the room from three enormous, squareish 'windows,' as if one were visiting some celestial aquarium."[39] These windows, relying on rather more conventional architectural references, manage to refer to depth while describing a volume of colored light that expands into one's visual field. Turrell says: "The sensuosity of *Amba* is almost voluptuous. It's more than I could live with."[40] He also makes the point that one's sense of time is heightened by being, as it were, suspended while the encounter with the work is occurring (Plate 6). Although we believe that this sort of temporal occlusion is relevant to an appreciation of spatial qualities generally, of importance here is the concept of light's ability to control the penetration of sight into a space, and to forge sensory boundaries. And so Turrell says: "True sensuousness comes from the act of sensing."[41]

The strikingly architectural character of *Amba* suggests a direction in which one might expect Turrell to proceed. In fact, he has been involved for the last twenty years in his Redon Crater Project, a group of built spaces within an extinct volcano located in Arizona's Painted Desert (Figure 10.6). Turrell has planned a total of twenty-five spaces in which different qualities of light can be perceptually experienced. In an

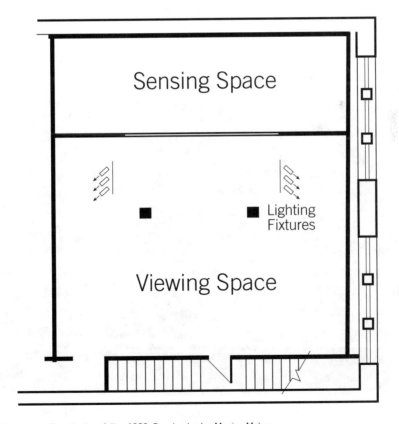

Figure 10.5. James Turrell, plan of *Iltar*, 1982. Drawing by Joy Monice Malnar.

article for *Metropolis,* Jeffrey Hogrefe describes three of them (Figure 10.7). The white chamber in the North Space (top section) acts as a camera obscura in which passing cloud patterns and light from the moon and other celestial bodies are projected on the floor, and the polestar Polaris can be viewed from the small chamber to the left. The Eye of the Crater (center section), located thirty-eight feet below the crater's floor, has an oculus that gives the effect of celestial vaulting. The South Space (bottom section) makes visible alignments of the sun, earth, and moon, with a bench (at the right) for viewing the north polar alignment.[42] The crater uses more than one thousand feet of tunnels to reach these spaces and at its top has an open-air observatory whose perimeter acts as a picture frame that perceptually flattens the sky, bringing it "closer" to the viewer. Turrell says that he creates "a world that deals with how we perceive, so that you look at yourself looking. At the same time there is a physicality to the light that makes it a material" (82). It is not surprising that Turrell influences the architecture of others. His own, he says, "is an architecture of space and light. A topological architecture" (100).

Inherent in Turrell's Redon Crater Project is the issue of light's counterpart, darkness, without which no light effect could have meaning. Thus illumination and darkness form a construct in which designers have usually stressed the former. It must be said that the determination to light space to the degree technically possible seems

Figure 10.6. James Turrell, *Roden Crater near Flagstaff, Arizona,* 1982. Photograph by James Turrell and Dick Wiser. Reprinted by permission of James Turrell.

Figure 10.7. James Turrell, *Sections of Roden Crater* (models of north space, crater's eye, and south space), 1998. Photographs courtesy of James Turrell.

primarily a Western obsession. In his book *In Praise of Shadows,* Junichirō Tanizaki describes the origin of the Japanese house:

> In making for ourselves a place to live, we first spread a parasol to throw a shadow on the earth, and in the pale light of the shadow we put together a house. . . . The quality that we call beauty . . . must always grow from the realities of life, and our ancestors, forced to live in dark rooms, presently came to discover beauty in shadows, ultimately to guide shadows towards beauty's ends. And so it has come to be that the beauty of a Japanese room depends on a variation of shadows, heavy shadows against light shadows—it has nothing else. . . . This was the genius of our ancestors, that by cutting off the light from this empty space they imparted to the world of shadows that formed there a quality of mystery and depth superior to that of any wall painting or ornament.[43]

Thus Tanizaki disapproves of the habituated use of electric lighting that had seemingly taken over by 1933. He does not call for a complete rejection of technology, only for an appreciation of its injurious effect on those things designed for a setting characterized by shadows (Figure 10.8).

Actually, the approach described by Tanizaki is a reasonable response to the reality of the pre-electric millennia that all of Earth experienced. Low-level lighting, that obtained from fire (hearth, candle, and coal oil), characterized the human condition prior to the early twentieth century. One might ask why certain cultures accommodated "the realities of life," turning them into an aesthetic, and other cultures did not. Western houses, in sharp contrast to Japanese tradition, are usually constructed so as to admit as much light as possible. This is consistent with the Western worldview, which has theologically and philosophically considered light a form of revelation. (Hence the ascendancy of "rational thought" in the West, the *Enlightenment.*) Light has even been seen as an element of social transformation; thus Bruno Taut's vision for a better humanity is one of a world of glass houses. Indeed, all-pervasive lighting has also become a hallmark of the modernist movement, supporting its rationale of hygiene, function, and morality. Thus has shadow been reserved for the landscape of our fears, except for those moments when a contemplative or romantic mood is desired.[44]

What we may be doing, in either of these cases, is reducing the amount of sensory input so as to better concentrate on the data of interest. This also has the effect of adjusting our cognitive timekeeping mechanism to a slower mode. The Russian poet Zinaida Hippius succinctly stated the nature of our interaction with time in her poem "L'Imprévisibilité":

> According to the word of the Eternal Being,
> The stream of time is continuous;
>> I only sense an oncoming breeze,
>> The chime of a new moment.[45]

Figure 10.8. Yoshijima House, Takayama, Japan. Photograph by Botand Bognar; copyright 2002.

It is arguable that this, in fact, is an accurate representation of time as a succession of relatively discrete sensations—the retinal "snapshots" noted by Heft and Wohlwill—that seamlessly blend into one another in retrospect. This, of course, refers to time experienced; time as historical representation is usually invoked symbolically through referential imagery. There are therefore two sorts of time passage; the first is sensory, and the second cognitive.

When Henry Plummer describes Venice, it is in almost purely sensuous terms: "Venice sways and flickers with time. . . . Canals and lagoons give off a moist atmosphere ranging from brittle clarity to dense fog, but which is usually a very soft and faint mist filtering the sun into a slightly powdery glow. . . . The breathy light of the skies is matched by an even more evanescent light in the shimmering green waters, whose liquefied crystal shifts with every wind into a new kind of mirror. . . . Richly colored facades are thus clothed in a living light, one that is tremulous and quivering, yet sensuous and soothing."[46] The key part of this description is its ending, that the suspension of time induced by the Venetian atmosphere is "sensuous and soothing." And yet Plummer is also aware of Venice through literary description and quotes Shelley to good effect.

Frank Lloyd Wright has said that "day lighting can be beautifully managed by the architect if he has a feeling for the course of the sun as it goes from east to west and at the inevitable angle to the south. The sun is the great luminary of all life. It should serve as such in the building of any house."[47] Tadao Ando's Church of the Light, a chapel located in Ibaraki City, Osaka Prefecture (Japan), is a splendid example of the effects obtainable from creative solar orientation. (The chapel in fact serves as an addition to an existing church and home.) While the building is based on a stable mathematical premise—a cuboid in which three spheres, each with a 5.9 meter diameter, could be inscribed—its dynamic quality is enhanced by a wall that penetrates this form at an angle of fifteen degrees to the structure's length (Figure 10.9). An opening behind the altar, in the shape of a cross, allows the morning sun to create a

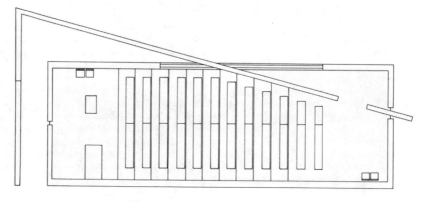

Figure 10.9. Tadao Ando, plan for Church of the Light, Osaka, Japan, 1989. Courtesy of Botand Bognar and Tadao Ando Architect and Associates.

Figure 10.10. Tadao Ando, interior of Church of the Light, Osaka, Japan, 1989. Photograph by Botand Bognar; copyright 2002.

cross of light. Ando comments: "I made as few openings as possible in the building, because the light becomes brilliant only against a very dark background. The only natural element here is the sunlight. . . . The architecture, adapting to this light, becomes purified."[48] He also points out that the light forms a distinctive pattern on the floor, where "one may come to recognize in a fundamental way the relationship of humanity to nature."[49] Thus does the sunlight solemnly mark cosmological time (Figure 10.10).

Another example of a building that uses the shifting characteristics of light, although to different ends, is L'Institut du Monde Arabe in Paris (1987), designed by Jean Nouvel. The institute comprises two parallel masses, one of which has a long curved facade that echoes the Seine River, the other a rectangle whose facade faces a courtyard. These two wings, connected underground, are separated by a narrow open space suggesting a duality in their juxtaposition. The building is multipurpose, as it contains an auditorium, offices, a library, and a museum. Our interest is in the south facade, the one that faces the courtyard. It is covered with hundreds of solar-activated mechanical diaphragms arranged in geometric patterns (Figure 10.11). These stainless steel irises provide shifting patterns in accordance with the available light, evoking traditional Arabic designs as well as providing active sun shielding for the interior. Zeynep Çelik comments that the "design has been hailed by critics as a particularly sensitive response to the site, context, materials, and modernism at large."[50]

What, then, do we make of a house designed to deny the passage of time as marked by the course of the sun? Il Girasole was designed by Italian engineer Angelo Invernizzi in the early 1930s, to rotate 360 degrees over a twenty-four-hour period in order to maintain the relationship between building facade and exposure. This villa, clad in metal, is sited amid vineyards near Verona (Italy). The structure rotates around a static central core containing a spiral stair and elevator. The remainder of the 1,500-ton house rests on a huge cylindrical block in turn mounted on wheeled trolleys driven by two small motors. The wheels run on iron tracks set in the ground, and gardens radiate from them. In all, it represents a stunning attempt to arrest time by the careful control of sensory input (Figure 10.12). Todd Williams poignantly notes: "Despite its noble conception and brilliant realization, there is something sad and temporal about this powerful structure."[51] And it stands in sharp contrast to the Japanese house that bows to the light's passing, or Ando's chapel in which a dialogue is created between darkness and light.

Another phenomenon—dependent on light—that has had an uneasy relationship with architectural design is color. This is no surprise. The study of color is complex and is made difficult by the many systems in which it manifests its capacities. These include the aesthetic, psychological, physiological, and symbolic, each with its own purpose. Color has extraordinary emotional power, involving a range of sensori-emotional references. Thus Emil Nolde exclaims: "Colors, the raw material of the painter: colors in their own individual life, weeping and laughing, dream and happiness, hot and holy, like love songs and lovemaking, like tunes and like magnificent chorales. Vibrating colors like tinkling silver bells or pealing bronze bells announcing joy, passion, love, soul, blood, and death."[52]

Designers have long recognized the importance of color, even when they have been uncertain about its application. This is especially true in architecture, where eighty years of modernism has held "decorative" elements to be ideologically unacceptable. This has often included applied color, resulting in an odd admiration for the bleak. Frances Anderton dryly notes: "Ever since the poor penguins gave stark, graphic relief to a concrete abstraction in chemical snow-white, a monochrome environment has been seen as the epitome of elegance."[53] The author maintains that although Greek temples were polychrome, Georgian houses were built sans white window frames, and the Japanese used blended colors and rich materials to achieve a subtle palette, monochrome images of these antecedents have tended to confirm black and white as "intrinsically Classical and intrinsically good."[54] There are certainly cultures—particularly those of Asia—where color has been used both expressively and dynamically. Especially startling to Western eyes is the use of full-intensity complementary hues on highly detailed architectural exteriors, as can be seen at Ch'angdok Palace in Seoul (Plate 3).

Color has been the subject of considerable investigation, leading to discoveries of its psycho-physiological attributes. Our understanding of light and color was aided by Sir Isaac Newton's discovery that white light contains all visible color. We see

Figure 10.11. Jean Nouvel, L'Institut du Monde Arabe, Paris, France, 1987. Photograph by Scott Frances; copyright Scott Frances/Esto. All rights reserved.

Figure 10.12. Ettore Fagiuoli (architect) and Angelo Invernizzi (engineer), Il Girasole (the sunflower), Marcellise, Italy, 1929–1935. Photograph by Oberto Gili. Copyright *House and Garden,* The Condé Nast Publications, Inc.

colors because wavelengths of light vary; high-energy, short-wavelength light is seen as violet, whereas low energy, long-wavelength light is seen as red. When projected light strikes a surface, it becomes reflected light. As surfaces absorb certain wavelengths of light, it is the reflected wavelengths that are identified as an object's color. As this light falls on the retina, the light-receptive area at the back of the eye, it is recorded by rods (brightness receptors) and cones (color receptors). Under bright light, the cones are operative, but as light dims, color perception decreases (beginning with low-energy hues) until there is insufficient light to see color at all. The rods then allow a full range "night vision" in value. (Curiously, we can accurately judge the similarity of colors in different light intensities, a phenomenon known as color constancy.) In this way do we understand color to be an inherent attribute of objects, as well as an independent, and constantly changing, sensory phenomenon.

Moreover, emotion and prior association play a major role in our comprehension and valuation of color. Hazel Rossotti points out "that colour is a *sensation*, produced in the brain, by the light which enters the eye; and that while a sensation of a particular colour is usually triggered off by our eye receiving light of a particular composition, many other physiological and psychological factors also contribute."[55] As these psychological and physiological factors are decisive in our final perception of a color, attempts at scientific definition must be somewhat suspect. The Commission Internationale de l'Eclairage (CIE) has devised a system based on spectrophotometric measurements of color in light, but such a system cannot predict the character of reflected color or its perception. In an effort to overcome these drawbacks, the Natural Color System (NCS) of Sweden has been devised. This system is based on the perception of color in the environment and posits red, yellow, blue, and green as elementary colors. As it is based on how we see colors rather than how we mix them, black and white are included even though they are achromatic. (The color solid used in this system relies on a black-white vertical axis intersected by red-green and blue-yellow axes.) Anders Hård has pointed out that "first of all we need a colour language which will communicate our experiences, findings and thoughts."[56] It is primarily this aspect—the phenomenological structure of the system—that suggests its future value for design purposes.

Still, what we mean by a particular color term may be quite different from what others mean. In his remarkable and still used work *The Elements of Color*, Johannes Itten provides this rationale for his theories:

> The physiologist investigates the various effects of light and colors on our visual apparatus—eye and brain—and their anatomical relationships and functions. . . . The psychologist is interested in problems of the influence of color radiation on our mind and spirit. . . . Expressive color effects—what Goethe called the ethico-aesthetic values of colors—likewise fall within the psychologist's province. The artist (or designer), finally, is interested in color effects from their aesthetic aspect, and needs both physiological and psychological information.[57]

In fact, the sheer quantity of reliable information about the effects of color has increased throughout the past half century. We know that children peak for form dominance at twenty-two months, for color dominance at age four and one-half, and then return to form dominance by age six.[58] Thus a beneficial color scheme for the first two years of life would be saturated red, blue, and yellow, de-emphasizing yellow, as it is less preferred than blue and red.[59] In their remarkable *Painting and Personality: A Study of Young Children,* Alschuler and Hattwick conducted an extensive study of children as they expressed themselves in primarily pictorial media (paint, crayons, clay, etc.) to discern relationships between personality and activities. They found that there was a strong parallelism between color emphasis and strong emotional drives, that this was more pronounced in girls than in boys, and that it tended to manifest itself in color preference.[60] "The relatively free and easy emotional pattern exhibited by most of the children who used warm colors, together with age data, indicate that warm colors are the expected color preference of nursery-school children who are developing in usual or typical fashion."[61] Children who consistently favored cold colors, on the other hand, tended to stand out for their highly controlled, over-adaptive behavior (18).

As children progress, the authors point out, from impulsive behavior to the level of conscious control—and from mass techniques to line and form—a preference for cold (or cooler) colors is entirely natural. This shift takes place, their data show, between ages three and three and one-half and thus precedes the period of maximum form emphasis that occurs between four and four and one-half years (103–4). More specifically, the transition is toward favoring blue over red, a tendency that continues over one's life.[62]

Nevertheless, in individuals between the ages of six and seventeen, it has been shown that in general, females prefer warm colors and males the cool ones.[63] Thus there is an active hue preference; at least one study found that when the gender of the candidate was unspecified, men tended to vote for names printed on the green ballots, while women voted for those on the pink ballots.[64] (At this point we might remember Knez's study demonstrating that cool light generated less negative affect in males and warm light less in females.) A study conducted by Silver and Ferrante indicated that the male preference for blue was stronger than for all other seven possibilities in the study combined—with red a distant second—while red was a stronger second choice for females, especially if combined with pink (Table 10.1).[65] An interesting corollary to the early childhood data is the preference by older adults (over sixty-five) for bright primary, secondary, and tertiary colors over pastel shades, a preference that stands in sharp contrast to popular institutional opinion.[66] The reasons for this may be partly physiological in nature; yellowing eye fluids account for a severe drop in color acuity over the span of one's life, particularly (and ironically) for the color blue.

Studies indicate that colors have been identified in conjunction with temperature, weight, smell, sound, and even taste (as in variations of red, which aids in the sensation of sweetness).[67] Collectively, such experiences are referred to as synesthesia, the involuntary physical experience of a cross-modal association. That is, the stimulation of one sensory modality reliably causes an involuntary perception in another modality. Such percepts are, moreover, durable, discrete, stable, and memorable. (Thus the criteria for synesthesia are somewhat more stringent than for simple cross-modal associations.) The Neonatal Synesthesia hypothesis suggests that all human babies (probably to age four months) experience sensory input in an undifferentiated way and hence experience synesthesia.[68] Thus have we all. Andrew D. Lyons points out that as we grow older, our perceptual development is characterized by gradual differentiation, but we nevertheless maintain a high degree of sensory integration in the frontal lobes of our brains.[69] (This would go far toward explaining our predisposition to grant taste characteristics to colors.)

Color relies largely on vision, and in fact vision/sound synesthesias have long been recognized. Such has not been the case with the so-called minor senses of taste, smell, and touch, where synesthesia has been considered more erratic and idiosyncratic. In a fairly recent set of experiments by Gilbert, Martin, and Kemp, the results suggested strong correspondences between vision and olfaction: "The results, from both a color name task and a color matching task, suggest that odors can evoke characteristic hues."[70] Moreover, these color-odor correspondences "are on as firm an empirical footing as other forms of cross-modal correspondence, in that they show a similar degree of intersubject consistency."[71] (They do point out, however, that the results are not as invariant as in clinical cases of synesthesia.) In a following study, Kemp and Gilbert found that there was a considerable amount of dimensionality in visual-olfactory correspondences. Strongly perceived odors, for example, corresponded to darker colors, as well as to greater color saturation (but in one case only). Thus while hue and intensity have some relationship to olfactory perception, it is relative brightness (or value) that is related to odor strength. Perhaps more important, the

Table 10.1. Percentages of color preferences across sexes

Color	Total Sample	Men	Women
Blue	45.07	56.63	36.36
Red	12.43	14.46	10.91
Green	8.29	8.43	8.18
Black	5.69	2.41	8.18
Pink	5.69	1.20	9.09
Purple	4.14	3.16	4.55
Yellow	4.14	2.41	5.45
Other	14.50	10.84	17.27
n	193	83	110

Source: N. C. Silver and R. Ferrante, "Sex Differences in Color Preferences among an Elderly Sample," *Perceptual and Motor Skills* 80 (1995): 920–22.

relationship "parallels those reported for vision and other sensory modalities"[72] Indeed, relationships between color and all the sensory modalities have been reported as increased research has been conducted.

Some data indicate that blue extends the sense of time; thus blue might be a poor choice for children's environments, as their sense of time is already extended.[73] Temperature-perception studies indicate that a blue room is perceived to be three or four degrees cooler than a red one.[74] Another study appears to confirm that the opposite is true as well.[75] Thus a marked difference in perceived temperature is obtainable through painted surfaces alone. Color has also been thought to influence task performance; specifically, that long-wavelength colors facilitate gross motor tasks, and short-wavelength colors fine motor and cognitive tasks. In a study conducted by Etnier and Hardy, the results "indicated that environmental color did not affect performance or arousal. However, color and time did interact to impact positive affect."[76] Thus willingness to complete the assigned tasks over time may correlate to increased subsequent task performance. Specifically, positive affect decreased more in the warm room prior to performance of the cognitively demanding task, and less prior to the physically demanding task.[77] It should also be noted, however that the only dimension of color considered in this experiment was hue; in fact, brightness and saturation are more likely to be determinant.

More recent studies have both questioned past findings and, more commonly, supported them. Questions have tended to center on the comprehensiveness of the methodology, in particular whether color brightness and saturation levels were considered along with hue. For example, while red appears to produce high arousal, precisely the opposite effect occurs when its value is raised to pink. In fact, Bismuth pink (also known as Baker-Miller pink) has been shown to lower anxiety, whose components include displeasure and high arousal.[78] In a study by Weller and Livingston, subjects were asked to read the details of murder and rape incidents—printed on white, blue, and pink paper—and report their emotional reactions. The result was that "the color pink produced less emotional responses than did the color blue."[79] That is, the events appeared less disturbing when appearing on the pink paper.

In a major study conducted by Valdez and Mehrabian, the effects of all three parameters of color—hue, saturation, and brightness—on emotional response were studied using the pleasure-arousal-dominance (PAD) emotion model. In fact, saturation and brightness both "evidenced strong and consistent effects on emotions."[80] The corollary to this is that the relationships between hue and emotions were weaker than anticipated, except perhaps green-yellow, which was consistently low for pleasure, but high for arousal. Thus the authors note that the current trend to use this color for fire department equipment is quite appropriate (402). They summarize their findings as providing highly consistent evidence relative to the PAD model: pleasure was a joint positive function of color brightness and saturation, being influenced more by brightness than saturation; arousal increased linearly and strongly with saturation; and dominance increased linearly and moderately with saturation and decreased sharply with increases in brightness.[81] There is one other finding of interest; a small but statistically significant difference appeared showing that women were more sensitive to brightness and saturation than men, as demonstrated in more extreme emotional reactions to varying brightness and saturation levels.[82]

A major difficulty in attempting to predict how any audience will react is that of cultural relativity. Studies have shown, for example, that while Japanese and Americans may agree on the affective measures of color, they disagree in their evaluation of them.[83] Another factor may lie in our favoring a color in some situations but not in others, or associating a particular color with a personal experience. The data on human color preferences are surprisingly consistent, however, and this raises questions about whether these preferences are learned or innate. J. P. Guilford has stated that this communality of color preferences "probably rests upon biological factors, since it is hard to see how cultural factors could produce by conditioning the continuity and system that undoubtedly exist."[84] On the other hand, some studies on the properties of color indicate that the debate between the universalist and relativist positions on color categorization is ongoing.[85] Abramov and Gordon point out that perceived changes in color identification—in any case—may depend on the observer's perceptual set.[86] Certainly the recent studies indicating that visual perception may be shaped by culture should give pause to design applications involving color. Put differently, the "blue phenomenon" that so consistently characterizes favorable subject responses in the United States is not necessarily universal.

There is a question of how space and color interact. In a study of the ways in which physical elements within child care facilities affect children's behavior, Read, Sugawara, and Brandt found that differentiation in ceiling height or wall color was related to higher levels of cooperative behavior among the preschool children they studied.[87] Four possibilities were tested: change of wall color, differentiation of ceiling height, alteration in both color and ceiling height, and no change at all. The findings are interesting: "the physical space that was the least differentiated was the environment in which preschool children displayed the lowest levels of cooperative behavior whereas physical spaces that were differentiated in ceiling height *or* wall color, in that order, respectively, were environments in which preschool children displayed the highest levels of cooperative behavior."[88]

Curiously, the room with both ceiling and color change fared only slightly better than the undifferentiated space. The authors hypothesize that changes of both types may have been too stimulating, particularly in a fairly small space. In any case, a fairly inexpensive solution is suggested for the fruitful differentiation of spaces, one that is easily under the designer's control. Now, the data that we have cited deal—in the main—with interior environments, where designers have both control and an inclination to use it. Less control and little inclination tend to be the case for the exteriors of buildings.

Michael Lancaster has pointed out that the appearance of environmental color depends on light, surface, and distance, and that each of these factors is, to some extent, within the control of the designer.[89] Light can be controlled through orientation, alignment, and artificial sources, the surface through shape, texture, and pigmentation, and the views by control of distance (23). This observation makes clear the importance of both the ostensible color of surfaces and their textural qualities. That is, textured surfaces tend to diffuse light, while polished surfaces are highly reflective, and this alters the appearance of the color. Lancaster thus concludes: "Differences in texture can be fundamental in the distinction between the old and the new or between the natural and the manufactured—for it is perhaps texture above all that distinguishes nature" (25).

In short, aspects of surface may make things "what they are" at any given moment, a fact that various cultures have exploited. Lois Swirnoff, for example, points out that "form, surface, color, and texture are integrally considered in Japanese architectural traditions."[90] She goes on to similarly praise the traditional architecture of Persia, in which surfaces are devised to draw the eye by the use of light and color transcribed to pattern on planes. That is, from a distance a Persian building is distinct as an architectural mass, relatively simple in shape and solidly placed, while at close range the superimposed patterning of its planes replaces that solidity with a fluid, changing order (14). And Swirnoff notes the distance effects referred to earlier: "From a distance the fine scale of a pattern will assimilate, so that the surface disintegrates altogether, like a hallucination, or meshes like as a film, suspended in space."[91]

An oddly similar experience can be had when looking at the soaring cast-concrete shells of the Sydney Opera House. The result of an international competition held in 1957, won by Jørn Utzon, the structure was not completed until 1973. The sail-like shells, resting on precast concrete ribs, appear smooth from the distance, but when viewed at closer range they reveal a finely textured surface pattern that effectively alters the scale (Figure 10.13). Coupled with differences in the size of the shells resulting from the remarkably complex program requirements, the result is a structure that satisfies at multiple scale levels and provides different views from various locations around the harbor. And when viewed from across the blue water of the bay, the white vaulted roofs fit contextually with the ever-present armada of sailboats.

In fact, one approach to architectural color might involve the examination of context, the characteristic colors of the physical setting. These might be the colors historically favored, or simply those occurring naturally in the vicinity. In this case, of course, some form of analytical tool or methodology becomes necessary so as to clearly understand existing paradigms. This would, in turn, permit the use of color systems for new construction that harmonizes with the larger context. Lancaster points out that color analysis "reveals the evidence of successive historical cultures, identifying new objects and buildings, colours and even colour traditions . . . that might be considered intrusive, disturbing the integrity of the place . . . whether or not they have been designated as conservation areas."[92]

In this context, the method developed by Jean-Phillipe Lenclos is instructive, as it is based on the analysis of existing artifactual color. Lenclos first developed his idea of a "geography of color" while he was a student in Japan, where he became aware of the peculiarity and subtlety of local color. Upon his return to France, he became the artistic director of the Gauthier Paint Company and was given the task of developing color palettes for the different regions of France. He based his conclusions—essentially a color typology—on a variety of color sources. These included naturally occurring materials in the vicinity such as rocks, soils, and vegetation, as well as the traditional colors used on the facades, roofs, and window frames of local buildings. Lenclos relies heavily on actual samples of materials, including paint chips. When such samples are not available, he uses sketches made with crayons. The result is a color analysis of a local area, which provides a database for any future restoration, alteration, or design in that area that is contextually sensitive. It is also worth noting that Lenclos has, since his work in France, gone on to work in various parts of the world. Lenclos's objective, he says, "is nothing more or less than to harmonise architecture with the surrounding landscape and with the inhabitants. It was no longer possible to think of architecture in isolation."[93]

Still, there are many situations that inherently offer a great deal of latitude in exterior color selection. When Regina Pizzinini and Leon Luxemburg began their practice, their first design was for a guest house for film producers Roger and Julie

Figure 10.13. Jørn Utzon, Sydney Opera House, Australia, 1973. Hall, Todd and Livermore, architects; Ove Arup and Partners, engineers. Photograph by Frank Vodvarka.

Corman. The structure of the Corman Guest House clings to the side of the hill, and the stairs thus form a striking axial note as well as a necessary ingress. The brilliant red retaining walls and yellow skylights of the structure combine with the blue California sky to form a primary triad whose intensity depends on weather conditions. At the base of the stair are two rooms, a blue studio and a green apartment. Michael Webb notes that "the stairs are only three feet wide; when the walls reflect the sun, the color is penetrating, and you feel the increase in temperature. At the bottom it's cooler, and the interiors, with their soft colors and natural materials, feel calm and intimate after the drama of the descent."[94] While the materials are entirely conventional—wood and stucco—the color is highly expressive. All in all, an idiosyncratic structure oddly suited to California (Plate 9).

Indeed, idiosyncrasy can form the basis of a highly delightful spatial experience, such as the Piazza d'Italia in New Orleans, designed by Charles Moore for a competition in 1974. Moore, as a member of the Urban Innovations Group, shared the commission as creative consultant with Perez and Associates, who oversaw the daily management of the project in New Orleans. As a place of gathering, the piazza makes reference to the piazzas of Rome, and more specifically to the Piazza d'Trevi, with its famed fountains. As the piazza is characterized by both painted surfaces and the use of colored light, it is arguable that it is most attractive in the evening hours. The surfaces themselves—while recalling the shapes of Rome's baroque structures—in fact are flatter and less detailed. This "flatness" has been perceptually altered by virtue of complementary hues that enhance the dimensionality of the surfaces (Plate 7).

The piazza also reflects Moore's long-standing affection for water. Kevin P. Keim notes that "at the Piazza d'Italia, Moore summoned the lessons of the Trevi and created a monumental stage-set backdrop against which water once played: tiny squirts (wetopes) sprung from the column capitals and bases, and then collected in basins."[95] In a confirmation of his delight in water, Moore has said: "Flowing water speaks of time and sometimes delight," and that at the Trevi Fountain, "the magic endures."[96]

On the subject of idiosyncratic designs, the work of Friedensreich Hundertwasser immediately comes to mind. Of his many designs, his Hundertwasser House in Vienna seems particularly instructive, as it represents a design that not only passed through multiple, fascinating stages but was in fact built. It was designed over a period of years (1977–1986) and reflects many of Hundertwasser's notions of aesthetics. The city council of Vienna's initial choice of architect to work with Hundertwasser designed a structure in the modernist tradition that the architect apparently assumed would simply be painted and landscaped by Hundertwasser. After the absurdity of this arrangement became clear, the architect Peter Pelikan took over as Hundertwasser's architectural partner, resulting in the construction of a rather extraordinary building.

In an effort to "overcome the geometric grid system supplied by the (original) architect," Hundertwasser turned to the use of a model made of fifty irregularly stacked matchboxes. These delineated a series of seven terraces that he characterized as "a melody of the seven notes of the scale."[97] Vital to his ecological view is as

Plate 1. J. R. R. Tolkien, Rivendell (the pleasance), 1937. Reproduced with permission of the Bodleian Library, University of Oxford, from its holdings labeled "MS Tolkien Drawings, 27 rectos." Copyright 1937, 2002 The J. R. R. Tolkien Copyright Trust.

Plate 2. Emilio Ambasz, *Emilio's Folly: Man Is an Island,* 1983. Dwight Ashdown, illustrator; Toshio Okumura, model maker. Photograph by Louis Checkman. Courtesy of Emilio Ambasz.

Plate 3. Songjongjon, Ch'angdokkung (Palace), Seoul, Korea, built by King T'aejong, 1405; rebuilt in 1647 under King Injo. Photograph by Frank Vodvarka; copyright 2002.

Plate 4. Sir John Soane, library, Soane House, London, 1812. Photograph by Richard Bryant, Arcaid.

Plate 5. Kirin Plaza Osaka, Namba, Osaka, Japan, 1991. Photograph by Henry Plummer; copyright 2002.

Plate 6. James Turrell, *Amba,* as installed at Center on Contemporary Art, Seattle, Washington, 1982. Photograph by Mark Sullo. Photograph courtesy of James Turrell.

Plate 7. Charles Moore, Piazza d'Italia, New Orleans, 1978. Photograph by Norman McGrath; copyright 1999 Norman McGrath.

Plate 8. Friedensreich Hundertwasser, Original Poster Hundertwasser House, Vienna, Austria, 1988. Photograph by Peter Dressler; overpainted and adapted by Friedensreich Hundertwasser. Copyright 2002 Joram Harel, Vienna.

Plate 9. Corman Guest House, Santa Monica, California, by Pizzinini and Luxenburg, 1992. Photograph by Dominique Vorillon.

Plate 10. Steven Holl, Chapel of Saint Ignatius, Seattle, Washington, 1997. Photograph by Paul Warchol; copyright 2002 Paul Warchol.

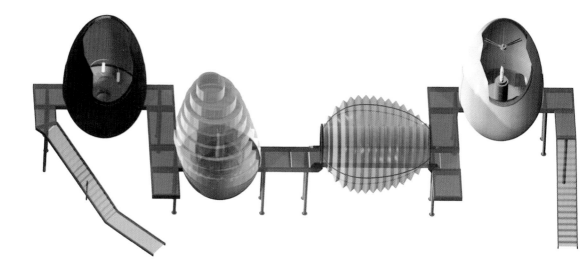

Plate 11. Mats Bigert and Lars Bergström, Climate Chambers, Swedish Pavilion World Expo 98, Lisbon, 1998. Courtesy of Bigert and Bergström, Sweden.

Plate 12. Peter Zumthor, thermal baths, Vals, Switzerland, 1996. Photograph by Ogawa Shigeo, Shinkenchiku-sha.

complete an access as possible to the terrace gardens by the resident. The successive models—next in cardboard, then in plexiglass—reveal a continuously developing aesthetic, primarily in the area of color application. We chose the photo-based poster designed by Hundertwasser himself as the most representative view of the finished work (Plate 8).[98] The garden terraces are luxuriant with vegetation, including trees (for which he has a special affinity).

At a 1980 press conference with the mayor of Vienna, Hundertwasser stated: "Man has three skins: his own, his clothing, and his dwelling. All three skins must continually change, be renewed, steadily grow and incessantly change or the organism will die. When the resident moves in, his creative building activity must begin; it must not be finished when he moves in."[99] This "creative building activity" includes "window rights"—the freedom to re-create the apartment space as well as paint the outside wall of the unit as far as one's arm can reach—and "tree obligation"—the duty to allow nature to grow as wild as it may in the complex. He goes on, listing a "bill of rights" that maximizes the creative potential of the resident, concluding: "It is an unusual house. For it is meant to be an oasis of humanity and nature in the sea of rational buildings, the realization of the longing of people for romanticism" (260).

As Hundertwasser is a painter practicing architecture, his observations on architectural color are more than usually interesting. He states: "It is absolutely clear that color in architecture has to do with nature and that the colors in architecture either have to adapt to nature or must be a counterpoint to nature or a contrast, but a good contrast to nature, one which underscores nature and underscores architecture" (62). While there is a distinction between natural and artificial, the real point is not their uniqueness but how they work to enhance each other. Color, he says, must not be uniformly applied. This can be accomplished by varying the color or the surface it is applied to. The color should, moreover, never be conceived as final; only the resident can do that. This can be facilitated by expressly giving the residents license to alter their portion; nature, too, should be allowed to take its course in terms of rain and vegetation. In short, architectural color should be allowed to evolve. He has yet other suggestions—endless numbers, really—that are for the most part both provocative and refreshing.

Nor does he neglect the more prosaic arenas of human activity. Hundertwasser had, for many years prior to his death in 2000, divided his residency among three locations: Vienna, Venice, and New Zealand's Northland. It was in New Zealand that he designed the public lavatories in the town of Kawakawa. Here he provided not only the design but part of the building fund as well. These toilets are best seen as a practical fantasy, a stunning collection of shaped columns, undulating walls and floors, and complex tile work. The materials—seemingly exotic—are actually common (and largely recycled) materials used in uncommon ways. His color is brilliant in execution and appearance and is used on both the glazed surfaces of the architectural elements and the glass embedded in windows and walls (Figure 10.14). In all, a wonderful way to improve the ablutions of locals and tourists alike.

We include these last designs by way of indicating that light and color have various aspects, sometimes requiring a degree of civilized circumspection on the part of the designer, but quite often allowing for whimsy and delight. What light and color are decidedly not are relatively superficial design aspects requiring minimal attention or attention after the fact, or—worse yet—merely the coincidental characteristics of the materials used. Their biological and psychological properties alone would argue against that. Moreover, many of our most revered structures clearly are tributes to light and color, implying that their expressive, sensory aspects are likely more important than the form that contains them.

Figure 10.14. Friedensreich Hundertwasser, public toilets, Kawakawa, New Zealand, 2000. Photograph by Frank Vodvarka.

11. Sensory Schematics

We begin this chapter by returning to Belk's tests for nonrational relations with objects, the fifth and sixth criteria in particular. These are feelings of elation or depression due to the object, when our sense of self is enlarged or diminished by objects; and personification, the anthropomorphizing of objects.[1] Thus Werner Muensterberger's comments that the source of the collecting habit is an emotional state in which one seeks to surround oneself with magically potent objects.[2] We also noted that Eugene Rochberg-Halton has made a strong argument for the significance of objects, proposing that "objects are not merely inert matter but are living signs whose meanings are realized in the transactions we have with them."[3] He proposes a view that could be termed critical animism, referring to the belief that things have within them a spiritual energy. We have tried to keep this essentially phenomenological position in mind as we develop the structure for a sensory typology.

As a prelude to this task, we should note the various authorities we have so far cited in support of our ideas. That there cannot exist any normative definition of human interactivity with the milieu is reflected in Arnheim's insistence that there is no apparent hierarchy of human needs satisfied by built form. That all of built reality is content laden is reflected in Bachelard's anthropomorphic description of houses, and his observations on the potency of memory. And so on. Indeed, virtually all our sources have, by the very nature of their positions, implicitly relied on a phenomenological view. Thus we appreciate the phenomenological position, in much the way we do the Jungian construction of archetypal experience, the developmental principles of Piaget, and the impact of culture on the shaping of perception—as reasonable explanations of human activity and a much-needed revaluing of sensory experience. We suspect that when designers use the term, they primarily refer to the sensory and emotional qualities fundamental to design and the materials it makes use of, rather than to a philosophical structure per se.

David Seamon points out that phenomenology has become important to the literature of both environment-behavior research and design, but for different reasons; the former for the philosophical alternative that it offers to positivism in understanding the motives and meanings of human actions, and the latter for more useful reasons. "Architects and other designers have become interested in phenomenology largely because of a *practical* crisis: the frequent failure of both architectural formalism and functionalism to create vital, humane environments."[4] Thus phenomenology offers a philosophical alternative to positivism, a more realistic way of understanding daily environmental experiences and behaviors.[5] By way of contrasting positivism and phenomenology, Seamon points out that the latter is radically empirical, avoids predefinitions, is holistic and qualitative in nature, and verifiable in terms of one's own experience. The aim, he says, is understanding, a search for meanings rather than a search for causes.[6] This definition stands in sharp contrast to positivism, many of whose tenets have been embraced by the modernist impulse, particularly its insistence on independence from idiosyncrasy. Perhaps most important for us is the first point, which suggests that a wide range of evidence—sensory, mnemonic, and experiential—is used in a fairly open definition of what constitutes reality. Accordingly, we consider the most useful aspect of the phenomenological stance to be its insistence on the vitality of sensory experience.

Maurice Sauzet says: "Between the inhabitant and his dwelling there is a dialogue. . . . I have tried to make use of sensory phenomenology in my projects. To imagine places to be lived in, and for the relationship of the occupant to his dwelling in which every space tends towards an awakening of the deepest recollections of the self."[7] Sauzet distinguishes four aspects of a sensory arrangement for design: the dialectics between inside and outside (orchestrated passages from one to the other); the hidden unity (unfolding views that suggest mystery factors); framing of views (in hierarchical arrangement); and the kinesthetic imprint (haptic information as it affects perception) (153). He appears to have derived these principles in some measure from an examination of the Jiko In Temple, for which he provides a plan. He notes that through their arrangement of space and itineraries in their temples, the Zen Buddhist monks of the seventeenth and eighteenth centuries expressed a philosophy of existence (155).

This itinerary manifests itself in the 1988 design of a school building at the Collège de Gareoult, Var (France), where the itinerary is fundamental to the design conception. The center of the school occupies a raised position on the site, denoting the end of the itinerary, thus making it topologically analogous to the temple plan. The goal, he says, is "a sensory arrangement of space with constant reference to the notion of itinerary" (153). What Sauzet has done is define the characteristics of spatial constructs, forming a broadly applicable, typological schematic. He has, in fact, relied on this typology in the design of his own house, where he used as his guide pleasures he attributed to imaginary anticipation coupled to memories "and in so doing discovered that the essential quality for an architect is the facility to anticipate sensations."[8]

Rather than depend on formal or mathematical order, Sauzet bases his method on the perception of architecture at 1.6 meters height as a person moves through space. The role of the architect is to organize the sensations that will thus be encountered: light and shadow, thresholds, views, textural changes, and dimensional variations (Figure 11.1). Sauzet continues: "Experiences, memories, become the matter of creation itself. But what is the keyboard on which this journey will be played?" (99). His answer is related to his typology: the relationship between within and without, typically represented by passages; selectively framed views; and kinesthesia based on bodily rotation, level alteration, and directional change (99). He concludes that while sensorial dimensions are rarely a major element of current architectural projects generally, they are nonetheless being increasingly experimented with and will "replace man at the heart of the conception, not in an abstract, but a concrete manner" (99).

Sauzet's concerns—the relationship between within and without, selectively framed views, and kinesthesia—as well as a detailed itinerary, have been addressed by Brit Andresen and Peter O'Gorman in the design of Mooloomba House. Located in North Stradbroke, a semitropical retreat near Brisbane, Australia, the house is sited in tall grasses and ferns, alongside a grove of Banksia trees. The materials used are an unusual combination of native hardwoods (including cypress), plywood, and fiber cement. Still more unusual is the private yet transparent quality of the interior space,

Figure 11.1. Maurice Sauzet, house at Cabasson, France, 1990. Photograph by Monsieur Massi. Reprinted by permission of Maurice Sauzet.

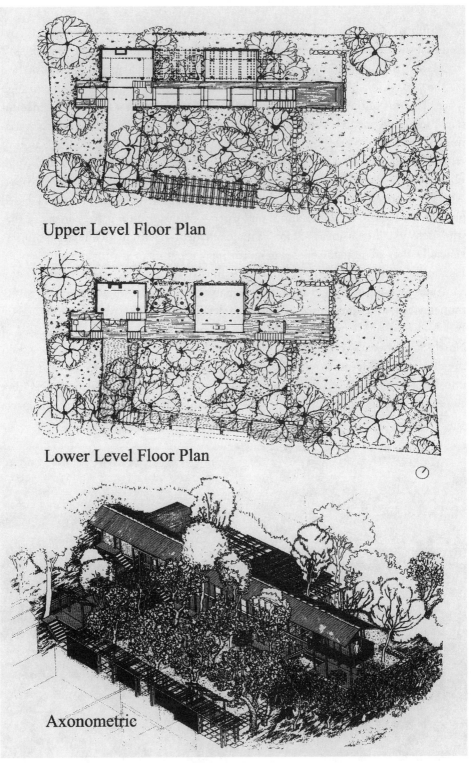

Upper Level Floor Plan

Lower Level Floor Plan

Axonometric

Figure 11.2. Mooloomba House, Queensland, Australia, 1999. Andresen O'Gorman Architects Pty. Ltd., architects; Graham Mellor, carpenter; Peter Nelson, carpenter assistant. Floor plans drawn by Fuller Pratt. Aerial perspective drawn by Michael Barnett. Courtesy of Brit Andresen and Peter O'Gorman.

and the way in which the visitor is sequentially led through a narrow structure to a balcony with a view of the ocean (Figure 11.2). Anna Jackson and Chris Johnson note that as the format masks sea views until one arrives at the bird's nest belvedere, this balcony dramatically culminates a journey through many different resting places.[9] These "resting places" are variously open or closed, roofed or not. The conclusion that is reached is a familiar one: "The whole ensemble—the framed path opening to the viewing decks and finally to the unfolding passages and spaces of the house—recalls Japan's Zen temples and stroll gardens of the 16th and 17th centuries."[10] In short, qualities of both temple layout and tearoom *rōji* have been exploited in this structure, as well as the sensitive use of materials. It also has a persuasive sense of place.

We began this book by quoting Henry James's description of the Boschetto. Here he offers us an implicit set of spatial principles: places are specific, but their elements are general; we comprehend places through sensory data; our understanding of place is filtered through memory; and our delight in place is enhanced by a degree of mystery. This simple construct is echoed by others in one respect or another. For example, Yi-fu Tuan maintains that space becomes place through experience; alternatively, E. V. Walter says that places are the locations of experience and as such evoke and organize memories, images, sentiments, and meanings. More specifically, Rudolf Arnheim refers to architecture as a temporal construct formed from a complete perceptual image shaped by experience. All of these characterizations are compatible with recent studies in the environmental sciences.

Because there are strong corollaries between James's notion of place and the patterns of human behavior earlier forwarded by Rachel and Stephen Kaplan, we have conflated the two characterizations. The Kaplans distinguish four distinct patterns in the discernment of spatial configurations: complexity, coherence, legibility, and mystery.[11] As the Kaplans are examining these factors as distinct phenomena, they tend to consider them equally. They remain, however, functionally discrete. The complexity of the individual part is only understood against the coherence of the larger paradigm, an approximation of James's first two ideas, and it is the clarity of this relationship that grants legibility. And while mystery indeed gives delight, it is likely not critical to our understanding of spatial constructs in quite the same way that the other factors are. Still, these four concepts go far toward explaining James's spatial view, and we have accordingly devised a schematic to describe it (Figure 11.3).

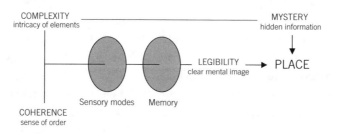

Figure 11.3. Character of place schematic. Created by Joy Monice Malnar and Frank Vodvarka.

In this construction, complexity refers to the intricacy of the information or detail present in the specific location. The Kaplans point out that humans prefer an information level neither too high nor too low, a concept that oddly reflects Gombrich's comment that delight lies between chaos and boredom. Coherence refers to our sense of order, our knowledge of the larger milieu. These two aspects, taken together, suggest a figure-ground relationship. In fact, we contend that legibility, the ability to form a clear mental image, relies on this correlation. The data that comprise complexity and coherence, however, are comprehended through our senses and subjected to memory; hence we have made provision for these two elements. Finally, mystery refers to the hidden (albeit available to extended scrutiny) information in locales that provides a measure of delight in their contemplation.

A question arises as to the mechanism that filters sensory information through the "present" into memory, and the degree of reciprocity that obtains. In short, what is the precise relationship between sensory modes and memory? How does sensory information pass into human awareness? Here the developmental work of Piaget has proved helpful. In an intriguing article on the mechanisms of awareness, Charles W. Rusch suggests that awareness may have developed from the human need to reduce the sheer amount of information in the environment to the ends of survival. This entailed the "filtering out" of certain (less immediately vital) material, and the concomitant "structuring" of the remainder, that is, giving it meaning.[12] Such "recoding" of information is used to symbolize a large amount of detailed data and leads to the ongoing process known as reflection. Awareness, according to Rusch, assumes two forms, that of external awareness of the environment, and that of inner awareness, the attention paid to one's thoughts and bodily processes (58). In his explanation of how sensory information from the environment enters human awareness, Rusch relies on Piaget's four-stage developmental model: the period of emotions, the sensory-motor period, the imaginal period, and the period of formal operations. He notes that each period represents a phase of development during which we learn to "structure" our experience, referring to the objects and events we encounter in our environment (62). Finally, he maintains that through our immediate experience we absorb information from three sources: perception, conception, and memory.

Memory is especially vital, as it constantly recycles the information fed into it. Rusch says that "the memory structure is by no means static or rigid; it is dynamic and constantly undergoing modification during recall when it is fed back through the constructive activity of immediate experience. . . . Thus, just as immediate experience is continuously changing, so also the memory structure is continuously being reconstituted" (63). From this position, Rusch has developed a diagram that seeks to explain the mental process (Figure 11.4). In this diagram, the basic divisions are between sensory experience, reflection, and memory, with the emphasis on the schematization loops that dominate the reflective process. Sensory information is seen as reduced through "perceptual readiness filters" based on anticipation of the future, and then further reduced into categories of preferred meaning. The information is then either acted on or passed on through the process of schematization into memory (or both). In the latter case, the information is represented symbolically and interwoven into the person's memory, a process that is represented in the diagram by a series of inter-connected loops. The inputs to each loop are from previous memories, immediate experience, or other loops, and these together construct new symbols or modify old ones. The outputs in turn form the fabric of memory, initiate muscular response, and operate the perceptual filter (64).

Thus perceptual information enters immediate experience, is condensed into a meaning category, and is either rejected or placed into this active memory structure. It will also be noted that the rising levels the diagram portrays—from emotional to formal—correspond to Piaget's stages of childhood development described earlier.[13] In this model, sensory information is categorized into these levels of meaning with

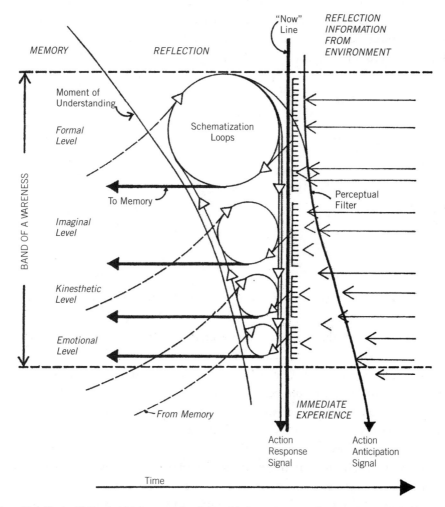

Figure 11.4. Charles W. Rusch, total diagram: a function model of mental process. Courtesy of Charles William Rusch, Eugene, Oregon.

corresponding schematization loops, and the memory fabric is thus woven according to the same levels. Rusch believes that this theoretical framework has three implications: first, it calls for an attitude that addresses the education of the whole mind; second, it makes clear research issues surrounding environmental awareness by revealing the balance between the conceptual and perceptual; and third, it helps elucidate a design process that relies on imagery as the medium of design thinking (79). All in all, an interesting and elegant explanation of a complex process.

There are, of course, alternative ways of understanding the manner in which we perceive spatial constructs. The Kaplans believe that perception is strongly influenced by prior experience, that preference factors include contents and organization, and that variations in preference are the result of cultural and ethnic patterns, as well as personal experience.[14] Human beings, they say, assess their environment in terms of its compatibility with needs and purposes, an idea clearly related to Gibson's concept of affordances. In chapter 3 we advanced a formula, PS / CM = CP (perceptual systems / cultural modifiers = contextual percept), which attempts to explain perception as the product of learned cultural inference. We have thus derived a more fully developed schematic to account for this (Figure 11.5).

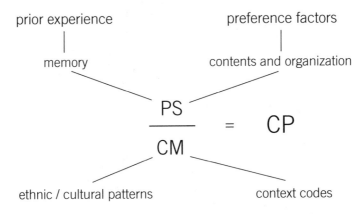

Figure 11.5. Contextual percept schematic. Created by Joy Monice Malnar and Frank Vodvarka.

In this construct, the theories of the Kaplans are brought to bear on our own explanation of perception as it occurs within a cultural context. Thus our perceptual systems are influenced by both prior experience as manifested in memory and preference factors as they affect the perception of the contents of our milieu and their organization. Cultural modifiers are shaped by both culture and position in regard to context codes, that is, our position on Hall's low-context/high-context scale.[15] In both schematics, however, what are critical are the sensory modalities for the understanding of place. This importance is further emphasized when we combine the two schematics to account for the effects of culture on both *how* we use our senses to understand spatial constructs, and the *contents* of the memory base we use for comparison (Figure 11.6).

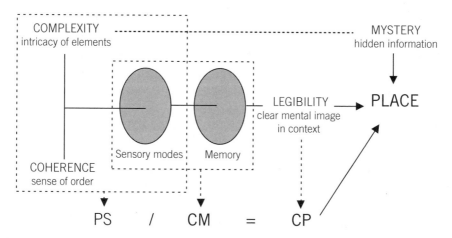

Figure 11.6. Integrated place schematic. Created by Joy Monice Malnar and Frank Vodvarka.

Two aspects of this construct are immediately apparent: first, that there is considerable interaction between perception and culture; and second, that sensory modalities are fundamental to both domains. In fact, it is through our senses that we interact with the "facts" of our particular environment. If the sense we most depend on in Western culture is the visual, it is at least in part because we have been habituated by our designed world to consider it the most crucial. (That is, our built form has reinforced our cultural bias.) Currently, what is not seen tends not to matter, at least until one or another of our nonvisual senses is impinged upon, or until we lose our visual capacity. A pity, as our interaction with the milieu is eminently multisensory.

In *The Urban Stage,* A. Richard Williams offers the reader a succinct definition of the "sensory realm": microenvironments—the smallest spatial components of the cultural or institutional fabric, or urban mosaic—as perception domains of all the senses: visual, tactile, sonic, thermal, and olfactory.[16] Williams points out that designers have been trained to optimize form/function relationships that emphasize vision. "Aside from meeting common standards of performance, architects do little creatively with acoustical, thermal, olfactory, and tactile sensory responses" (5). His experience with theatrical performances, where organized sensory information is critical to success, suggests a new goal for architectural settings: "to orchestrate and 'tune' them over a full range of sensory responses, as flexibly as can be done on stage" (5). To succeed, one would need to examine the detailed and ensemble nature of human settings. Williams concludes that a greater understanding at these intimate scales, especially of the full range of sensory responses that better design can reinforce, "is as important as the need to design better communities, cities, and regions" (6). Continuing the theater analogy, Williams insists that all aspects of the setting must be linked with the "performances" for which they are intended, and that this "places greater emphasis on the design of the full sensory realm of sound, heat, taste, smell and touch, as well as vision in establishing form/function relationships" (39).

Williams identifies five "components of essence" in his design synthesis: program, space, structure and material, environmental systems, and sensory perception (141). While one or more of these elements might dominate in a particular situation, all need to be considered. We find the last two most interesting for our purposes. Williams points out that environmental systems become more important as one considers the design of settings at the microscale. This will involve knowledge of physiological, metabolic, sensory, and psychic stress, and the means of ameliorating them to the "enhancement of well-being" (151). This, of course, requires that more attention be paid to the sensory environment, and the ways in which we experience it (Figure 11.7). Williams concludes that this raised consciousness has two levels, one of which is to design with the senses in the simplest, most natural, direct way: "The other is to develop a repertoire in sensory media reinforcement that may be sensitively applied where appropriate" (153).

Figure 11.7. A. Richard Williams, *Sensory Realm,* 1980. From A. Richard Williams, *The Urban Stage: A Reflexion of Architecture and Urban Design.* Courtesy of A. Richard Williams.

Of course, for multimodal sensory perception to occur, we must be prepared to use all our senses. After a walk in the woods, a friend of Helen Keller remarked that she had seen nothing particularly notable. Keller had this reaction:

> How was it possible, I asked myself, to walk for an hour through the woods and see nothing worthy of note? I who cannot see find hundreds of things to interest me through mere touch. I feel the delicate symmetry of a leaf. I pass my hands lovingly about the smooth skin of a silver birch, or the rough, shaggy bark of a pine. . . . I who am blind can give one hint to those who see. . . . Use your eyes as if tomorrow you would be stricken blind. And the same method can be applied to the other senses. Hear the music of voices, the song of a bird, the mighty strains of an orchestra, as if you would be stricken deaf tomorrow. Touch each object you want to touch as if to-morrow your tactile sense would fail. Smell the perfume of flowers, taste with relish each morsel, as if to-morrow you could never taste or smell again. Make the most of every sense.[17]

This would be excellent instruction indeed, for any designer. But for this to actually happen, we will need to revalue the nonvisual senses and learn a new vocabulary as well.

There exist, of course, "environmental" designs that do appeal to our various senses. While most of these are the projections of artists, we believe they could all enjoy architectural application, were a broader view of that discipline common. We have on several occasions referred to the phrase "flatlands," which was coined by Edward Tufte in his highly influential book *Envisioning Information.* His point in this regard is that the various means developed for communicating three-dimensional information are almost invariably two-dimensional, a dilemma with which architects are surely familiar. At about the same time that Tufte worked on the book, he also designed a multiplanar sculpture, *Escaping Flatlands,* so complex that no single, flattened view could capture it. On the contrary, the mirrorlike surface reflects the characteristics of color, but not the shapes it occupies.[18] It is, in short, a constantly changing, sometimes dematerialized collection of color-field studies dependent on the quality of the light and our viewing position.[19] It is also a rather amusing way to make his point.

Thus space is both delineated and alluded to, and the search for full comprehension of the work actively involves the viewer. The idea of an essentially borderless space has also interested Jesús Rafael Soto, especially as seen in his series of *Pénétrables.* Soto notes that in these "sculptures," the beholder is fundamentally a part of the work. "The Pénétrable . . . throws light on the question of sensitive space, continually filled with the purest structural values, such as energy, time and movement. The reality of the experience of the beholder who takes part by going into the Pénétrable, and so into a different time-space, will be clearer for him the day he can move freely in weightless surroundings."[20] In fact, in the *Pénétrable Washington* (1975), the aqueous space provides the viewer with both visual and haptic experience. Notably, a part of its success rests on enhancing the haptic aspect via touch while restricting the visual (Figure 11.8). And still other sculptors have created works that exploit the capacity of sound and odor to elicit spatio-emotional response.[21]

Bernhard Leitner has developed an extraordinary series of sound spaces, whose form and content are determined by sound movement. Such spaces rely on both hearing with one's ears and feeling with one's entire body. At the outset of his book *Sound:Space,* Leitner states that a line is really an infinite series of points, and space can be defined by lines; therefore space can be defined by the line of sound that is produced by a series of points marked by loudspeakers.[22] More specifically, "the lines delineate the configuration of space and simultaneously make it a specific expressive experience" (13). The space that is thus described is different from the usual definition of space in several important ways: it is sonic rather than solid; it is linear—and thus temporal—rather than fluid; and it relies on an auditory-haptic definition of spatial sensation. "Space unfolds in time; it is developed, repeated and transformed in time" (13). Leitner points out that this is a fundamentally new form of spatial experience: "It is above all the intensity, the rhythm, the speed of the moving sound and their interrelated variations that determine the shape of a space" (15). Sound spaces are characterized, however, by very physical qualities such as pushing and pulling, contracting and stretching, confining and expanding, rocking, embracing, guiding, and so on.[23]

Figure 11.8. Jesús Rafael Soto, *Pénétrable Washington,* 1975. Copyright 2002 Artists Rights Society (ARS), New York/ADAGP, Paris.

We find two of Leitner's spaces particularly relevant. The first is the *Soundcube,* "an instrument for producing space with sound." It is a visually neutral cube with loudspeaker grids on each of its six internal sides that project sounds containing changes in pitch and intensity. The sound is programmed to go from speaker to speaker in order to depict a specific spatial sensation, and an infinite number of these can be created. Leitner regards the cube as "a laboratory for studies in the definition and character of space and for investigations into the relationships between motions of sound and their audio-physical experience" (18). The participant is surrounded by this flexible "sound structure," whose various outlines are heard and felt inside the visible structure that contains the speakers (Figure 11.9).

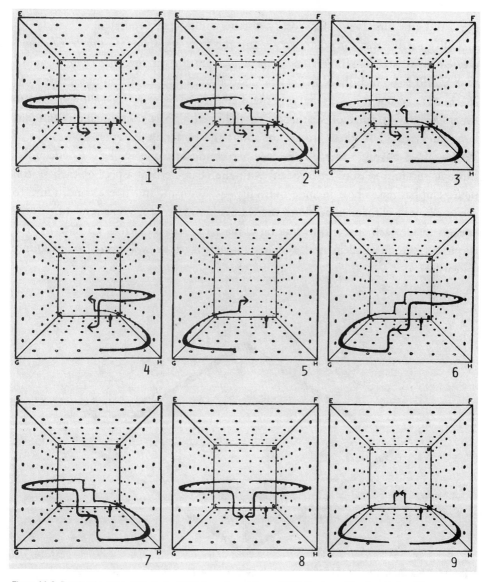

Figure 11.9. Bernhard Leitner, *Soundcube,* 1969. From *Sound:Space,* 1978. Courtesy of Bernhard Leitner, Vienna, Austria.

The "shaping of space" is a familiar concept to the architect, and thus the second space we are interested in is one Leitner calls *Sound Gate*, one of the series *Guiding Spaces*. The gate itself is a four-meter square with two floor extensions, one on each side of the vertical elements. Seventeen speakers are mounted on each of these modular structures. Leitner says that the moving sound acoustically alters the shape of the gate, articulates through changing intensity the vertical dimension of the gate, and transforms the gate into a directional space. The result is that "the line of sound leads the person through the gate. The gate performs a leading, directing gesture" (42). The design implications are likely obvious (Figure 11.10). Leitner concludes: "Superimposing a sound-dynamic secondary space over a static primary space modifies, enriches, intensifies in various ways the original meaning of the primary space" (42). And, of course, yet other sensory systems could be incorporated.

Of great interest for our purposes are the four egg-shaped *Climate Chambers* created by artists Mats Bigert and Lars Bergström for the Swedish Pavilion at the 1998 World Expo in Lisbon. In an article for *Metropolis,* Saul Anton notes that these spaces were arranged in seasonal order and connected by walkways, allowing one to experience a wide range of weather. "Part architecture, part conceptual art, and part amusement ride . . . these spaces are about the buffeting extremes of weather."[24] Within these chambers are all the weather conditions one is likely to encounter through the four seasons in Sweden, with the characteristic aspect of each season being emphasized. These include humidity, heat, storm, and freeze conditions. To accompany the climatic conditions, there are other material references relating to the seasons inside each space, thus linking climate to aspects of culture (Plate 11). For the artists, this link is elemental, as climate is central to the evolution of every culture on earth.[25]

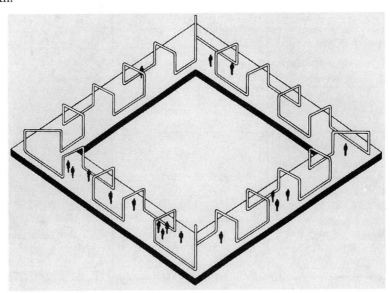

Figure 11.10. Bernhard Leitner, *Sound Gate,* 1971. From *Sound:Space,* 1978. Courtesy of Bernhard Leitner, Vienna, Austria.

Another intriguing and multireferential work—linking culture artifact to climate—has been produced by the innovative landscape architect Michael Van Valkenburgh. His *Krakow Ice Garden* was designed for a private residence on Martha's Vineyard, Massachusetts (Figure 11.11). The design makes reference to the changing seasons through the use of climbing plants—purple clematis in the spring, blue morning glories in the summer, and red ivy in the fall—and a wall of ice (produced by a drip irrigation fixture) in the winter. The structure surrounds formal planting beds and movingly suggests the passage of time. James Corner writes:

Figure 11.11. Michael Van Valkenburgh, *Krakow Ice Garden,* Martha's Vineyard, Massachusetts, 1990. Photograph by Mark Darley; copyright Mark Darley/Esto. All rights reserved.

With a rare and graceful clarity, the built landscapes of Michael Van Valkenburgh modestly demonstrate these simple, though radical, premises: that knowledge of a place derives more deeply through the experience of material, time, and event than through visuality alone, and that landscape experience is fuller and more profound when it accrues through inhabitation than through the immediacy of the image or the objectification of the new.[26]

These few examples of sensory designs being produced by artists, designers, and landscape architects offer some suggestion of how rich a sensory architecture could be, especially when sensory systems are combined. Of course, to become useful, this requires a larger context.

In his explanation for why people experience either overestimations or compensations in regard to spatial illusions, Jean Piaget explains that "in visual perception (without necessarily excluding other perceptual modalities), space, as constituted by a collection of objects, is not homogeneous; even in the case of objects of equal size . . . some are over- and others under-estimated as a function of the five following factors: the area of the retina which they stimulate (central or peripheral); the duration of their centration; the temporal order of their centration; the intensity of their centration (attention); and their visual clarity, as a function of illumination, distance from the observer, etc."[27] These observations refer to visual perception, but—as suggested by Piaget—there are analogous structures in the other sensory modalities. These five factors in an auditory reference, for example, might be locational or ambient sound, duration, order of notes, intensity in decibels, and distinctness or articulation. Odor, as well, likely follows a similar delineation of aspects.

We believe that we can, by altering the terminology in appropriate manner, form a matrix of common aspects of sensory response as it relates to space, the first step in a sensory typology. Piaget's distinctions provide a logical place to start. His five factors, restated, are type of stimulation (locational or ambient), duration (length of stimulation), order (sequence of information), intensity, and clarity (or articulation). We have already suggested—per Piaget—that these aspects are not necessarily restricted to vision, and we have accordingly devised vocabulary and legibility cross-references (Figure 11.12). In the first instance, it might be noted that for each sense, there are two types: precise (and limited), and general (forming a context, or ground). While the terms used for vision are likely familiar, the others may not be. Immediate and episodic odor types refer to that immediately experienced and that recurring through memory, while the entries for the haptic remind us that it is multifaceted. The duration category particularly reveals real differences between the visual and auditory, on the one hand, and the haptic and odor, on the other. Indeed, the references for the latter are both wider-ranging and more fundamental (as suggested by the terms "involuntary" and "visceral") than those for the former, suggesting that their role in design is correspondingly profound.

VOCABULARY

Sense	Type		Duration		Order	
Visual	Foveal	Peripheral	Focused	Subliminal	Detail	Mass
Sound	Locational	Ambient	Clear	General	Hi-fi	Lo-
Odor	Immediate	Ambient	Involuntary	Episodic	Olfactory	Associate
Haptic	Tactile	Visual	Visceral	Cognitive	Inherent	Associativ
Orientation	Containment	Space	Self	Location	Balance	Entension

Figure 11.12. Common vocabulary schematic. Created by Joy Monice Malnar and Frank Vodvarka.

The legibility schematic relies on the old and hallowed figure/ground concept, but placed in a different organizational format. Here we use the complexity/coherence concepts illustrated in earlier figures. We have added a category called contextual, which refers to sensory data that seem to be neither figure nor ground but are nonetheless fundamental to the identification of particular places. They are the specialized things, sounds, odors, and so on, that are so integral to the character of a place that we cease noting them in figure-ground terms. (This might include street signage, church bells, and urban ozone.) Thus the figure/ground/icon relationship in the visual finds its counterpart in sound as signal/keynote/soundmark (per Schafer), and the immediate/ambient/episodic for odor (per Engen). We have subdivided the haptic aspect into touch, kinesthesia, plasticity, and temperature/humidity awareness.

Texture, for example, is both felt and seen as a gradient, kinesthesia is really represented by muscular tension exerted against bodily mass, plasticity describes the effects of spatial compression and expansion on human awareness, and temperature is understood as degree against normative range. The extent of texture gradient is always understood in context, that is, as an aspect of the thing it provides a surface for. Attribute refers to characteristic texture, that which identifies certain things for what they are. Basic-orienting is represented by the self in space, a concept that modern dancers often refer to as centering. And, of course, certain activities require specialized body-space attitudes, which we refer to with the term "task." Of interest is that the tripartite relationship, which forms a legibility gauge, applies to all the senses, suggesting design suitability (Figure 11.13).

Sense	LEGIBILITY		
	Complexity	Coherence	Contextual
Visual	Figure (detail)	Ground (context)	Icon
Sound	Signal (note)	Keynote (ground)	Soundmark
Odor	Immediate (context)	Ambient	Episodic (memory)
Haptic ①	Gradient (surface)	Context (type)	Attribute
Haptic ②	Tension (muscular)	Resistance (mass)	Task
Haptic ③	Compression	Expansion	Expected
Haptic ④	Degree	Range	Comfort
Orientation	Self (body)	Space (surround)	Activity

Figure 11.13. Legibility schematic. Created by Joy Monice Malnar and Frank Vodvarka.

In our previous book *The Interior Dimension: A Theoretical Approach to Enclosed Space,* we discussed the Scanner, a remarkable device designed by Gordon Cullen in 1966. Cullen divided the built environment into two areas: human factors and physical factors. Each section or layer of his paradigm has as its nominal title "Have I considered . . ." followed by a vast array of design factors related to the two categories grouped under area headings. For human factors, they are zests, integration, association, work/leisure, and tenure; and for physical factors, identity of place, optics, landscape, pattern, and community. In neither case do the areas refer to narrow, programmatic concerns. We were (and are) struck with the complexity that he portrayed, and the fact that it formed a reference point or goal. We regard our schematics in much the same way, as references rather than prescriptions.

It is in this spirit that we have devised a design tool based on our legibility schematic, which we refer to as the *Sensory Slider* (Figure 11.14). The schematic is composed of eight bars, each one describing the extent of figure/ground clarity for a particular sense. It will be noted that there are a number of categories devoted to the haptic. This reflects its complexity as a sense, as well as the commensurate number of opportunities offered the designer for its exploitation. Spatial structures that have a clear and pronounced figure aspect, as seen against the prevailing ground, or milieu, we denote as *high intensity.* To integrate this information into the schematic, one would place a symbol (■) at the appropriate place on the slidebar. Icons, or the characteristic images of place described earlier, which are neither figure nor ground, might be more or less present in any particular place. This fact would be denoted by an alternative symbol (●) to mark their extent. As no human beings prefer conditions of overload or deprivation, most of the notation will likely fall into the central area, though surely not equally.[28] In this way, a space can be charted in terms of its sensory characteristics in an analytic manner, although it is our hope that the Slider will be used in the predesign stage of planning.[29]

Of course, any tool is judged by its usefulness. We have thus illustrated how the *Sensory Slider* functions by applying it to two Chicago buildings, the Rookery and 333 Wacker Drive. The Rookery was designed in 1885 by Daniel H. Burnham and John W. Root, the principals of one of Chicago's best-known firms. The building depends on many design innovations by Root, including a rail-grillage foundation (a "floating raft" concept), and an early use of iron framing, plate glass, and hydraulic elevators. However, Root's ideas about space and its decorative elements—being the most apparent and manipulative—really account for our sensory response to the building. Its shape is that of a square doughnut, with a central court that is covered by a two-story skylight. The ornament is both visually rich and referential, inside and out. While the exterior is notable for its use of red granite, brick, and terra-cotta, the early interior was awash in light and complex displays of black wrought iron (Figure 11.15).

Frank Lloyd Wright was commissioned in 1905 to rework the interior court and lobbies; in the process, he covered the wrought iron with marble panels. These are decorated with low-relief incisions filled with gold. William Drummond later reduced the height of the lobbies that opened onto the court, and enclosed the elevators with solid doors. Still later, the glass of the court was tarred over, resulting in a dependence on artificial light. In 1992 McClier Corporation undertook a restoration, which took the building back to approximately 1907, when both Root's design and Wright's alterations still remained clear (as did the glass).

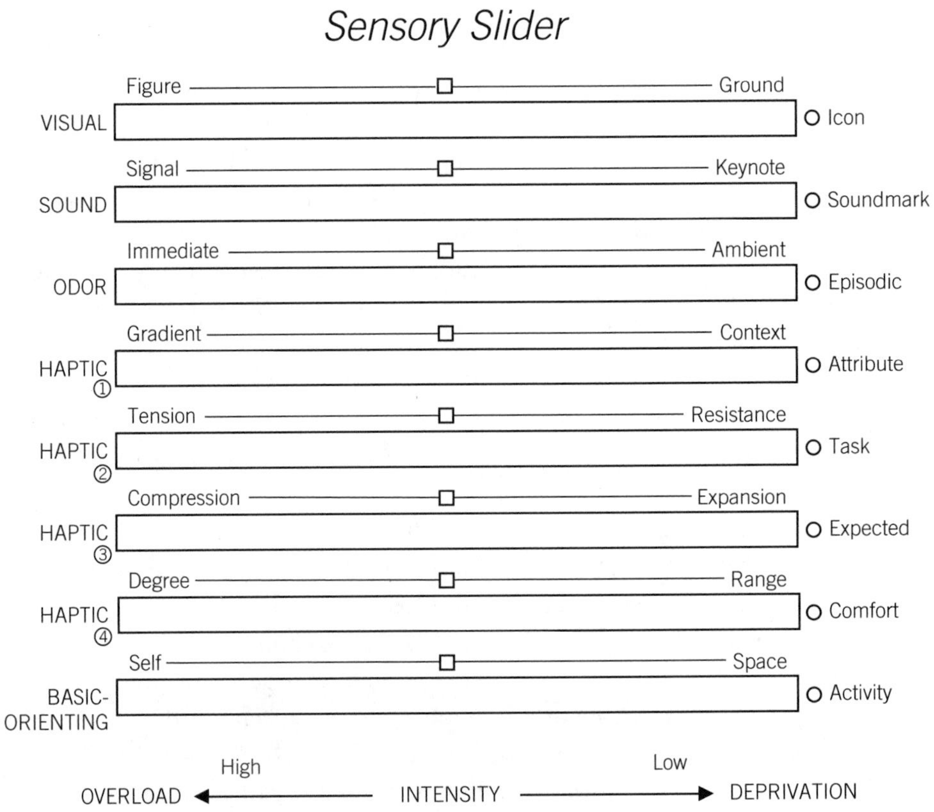

Sensory Slider

	Figure ——————————□—————————— Ground	○ Icon
VISUAL		
	Signal ——————————□—————————— Keynote	○ Soundmark
SOUND		
	Immediate ——————————□—————————— Ambient	○ Episodic
ODOR		
	Gradient ——————————□—————————— Context	○ Attribute
HAPTIC ①		
	Tension ——————————□—————————— Resistance	○ Task
HAPTIC ②		
	Compression ——————————□—————————— Expansion	○ Expected
HAPTIC ③		
	Degree ——————————□—————————— Range	○ Comfort
HAPTIC ④		
	Self ——————————□—————————— Space	○ Activity
BASIC-ORIENTING		

High   Low

OVERLOAD ◄———————— INTENSITY ————————► DEPRIVATION

Figure 11.14. *Sensory Slider.* Created by Joy Monice Malnar and Frank Vodvarka.

Figure 11.15. The Rookery, Chicago, by Burnham and Root, 1886. Photograph by Frank Vodvarka.

By adjusting the relative position of the marker (■) between figure and ground, and the intensity of the icon (●), we can describe the sensory nature of the structure (Figure 11.16). The slider for the visual bar, for example, is set at a high intensity. This reflects the saturated quality of figural elements, both in visual terms (detail and contrast) and in symbolic reference (rooks and botanic data). One's eye moves slowly into and through this space and is constantly attracted by the highly organic but well-organized surfaces. Because characteristic, identifying motifs reoccur, we have also rated the building as high in iconic content. Sound, in part a result of sharply differing spatial characteristics, in part a result of reflective materials, also has a fairly high signal/keynote ratio, although the soundmark does not have the icon's pronounced

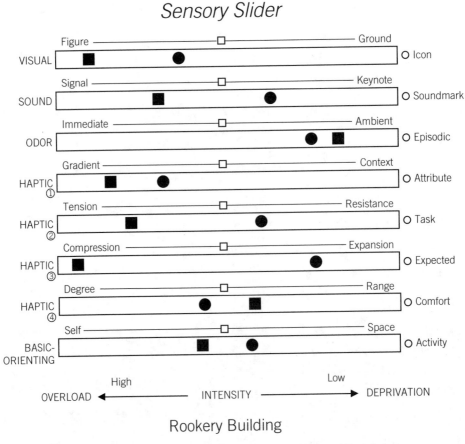

Figure 11.16. *Sensory Slider* analysis of the Rookery. Created by Joy Monice Malnar and Frank Vodvarka.

presence. Odor, as one might expect, is negligible in all the categories. The Rookery is, however, rich in haptic attributes. Touch (H1) enjoys a high intensity rating, which is consistent with the visual rating. Masses of detail having a high degree of contrast provide a pronounced gradient. And as the motifs are repeated, they tend to become an attribute of the surfaces they cover. Kinesthesia (H2) is also relatively high, as the multiple staircases offer complex invitations to their use and have differential height/tread ratios. We kept the task category somewhat lower, as the presence of elevators makes the stair climbing unnecessary, though appealing.

The plasticity category (H3) is very intense, in large part the result of the spatial manipulation of the lobbies referred to earlier. The continuum—outside to lobby to court—is now one of expansion to compression to expansion again, as can be seen in our illustration (Figure 11.17). The stairwells, too, follow a similar pattern of abrupt spatial alteration. The temperature/humidity (H4) category is denoted by a central rating, as the coolness is slightly surprising (a result of the use of marble), but not unusual in the modern context of air-conditioning. (One can only guess what a pleasant experience it would have provided in the 1880s.) The final category, basic-orienting, receives a rating somewhere in the center of the Slider. That is, while there are quite a few stairs and level changes, such changes are not the point of the space. Still, we note that the rating is more intense than would likely be the case in most contemporary commercial buildings. The visual and haptic categories are, as with most nineteenth-century buildings, of relatively strong intensity. Overall, the image that emerges from this analysis is one of a high-intensity sensory environment.

We would expect a comparison with current buildings to reveal real differences in attributes. Our second example, 333 Wacker Drive—designed in 1979 by Kohn Pedersen Fox (with Perkins and Will)—represents such a building. The lead designer, William E. Pedersen, relied on a modernist vocabulary sensitively adapted to a difficult (though striking) site, and a distinctly Chicago context. The sloped, triangular site is located on a bend in the Chicago River, with streets on three sides. The site's hypotenuse, which faces the river's bend, was the one chosen by Pedersen for a long, tautly curving wall of green glass that reflects the turning of the river in shape and color. The strong tripartite statement of the structure's development reflects both a long-standing design position of the firm and a marked characteristic of Chicago buildings generally. The base, in particular, suggests the local traditions (context, if you will) in development and materials. It meshes with the upper shaft of glass curtain wall in a staggered, integrated formation in such a way that the tower seems to grow from it. The base itself is made of gray granite with horizontal green marble banding, and both colors are repeated in the multiple columns (Figure 11.18). The building affords strikingly different profiles depending on the view, offering what Jim Murphy has described as "a feeling of permanence, of confidence, and of command over the area."[30]

Terazzo floors in the two lobbies—one on the river side and one at the apex side—lead almost continuously out to the plaza surfaces. Due to the sloping site,

Figure 11.17. Frank Lloyd Wright, interior of the Rookery, Chicago, 1907. Photograph by Frank Vodvarka.

Figure 11.18. 333 Wacker Drive, Chicago, by Kohn Pederson Fox, 1983. Photograph by Frank Vodvarka.

these two lobbies are not on the same level; in fact, one climbs two sets of stairs on the apex side—one outside the building and one inside—to get to the same level as the riverside lobby and elevator core. This transition is handled rather well, in part because of the intriguing spaces and in part because of expensive details like stainless steel handrails, grilles, and trim. Indeed, it has been pointed out that the quality of the materials, finishes, and workmanship is far higher than is customary for speculative construction.[31] As is clear in the illustration, this is no exaggeration (Figure 11.19). It is, all in all, a fine building that nonetheless is different in sensory character from the Rookery. The materials, for example, are flat in character, ranging from the low relief of the granite to the high polish of the marble and stainless steel, resulting in a high degree of reflectivity. Thus the visual bar on the Slider is set at a medium level, as there is neither a strong figural content nor a high level of differentiation from ground. Nor is there any program to the details other than their reference to an industrial aesthetic. Because they are largely self-referential, they are also low in iconic value (Figure 11.20).

Figure 11.19. Entry and interior of 333 Wacker Drive, Chicago, by Kohn Pederson Fox, 1983. Photograph by Frank Vodvarka.

Sensory Slider

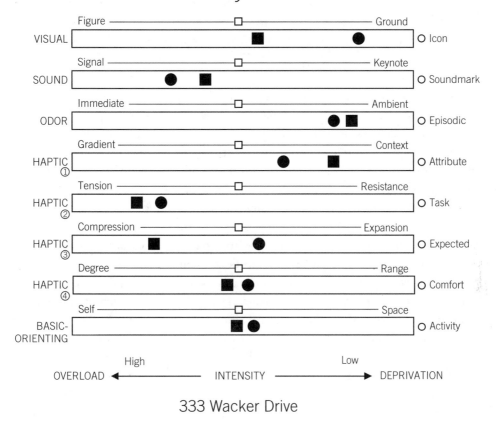

333 Wacker Drive

Figure 11.20. *Sensory Slider* analysis of 333 Wacker Drive. Created by Joy Monice Malnar and Frank Vodvarka.

The sound bar is set fairly high, the result of sonically reflective materials. Because the sound grants an extraordinarily characteristic sound, we judged it higher as a soundmark. Odor is once again a negligible component. The haptic attributes reflect the comparatively low visual rating. Touch (H1) is fairly low; while the smooth, polished character of the materials certainly has character, it is low stimulus and comparatively limited in contrast levels. Kinesthesia (H2) is rated somewhat higher, as the stairs are necessary to passage through one of the lobbies and offer vital spatial definition. Thus the task level is also high. The plasticity (H3) category— in common with the Rookery—is fairly high, for much the same reason, that is, the effects of compression and expansion, and the relative complexity of the lobby spaces. The temperature/humidity (H4) bar is set at a central rating, which would be common for a fully air-conditioned building, and moreover expected. Finally, the basic-orienting category is set at a central point, much as in the Rookery, but at a slightly lower intensity, as the tread/riser ratios are standardized, and their regularity clearly communicated.

There are two points to be made here: first, the two *Sensory Slider* analyses—the Rookery and 333 Wacker Drive—are closer than would probably be the case with a more conventional "modernist" structure; and second, although the analysis centered on the interiors of the buildings, it would likely not have been too very different for the facades. This is especially true for 333 Wacker Drive, where the exterior materials reappear on interior surfaces. (This speaks to the fundamental consistency with which the two architects approached their projects.) If Pedersen comes surprisingly close to Root in his consideration of haptic qualities, it may in part be due to the constraints of site, and Pedersen's obvious desire to maintain contextual reference points. The result is a building, in our opinion, that returns to a fundamentally modernist aesthetic at least some of the sensory attributes that would otherwise have been omitted. Alas, such sensitivity is rare in contemporary manifestations of modernism.

This leads us to consider whether any current structures *do* exploit a wide range of sensory information in a calculated, proactive manner. Happily, the answer is yes. We made reference in the previous chapter to Tadao Ando's Church of the Light, in which light is carefully manipulated to produce a spiritual aura on the interior surfaces. Yet another project that relies on the effects of light and the subtle coloration that light imparts to surfaces is the Chapel of Saint Ignatius, located on the campus of Seattle University. The architect of this intriguing structure is Steven Holl, who based its design on *The Spiritual Exercises* written by Ignatius Loyola in 1548 as a guide for an extended process of personal prayer. The idea was to assist the individual in discerning among interior lights and darknesses—what Saint Ignatius termed *consolations* and *desolations*—which will allow that individual to make just decisions. From this idea, Holl developed the chapel's concept, "a gathering of different lights."

More precisely, the chapel took form around the image of "seven vessels of light" contained within a "stone box," each vessel representing a different physical area or program element of the building (Figure 11.21). Gerald T. Cobb, S.J., describes the play of light entering the chapel through openings that demarcate spaces corresponding to particular aspects of worship. "In a powerful paradox Holl has filled these vessels with light that acts like liquid, an aqueous medium spilling across interior surfaces."[32] And Cobb notes that the cedar doors at the threshold of the chapel contain glass discs set at different angles that admit light into the interior by day and permit it to stream out at night.[33]

In fact, Holl went to great lengths to ensure that all the senses are attended to. Saint Ignatius held that the auditory sense was the most important, followed by touch and then sight. The acoustics are exemplary, in part due to the curved ceilings being checked during design to make certain that reflected sound did not focus at ear level. According to Timothy Bade, Holl's project architect, this allowed the reflected sound to be distributed evenly throughout the space.[34] As total acoustic isolation of the separate spaces is not possible without walls, a sound system was installed—for the most part unused. The haptic is provided for by virtue of custom-designed furnishings and fixtures out of materials such as bronze, granite, and sand-cast glass. Cobb makes an interesting point about the broader aspects of sensory experience:

> The haptic or sensory dimension of a building becomes the place of disclosure or revelation of something more than the obvious form: the chiseled surfaces in the Alaskan cedar doors reveal the ligneous interior, which catches and disperses sunlight; light spills and moves across the hand-textured plaster walls; the polished black concrete flooring becomes a reflective watery surface flowing in visual continuity from the pool into the chapel proper.[35]

This also provides a clear reference to the increased efficacy of the haptic coupled to the visual, a phenomenon referred to in an earlier chapter.

Odor results from the use of carefully chosen aromatic materials; for example, the Alaskan cedar already referred to. Even more intriguing is the chapel of the Blessed Sacrament, whose walls were finished by artist Linda Beaumont. Here gold leaf prayer texts lie under layers of beeswax, scenting the air with a sweet odor.[36] (Here is one project that would score much higher than normal on the odor portion of the Slider.)

Figure 11.21. Steven Holl, Chapel of Saint Ignatius, Seattle, Washington, 1997. Photograph by Paul Warchol; copyright 2002 Paul Warchol.

It is, however, the light that is especially responsible for the interior ambience. Holl describes the lighting program:

> In the narthex and processional hall, the natural light of the sun creates a play of shadows. Moving deeper into the chapel, the light glows mysteriously from the reflected color fields. Each "bottle of light" contains a unique reflected color with a colored lens of a complementary color. . . . The twofold merging of concept and phenomena in the chapel is communicated in this visual phenomenon of complementary colors.[37]

Each spatial element has its own paired color field and complementary or split-complementary lens: orange field with purple lens in the chapel of the Blessed Sacrament, green field with red lens in the choir, and so forth (Plate 10). The processional hall is adorned by four fused glass windows by Doug Hanson, each depicting one of the spiritual exercises. Added to this ambitious program are the bell tower and reflecting pool, which are lit with both natural and artificial light, sometimes through the night. Indeed, it is Holl's careful combining of natural light with devices that alter its character that most interests us here. And in common with Ando, Holl claims that time, or duration, is a central theme of the chapel's interior.[38]

Indeed, one can almost imagine the state of suspended time induced by the careful control of sensory input in these two chapels or, for that matter, Il Giarasole. In fact, the estimation of time alters significantly in conjunction with alterations in the sensory environment. In Joseph Glicksohn's study of the effects of alterations in auditory and visual stimulation on subjective time estimation, two results emerged. First, he found that visual and auditory stimulation interact with each other in their production of an altered sensory environment, and second, that the rate of functioning of the cognitive timer (our internal clock) is environment dependent.[39] The operative hypothesis is that the more varied the sensory environment (i.e., perceptual overload versus perceptual deprivation), the faster would be the rate of functioning of the cognitive timer. "To conclude, visual and auditory stimulation interact in their production of an altered sensory environment. Underload in both modalities produces a situation of perceptual deprivation, resulting in a slower rate of functioning of the cognitive timer. . . . When overload in one modality is coupled with underload in the other, the cognitive timer runs at a faster pace" (649). And, perhaps not unexpectedly, overload in both modalities eventually results in the system slowing down because "a fast tempo of extraneous events leads to overestimation of time, and a slow tempo to crashing" (649).

There are other such studies. One found there to be an underestimation of time with varied events.[40] (Apparently the difference between *tempo* and *varied* is quite significant.) In yet another study, it was found that the internal clock advances faster when the tempo of events increases in regard to the estimation of mean velocity and time.[41] The concept of time passage therefore depends on the extent and type of sensory data that is experienced. These studies emphasized sound and sight, and movement estimations variously; but time estimation, we believe, is similarly influenced by odor, taste, and touch. Certain designers have used aspects of time to both psychological and symbolically referential ends. In this regard, Williams maintains that "time as a creative dimension for design becomes significant as variations in sensory responses in light, color, sound, and other properties of a setting become positive parts of the design process."[42] In addition to the future inclusion of time-notation systems in the full range of design tools (such as drawings and models), "greater knowledge, experience, and sophistication in the handling of all sensory reinforcement will be expected in the qualifications of environmental designers."[43]

In 1993 Juhani Pallasmaa was asked to design the lighting and traffic guidance fixtures at the end of the entrance driveway for the Cranbrook Academy in Michigan. This crossing became the "Arrival Plaza 'Analemma' (Calendar Teacher)," which has the effect of slowing one's accelerated eye movement while being transported by car. Pallasmaa invites the passengers to get out and feel the air and sun, as well as setting up a situation for contemplating the passage of time by exploring materials and light. The six slender plaza columns are made of the different kinds of granite found in the stone wall of the academy, whose geographic location marks the southern limit of an Ice Age glacier. They were in fact cut from the Canadian bedrock from whence the glacier had originated (Figure 11.22).

The columns are compiled of parts that "grow" in the Fibonacci sequence, not only creating an upward sweep but referring as well to the golden mean (Ø), for which the sequence provides an analogy.[44] As placed, the columns form a sundial, with the points showing the position of the shadow of the midday sun (as it is reflected by a lens located on top of the second column) marked in different metals. Thus the design combines sensory aspects with an applied intellectual content: "Although the criteria applied to the design were the aesthetics of the eye and bodyscale, the outcome was an accurate cosmic device."[45]

In a sensitive article on Pallasmaa's approach to design generally, Peter MacKeith contends that his intent is to slow down our experience of the spaces that he has designed by the "thoughtful placement of architectural elements, by the careful use of coloured surfaces . . . by the considered juxtaposition of materials, by the subtle imposition of ordering geometries in both plan and section, and by the intense concentration on the precise crafting of each specific component and detail."[46] What *is* left to chance, he says, is the individual sensory experience, the tactile memories. "It is, then, the slowed passage of time that allows the tactile experience to resonate within one's consciousness long after departing from the design."[47]

This way of thinking is also extraordinarily appropriate for the design of a museum, as can be seen in Pallasmaa's design for the Sámi Museum in Finland. This museum celebrates the Sámi culture of Lapland (northern Finland) with the provision of exhibition space combined with a visitor's center, as well as caretaker's quarters. Some of the few old Sámi structures—log cabins, essentially—that have survived

Figure 11.22. Juhani Pallasmaa, Cranbrook Academy Driveway Square, Bloomfield Hills, Michigan, 1993. Photograph by Balthazar Korab. Reprinted by permission of Juhani Pallasmaa.

are located next to the museum and have obviously served as vernacular guides to his design (Figure 11.23). Joseph Giovannini succinctly states the cultural program: "The design demanded architectural character that was as strong as the old farm structures: simple materials, simply fitted to their function. It had to be a direct and unpretentious invention with strong cultural recall."[48]

While no one would mistake Pallasmaa's complex for a Sámi structure, it maintains its character. To account for the extremes of light in Lapland, Pallasmaa relies on a mixture of artificial and natural light sources, which have the effect of both referring to time passage and revealing the variety of materials that he uses. These include copper, concrete, plaster, glass, and—above all—a variety of woods. In fact, Pallasmaa used wood as the primary material: wood siding, a wood canopy, and wood studs stained red. His belief in the tactile qualities of wood can everywhere be found, perhaps an echo of the local dependence on it. Giovannini concludes: "Pallasmaa's sense of tactility and architectural presence lends his design the immediacy exhibited by the Sámi farm structures. . . . His building is a genuine salute to Sámi culture."[49] It is also a tribute to the sensory power of natural materials, and an implicit affirmation of the vernacular tradition.

Figure 11.23. Juhani Pallasmaa, Sámi Museum, Finland, 1998. Photograph by Jussi Tiainen. Reprinted by permission of Juhani Pallasmaa.

There are still other designers who have manipulated sensory data. In 1990 Peter Zumthor designed the Thermal Bath Vals, in Graubünden, Switzerland. He states:

> Right from the start, there was a feeling for the mystical nature of a world of stone inside the mountain, for darkness and light, for the reflection of light upon the water, for the diffusion of light through steam-filled air, for the different sounds that water makes in stone surroundings, for warm stone and naked skin, for the ritual of bathing. . . . So our bath is not a showcase for the latest aqua-gadgetry, water jets, nozzles or chutes. It relies instead on the silent, primary experiences of bathing, cleansing oneself, and relaxing in the water; on the body's contact with water at different temperatures and in different kinds of spaces; on touching stone.[50]

The cavelike rooms are sequenced and sized based on temperature, smell, and sound, and the body has direct contact with varying degrees of texture (Plate 12).

Raymund Ryan described Zumthor's design as "archaic and primary" and noted its extremely sensuous character: "Inside one apparently solid shaft is a chilly 10 degrees Celsius plunge pool, inside another an aromatic 30° C bath with petals; both are entered at right angles and surround the bather immediately in stone. You step down directly into the hottest pool (42° C), then rest on submerged shelves as small waves drop noisily into a deep perimeter trough."[51] In fact, the room plan is labeled by temperature notation. In his use of curving tunnels, tubular turnstiles, and shadowy corridors, Zumthor stresses the connections (or interstices) between the pool elements, and the clever use of dripping water and slivers of light provides signal and figural elements against an atmospheric field. Far from having the sculptural character that most structures aspire to, the building is hidden beneath a meadow, almost invisible to the casual observer. Zumthor relies instead on the pure sensory nature of his interior spaces to carry the structure's persona. Indeed, Zumthor's design is unusual in that it would score at the high intensity end of the *Sensory Slider* in all of the eight categories, if not equally.

Clearly there are certain architects who have made design decisions affirming the intrinsic value of sensory response. That is, their designs exploit the entire range of sensory information available. Of course, for such an approach to become general, we would need to have a broad and perceptive knowledge of the sensory environment, as well as methodologies to make that knowledge material. This is the subject of the next chapter.

12. Getting Somewhere

John Summerson observes, "Architecture, by virtue of its actual limitations, can exploit our capacity for dramatizing ourselves, for heightening the action of ordinary life; it can increase man's psychological stature to an angel's."[1] Well, perhaps; but not if we persist in the myth of architecture as *un machine d'habiter.* Indeed, writer Philippa Tristram observes that the house can never be regarded as a machine for living: "No building, however new, can be totally divided from its history, even where designers have forgotten it." Still, she continues: "The arrival of electricity, central heating, and television has changed our houses more than we assume. With the disappearance of the hearth as the major source of light, heat, and interest, the Victorian notion of 'home' is unavailable, and the relation of the house to the world outside is now of a different kind."[2] Of course, far more is involved than the hearth; television, personal computers, vocational insecurity, and the radical redefinition of family all contribute to our state of anomie.

But, say some analysts, the situation may be even more serious than the dissolution of cultural memory. In chapter 8 we referred to Meyrowitz's observations about the impact of electronic media on the separation of social place from physical place. "As a result of electronically mediated interactions, the definition of situations and of behaviors is no longer determined by physical location. To be physically alone with someone is no longer necessarily to be socially alone with them. . . . By altering the informational characteristics of place, electronic media reshape social situations and social identities."[3] Meyrowitz points out that electronic media today may be responsible for the trend toward fewer distinctions among places because they merge many social information systems and weaken the usefulness of places as secure information systems (182). "Television," he says, "not only demystifies the places actually exposed on it but also promotes a new sense of access and openness to all places" (181). Of course, "access and openness to all places" implies that no place is distinctive or special or empowering.

He of course refers to what we fill our homes *with*. The situation can be made worse by the ways in which we build those homes; that is, with little concern for sensory qualities, memory, or cultural affirmation. In his "Making Sense of Architecture," David Pearson notes Christopher Day's position that our surroundings can desensitize us morally and socially or support the inner processes of growth that are the foundation of health, contributing to stress or balance.[4] The question is whether or not these current trends are simply the distressing result of an increasingly pervasive technology on our spatial constructs. Is it, as some would maintain, an inherent characteristic of technology to be distressing?

In the epilogue to his intriguing work *The Urban Stage,* A. Richard Williams proposes certain courses of action if architecture is to be a "gentle, compassionate response to human needs." Thus he says that "the fine tuning of a setting requires a balancing act of design decisions over the full sensory realm, well beyond the static, fixed sets of present and past high fashion architecture, interior and urban design."[5] He notes that this should not be interpreted as a call for high technology, but at the same time observes that where appropriate, such technology ought not to be disdained.[6] In fact, technology has, on the positive side, given us the means of both identifying the sensory characteristics of spatial environments and using that information in their design. Unfortunately, design seldom avails itself of such data and views it as primarily visual when it does.

In fact, human sensory systems mediate four attributes of a stimulus capable of being quantitatively correlated with a sensation: modality, intensity, duration, and location. The last three attributes—intensity, duration, and location—apply to all sensory modalities and hence form the basis of most measures of the sensory environment. And despite our sensory abilities remaining relatively constant over the millennia, the means of obtaining relevant design information has radically increased in recent years.

In chapter 8 we discussed the work of two significant researchers, Buswell and Yarbus, and noted that the equipment used by the latter was a great improvement over that of the former. There have been many other developments since then. S. Carr, an urban designer, and D. Schlisser, a psychologist, conducted experiments in which they used a head-mounted eye-movement recorder. Using the eye movement device coupled to a movie camera that recorded their impressions, the subjects took a trip via elevated expressway into the center of a city. The object of the investigation was to discover the subject's interest in specific elements as measured by direction and duration. The researchers found that there was substantial agreement concerning items of visual interest, as well as a tendency to orient attention in similar directions.[7] What interests us, however, is the apparent usefulness of such a system in the assessment of the interior and exterior aspects of buildings.

Since then, the number of eye tracking devices has grown both in number and in capability. The Eyetracking Facility at the Beckman Institute for Advanced Science and Technology at the University of Illinois at Urbana-Champaign currently lists no fewer than six types of equipment. The most sophisticated of these is likely the fifth-generation Dual Purkinje Image Eye-tracker, which can sample eye position one thousand times per second without requiring any physical contact with the eyes. The most useful for design purposes—essentially an updated version of the recorder previously discussed—is the Eyelink Video Eye-tracker System. It is a lightweight head-mounted eye-tracking system that samples eye position 250 times per second with spatial and temporal resolution nearly as effective as the Purkinje Eyetrackers.[8] Some of the software developed at the Beckman Institute include programs to make dynamic changes in computer imagery in response to the observer's eye movements while recording the nature of those changes, programs to detect differences in eye movement patterns produced under different conditions, and programs to display images overlaid with the eye movement patterns of the observer.[9] One can only imagine what extraordinary design information might be generated by combining these advances with the capability of immersive virtual reality.

Of course, most complaints relating to building design concern common sensory changes to the local fabric. Put differently, the locale in which the building is constructed—the ground, if you will—is typically chosen by the occupants for its specific character and amenities. When a figural element, such as a new structure, reflecting neither the character nor the scale of the area is added, the result is an often visceral rejection of the addition. This is, of course, at the other end of the spectrum from the sort of research we just discussed. It moves from the esoteric to the prosaic—from fifth-generation eye-tracking devices to rational city building codes that place restrictions on gross disruptions of accepted ground texture. In Chicago, certainly, grotesque fifty-foot slabs of buildings that effectively obliterate both local residential scale and urban views are entirely ordinary. Consideration of how proposed additions might affect local housing stock should be an easy matter for architects and developers, as they are amenable to both scale model analyses and computer-generated modeling.

Seaside, in the Florida panhandle, has been one of the more intriguing residential developments of the past twenty years. An eighty-acre planned town, Seaside was designed by Andres Duany and Elizabeth Plater-Zyberk with the assistance of Leon Krier. Success depended on their ability to create a homogeneous fabric that nonetheless accommodated a certain amount of diversity. The result is a curious reflection of the traditional small southern U.S. town, but with a more complex—even urban—character, and boasting a more sophisticated level of architectural design than would ordinarily be the case. Perhaps the most unusual feature of Seaside is the relative proscription of automobiles and the entire infrastructure they necessitate. Indeed, everyone is guaranteed an unfettered (and quite charming) walk to the seaside pavilions, one of which we illustrated in chapter 2 (Figure 2.1). In fact, much of the planning effort went into providing street vistas that terminate at points of architectural or geographic interest, and multiple connections to various points of the town. We are interested here, however, in the mechanisms that were employed to guide the town's development without their resulting in a stifling similarity of housing stock.

Richard Sexton notes that Seaside is composed of eight defined areas, each with a prescribed house prototype—height limits, buildable footprints, setbacks, and so forth—for the lots contained within them.[10] The approach that the designers used was to code building type rather than to zone building use. Sexton states: "The architectural diversity of Seaside houses is based on the prescriptions in the Seaside Urban Code, a document whose purpose is to establish a coherent building pattern of integrated use. . . . A further purpose of the code is to ensure that the details of a given building type are appropriate and compatible with neighboring houses. It is not, however, intended to mandate style."[11] This code has as its counterpart the construction regulations, which provide for a commonality of materials and roof types. Thus houses of familiar type, materials, and style form the basis for the community. The only element conspicuously missing is the effect of time passage, although it likely goes without saying that time itself will take care of that. Seaside should be even more interesting in another twenty years.

The point of interest for us is not whether Seaside itself can serve as a model for other communities; clearly it could do so only in a limited way. It is rather its emphasis on codifying building type for particular areas—neighborhoods, if you will— that we believe to be useful. In Chicago, this would have prevented grossly outscaled structures from marring neighborhood vistas, while permitting the earlier conversion of commercial buildings (such as loft spaces) to residential use. Nor do we believe that it is too late even now to employ this method, or some variant of it. It could apply not only to views but to thermal comfort (solar access and favorable wind conditions) and sonic conditions as well.

An example of this is the study conducted for the city of Toronto for use in reviewing its Master Plan for the Central Area (Cityplan '91), which investigated pedestrian thermal comfort on the streets, sidewalks, and open areas, and the effect of urban development on climatic conditions.[12] The study used wind tunnel studies, solar analyses, computer comfort simulations, and field measurements and evaluated ways of regulating the height and mass of future development in order to optimize microclimatic conditions for pedestrians (97). The study calls for mandatory street wall heights in the vicinity of open spaces to provide solar access and protection from the wind (97) (Figure 12.1). Such building coding would result in structures far more sensitive to the needs of the pedestrians who walk the streets, as well as guarantee some continuity in the urban fabric, while doing little to limit design creativity.

The solar access and wind patterns that this study addressed are increasingly a critical issue in large urban areas, especially where older structures are being demolished to make room for ever-taller buildings. The primary authors of the previous study, Edward Arens and Peter Bosselmann, earlier described a procedure to predict the thermal comfort of people in outdoor spaces in order to determine height and mass regulations in downtown San Francisco. Their paper, presented at the annual convention of the American Society of Civil Engineers, details a method based on a computer model of the human thermoregulatory system run on a typical year's hourly climate data, to produce the seasonally adjusted number of hours that comfort or discomfort are to be expected.[13] The climate data are then synthesized to take into account the city's influence on climate and are made distinct for seven separate areas. Each area is then assigned a comfort percentage based on wind results and sun shading patterns, which, in turn, can be used to mitigate such building regulations as are being considered by the city. Thus the procedure—elegantly described in their paper—provides designers and urban planning officials with quantified information about various building strategies.[14]

Such studies are hardly unique to North America. Ulla Westerberg in Sweden points out that despite all our advances in stretching our climatic limits via technology, "the external climate—sunshine and wind—represents natural values that continue to have a physical and symbolic meaning in our everyday lives."[15] Planning the outdoor climate means the influence on and by variations between sun and shadow, as well as wind velocity and type. Unfortunately, official weather maps, Westerberg points out, generally conceal those variations significant for individual activities and

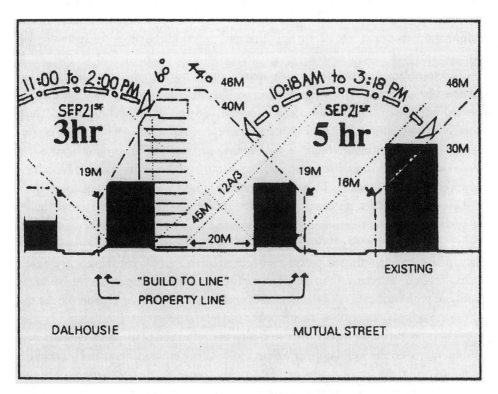

Figure 12.1. Toronto mitigated development chart, 1992. Courtesy of City of Toronto Urban Development Services, City Planning.

experiences. He goes on to say: "The interaction between man, climate and the physical structures has biological, material and cultural dimensions. The biological one, with which we integrate consciously and unconsciously, functions without regard to our wishes or choices and includes the climate's direct and physical influences on mental conditions, bodily activity and experiences" (51). Westerberg goes on to discuss the material dimension, which exists in physical structures, and the cultural dimension—what we know and have experienced. The physical dimension particularly interests us, as it is assumes sensory response.

In his paper, which was prepared with Sweden specifically in mind, Westerberg analyzes methods of, and criteria for, planning with reference to wind and solar access. In the case of the former, a "wind-comfort scale" was used to describe the effects of wind on people. Requiring maps and diagrams, but no extensive calculation (at least for Sweden), the scale is used to estimate windiness in terms of median velocities in eight directions, and to suggest means of wind reduction.[16] The scale takes into account factors such as base wind velocity, a reduction for the surface roughness of structures, and corrections for topography and building height. A second scale is used to calculate solar access, which in Sweden is formulated as the potential amount of sunshine at equinox. Thus the "sunshine planning diagram" indicates the length of shadows made by obstacles of different heights at different times of the day relative to equinox. Westerberg points out that in principle such a diagrammatic analysis can be designed for any time of the year. Combined, these two diagrams would provide information about any site before building, and the effect the proposed structure will have on that site.

The problem with most of the research on the thermal environment is that it has centered on thermal comfort (satisfaction with the thermal environment) or thermal neutrality (wherein one would prefer conditions to be neither warmer nor cooler). Forrest Wilson comments: "As with the auditory area of research, the approaches concentrate on preventing feelings of discomfort, rather than on producing positive responses—such as interesting, invigorating—to thermal conditions."[17] It is perhaps with this in mind that F. J. Langdon commends a new way of thinking about thermal comfort, in which an essentially passive model is replaced by "an active model of a self-regulatory system in open-ended interaction with the physical environment in forms governed by social constraints."[18] (He is speaking of conditions inside buildings, which have fared little better than the results of urban planning.) The result would replace the relatively narrow temperature-humidity ranges currently thought sufficient with wide ranges of temperatures (and other variables) and promote the use of more responsive control mechanisms for use by the occupant.

These are no small things. In a study on the influence of air ions, temperature, and humidity on the well-being of workers in an office environment, L. H. Hawkins found that all these factors had a significant effect on subjective evaluations of health and well-being.[19] Of course, these are not the only negative factors in modern office environments, but, Hawkins notes, "the present paper provides evidence that a lack of control of temperature and humidity will contribute to the day-to-day variation in complaints of illness and discomfort" (290). It is also apparent, he points out, that air ionization is a factor in the level of illness, both of itself and in combination with other variables (290). Now, these factors clearly reflected on the subjects' evaluation of their comfort and health; is it too much to suppose that such evaluations were extended to the spaces in which the discomfort occurred?

Visual and thermal factors are hardly the only sensory attributes of the built environment to invoke concern. In chapter 7, we noted Southworth's contention that sound constituted a major aspect of the urban experience. Thus sonic conditions are crucial to our evaluation of cities, and he makes several proposals to improve them. His 1969 study, conducted in Boston with both auditory and visual-auditory subjects, suggests certain types of action. In the first place, he says, before attempting sonic design, it will be necessary to confront the problem of existing city noise, which he defines as sound that is not culturally approved, is dull and uninformative, interferes with human activities, or is attention demanding because of high frequency or intensity.[20] Traffic, he points out, creates much of the noise in urban areas, and he suggests four solutions to mitigate it: careful location of noisy activities, new types of street design, special vehicle design, and the masking of existing noise by added sound (to break its monotony).

Beyond noise reduction, changes in the soundscape are needed to increase the identity of the soundscape, provide responsive settings that contain novel sounds, and increase the correlation between sound and the visible spatial and activity form. Southworth identifies three types of form elements that seem to have potential in terms of these needs: large, open spaces; small, sonically responsive spaces; and sonic signs (67). The last item is the most intriguing in his list. Sonic signs are a shorthand for an event or activity, as in clocks, sirens, or, for that matter, food sizzling on the grill. Southworth suggests that networks of commonly used streets could be programmed with sonic signs of unseen activities, and with sounds that prepare one for major events and decision points, which orient passersby or reinforce or explain (67). In short, he considers sound an active design parameter.

This raises the question of how we can know the sonic characteristics of neighborhoods. Southworth used a "sound event map," for which subjects recorded their impressions as they walked through the area. (Hence it was anecdotal in nature.) R. Murray Schafer says that because the soundscape is a field of interactions, to determine the ways in which sounds affect each another and ourselves is far more difficult than it would be in a laboratory situation. He suggests a system of notation that could be read and comprehended by professionals in many fields (including design), which he refers to as aerial sonography.[21] The isobel contour map is an example of aerial projection technique applied to sound intensity (Figure 12.2). It derives from the contour maps of mapmakers and meteorologists and "consists of hundreds or thousands of readings on a sound level meter averaged out to produce bars of equal intensity. . . . On such a map the quietest and noisiest sections of a territory can be immediately identified" (131). However, Schafer also recommends the sound event map, for which he provides as an example a city block that has been circled—and listened to—at two different times (Figure 12.3). The symbols for sound types are obvious enough; the dark areas reflect the character of the sound, whether it is soft, medium, or loud, and are tabulated to show activity and intensity (267).

These sorts of diagrams pertain to larger areas or neighborhoods. The problem changes somewhat when it is a building under discussion. Rubin and Elder state: "To describe design goals for the auditory environment in the household . . . one must first determine the nature of the activities to be performed, and the possible impact of the auditory environment. . . . One would then tentatively plan where these activities are likely to be performed in order to minimize conflicts among incompatible ones."[22] The activities that they describe are the ordinary actions of everyday life, such as reading, talking, eating, sleeping, listening to music, performing household tasks, and so forth. Their commonsense recommendation is to separate noise-producing equipment and activities from those spaces requiring quiet. This raises the question

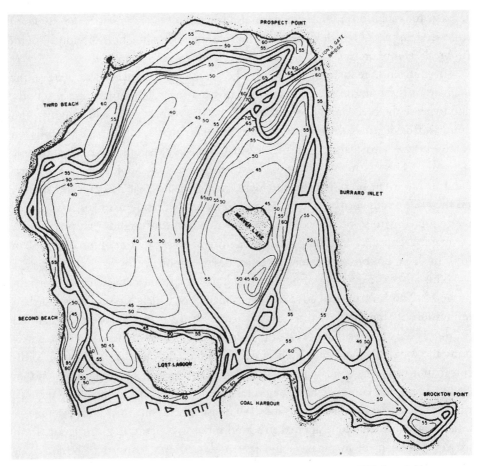

Figure 12.2. R. Murray Schafer, isobel map of Stanley Park, Vancouver, British Columbia, 1977. From R. Murray Schafer, *The Tuning of the World*. Copyright 1977, 1994 by R. Murray Schafer.

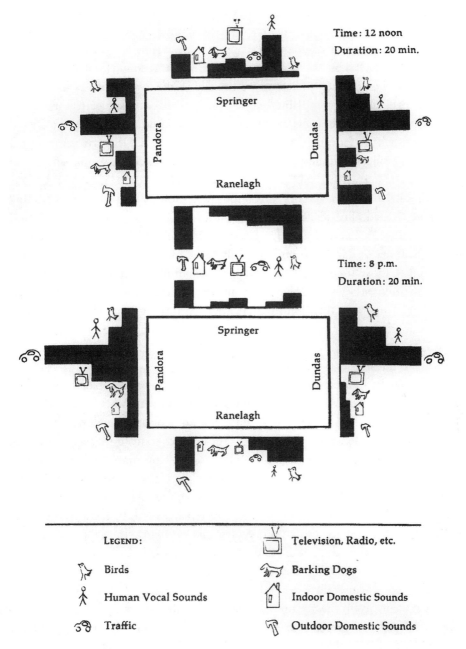

Time: 12 noon
Duration: 20 min.

Time: 8 p.m.
Duration: 20 min.

LEGEND:

Birds

Human Vocal Sounds

Traffic

Television, Radio, etc.

Barking Dogs

Indoor Domestic Sounds

Outdoor Domestic Sounds

Figure 12.3. R. Murray Schafer, sound map of city block, 1977. From R. Murray Schafer, *The Tuning of the World.* Copyright 1977, 1994 by R. Murray Schafer.

of how one is to precisely know how noisy a particular activity is. The available criteria tend, on one hand, to describe the acoustic environment of spaces, and, on the other, the noise transmission characteristics of building components and their materials. And there are many such guides available to designers from corporations and governmental agencies. The authors caution, however, that the adequacy of these tools depends on how they relate to the activities to be performed, the human behavior that takes place.[23] Thus both noise criteria curves and sound transmission class ratings will need to be used judiciously, especially as they were both developed for the criterion of "minimal complaints" rather than optimal acoustic performance.

A fairly simple "Noise Assessment Guideline" has been developed by the United States Department of Housing and Urban Development (HUD) to assess the overall noise level of a site. Rubin and Elder point out that it is really a simplified version of the technique known as the "Walk-Away Test," designed to measure speech intelligibility (136). To perform the test, a 100-foot tape measure and unfamiliar reading material are needed. The reader backs away until the listener can only understand the occasional word. Because noise levels vary over time, multiple tests are necessary, especially at times of day when noise is likely to be most severe and at times when noise would be most annoying. Unfortunately, the authors point out, "the design of acoustic environments which enhance or support activities has not received much research attention," and the "information available dealing with the *disruption* of activities in buildings by noise is not much better" (141). The reason for this, as virtually everyone concerned seems to agree, is that knowledge of positive sonic design has largely been lost.

Unfortunately, information dealing with odor is even scarcer. Not only are the techniques and technical equipment primitive compared to what is available for visual and auditory studies, but even a universal nomenclature is nonexistent. We discussed odor at some length in chapter 7, but here we want to suggest a measurement device of use to design. The Copley International Corporation devised an odor test for use in a national study on air pollution for the United States Environmental Protection Agency (EPA). Training sessions were conducted with the individuals who were to serve as panel members, using reference standards. Field studies then took place—near refineries and a rendering plant—in which the subjects recorded odor intensities relative to the four-point dilution scale used in the laboratory (201). In the field a scentometer was used as a measurement instrument, which allowed the subjects to cross-check impressions back in the laboratory.[24] It can be seen that the measurements made by the scentometer are essentially useless by themselves; it is rather the human interpretation of the data that has relevance. In fact, all the odor measurement studies that we are aware of rely on subjective responses expressed in words. While we see nothing wrong with human beings responding as such, it does make generalization difficult. This also helps to explain why the majority of these studies—like those for sound—concentrate on ways to alleviate the negative conditions rather than emphasize the positive opportunities.

This has not stopped people from trying to exploit odor's powerful capacities. In chapter 7 we noted Shimizu of Japan, a corporation that manufactures scent distribution systems using a building's ventilating system. In the United States, Dexster Smith and Joel Lloyd Bellenson have founded a company called DigiScents to provide odor on call. In an article for *Wired,* Charles Platt comments that the founders "claim they've developed a highly secret process to encode odors as digital data. Just as we can download digitized music and play it through speakers attached to a computer, we should soon be able to acquire online scent data that a little gadget can play back as smells."[25] A small box with a vent is attached to a computer, which sends signals to heat the small vials of oils in the box. Mixing complete, the box emits the selected odor. Smith and Bellenson believe that "scentography" will transform the entertainment industry. Platt notes that smell bypasses our conscious brain and communicates directly through the limbic system (discussed in chapter 7). Hence, he says, "It's an opportunity for filmmakers, advertisers, and Web designers to evoke emotions that are literally uncontrollable. That's the power—and perhaps the danger—of communication via smell."[26] As this is not the only attempt being made to incorporate odor into communication devices, we will almost certainly see more use made of odor in the future.[27]

There are many ways of measuring aspects of the haptic and basic-orienting systems as well, ranging from the anthropometric data that informs ergonomics, to tactile studies (including temperature analyses), to field studies of building movement and vibration. There are so many, in fact, that entire books have been compiled with the resulting data, and handbooks detailing standards are commonplace. As the population ages, data will become increasingly vital. And to reiterate, this is *all* sensory data under discussion. At the outset of his book, Forrest Wilson observes: "The meanings in our surroundings, the significance of form, line, color are consciously pursued by artists, but below the surface, in the atavistic stirrings of our subconscious, the meanings in the jumble of built form that surrounds us nag at our consciousness spurred by all the primordial fears that directed our senses in the first line of defense against lurking fang and claw."[28] At the close of the book, he says: "What kind of architecture will we fashion when we realize that the question is not art or architecture but humankind itself?"[29] This is likely the real value of the instruments available to discern the characteristics of our sensory environments. Of course, the will to use these instruments and data requires sensitivity on the parts of designers, developers, and politicians.

Not only has technology altered the ways in which we understand spaces, but it has provided increasingly sophisticated tools with which to design them. We are not referring here to the various computer design and drawing systems (CADD) that have become ubiquitous in architectural offices. These are, for the most part, simply electronic extensions of the visualization processes that have been used for hundreds of years. As such, they do little to ameliorate the fundamental design contradiction. That is, designs intended to be experienced in three dimensions are conceived in sketches, elaborated in plan, elevation, and section, presented in perspectives, and specified in technical drawings—all two-dimensional techniques.[30] In this manner have the visual "truths" relied on by artists been extended to architectural design.[31]

In chapter 6 we discussed Edward R. Tufte's position that although we travel through a perceptual world of three dimensions, the world portrayed on our informational displays—*flatland*—is two-dimensional. And "flatland" is an apt description of current architectural communication, whether on paper or monitors or in photographs. As Juhani Pallasmaa pithily notes, "The architecture of our time is turning into the retinal art of the eye. Architecture at large has become an art of the printed image fixed by the hurried eye of the camera. The gaze itself tends to flatten into a picture and lose its plasticity; instead of experiencing our being in the world, we behold it from outside as spectators of images projected on the surface of the retina."[32]

We have already discussed the highly ocularcentric relationship that developed between the observer and the observed, in large measure the result of Renaissance systems of perspective. Edmund N. Bacon has referred to this as the "tyranny of the single point-of-view of perspective," which, we note, has become the basis for many architectural assumptions.[33] The current tools and techniques of the design profession have had a profound influence, with the use of drawn plan, elevation, and section, and foam core models typically resulting in buildings conceived as an assemblage of flat planes set at ninety-degree angles. Nor are most of the available computer programs capable of putting into drawn specifications the complex layering and compound curves possible when advanced modeling techniques are used. There are, of course, notable exceptions. Frank Gehry's handcrafted models, for example, have been converted into rather dynamic architecture by the computer program CATIA, commonly used by the automobile and aerospace industry to design cars and supersonic jets.[34] Gehry's studio has extensive model-making facilities, and thus the ability to produce both scale building models and full-scale mock-ups. In fact, he is known for his use of models at different scales in the evolution of a particular design.

The problem inherent in this approach is that converting the complex three-dimensional models that Gehry creates into the two-dimensional construction drawings needed for obtaining contractors' cost estimates is time-consuming, costly, and unnecessarily complex. In 1990 Gehry's staff began looking for software that could translate the complex 3-D models without limiting Gehry's physical-model-based design process itself.[35] As CATIA has the capacity to define surfaces with descriptive, geometrical, and mathematical formulas amenable to industrial fabrication, Gehry used it in the design of the Guggenheim Museum in Bilbao, Spain (Figure 8.3). In fact, it was used to define all the complex surfaces of the 24,000-square-meter facility, after which Gehry integrated the application of CATIA models for construction and fabrication with the production of traditional construction documents in Auto-CAD. This required a complex translation using an in-house IGES process. Interestingly, it was the CATIA model containing face and surface elements that was sent to the machine shop. Thus Gehry uses CATIA as an intermediary process between finished model and initial construction drawings, after which he completes the project with the more prosaic computer usage.

More recently, Gehry used CATIA to design the Experience Music Project (EMP), a museum in Seattle devoted to the history of rock and roll. Its rather unconventional multicurved form—suggestive of the shapes found in a guitar—uses curved steel ribs that support a steel mesh substrate for a five-inch layer of shotcrete topped by two inches of insulation. The exterior consists of metal panels attached to aluminum framing supported on steel pedestals, differentially rising above the shotcrete. The program allowed Gehry's model to be digitized into an electronic model, and the data used to develop the specific design of the metal skin, structural concrete and steel elements, and routing for mechanical and electrical systems.[36] The exterior skin is particularly complex, consisting of about 20,000 pieces of trapezoidal-shaped metal sheets, formed into 3,180 panels, none of which are identical. The fabricator, A. Zahner Co., paid CATIA a compliment by noting that the project would have been impossible without the program to create a surface model.[37] Thus CATIA, in its ability to efficiently and accurately model three-dimensional material, represents a major advance in the ability of architects to complete designs previously thought too complex to be realized.

Architectural critic Paul Goldberger comments: "By the standards of a new generation, Gehry is old-fashioned. He has always designed in his head, put his ideas down on paper, and developed them further by playing with wood and foam models."[38] Goldberger is referring to the fact that Gehry only involves the new computer systems after the design is pretty much set in his mind. This is quite different from designing directly on computers and, perhaps more important, permitting the computer to become an active participant in the process. Goldberger made his comment in an article for *The New Yorker,* in which he looks critically at an exhibition titled "Folds, Blobs, and Boxes: Architecture in the Digital Era."[39] The exhibition goes far, he says, towards demonstrating the nature of the new aesthetic generated by technology, and how it relates to architecture of the past. While the visual character of the projects tends to fall into the categories denoted in the exhibition's title, Goldberger notes that the similarities outweigh the differences; to wit, they all consist of self-referential, abstract shapes.[40] He notes that the computers produce shapes of extraordinary complexity, and, moreover, they are perfect shapes seemingly easy to achieve: "Digital architecture has little patience for funkiness, for casualness, for incompleteness. It is a celebration of surfaces" (98).

It is not our intention to become involved in a discussion of these designs as architecture in the conventional sense, for many—perhaps most—of these projects clearly exist in a theoretical form. It is perhaps for this reason that Joseph Rosa, curator of the show, says: "Terms such as beauty, scale and proportion that were once used to describe the massing, articulation, and texture of predigital architecture have given way to adjectives like smooth, supple, and morphed, derived from digital-age vernacular" (98). But surely there is a difference between these sets of terms, if only because the former have for millennia developed a rich content; it is the difference, perhaps, between nouns and adjectives. One of these designs is Greg Lynn's Embryologic House, which Goldberger refers to as a prototype for mass-produced houses in which he used a software system that helped him generate variations on a blob (98). In fact, Lynn himself has used the word "blob" to describe the amorphous shapes that often characterize the new computer-generated designs where the compound curves, liquidity, and mutability strangely suggest no structure is necessary at all.

The Embryologic House offers an opportunity to examine the theoretical position that underlies Lynn's design. The key to this shell-like structure is to understand it as the product of "a rigorous system of geometrical limits that liberate an exfoliation of endless variations."[41] Thus this house form has a fundamentally generic character, without any two ever being identical. On the contrary, he conceives of it as adapting to a vast number of social, climatic, and functional contingencies. More specifically: "The variations in specific house designs are sponsored by the subsistence of a generic envelope of potential shape, alignment, adjacency and size between a fixed collection of elements."[42] Window and door openings do not appear as such; rather, their function is accommodated by "tears, shreds and offsets." The house, as one might expect from such an open-ended formulation, has a primitive character, not unlike a trilobite, which the house resembles. The means of its generation, on the other hand, are quite sophisticated. Lynn's own Web site states: "The office views the incorporation of state of the art hardware and software—*SGI Indigo* and *Indigo Extremes,* running *Alias, Wavefront* and *SofImage*—as a set of tools to investigate architectural performance within the framework of theories based on performance parameters only now being theorized in architecture."[43]

Some of Lynn's other design theories are quite interesting. In his *Animate Form,* he suggests that because of architecture's dedication to permanence, it remains a mode of thought based on the inert; that even more than shelter, architects are supposed to provide culture with stasis.[44] Thus the architectural obsession with formal purity. In design fields other than architecture, space is considered to be an environment of force and motion, so that "form can be shaped by the collaboration between an envelope and the active context in which it is situated."[45] Thus a dynamically conceived architecture may be shaped by the virtual motion and force of its environment without altering its basic form. He proposes a proactive, contextual architecture that arranges itself in a manner best suited to interaction with dynamic forces.

Of course, research on the ways in which large urban structures can be designed to interact actively with the climatic conditions of their site is an ongoing concern in architecture already.[46] That is, design that sympathetically resonates with the conditions of its environment is already being examined in situations where self-referential, structural concerns once dominated. But one might also examine the vernacular construction techniques extant in any geographic area in order to see millennia of social-climatic collaboration at work. Nor do vernacular buildings, even those located in similar climates, necessarily resemble each other except in their dedication to appropriateness of construction technique and materials. In the June 2001 issue of *National*

Geographic, an article featured the west African city of Djénné, a city built of mud brick that is replastered annually.[47] The result is a remarkable and elegant group of buildings in sub-Saharan and North African style that the centuries of plastering by master masons have turned into a kind of free-form fantasy. And despite some similarities in appearance, this is not "blob" architecture but a continuously evolving, fully sensory, culturally revered building form.[48]

While we understand the fascination with the seemingly endless possibilities that "digital architecture" offers, we are troubled by the theoretical design approach, in which the goal is not the desirable but the possible. Nor are the results, to the degree that they can be judged as habitable built form, an improvement over theory. The designs that result are, for the most part, as devoid of memory, cultural reference, and positive sensory characteristics as the products of the modernist impulse that preceded them. Thus we regard them as the products of an alien procedure. While programs such as CATIA are used at the end of the creative process to enable construction, these newer digital programs are involved at the beginning. They are, moreover, extraordinarily sculptural in nature, encapsulating the worst aspects of the modeling process by desensitizing architects to the smells, textures, sounds, and movement within the environment.

But there are even newer technologies that *do* permit a multisensory understanding of spatial design, as well as the ability to sketch in space. Because new tools such as the CAVE and Infinity Wall allow us to design in three-dimensional, multisensory environments, they surpass both the desktop computers that are simple extensions of the drafting board and the animated modeling systems that the digital architects use.[49] The concept of the CAVE was developed by Tom DeFanti and Dan Sandin in 1991 at the University of Illinois Chicago's Electronic Visualization Laboratory (EVL). It was here that the first CAVE was built in 1992. (The second CAVE was built by the National Center for Supercomputing Applications, located on the University of Illinois Urbana-Champaign campus.) In 1995 EVL developed the ImmersaDesk, a portable virtual reality drafting table.[50]

The CAVE consists of three screens arranged to create a ten-foot cube placed within a darkened thirty-by-thirty-foot room. High-performance graphics computers generate stereoscopic, high-resolution, full-color images that are sent to three rear projectors and one projector aimed at a Mylar mirror. Ten people wearing liquid crystal shutter glasses can enter and walk freely within this environment (Figure 12.4). Their bodies are surrounded by the images, which can be directed with a handheld device.[51] It is the gradual inclusion of the other, nonoptical senses in this spatial construct that interests us, however.

William Sherman and Alan Craig, senior research programmers at the National Center for Supercomputing Applications (NCSA) offer the following definition of *virtual reality:* "a medium composed of highly interactive computer simulations that sense the user's position and replace or augment the feedback of one or more senses— giving the feeling of being immersed, or being present in the simulation."[52] They point out that a typical VR system will substitute at least the visual stimuli, with sound frequently provided as well. Data, or "phantom," gloves allow for detection of textures, as well as other physical interaction with the virtual world. Thus planes exhibit the tactile characteristics that they are programmed to have. Experiments are also being conducted on how to simulate the kinesthetic sensations of movement over distance, and up stairs and ramps. Directional sound is reproduced by multiple stereo speakers, which permit the sonic location of moving objects. Finally, it is probable that air movement and odor can also be introduced for a truly multisensory environment, although this aspect remains experimental.

"CAVE" is an acronym for Cave Automatic Virtual Environment. It is also descriptively appropriate. In it, one is removed from all normal light sources, and thus any sense of time. Richard Powers opens his *Plowing the Dark* with its poetic description:

> *This room is never anything o'clock.*
>
> *Minutes slip through it like a thief in gloves. Hours fail even to raise the dust. Outside, deadlines expire. Buzzers erupt. Deals build to their frenzied conclusions. But in this chamber, now and forever combine.*
>
> *This room lingers on the perpetual pitch of here. Its low local twilight outlasts the day's politics. It hangs fixed, between discovery and invention. It floats in pure potential, a strongbox in the inviolate vault.*

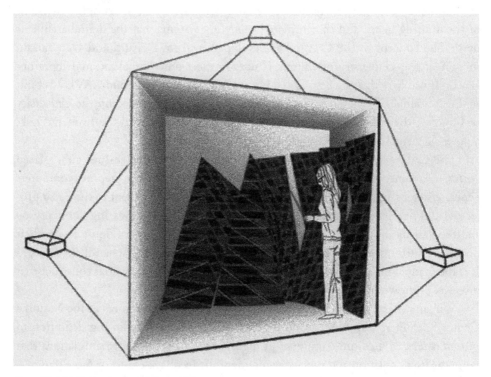

Figure 12.4. CAVE. Drawing by Joy Monice Malnar.

Time does not keep to these parts, nor do these parts keep time. Time is too straight a line,
too limiting. The comic tumbling act of causality never reaches this far. This room spreads
under the stilled clock. Only when you step back into the corridor does now revive.[53]

The CAVE was actually developed for the scientific visualization of biological materials and large data sets such as are necessary for weather prediction and the study of the solar system. Rachael Brady, former director of the Integrated Systems Laboratory at the Beckman Institute, was instrumental in the development of CRUMBS and was able to add functions that allowed an interactive virtual environment application designed to explore, mark, and measure three-dimensional fibrous material to serve as a sketching tool for design.[54] ShadowLight-Mirage, a recent development, was designed by Kalev Leetaru with assistance from his supervisor Alan Craig and has extended the ability to directly model large complex buildings at full scale at the University of Illinois School of Architecture.[55] Programs under development will permit the creation of a single room—or an entire building—within the ten-foot cube.

In 1988 Edmund Bacon wrote, "The hologram, each fragment of which contains within it the whole, frees us from the tyranny of the single point-of-view of perspective. . . . It is holistic and simultaneous. At least in the not too distant future it will give a very practical aid to design."[56] He further noted that it would soon be possible to draw three-dimensionally into the hologram and transmit design information directly to both the builder and the client. In fact, the future he described is arriving now with virtual reality immersion, an even more useful tool than Bacon had envisioned.

Karen A. Franck notes that the world of virtual reality does not replicate experiences of gravity, density, weight, mass, and distance. "The objects we see or create and the spaces we occupy in virtual worlds have very different visual and kinesthetic qualities from those in the physical world. Objects/spaces can appear, disappear, occupy the same location, and change appearance instantaneously. . . . There is both a fluidity and speed of movement that are more akin to dreams than waking life."[57] There is a great deal of truth in Franck's observations, although recent advances have brought an increased physicality to the virtual world. Moreover, the user interface is being enhanced at a remarkable rate, especially with the latest-generation VR environments. In fact, since 1998, five six-sided VR environments have been constructed worldwide.[58]

As an immersive environment, the CAVE can perhaps bring us back to Geoffrey Scott's "architecture of humanism," where he speaks of an architecture in which "arches 'spring,' vistas 'stretch,' domes 'swell,' Greek temples are 'calm,' and baroque facades are 'restless.'" It is his view that "the whole of architecture is, in fact, unconsciously invested by us with human movement and human moods. . . . *We transcribe architecture into terms of ourselves.* . . . This is the humanism of architecture. The tendency to project the image of our functions into concrete forms is the basis, for architecture, of creative design."[59]

Robert Ousterhout has speculated about how other cultures have designed buildings in the past. "Following contemporary conventions, we might automatically assume that the process began with a drawing. But, for medieval Europe, Byzantium, and the Islamic world, however, the historical evidence most often indicates the absence of architectural drawings."[60] His research has in fact revealed evidence that ashes and cottonseed were laid out on one building site and then ignited to see the flames provide a three-dimensional illustration of the proposed building. It is within reason that VR technology can advance to the point where we could similarly project a fully sensory image of the conceived building on its site. But, of course, the CAVE is not yet the Holodeck featured in *Star Trek.*

What exactly is its future? Design students at the University of Illinois at Urbana-Champaign have been exploring the potential of this technology. Comparative analyses of traditional perspective drawings, animated computer screen models, and full-scale environments have made students aware of the need to design haptically. This sensitivity may be gauged by the "sensory experience chart" prepared by an architecture student, in which the architectural experience is seen as a story, with a beginning, middle, and end, each with its own sensory qualities (Figure 12.5).[61] Other students have used the CAVE technology to explore spatial concepts and reactions to color. These are, of course, simply the first steps of an ongoing process. By collaborating with computer researchers, architects can create applications that address particular design questions, for example, enclosure, entry, and path distinctions, surface texture, and so forth (Figure 12.6). Plans are currently under way to account for daily and seasonal light incidence patterns, as well as seasonal weather characteristics.

We have focused on these immersive VR developments as an affirmation that technology per se is not the problem; on the contrary, much is happening that is potentially liberating.[62] The problem is a flawed typology based on abstract elements given rectitude by a belief that they are inherently pure, even healthy. Nor are we claiming that various forms of new technology will be able to rectify the situation by themselves. These are simply the tools of our good intentions. What is required is a different view of what constitutes design. As we have argued, throughout history there have been designers who have made use of sensory data (with and without technology). We are thinking at the moment of the figures from our own lifetimes responsible for a broadly humane design approach. Luis Barragán has shown how color and texture can be put to intense effect, Charles W. Moore has confirmed how central objects are to the designed environment, and Carlo Scarpa has pointed to the design potential of elements such as light, water, and time itself.

We admire individuals for different reasons, but the common feature of their work is the emphasis on the sensory and mnemonic aspects of architecture, as well as respect for vernacular antecedents. They include individual designers like Steven Holl, Juhani Pallasmaa, Peter Zumthor, and Laurie Baker, and design teams like Enrique Browne and Borja Huidobro, Peter Stutchbury and Phoebe Pape, and Jacques Herzog and Pierre de Meuron. All do "cutting edge" design, by which it is usually

SENSORY CHART . . . JOURNEY OF SPACE

Architecture can be interpreted as a story, with a beginning, middle, and end. There are various haptic clues to aid one in differentiating qualities of space. This chart is intended to provide the occupant with questions pertaining to seven systems of sensual appreciation. These questions will lead to answers that can help the occupant gain a full sensory interpretation of the architectural space at hand.

Approach	Entry	Interior Space 1.2.3...	Exit	Path Out
Auditory System • are sounds in open/close space • where are keynote sounds • what are the soundmarks	**Auditory System** • what sounds signify enclosure • can you sense new scale	**Auditory System** • are the sounds contained/dispersed • are there new keynote sounds	**Auditory System** • is there a blend of interior/exterior sounds	**Auditory System** • is the path out similar to the approach • can you sense what direction to proceed
Haptic System • is ground hard/soft • is ground one/many surfaces	**Haptic System** • did the ground surface change • what materials enclose you • what did you touch upon entry	**Haptic System** • do the materials want to be touched • are the surfaces hard/soft/edges/curves	**Haptic System** • does the ground prepare you for exiting the space • are there new materials	**Haptic System** • is ground hard/soft • is ground one/many surfaces • is the ground like the interior/exterior
Taste/Smell System • is the air salty/dry/wet • is there nostalgia in the smell • why is the smell specific to the place	**Taste/Smell System** • is the air manmade/natural • did the taste change • are smells eliminated/enhanced	**Taste/Smell System** • does the air taste different room to room • is there a different smell in each room	**Taste/Smell System** • is the air closer to inside or outside smells • is it distinctive	**Taste/Smell System** • is the air like the approach • why is the smell specific to the space
Basic-Orientation System • are you the north/south/east/west • is the ground high/low • is the space near the edge of land/inland	**Basic-Orientation System** • what elements direct • are you higher/lower than at the approach	**Basic-Orientation System** • are the spaces aligned with the north/south/east/west • do you feel lost • is the space warm/cold	**Basic-Orientation System** • are you facing the same direction as the beginning • do you know what is next	**Basic-Orientation System** • are you north/south/east/west • is the ground high/low • is the space near the edge of land/inland • where are you in relation to the traveled space
Temperature/Humidity System • is the space hot/cold/damp/dry • is the air heavy or light	**Temperature/Humidity System** • did the temperature/humidity change • is the space better/worse for comfort	**Temperature/Humidity System** • is the space warm/cold • is the humidity good for breathing	**Temperature/Humidity System** • is the temperature like the interior/exterior	**Temperature/Humidity System** • is the space hot/cold/damp/dry
Visual System • what colors surround the space • what shapes do you see • what scale is the space • is there manmade intervention	**Visual System** • what colors surround the space • what shapes do you see • what scale is the space • is there manmade intervention • what signifies a change in space	**Visual System** • what objects are included • are the objects part of the space or an addition to the space	**Visual System** • what colors surround the space • what shapes do you see • what scale is the space • what symbols identify the exit • what leads you out	**Visual System** • what colors surround the space • what shapes do you see • can you see where to go next

Figure 12.5. Marina Panos, sensory experience chart, 2001. Courtesy of Marina Panos, Chicago.

meant that it is well outside the mainstream. Time will correct that, of course, but we wish to mention a few of them here.

In 2001, architecture's most prestigious recognition, the Pritzker Prize, was awarded to Jacques Herzog and Pierre de Meuron. Their Dominus Winery in California is a result, they say, of their phenomenological approach to design.[63] Wilfried Wang points out that buildings in the United States typically depend on mechanical systems to maintain a constant room temperature, and thus design strategies that incorporate the actual walls for climate control are rarely employed. Not so with Herzog and de Meuron:

> For the facade, Herzog & de Meuron used metal grids combined to form baskets filled with stones. These stones form an inert mass in front of the inner building wall and insulate the interior spaces. A local basalt, ranging in color from dark green to black, was chosen to beautifully fit into the landscape. According to the spatial requirements, the gabions are filled at different densities. Thus, different zones are created in the masonry: in some places, it is totally impermeable, in others, daylight is allowed to enter into the interior space, and at night, the artificial light shines

Figure 12.6. Philip Covarrubias and Brandon Welborn, Thoreau Room. Courtesy of Philip Covarrubias and Brandon Welborn.

through to the outside. A stone weaving with varied transparency: more comparable to a skin than to a traditional stone wall.[64]

This is a unique approach that provides long-term energy efficiency while permitting the use of materials for their color, light, texture, and temperature control (Figure 12.7).

Enrique Browne and Borja Huidobro reinterpreted the paradigm of the Mediterranean pergola for use on a large-scale office high-rise located in Santiago, Chile. Such pergolas, a staple of vernacular buildings in hot, dry climates, are used to diffuse light and offer shade and are entirely typical of Santiago. This building is stepped back in three sections, each screened with two-to-four-story planted trellises based on pergolas. The plantings change color with the seasons, filter the heat and glare of the intense sun, and screen the noise from the busy main business district (Figure 12.8). The east elevation, which faces the mountains, is entirely glazed; the west facade is vulnerable to solar gain, and it is here that the plantings are employed. This approach has resulted in a 60 percent reduction in solar gain, as well as offering west-facing offices a green view.[65]

Figure 12.7. Jacques Herzog and Pierre de Meuron, Dominus Winery, California, 1998. Photograph by Margherita Spiluttini; copyright Margherita Spiluttini.

Figure 12.8. Enrique Browne and Borja Huidobro, Consorcio-Vida Offices, Santiago, Chile, 1993. Photograph by Guy Wenborne. Courtesy of Enrique Browne.

The architecture of Peter Stutchbury and Phoebe Pape reflects a respect for the Australian landscape, as seen in their design for the Olympic Archery Park in Homebush Bay outside Sydney. Thus they describe their concept:

> We have always seen the building as the restrained formal partner of the land. . . . The awning roof, not dissimilar to the mighty "razor blade" roofs of inland Australia, is a direct solution to shelter. . . . the site has been spatially qualified by the placement of two linear pole forests, which run in decreasing heights from north to south and create deliberate physical boundaries that challenge human scale and introduce a person dramatically to the site.[66]

In fact, Stutchbury has done extensive study of indigenous buildings with particular concern for their ability to use natural climate control (Figure 12.9). The result, according to James Weirick, is that the building and its landscape "are simply beautiful forms, poised and balanced in relation to each other, charged with an inner energy and expressing one idea: excellence."[67] This makes the building a fine metaphor for the sport of archery as well.

Figure 12.9. Sydney Olympics Archery Centre, Homebush, Australia, by Stuchbury and Pape, 2000. Photograph by Patrick Bingham-Hall; copyright 2002.

As will become evident, there have been more than a few site-sensitive designs realized in the Southern Hemisphere of late. The work of Fraser Cameron in New Zealand represents such a trend. He received the 2001 NZIA-RESENE local Waikato Bay of Plenty Award for Architecture for four of his buildings. Three of them are residential in nature—interesting in their own right—and one is essentially civic, a pavilion and fish-viewing conservation station. Because diminutive, understated designs seldom receive accolades, we especially note the latter, his Tongariro National Trout Centre Observation Chamber in Turangi, near Lake Taupo (Figure 12.10). The early 2002 issue of *New Zealand Architecture* states that the "well-handled forms sympathetically integrate the structure with the natural environment allowing light and a sense of openness within the underground space."[68] In fact, the underwater observation area, deck, and curved roof forms blend almost seamlessly into the surrounding plant life, which is as it should be. The review praises the precise detailing and use of materials as well; indeed, such praise justly characterizes all four of the reviews.

One of the more interesting figures in architecture practices in India, where he has long attempted to use the local traditions, craftsmanship, and materials of that country. Laurie Baker's pragmatism is demonstrated by his sympathy with the local conditions of topography and climate, which in his estimation produced a natural building type. Sloping roofs, ground level wall openings, circular structures, and the use of the *jali* (small wall openings that allow air to circulate) all typify Indian buildings for excellent reasons. This is particularly true in the state of Kerala, where Baker lives. Baker

Figure 12.10. Tongariro National Trout Centre observation chamber, Turangi, New Zealand, by Fraser Cameron Architects, 2001. Photograph by Frank Vodvarka; copyright 2002.

excels in combining these vernacular elements with his own invention and a real concern for the client. Mohsen Mostafavi states: "Baker pays great attention to the specific requirements of his clients. Rather than conceiving of architecture as *Gesamtkunstwerk*—a total work of art dominated by the architect—he constructs an architecture that, in its attention to the desires and habits of its occupants, becomes a stage for their own everyday performance."[69] Baker has, over the years, also maintained a cost sensitivity such that the best possible building can be provided for the least money.

Baker's own house, built with salvaged materials, illustrates a responsive growth over a thirty-year period. This has included old fish tiles, recycled roofing and dormer material, and the odd pieces of tile and stone. This method has the added result of being a "visual feast of different textures, and has a wonderfully tranquil feel about it."[70] The house has grown down the hill with each portion relating to the one that preceded it in four different stages, but the heart of it remains the veranda (Figure 12.11). Baker has thus combined his own British-trained design sensibility with a real appreciation for the local vernacular tradition and imbued the result with living memory. Quite a feat, not unlike Carl Jung's at Bollingen.

In fact, we began this book with an extended reference to Jung, particularly his concept of type and archetype. Carl Jung's house at Bollingen, built on the shore of Zurich's upper lake, is a structure built of archetypal form. Jung says: "I had to achieve a kind of representation in stone of my innermost thoughts and of the knowledge I had acquired . . . I had to make a confession of faith in stone."[71] This "confession" began in 1922 as a simple hut surrounding a hearth but was later altered to produce a low tower. He comments: "The feeling of repose and renewal I had in this tower was intense from the start. It represented for me the maternal hearth" (224). He added an annex in 1931, containing a "retiring room," and a courtyard and loggia by the lake in 1935. When his wife died in 1955, he added an upper story. Thus the building represents the work of almost thirty-five years (Figure 12.12). When Jung speaks of this building, it is with introspection:

> From the beginning I felt the Tower as in some way a place of maturation—a maternal womb or a maternal figure in which I could become what I was, what I am and will be. . . . There is nothing in the Tower that has not grown into its own form over the decades, nothing with which I am not linked. Here everything has its history, and mine; here is space for the spaceless kingdom of the world's and the psyche's hinterland. (226)

Throughout his descriptions of this remarkable house, Jung refers to the qualities of materials, textures, hearth light, and so forth. In fact, he made a point of including as few modern materials—or amenities, for that matter—as possible, including electricity. It is truly a house constructed of sensation and memory.

For the last twelve chapters, we have argued for an architecture that views the sensory response and memory of human beings as critical functions of the building,

Figure 12.11. Laurie Baker, view of veranda, the Hamlet, Trivandrum, Kerala, India, 1969. Photograph by Kenichi Suzuki, Shinkenchiku-sha.

and thus vital to the design process. We have suggested multiple ways in which sensory response can be calculated and, more importantly, predicted. We have supplied several schematics and some tools that can be used to design ends. And we have suggested ways in which our current (and near-future) technologies can aid in this process. Which of these tools and methods are employed, and to what degree, we leave to designers. But we implore designers to once again consider sensory response a primary consideration in the making of architecture, even as they once did.

When Alice ran into the Cheshire Cat, she thought to get some help in finding her way:

> "Would you tell me, please, which way I ought to walk from here?"
> "That depends a good deal on where you want to get to," said the Cat.
> "I don't much care where—" said Alice.
> "Then it doesn't matter which way you walk," said the Cat.
> "—so long as I get *somewhere*," Alice added as an explanation.
> "Oh, you're sure to do that," said the Cat, "if you only walk long enough."[72]

Well, just so. And this has been architecture's fate—for better *and* worse—for well more than a century now. But there are new social and cultural imperatives to bring about a design centered on the nature of human beings, and the means to accomplish it. At the least, a path is suggested that ought to get us *somewhere*.

Figure 12.12. The house of Carl G. Jung, Bollingen, Switzerland, 1922–1955. Copyright The Estate of C. G. Jung.

Notes

Preface

1. Rafael Moneo, "On Typology," *Oppositions* 13 (summer 1978): 27.

2. Ibid., 23.

3. Jean-Nicolas-Louis Durand, *Précis des leçons d'architecture données à l'École royale polytéchnique* (1802–1805), quoted in *Neoclassical and 19th Century Architecture*, by Robin Middleton and David Watkin (New York: Harry N. Abrams, 1980), 20.

4. Kent C. Bloomer and Charles W. Moore, *Body, Memory, and Architecture* (New Haven: Yale University Press, 1977), ix.

5. Ibid.

6. Vincent Scully, "Buildings without Souls," *New York Times Magazine*, 8 September 1985, 116.

7. E. V. Walter, *Placeways: A Theory of the Human Environment* (Chapel Hill: University of North Carolina Press, 1988), 21.

1. Spatial Constructs

1. Henry James, *Henry James on Italy* (New York: Barrie and Jenkins, 1988), 130.

2. Ibid. Indeed, so persuasive and meaningful is the space that to do anything in it was in itself consequential.

3. Gaston Bachelard, *The Poetics of Space,* trans. Maria Jolas (1958; Boston: Beacon Press, 1969), xxxi.

4. Ibid., xxxii.

5. Thomas Wolfe, *You Can't Go Home Again* (1934; New York: Harper and Row, 1973), 123.

6. Ibid., 122–23.

7. Jorge Luis Borges, "The Immortal," in *Labyrinths* (Middlesex, England: Penguin Books, 1970), 141.

8. Romedi Passini, *Wayfinding in Architecture* (1984; New York: Van Nostrand Reinhold, 1992), 2. Actually, Passini also notes three other possible derivations for the term: first, a dance pattern for the worship of an earth goddess, possibly Ariadne; second, a linguistic analysis based on Latin roots; and third, another linguistic analysis linking the term to megalithic cults. All refer to ancient phenomena, all are possible; but the derivation cited remains the most credible on both historical and linguistic grounds.

9. The City of the Immortals that Borges's protagonist has sought for so long ceased to exist some nine centuries previously, torn down by the race that built it. Indeed, it was these Immortals who consequently erected this second "mad city" with its labyrinths from the ruins, as both a parody and a temple of the "irrational gods who govern the world and of whom we know nothing." (The Immortals themselves had reverted to the form of troglodytes living in the caves that surrounded the city, lost to pure speculation of thought and indifferent to the physical world.)

10. Rafael Moneo, "On Typology," *Oppositions* 13 (summer 1978): 23.

11. Malcolm Quantrill, *The Environmental Memory* (New York: Schocken Books, 1987), 47.

12. Terrance Goode, "Typological Theory in the United States: The Consumption of Architectural 'Authenticity,'" *Journal of Architectural Education* (September 1992): 2.

13. Quantrill, *The Environmental Memory*, 81.

14. Ibid., 95. Thus Quantrill's understanding of architecture is that of socio-spatial construct, a built response to myth and ritual. The notion of cultural analysis through architectural classification is surely a familiar one.

15. Micha Bandini, "Typology as a Form of Convention," *AA Files*, no. 6 (1984): 73.

16. Ibid., 75.

17. Ahmet Gulgonen and François Laisney, "Contextual Approaches to Typology at the Ecole des Beaux-Arts," *Journal of Architectural Education* (1982): 26.

18. Ibid., 26. This is perhaps true of Durand—although it is at least arguable that the spatial and formal character of space also entered into his calculations—but is surely not so of Quatremère, whose view seems far more catholic. In any case, the authors are simply proposing a design strategy within an academic context that freely uses one, two, or all three of these categories.

19. Hassan Fathy, *Architecture for the Poor* (Chicago: University of Chicago Press, 1973), 24, found in Kathleen Dugas Arceneaux, "Value Based Opportunities in Architectural Education," in *Debate and Dialogue: Architectural Design and Pedagogy,* Proceedings of the 77th Annual Meeting of the Association of Collegiate Schools of Architecture, Chicago, ed. Tim Mcginty and Robert Zwirn (Washington, D.C.: Association of Collegiate Schools of Architecture, 1989), 13.

20. Alan Colquhoun, "Typology and Design Method," in *Meaning in Architecture,* ed. Charles Jencks and George Baird (New York: George Braziller, 1969), 275.

21. Jacques François Blondel, *Cours d'architecture* (Paris, 1771–1777), in Anthony Vidler, "The Idea of Type: The Transformation of the Academic Ideal, 1750–1830," *Oppositions* 8 (spring 1977): 101.

22. Vidler, "The Idea of Type," 95.

23. Blondel, *Cours d'architecture*, vol. 2, 229, in Vidler, "The Idea of Type," 99.

24. Quatremère de Quincy, *Encyclopédie méthodique 1* (1788), in Anthony Vidler, "Type: Quatremère de Quincy," *Oppositions* 8 (spring 1977): 147.

25. Quatremère de Quincy, in Vidler, "The Idea of Type," 104.

26. Jean-Nicolas-Louis Durand, *Recueil et parallèle des édifices de tout genre anciens et modernes* (1801), in Vidler, "The Idea of Type," 107.

27. Vidler, "The Idea of Type," 107.

28. Ibid. Vidler points out that Durand makes no mention of evolutionary theory, relying instead on the general idea of progress as related to architecture. But Durand's method and assumptions about organic growth both suggest the theory of evolution.

29. Jean-Nicolas-Louis Durand, *Précis des leçons d'architecture données à l'École Royale Polytéchnique* (1802–1805), vol. 1, in Middleton and Watkin, *Neoclassical and 19th Century Architecture,* 20. ["Soit que l'on consulte la raison soit que l'on examine les monuments, il est évident que plaire n'a jamais pu être son objet. L'utilité publique et de la société, tel est le but de l'architecture."]

30. Sergio Villari, *J. N. L. Durand (1760–1834): Art and Science of Architecture,* trans. Eli Gottlieb (New York: Rizzoli International Publications, 1990), 59.

31. Ibid., 60.

32. J. N. L. Durand, *Précis des leçons d'architecture,* in Villari, *J. N. L Durand,* 59.

33. Vidler, "The Idea of Type," 107.

34. Villari, *J.N.L.Durand,* 61.

35. Vidler, "The Idea of Type," 108. Vidler relates this anecdote as the remembrance, in 1810, of one of Durand's students.

36. Durand, *Précis de leçons d'architecture données à l'École Royale Polytéchnique,* vol. 2 (1805), 7. ["Que la disposition est dans toutes les cas la seule chose dont doive s'occuper l'architecte, si cette disposition aussi convenable et économique qu'elle peut l'être."]

37. Jean-Baptiste Rondelet, *Traité théorique et practique de l'art de batir,* vol. 1 (1802), in Middleton and Watkin, *Neoclassical and 19th Century Architecture,* 20. ["La théorie est une science qui dirige toutes les opérations de la pratique. C'est par le moyen de la théorie qu'un habile constructeur parvient à déterminer les formes et les justes dimensions qu'il faut donner à chaque partie d'un édifice en raison de sa situation et des efforts qu'elle peut avoir à soutenir, pour qu'il resulte perfection, solidité et économie."]

38. In fairness to Durand, it should be noted that he had conceived his system of basic elements placed in axial arrangement as a tool for educating his students at the Ecole Polytechnique. In any case, much of the support his system received came not from fellow architects but from engineers like Rondelet.

39. Hans Blumenberg, "Light as a Metaphor for Truth: At the Preliminary Stage of Philosophical Concept Formulation," in *Modernity and the Hegemony of Vision,* ed. David Michael Levin (Berkeley: University of California Press, 1993), 46. Blumenberg goes on to comment on how profound the confrontation between the Greek tradition, based on sight, and the Old Testament tradition, based on the Word, must have been.

40. Anthony Synnott, "Puzzling over the Senses: From Plato to Marx," in *The Varieties of Sensory Experience: A Sourcebook in the Anthropology of the Senses,* ed. David Howes (Toronto: University of Toronto Press, 1991), 62.

41. Ibid., 63.

42. Lest the utilitarian argument overawe the reader, it should be remembered that which sense is most useful depends in large measure on geographic and cultural conditions. For example, in areas with dense vegetation, smell and sound suddenly take on great importance and vision less.

43. We here refer to the new conception of a world in which all known elements could be ordered in a regular and predictable matrix, a system made to order for the absolutist rulers of the fifteenth and sixteenth centuries.

44. Marshall McLuhan, "The Gutenberg Galaxy," in *Essential McLuhan,* ed. Eric McLuhan and Frank Zingrone (New York: Harper Collins Publishers, 1995), 118.

45. Ibid., 117.

46. Aldo Rossi, *The Architecture of the City*, trans. Diane Ghirardo and Joan Ockman (Cambridge: MIT Press, 1982), 40. This became especially the case during the twentieth century when the role of architect became entwined, practically and ideologically, with that of engineer. It can be argued that the structural imperatives that characterize engineering increasingly dominated the traditional concerns of architecture, which during the nineteenth century only nominally recognized structural concerns. In this light, it seems reasonable that architects facing multiple demands on time and energy would turn to Durand's grid as design expedient, and pattern books as menu sources for the elements of design. Thus was the value of typology as a tool of expedience enhanced.

47. Carl G. Jung, *The Basic Writings of C. G. Jung*, ed. Violet Staub De Laszlo (1938; New York: Random House, 1959), 287.

48. Carl Gustav Jung, *Psychology and Religion* (New Haven: Yale University Press, 1938), 63.

49. Jung, *The Basic Writings of C. G. Jung*, 288.

50. Carl G. Jung, *Memories, Dreams, Reflections*, recorded and edited by Aniela Jaffe, trans. Richard and Clara Winston (1961; New York: Vintage Books, 1973), 392.

51. Jung, *Memories, Dreams, Reflections*, 392.

52. Jung, *Psychology and Religion*, 63.

53. Morris Philipson, *Outline of a Jungian Aesthetics* (Chicago: Northwestern University Press, 1963), 141.

54. Ibid., 142.

55. In the preface to his *Primitive Art*, the famed anthropologist Franz Boas states that as far as his experience dictates, "the mental processes of man are the same everywhere, regardless of race and culture." And in the conclusion, he asserts that formal principles—symmetry, rhythm, and emphasis of form—are "present in the art of man the world over." Thus Boas—in common with many anthropologists—assumes a common desire for aesthetic expression, as well as common standards and methods to achieve this.

56. Carl G. Jung, "The Spirit of Psychology," in *Spirit and Nature* (New York: Pantheon Books, 1956), 436.

57. In his *Outline of a Jungian Aesthetics*, Morris Philipson concludes that (1) if there are indeed such phenomena as symbols with prospective value, and (2) if the referents of such symbolic content cannot be reduced to instinct or environmental conditioning, then (3) "Jung's hypothesis of the source of such contents in a universally inheritable Collective Unconscious is as good, or as poor, a speculative suggestion for explanation as we have."

58. Jolande Jacobi, *Complex, Archetype, Symbol in the Psychology of C. G. Jung* (1957; Princeton, N.J.: Princeton University Press, 1959), 51–52.

59. Bettina L. Knapp, *Archetype, Architecture, and the Writer* (Bloomington: Indiana University Press, 1986), 192.

60. Jacobi, *Complex, Archetype, Symbol in the Psychology of C. G. Jung*, 73.

61. Quantrill, *The Environmental Memory*, 48.

62. Jung, *Memories, Dreams, Reflections*, 160.

63. Bachelard, *The Poetics of Space*, 4.

64. Martin Heidegger, *Poetry, Language, Thought*, trans. Albert Hofstadter (New York: Harper and Row, 1971), 157.

65. E. V. Walter, *Placeways: A Theory of the Human Environment* (Chapel Hill: University of North Carolina Press, 1988), 145.

66. Martin Pawley, "The Time House," in *Meaning in Architecture*, ed. Charles Jencks

and George Baird (New York: George Braziller, 1970), 135. The symbolic and mnemonic qualities of place, as well as the significant objects that fill it, are both notions that we will be pursuing throughout this book.

67. Thomas Wolfe, *You Can't Go Home Again* (1934; New York: Harper and Row, 1973), 10.

68. Bachelard, *The Poetics of Space,* 9.

69. Quantrill, *The Environmental Memory,* 46.

70. Ibid., 47.

2. The Mind's Eye

1. One of the authors visited with his paternal grandparents on numerous occasions as a child. As his room was over the kitchen below, he often awoke to the smell of a farm breakfast being prepared. To this day, the smell of cooking bacon immediately brings forth the detailed memory of that room.

2. Frances Downing, "Memory and the Making of Places," in *Ordering Space: Types in Architecture and Design,* ed. Karen A. Franck and Lynda H. Schneekloth (New York: Van Nostrand Reinhold, 1994), 233.

3. Marcel Proust, *Remembrance of Things Past: Swann's Way,* trans. C. K. Scott Moncrieff (1928; New York: Vintage Books, 1970), 5. "Its" here refers to his body, and its haptic recognition of particular places.

4. Ibid.

5. John Steinbeck, *Cannery Row* (New York: Bantam Books, 1945), 1.

6. Frances Anderton, "Architecture for All Senses," *Architectural Review* 189, no. 1136 (October 1991): 27.

7. David Abram, *The Spell of the Sensuous* (New York: Vintage Books, 1997), 35.

8. Ibid., 38. Thus if a sufficient number of individuals agree on the characteristics of the wood, it is taken to be a fact.

9. Edmund Husserl, *Cartesian Meditations: An Introduction to Phenomenology,* trans. Dorion Cairns (1929; The Hague: Martinus Nijhoff, 1973), 57.

10. Ibid.

11. Abram, *The Spell of the Sensuous,* 64. One is reminded of the assignation of spiritual qualities—called *mana*—to all manner of things, living and inert, in the cultures of New Guinea.

12. Ibid., 49.

13. Maurice Merleau-Ponty, *Phenomenology of Perception* (1945; London: Routledge and Kegan Paul, 1962), ix.

14. Ibid., 23.

15. Abram, *The Spell of the Sensuous,* 94.

16. David Pearson, "Making Sense of Architecture," *Architecture Review 10: Sensuality and Architecture* (October 1991): 68. As the same forces that Pearson decries were also responsible for the more pernicious aspects of the quasi-scientific typologies that dominated architecture in the late eighteenth century and the early nineteenth, we have little disagreement with him.

17. Ibid., 70.

18. Steven Holl, "Questions of Perception: Phenomenology of Architecture," in *Questions of Perception: Phenomenology of Architecture,* by Steven Holl, Juhani Pallasmaa, and Alberto Pérez-Gómez (Tokyo: a + u Publishing, 1994), 41. When Holl speaks of the "silence of perceptual phenomena," we assume he means that this communication is

wordless, not that sound is not part of a cathedral's perception. Indeed, few structures depend more on the quality of sound.

19. François Molnar, "A Science of Vision for Visual Art," in *Emerging Visions of the Aesthetic Process: Psychology, Semiology, and Philosophy,* ed. Gerald C. Cupchik and János László (Cambridge: Cambridge University Press, 1992), 225.

20. Nick Zangwill, "Aesthetic/Sensory Dependence," *British Journal of Aesthetics* 38, no. 1 (January 1998): 66. This is referred to as a weak dependence thesis, by which is meant that sensory properties are necessary, though not sufficient, for aesthetic properties.

21. Ibid., 67.

22. Ibid., 70. The implicit conclusion is that there can be no purely cognitive architecture, although this seemingly obvious statement will be found controversial by some.

23. Nathaniel Hawthorne, *The House of the Seven Gables* (1851; New York: Holt, Rinehart and Winston, 1962), 1.

24. Rudolf Arnheim, *The Dynamics of Architectural Form* (Berkeley: University of California Press, 1977), 3.

25. Ibid.

26. William J. R. Curtis, *Modern Architecture since 1900* (Englewood Cliffs, N.J.: Prentice Hall, 1983), 61.

27. "Hermann Muthesius: Aims of the Werkbund" (1911), trans. Michael Bullock (1970), in *Programs and Manifestoes on 20th-Century Architecture,* ed. Ulrich Conrads (1964; Cambridge: MIT Press, 1975), 238.

28. Reyner Banham, *Theory and Design in the First Machine Age,* 2d ed. (Cambridge: MIT Press, 1960), 72.

29. Curtis, *Modern Architecture since 1900,* 60.

30. Hans M. Wingler, *The Bauhaus,* ed. Joseph Stein, trans. Wolfgang Jabs and Basil Gilbert (1962; Cambridge: MIT Press, 1969), 32.

31. What is truly amazing is that at no point are human mental states taken as given; rather, they are examined as formats for structured possibilities. Put differently, visual formats do not conform to mental states but are valued for their potential to shape those states.

32. H. M. Wingler, "The Bauhaus and De Stijl," introduction to *Principles of Neoplastic Art,* by Theo Van Doesburg, trans. Janet Seligman (New York: New York Graphic Society, 1966), ix.

33. Ludwig Mies van der Rohe, *"G"* (no. 1, 1923) in *Bauhaus: 50 Years German Exhibition,* comp. Herbert Bayer, Ludwig Grote, Dieter Honisch, and Hans M. Wingler (Chicago: Illinois Institute of Technology, 1969), 164.

34. Ludwig Mies van der Rohe, *Zu Meinem Block in Bau und Wohnung,* ed. Deutscher Werkbund (Stuttgart, 1927), in Bayer et al., *Bauhaus: 50 Years,* 165.

35. Oskar Schlemmer, *Briefe und Tagebucher* (Munich, 1958), in Bayer et al., *Bauhaus: 50 Years,* 20.

36. Walter Gropius, "Neue Arbeiten der Bauhaus Werkstatten," in Bayer et al., *Bauhaus: 50 Years,* 20.

37. Walter Gropius, *Scope of Total Architecture* (1943; New York: Collier Books, 1962), 26. Gropius did note, however, that this dependence on standard types produced a fair amount of similarity in the work of the students.

38. Marcel Breuer, "The House Interior" (lecture given at the Technical University, Delft, 1931), in *Marcel Breuer: Furniture and Interiors,* by Christopher Wilk (New York: Museum of Modern Art, 1981), 184.

39. Karen A. Franck, "It and I: Bodies as Objects, Bodies as Subjects," *Architectural Design* 68, nos. 11–12 (November–December 1998): 16.

40. Ibid., 18. Thus Franck argues for a more human design methodology, one that takes into consideration the sensate character of people. And she warns that the propensity of architects to objectify humans can be all too easily enhanced by the use of computers.

41. Theo Van Doesburg, *Principles of Neo-plastic Art,* trans. Janet Seligman (1925; New York: New York Graphic Society, 1966), 2.

42. Daniele Baroni, *The Furniture of Gerrit Thomas Rietveld* (Woodbury, N.Y.: Barron's, 1978), 24.

43. CIAM, "La Sarraz Declaration," in *Programs and Manifestoes on 20th-Century Architecture,* ed. Ulrich Conrads (Cambridge: MIT Press, 1975), 109.

44. Baroni, *The Furniture of Gerrit Thomas Rietveld,* 106.

45. Banham, *Theory and Design in the First Machine Age,* 326.

46. Robert Marks and R. Buckminster Fuller, *The Dymaxion World of Buckminster Fuller* (1960; Garden City, N.Y.: Anchor Press, 1973), 19.

47. Ibid., 20.

48. Juhani Pallasmaa, *The Eyes of the Skin: Architecture and the Senses* (London: Academy Editions, 1996), 10.

49. Frank Lloyd Wright, *The Sovereignty of the Individual: In the Cause of Architecture* (Berlin: Wasmuth, 1910). Reprinted as an introduction to an exhibition catalog at the Palazzo Strozzi, Florence, Italy, 1951, 15. We are, of course, fully aware that this view was shared by others, notably Charles Rennie Mackintosh.

50. Ibid.

51. Frank Lloyd Wright, *An Autobiography* (New York: Longsmans, Green and Company, 1932), 143.

52. Frank Lloyd Wright, *The Living City,* in *Frank Lloyd Wright: Collected Writings, 1949–1959,* ed. Bruce Brooks Pfeiffer, vol. 5 (New York: Rizzoli, 1995), 335.

53. David A. Hanks, *The Decorative Designs of Frank Lloyd Wright* (New York: E. P. Dutton, 1979), 47.

54. Curtis, *Modern Architecture since 1900,* 203.

55. Ibid.

56. Gwendolyn Wright, *Building the Dream: A Social History of Housing in America* (New York: Pantheon Books, 1981), 168.

57. Ibid., 200.

58. Joseph B. Mason, *History of Housing in the U.S., 1930–1980* (Houston: Gulf Publishing, 1982), 14.

59. It should be noted that altruism—much less aesthetics—had little to do with Hoover's efforts; rather, it was the desire to limit labor unrest through the socioeconomic implications of home ownership for the working classes.

60. Mason, *History of Housing in the U.S., 1930–1980,* 15.

61. Robert T. Jones, ed., *Authentic Small Houses of the Twenties,* reprint of *Small Homes of Architectural Distinction: A Book of Suggested Plans Designed by the Architects' Small House Service Bureau, Inc.* (1929; New York: Dover Publications, 1987), 7.

62. By 1957, the FHA had financed over 4.5 million homes, all subject to its design approval.

63. Wright, *Building the Dream,* 251.

64. Franck, "It and I," 19.

65. George Eliot, *Adam Bede,* cited in *Living Space in Fact and Fiction,* by Philippa Tristram (New York: Routledge, 1989), 217.

66. Gaston Bachelard, *The Poetics of Space,* trans. Maria Jolas (Boston: Beacon Press, 1969), 6.

3. Sensory Response

1. Put differently, there seems to exist an assumption that the viewer will, when confronting architectural paradigms, see what ideologically *ought* to be seen.

2. Aristotle, *De Anima* (On the Soul), trans. Hugh Lawson-Tancred (New York: Viking Penguin, 1986), 218. "While the other senses, smell, sight, and hearing, perceive through other things; but anything that makes contact will, if it have no perception, be unable to avoid some things and acquire others. In which case it will be impossible for the animal to be preserved."

3. Geoffrey Scott, *The Architecture of Humanism: A Study in the History of Taste* (1914; Gloucester, Mass.: Charles Scribner's Sons, 1965), 95.

4. Ibid., 173.

5. James J. Gibson, *The Senses Considered as Perceptual Systems* (Boston: Houghton Mifflin, 1966), 53.

6. This sounds, though one hesitates to say so, very much like a kind of "physical gestalt"—that is, Gestalt principles applied to the mechanical aspects of the organism.

7. Gibson, *The Senses Considered as Perceptual Systems,* 53.

8. Eugene V. Walter, *Placeways* (Chapel Hill: University of North Carolina Press, 1988), 135.

9. Paul Zucker, *Town and Square* (Cambridge: MIT Press, 1970), 6.

10. Arthur I. Rubin and Jacqueline Elder, *Building for People: Behavioral Research Approaches and Directions,* special publication 474 (Washington, D.C.: National Bureau of Standards, 1980), 143.

11. Kurt Koffka, *Principles of Gestalt Psychology* (New York: Harcourt, Brace, 1935), 110. In this case, the term "good" is taken to mean regular, concise, symmetrical, unified, harmonious, and simple.

12. David Canter, *Psychology for Architects* (New York: John Wiley and Sons, 1974), 34. As will become clear later in the chapter, other psychologists (Segall et al.) adhere to precisely the opposite position: that the (cultural) environment actively structures perception.

13. David Katz, *Gestalt Psychology: Its Nature and Significance* (New York: Ronald Press, 1950), 51.

14. Wolfgang Köhler, *Gestalt Psychology* (New York: Liveright, 1947), 103. He goes on to argue that this viewpoint would explain why, given a constant local stimulus, local experience varies when the ambient stimulation is altered. This position contrasts with that of both the empiricists and S-R theorists, who maintain that sensation is fundamentally a mosaic of information.

15. Ibid., 214. Köhler believes, furthermore, that all these phenomena have a direct relationship to visual facts. Perhaps so; but it might as well indicate the degree to which Gestalt depends on sight factors to infer broader principles.

16. David Levi, "The Gestalt Psychology of Expression in Architecture," in *Designing for Human Behavior,* ed. Jon Lang, Charles Burnette, Walter Moleski, and David Vachon (Stroudsburg, Pa.: Dowden, Hutchinson and Ross, 1974), 112.

17. In this, the Bauhaus (under Gropius) was continuing an older position taken by the Deutscher Werkbund, that is, the notion of design in the service of normative types that could serve as standard for mass production. The visible result of that thrust can be seen

in the Werkbund Model Factory Pavilion, designed in 1914 by Walter Gropius and Adolf Meyer. See chapter 9 of *The Interior Dimension: A Theoretical Approach to Enclosed Space*, by Joy Monice Malnar and Frank Vodvarka, for a fuller explication of this development.

18. Kent C. Bloomer and Charles W. Moore, *Body, Memory, and Architecture* (New Haven: Yale University Press, 1977), 32. The authors speculate that the tendency to quickly accept an architectural position based on visual phenomena (especially that of geometric simplicity) might simply reflect the powerful influence of Platonic thought in Europe. That tendency was reinforced, moreover, by the strong presence of two-dimensional artists on the Bauhaus faculty in the early years.

19. Julian Hochberg, "Visual Perception in Architecture," *Via: Architecture and Visual Perception* 6 (1983): 37.

20. Gestalt has maintained that direct sensation is insufficient to explain either the workings of the nervous system or the actual, and often complex, appearance of things. The Gestalt theory of perception, moreover, also relies on visual organization through spatial inference; the question is really whether that inference is innate and whole, or learned and constructed.

21. Hochberg, "Visual Perception in Architecture," 43.

22. A major weakness in this theory, acknowledged by J. J. Gibson, is that there "must be certain little-known neural processes" at the last stage of perception that are responsible for the imagery's integration. These processes are not, however, defined.

23. James J. Gibson, *The Perception of the Visual World* (Boston: Houghton Mifflin, 1950), 3.

24. Ibid., 76. It is, of course, the visual *world*—the very area Gibson has the most difficulty with—that Gestalt theory claims to represent.

25. Ibid., 211. This last item—the virtual ignoring of local social norms—is precisely what endears this theory to the developers of our own age. Perhaps of equal value is the theory's preoccupation with purely visual phenomena.

26. Hochberg, "Visual Perception in Architecture," 40.

27. This is perhaps recognized by Gibson himself when he notes that the visual world "is filled with things that have meaning." Meaning, at least as usually understood, is the direct product of acculturated learning. This results in an understanding of perception as *interpreted sensation,* whatever the mechanism.

28. Gibson, *The Perception of the Visual World,* 23.

29. Köhler, *Gestalt Psychology,* 82.

30. Ibid., 93. Such a distinction—that stimuli can be thus separated into a distinct category—should make it clear why Köhler considers empiricism (in a limited sense) a derivation of S-R theory.

31. Jean Piaget and Barbel Inhelder, *The Child's Conception of Space,* trans. F. J. Langdon and J. L. Lunzer (1948; London: Routledge and Kegan Paul, 1956), 3.

32. Ibid., 4. Piaget notes that if Gestalt principles held true, a baby should, at any age, recognize the shape of an object independent of perspective, as well as its size apart from its distance. This is not, however, supported by research in the field.

33. Ibid., 13. Piaget notes that despite the differences in these two constructions of space, the common factor linking them is motor activity. Thus there is both continuity of perceptual and representational space, as well as separation.

34. It can be seen, however, that Piaget and Inhelder conceive that process to be closely connected with the physical maturation of the subject. Moreover, they understand the Gestalt phenomena as clear and distinctive attributes of particular points in that process.

35. Jean Piaget, *The Mechanisms of Perception,* trans. G. N. Seagrim (1961; New York: Basic Books, 1969), xxv.

36. Ibid., xxvi. It should be noted here that Piaget refers to his theory as a third possibility (rather than a fourth), in an a priori dismissal of S-R theory.

37. After all, even Gestalt concedes this phenomenon.

38. Hochberg, "Visual Perception in Architecture," 35.

39. Reginald G. Golledge and Robert J. Stimson, *Spatial Behavior: A Geographic Perspective* (New York: Guilford Press, 1997), 191.

40. Ibid.

41. Edward T. Hall, *Beyond Culture* (Garden City, N.Y.: Anchor Press/Doubleday, 1977), 42. Hall goes on to note that such controls are usually so well hidden that they are experienced as innate.

42. Marshall H. Segall, Donald T. Campbell, and Melville J. Herskovits, *The Influence of Culture on Visual Perception: An Advanced Study in Psychology and Anthropology* (Indianapolis: Bobbs-Merrill, 1966), 73. The authors go on to note that this view seems to be shared by most contemporary perceptual theorists, even J. J. Gibson. It assumes that the past experience of the organism plays an important part in the construction of certain assumptions about the world in which it lives—assumptions that remain, however, largely unconscious.

43. Ibid., 49. Simply stated, the question here is whether our cultural experience predisposes us to look for, and respond to, certain features of our environment more readily than others.

44. Ibid., 50. Bagwell interpreted his findings as supporting a transactional theory of perception in which perceptual differences result from differences in past cultural difference. See also William H. Ittelson, *Visual Space Perception* (New York: Springer, 1960).

45. Segall, Campbell, and Herskovits do point out that the data are not as clear as they might have wished in all instances, but that the evidence nonetheless points in the direction they hypothesized it would. And, of course, they call for more study in the area.

46. David Howes, "To Summon All the Senses," in *Varieties of Sensory Experience: A Sourcebook in the Anthropology of the Senses,* ed. David Howes (Toronto: University of Toronto Press, 1991), 3.

47. David Howes, "Sensorial Anthropology," in *Varieties of Sensory Experience: A Sourcebook in the Anthropology of the Senses,* ed. David Howes (Toronto: University of Toronto Press, 1991), 173. One of the references cited by Howes is an article by Rosaleen A. McCarthy and E. K. Warrington, "Evidence for Modality-Specific Meaning Systems in the Brain" (1988). In their tests on a subject with progressive deterioration in his use of language and comprehension of the spoken word, the researchers found that his degradation deficit was confined to one modality and to one category within that modality, thereby refuting the notion of an "all-purpose" meaning store and providing positive evidence for multiple meaning representations.

48. Ibid.

49. Anthony J. Marsella and Walter Y. Quijano, "A Comparison of Vividness of Mental Imagery across Different Sensory Modalities in Filipinos and Caucasian-Americans," *Journal of Cross-Cultural Psychology* 5, no. 4 (December 1974): 451. The three hypotheses tested with the two groups were first, that Filipinos would manifest greater vividness of imagery; second, the order of preferences and capabilities in vividness of imagery across sensory modalities would differ; and third, the interrelationships in vividness of imagery among the different sensory modalities would differ.

50. Ibid., 460. The third hypothesis failed to find any support.

51. Walter J. Ong, "The Shifting Sensorium," in *Varieties of Sensory Experience: A Sourcebook in the Anthropology of the Senses,* ed. David Howes (Toronto: University of Toronto Press, 1991), 26.

52. Ibid., 28.

53. Mallory Wober, "The Sensotype Hypothesis," in *Varieties of Sensory Experience: A Sourcebook in the Anthropology of the Senses,* ed. David Howes (Toronto: University of Toronto Press, 1991), 33.

54. Constance Classen, "The Sensory Orders of 'Wild Children,'" in *Varieties of Sensory Experience: A Sourcebook in the Anthropology of the Senses,* ed. David Howes (Toronto: University of Toronto Press, 1991), 59.

55. David Howes and Constance Classen, "Sounding Sensory Profiles," in *Varieties of Sensory Experience: A Sourcebook in the Anthropology of the Senses,* ed. David Howes (Toronto: University of Toronto Press, 1991), 257.

56. Rudolf Arnheim, *Entropy and Art: An Essay on Disorder and Order* (Berkeley: University of California Press, 1971), 34.

57. Rudolf Arnheim, *The Dynamics of Architectural Form* (Berkeley: University of California Press, 1977), 263.

58. Arnheim, *Entropy and Art,* 2.

59. Ibid., 3.

60. David Canter and Stephen Tagg, "The Empirical Classification of Building Aspects and Their Attributes," in *Meaning and Behaviour in the Built Environment,* ed. Geoffrey Broadbent, Richard Bunt, and Tomas Llorens (New York: John Wiley and Sons, 1980), 1.

61. Ibid., 2. Thus, for Canter and Tagg, all space is cultural space, the result of mediated perception.

62. Ibid., 16. As will become apparent in a later chapter, this emphasis on the importance of objects should come as no surprise.

4. The Meaning of Meaning

1. William James, "What Is an Emotion?" in *The Emotions,* by Carl Georg Lange and William James (1884; New York: Hafner, 1967), 11.

2. Wolfgang Köhler, *Gestalt Psychology* (New York: Liveright, 1947), 227.

3. Ibid.

4. James chose in this argument not to discuss this particular kind of feeling, although he does return to such a discussion in his *Principles of Psychology* (published at a later date).

5. James, "What Is an Emotion?" 13. James refers to examples such as meeting a bear, becoming frightened, and then running; or alternatively, losing our money, becoming sorry, and then weeping. The more rational sequence would be that upon losing our money, we cry and thus feel sorry. That is, the physical response follows the event, immediately producing the emotion—indeed, so immediately that our experience of the response in fact constitutes the emotion.

6. Ibid. James maintains, moreover, that this sort of physical response is called forth *directly* from the individual, in advance of all experience of the stimulus. (One can readily see why Köhler would be favorably disposed toward this hypothesis.) Indeed, fairly recent research indicates that emotional response may be gender specific; that is, men appear to more consistently respond to emotional stimuli physically, and women tend to react on the symbolic level (*Chicago Tribune,* 27 January 1995).

7. This should perhaps be clarified. If James's assertion stands as is, it argues for a kind of "emotional gestalt," with all the attendant problems Gestalt has—primarily that of universal response. If one conceives, however, of perception as conditioned by experience, response to a particular stimulus will be stronger in some individuals than in others, and in some cultures more than others.

8. E. V. Walter, *Placeways: A Theory of the Human Environment* (Chapel Hill: University of North Carolina Press, 1988), 142.

9. Ibid., 143.

10. Charles Moore, Gerald Allen, and Donlyn Lyndon, *The Place of Houses* (New York: Holt, Rinehart and Winston, 1974), 49.

11. Ibid., 226. We will argue at a later point that such possessions play an even more critical role in the support of persona than these authors suggest.

12. William James, "The Emotions," in Lange and James, *The Emotions,* 125.

13. Ibid.

14. Phillipa Tristam, *Living Space in Fact and Fiction* (New York: Routledge, 1989), 23.

15. Martin Pawley, "The Time House," in *Meaning in Architecture,* ed. Charles Jencks and George Baird (New York: George Braziller, 1970), 123.

16. Ibid., 126. The truth of this observation is amply attested to by various studies.

17. Ibid., 138. And so argues Pawley: "The hostility that the public exhibits to consumer housing is thus as rationally based as its hostility to demolition and redevelopment."

18. Ibid., 129. This is especially critical if the current trend to stay indoors continues. The December 1999 cover of *Architecture* stated that "the average American spends only 72 minutes outdoors each day." They obtained this statistic from *American Demographics.*

19. Umberto Eco, "Function and Sign: The Semiotics of Architecture," in *Sign, Symbols, and Architecture,* ed. Geoffrey Broadbent, Richard Bunt, and Charles Jencks (New York: John Wiley and Sons, 1980), 11.

20. Geoffrey Broadbent, "General Introduction," in *Signs, Symbols, and Architecture,* ed. Geoffrey Broadbent, Richard Bunt, and Charles Jencks (New York: John Wiley and Sons, 1980), 3.

21. Ibid., 4.

22. Le Corbusier, *Towards a New Architecture* (New York: Holt, Rinehart and Winston, 1960), 54. Corbusier goes on to say: "The figures are terrifying, pitiless but magnificent: giving each employee a superficial area 10 sq. yds., a skyscraper 650 feet in breadth would house 40,000 people." Thus the density would be very high indeed, in spite of the surrounding park with trees and grass.

23. Rob Krier, *Urban Space* (New York: Rizzoli International, 1979), 75. It is notable that Mr. Krier, observations notwithstanding, has found it difficult to resist this sort of design effort himself.

24. We might consider, for example, Frank Lloyd Wright's 1932 plan for Broadacre City, an extraordinarily prescriptive plan from such a high-profile individualist.

25. In his autobiography, *A Life in Architecture,* Yamasaki comments that prior to his trip to Kobe, Japan, sometime after 1950, "my buildings were shallow imitations of those of Mies van der Rohe, who, I believe, was the most influential and best architect in the world at that time." Of course, as Yamasaki himself points out, such imitation was far from rare.

26. Minoru Yamasaki, *A Life in Architecture* (New York: John Weatherhill, 1979), 9. Yamasaki has listed this "sense of security" *after* the functional aspects (structure, environmental protection, and efficiency), and aesthetic concerns such as scale, proportion, form and arrangement, et cetera.

27. Ibid., 39.

28. Frances E. Kuo, William C. Sullivan, Rebekah Levine Coley, and Liesette Brunson, "Fertile Ground for Community: Inner-City Neighborhood Common Spaces," *American Journal of Community Psychology* 26, no. 6 (1998): 826.

29. Oscar Newman, *Defensible Space* (New York: Macmillan, 1972), 2.

30. We should point out that with the notable exception of the New Urbanists, a similar enthusiasm seems lacking among architects and developers.

31. Newman, *Defensible Space,* 8. The author points out that while the politicians, bureaucrats, planners, and architects were undoubtedly well intentioned, the results in hindsight are inadequate and irrational.

32. Moore, Allen, and Lyndon, *The Place of Houses,* 140. Fortunately, as the authors point out, the initial design was sufficiently generalized that the building's occupants could "enter into a continuing exchange with the buildings, to transform them to suit their own visions and wishes." This is certainly an optimistic way to view the situation.

33. Philippe Boudon, *Lived-In Architecture,* trans. Gerald Onn (1969; Cambridge: MIT Press, 1972), 2.

34. Ibid.

35. Not that the tenant's living modalities in Pruitt-Igoe were all that exotic. All the negative factors taken together made its occupants defenseless. It is arguable that no group is so fractured that it could long survive such conditions.

36. Edward T. Hall, *Beyond Culture* (Garden City, N.Y.: Anchor Press/Doubleday, 1977), 16.

37. Hall's position is that the linear quality of language inevitably results in the accentuation of certain things at the expense of others; that is, language can never replicate the rich actuality of an event. Of course, it is arguable that highly descriptive written language fails just as often in its lack of obvious inflection. Thus Hall notes that without context, the linguistic code remains incomplete, since that code comprises only a part of the message.

38. Hall, *Beyond Culture,* 90.

39. Ibid., 91. Thus, he points out, twins who have grown up together use a more economical HC code than two lawyers in a courtroom setting whose interests are quite disparate and thus must rely on an LC mode.

40. Ibid. This is not invariably so; Hall points out that China, a technologically advanced culture, is also high context. As a rule, however, the observation stands, and certainly in regard to the United States.

41. Thus designers of low-income housing often attempt not only to design the buildings and their interior spaces but to predict furniture placement within the rooms. All this without having met any of the inhabitants, or knowing anything more about them other than their median incomes. That they fail should come as no surprise.

42. Hall, *Beyond Culture,* 174. The ability to visualize three-dimensional space on a two-dimensional surface may, he suggests, present as many difficulties as opportunities.

43. Bill Hillier and Julienne Hanson, *The Social Logic of Space* (New York: Cambridge University Press, 1988), 1.

44. Jean-Paul Bourdier and Nezar Alsayyad, *Dwellings, Settlements, and Traditions: Cross-Cultural Perspectives* (Lanham: University Press of America, 1989), 17.

45. Ibid., 6. Their concern, they make clear, is with buildings that are produced by a process of "personalized thought and feeling" rather than formal utility, and represent the "activities and enterprises of ordinary people." Thus they are describing high-context design.

46. Emile Durkheim, *The Elementary Forms of the Religious Life* (London, n.d.), 12. Durkheim notes that the Zuni world, for example, is thought to have seven quarters, each of which is in intimate contact with the seven quarters of the pueblo where related clans reside. Each area has not only a connection to a compass point but its own distinctive color that symbolizes it. Thus the pueblo, or village, graphically represents a larger cosmology.

47. Fernandez contends, for example, that there are cosmological and theological explanations for the juxtaposition of contradictory qualities—which include formal, symbolic, and gender-related elements—in the sculpture of the Fang. He states: "Without this balance of opposite members, it was said . . . the figure would have no life of vitality within it *(enin e se ete)*."

48. James W. Fernandez, "Principles of Opposition and Vitality in Fang Aesthetics," in *Art and Aesthetics in Primitive Societies*, ed. Carol F. Jopling (New York: E. P. Dutton, 1971), 366. He points out that the minor segment of the clan *(mvogabot)* is often defined as those brothers who build their houses opposite each other, as it is better to openly shout insults across the court of the village than whisper them as neighbors.

49. Ibid., 367.

50. Suzanne Preston Blier, "Moral Architecture: Beauty and Ethics in Batammaliba Building Design," in Bourdier and Alsayyad, *Dwellings, Settlements, and Tradition,* 339.

51. Sarah Rossbach, *Feng Shui: The Chinese Art of Placement* (New York: E. P. Dutton, 1983), 2. She further points out that feng shui operates on many levels—superstitious and practical, emotional and physical, and so on—but that many believe its metaphysical operations are not dissimilar to modern physics, especially in its attempt at a unified theory.

52. Ibid., 16.

53. Carl G. Jung, foreward to *The I Ching or Book of Changes,* Bollingen Series 19 (Princeton: Princeton University Press, 1977), xxxii.

54. Ibid., xxii.

55. Nor, it might be added, does an ancient practice endorsed by millions of people need any such support; these days its strong following even includes corporate America.

56. Walter, *Placeways,* 15. Note that the definition of *genius loci* employed by Walter is slightly different from that used by Quantrill; Walter's view is more familiar, that is, the *spirit* of the place, while Quantrill's notion is sensory in character.

57. Ibid., 21.

58. Certainly modernism had concluded, in its solution to the fundamental issues of architecture, that it could be applied to building problems internationally. Hence the striking similarity in the works of Le Corbusier located in France, Algeria, and India, despite obvious cultural and climatic differences in location.

59. Alan Colquhoun, "Vernacular Classicism," in *Modernity and the Classical Tradition: Architectural Essays, 1980–1987* (Cambridge: MIT Press, 1989), 22.

60. Amos Rapoport, "Vernacular Architecture and the Cultural Determinants of Form," in *Buildings and Society,* ed. Anthony D. King (London: Routledge and Kegan Paul, 1980), 285.

61. Ibid., 287. This certainly represents a quite different view of *gestaltung.*

62. Moore, Allen, and Lyndon, *The Place of Houses,* 127.

5. The Talking Spring

1. Manolis Andronicos, *Delphi,* trans. Brian de Jongh (1976; Athens: Ekdotike Athenon, 1985), 9.

2. Aeschylus, *The Eumenides,* in *The Complete Greek Tragedies,* vol. 1, *Aeschylus I,* ed. David Grene and Richmond Lattimore (New York: Modern Library, 1942), 151. The "Earth," of course, refers to the mother of the gods, Gaia, and thus to a far older matriarchal tradition than is suggested by the connection to Phoebus Apollo. Indeed, the real subject of the play is the clash between the older divinities—the Eumenides, or Furies— and the newer Olympian hierarchy here represented by Apollo, and to some degree Athena. This is made clear when Aeschylus has the Eumenides speak the following line to Apollo: "A young god, you have ridden down powers gray with age" (p. 157, line 150).

3. The Pythia was always a woman, at least fifty years of age: who had to live a chaste, morally irreproachable life. Those very fortunate few who asked their questions never actually saw the Pythia, who was seated on the throne of Apollo behind a screen. Nor would they have understood the inarticulate cries she uttered in her ecstasy. These cries were "translated" by the *prophetai* into hexameter verse. The figure we have used is a largely fanciful version of events with an entranced (perhaps from laurel leaves) young Pythia holding snakes (a reference to Python) in front of the *prophetai.*

4. Andronicos, *Delphi,* 6.

5. Malcolm Quantrill, *The Environmental Memory* (New York: Schocken Books, 1987), 46.

6. Ibid., 47.

7. E. V. Walter, *Placeways: A Theory of the Human Environment* (Chapel Hill: University of North Carolina Press, 1988), 15.

8. Ibid., 21.

9. Allardyce Nicoll, ed., *Chapman's Homer: "The Iliad," "The Odyssey," and "The Lesser Homerica,"* vol. 2 (New York: Pantheon Books, 1956), 534.

10. Yi-Fu Tuan, *Space and Place: The Perspective of Experience* (Minneapolis: University of Minnesota Press, 1977), 5.

11. Ibid., 6.

12. It is arguable that despite the seeming continuity of the story line, details of character and plot are not really coherent. Moreover, the three plays have as their object such different points that they stand as essentially discrete stories and were surely not conceived as a trilogy in the narrower sense.

13. Sophocles, *"Oedipus at Colonus" and "Electra,"* ed. and trans. Peter D. Arnott (Northbrook, Ill.: AHM Publishing, 1975), 5.

14. Ibid.

15. Walter, *Placeways,* 120.

16. Sophocles, *"Oedipus at Colonus" and "Electra,"* 25.

17. Ibid., 26.

18. James C. Hogan, *A Commentary on the Plays of Sophocles* (Carbondale and Edwardsville: Southern Illinois University Press, 1991), 98.

19. Ernst Robert Curtius, *European Literature and the Latin Middle Ages,* trans. Willard R. Trask (1948; New York: Bollingen Foundation, 1953), 195.

20. Ibid., 185. Curtius goes on to quote a passage from the *Odyssey,* in which an island is described: "Here are meadows on the banks of the gray sea, moist, with soft soil; here vines could never die; here is smooth ploughing-land . . . just at the harbor's head a spring of sparkling water flows from beneath a cave; around it poplars grow." And he notes that the grotto of Calypso is surrounded by forests, flowers and spring-watered meadows. And so forth.

21. J. Wight Duff and Arnold M. Duff, trans. *Minor Latin Poets* (1934; Cambridge: Harvard University Press, 1954), 559.

22. Curtius, *European Literature and the Latin Middle Ages,* 197.

23. Ibid. Curtius does note an example involving Matthew of Vendome, in which he has managed to raise the number of "charms" to seven by the inclusion of fruit.

24. Curtius describes a wonderful instance in the epic of the Cid where Angelica flees through a wild forest only to stumble upon "un boschetto adorno," a place with a gentle breeze; clear brooks, lawns, and shade.

25. Dante Alighieri, *The Divine Comedy: II, Purgatory,* trans. Louis Biancolli (New York: Washington Square Press, 1966), 115.

26. *The Compact Edition of the Oxford English Dictionary* (New York: Oxford University Press, 1988), 983.

27. Nicolas Le Camus de Mézières, *The Genius of Architecture, or The Analogy of That Art with Our Sensations,* trans. David Britt (Santa Monica, Calif.: Getty Center Publication Programs, 1992), 101.

28. Ibid. In fact, Watelet was a garden designer in the picturesque sense, whose first great work was probably the garden at Moulin-Joli, an estate on an island in the Seine. Here he combined a formal design structure with a fairly "wild" sensibility in the plantings. The point, however, remains that the effect was a contrivance.

29. Charles W. Moore, William J. Mitchell, and William Turnbull Jr., *The Poetics of Gardens* (Cambridge: MIT Press, 1993), 13. In much the same vein as Le Camus de Mézières, the authors state: "Gardens are rhetorical landscapes . . . We can read gardens for content, and we can analyze the devices of structure and figure and trope by means of which they achieve their effects" (49).

30. Ibid., 198.

31. Without pressing the matter too far, it might also be noted that the canal axis bisects the semicircular planting axis at approximately the golden mean, or Ø. And if the reflecting pools are considered a secondary minor axis, the built layout can be seen as consisting of thirds.

32. Moore, Mitchell, and Turnbull, *The Poetics of Gardens,* 199.

33. Unfortunately for the master of Vaux, Nicholas Fouquet, the king also noted that the gardens' cost was well beyond Fouquet's salary as state treasurer. Fouquet was later imprisoned for mismanagement of royal funds and embezzlement.

34. Moore, Mitchell, and Turnbull, *The Poetics of Gardens,* 125.

35. J. Douglas Porteous, *Environmental Aesthetics: Ideas, Politics, and Planning* (London: Routledge, 1996), 68.

36. The ha-ha is really a sunken fence line that gives the illusion of there being no fence at all.

37. Porteous, *Environmental Aesthetics,* 82. The author goes on to describe such a garden's grass lawns, graveled parterres, clipped hedges, long avenues, and so on, all arranged in tedious geometry.

38. These consisted of herds of deer, sheep, and cattle; horses, as at Delphi, were apparently proscribed.

39. Thomas Hinde, *Capability Brown: The Story of a Master Gardener* (New York: W. W. Norton, 1986), 120.

40. Dorothy Stroud, *Capability Brown* (London: Faber and Faber, 1975), 157.

41. Ibid., 206. Stroud makes the point that there were some individuals (Holland, Lapidge, Spyers, et al.) who aspired to Brown's status, but none who attained it.

42. Julie V. Iovine, *New York Times Magazine,* 4 February 1996, 44.

43. The Adena and Hopewell are names given to early cultures (the Adena preceding the Hopewell) of central North America, and the Ohio River Valley in particular. They

were notable for their building of both burial and effigy mounds. Current research, however, indicates that the mound was constructed by a later group, the Fort Ancient people.

44. E. G. Squier and E. H. Davis, *Ancient Monuments of the Mississippi Valley: Comprising the Results of Extensive Original Surveys and Explorations* (New York: Bartlett and Welford, 1848), 97.

45. Emilio Ambasz, "Emilio's Folly: Man Is an Island," in *Follies: Architecture for the Late-Twentieth-Century Landscape,* ed. B. J. Archer and Anthony Vidler (New York: Rizzoli International, 1983), 34.

46. Emilio Ambasz, *Emilio Ambasz: The Poetics of the Pragmatic* (New York: Rizzoli International, 1988), 162.

47. Jon Meyer, "Follies," *Arts Magazine* 58 (January 1984): 23.

48. C. G. Jung, *Word and Image* (Princeton: Princeton University Press, 1979), 196.

49. Rachel Kaplan and Stephen Kaplan, *The Experience of Nature: A Psychological Perspective* (Cambridge: Cambridge University Press, 1989), 10.

50. Porteous, *Environmental Aesthetics,* 25. In this paradigm, aesthetic satisfaction is a spontaneous reaction to the habitat.

51. Kaplan and Kaplan, *The Experience of Nature,* 1. They cite, for example, Verderber's 1986 study indicating that the quality of the view from the hospital window is a significant factor in the recovery of patients in physical medicine and rehabilitation wards; and they note that Ulrich (1984) has demonstrated that if the content of a patient's view includes nature, the speed of recovery from surgery is enhanced. (And they cite still other studies, such as Moore's 1981 study that a view of nature decreases prison inmates' use of health care.)

52. Frances E. Kuo, William C. Sullivan, Rebekah Levine Coley, and Liesette Brunson, "Fertile Ground for Community: Inner-City Neighborhood Common Spaces." *American Journal of Community Psychology* 26, no. 6 (1998): 836.

53. Ibid., 843.

54. The intriguing (though unscientific) study carried out by the Russian artists Komar and Melamid determined that Americans highly rated landscape paintings that had water as their subject, or where water was at least present. They also ascertained other data that provided the basis for the complete, stereotypical American view, which was then encrypted into a paint-by-number layout.

55. Kaplan and Kaplan, *The Experience of Nature,* 88. In sharp contrast to this unanimity, group preference diverged when presented with scenes having no water, with each group preferring the more "foreign" landscape type.

56. Ibid., 26. The testing procedures relied on a fairly extensive series of photographs of natural settings, which they found produced subject responses similar to what was obtained from actual landscape. The authors point out that this should not be surprising, considering the quantity of information that reaches us daily in two-dimensional form. Indeed, people report a high satisfaction with the accuracy of such material, whether in photographs or on television.

57. Ibid., 29. More specifically, the first category pictured scenes of intensive development, and the second showed small structures in natural settings.

58. Ibid., 31. Categorization would seem to reflect the apparent importance of the domain, but such categorization is obviously not absolute.

59. Ibid., 37. The authors conclude that the research thus reveals both an empirical and theoretical basis for landscape categorization.

60. As the greater part of human history has been played out in a natural setting, it is perhaps to be expected that humans express a consistent preference for scenes based on nature alone.

61. Kaplan and Kaplan, *The Experience of Nature,* 29.

62. We might also recall the image of the retreat or teahouse high on the mountain, or on the lake, so ubiquitous in the paintings of Japan and China; while generally seen as more refined in appearance than the cabin, they are not substantively different.

63. Kaplan and Kaplan, *The Experience of Nature,* 52–55. Here we may recall Henry James's description of the Boschetto at the Villa Medici.

64. H. Randy Gimblett, Robert M. Itami, and John E. Fitzgibbon, "Mystery in an Information Processing Model of Landscape Preference," *Landscape Journal* 4, no. 2 (1985): 89.

65. Ibid., 92.

66. Porteous, *Environmental Aesthetics,* 27. Aesthetic satisfaction thus derives from a dialectical interplay between the complexity and chaos sought by the limbic system, the linear order needed by the left hemisphere, and the structure provided by the pattern-dominant right hemisphere.

67. Ibid., 28.

6. There . . . and Back

1. Hence the lines in *Purgatory:* "Without waiting any longer, I left the slope / And slowly started out across the field."

2. Eugene V. Walter, *Placeways* (Chapel Hill: University of North Carolina Press, 1988), 135.

3. James J. Gibson, *The Senses Considered as Perceptual Systems* (Boston: Houghton Mifflin, 1966), 53.

4. Thomas Thiis-Evensen, *Archetypes in Architecture* (Oslo: Norwegian University Press, 1987), 25.

5. Ibid.

6. Forrest Wilson, *A Graphic Survey of Perception and Behavior for the Design Professions* (New York: Van Nostrand Reinhold, 1984), 90.

7. Ibid.

8. Charles W. Moore, William J. Mitchell, and William Turnbull Jr., *The Poetics of Gardens* (Cambridge: MIT Press, 1993), 50.

9. Ibid., 100.

10. Hermann Schöne, *Spatial Orientation: The Spatial Control of Behavior in Animals and Man,* trans. Camilla Strausfeld (Princeton, N.J.: Princeton University Press, 1984), 274.

11. Moore, Mitchell, and Turnbull, *The Poetics of Gardens,* 103.

12. Marc P. Keane, "Japanese Entrances: Cultural Symbols in the Landscape," *Landscape Architecture* 78 (September–October 1988): 120.

13. Teiji Itoh, *Space and Illusion: In the Japanese Garden* (New York: John Weatherhill, 1973), 69.

14. Ibid.

15. A. C. Sewter, *Baroque and Rococo* (New York: Harcourt Brace Jovanovich, 1972), 202.

16. Vincent Scully Jr., *Modern Architecture* (New York: George Braziller, 1974), 11.

17. Thiis-Evensen, *Archetypes in Architecture,* 297.

18. Karen A. Franck, "Types Are Us," in *Ordering Space: Types in Architecture and Design,* ed. Karen A. Franck and Lynda H. Schneekloth (New York: Van Nostrand Reinhold, 1994), 366.

19. Jan C. Scruggs and Joel L. Swerdlow, *To Heal a Nation: The Vietnam Veterans Memorial* (New York: Harper and Row, 1985), 78.

20. Harry Heft and Joachim F. Wohlwill, "Environmental Cognition in Children," in *Handbook of Environmental Psychology*, vol. 1, ed. Daniel Stokols and Irwin Altman (New York: John Wiley and Sons, 1987), 179. The implication here is that we take these discrete "frames" and assemble them into a continuous film in our minds.

21. Ibid. This is clearly an effort to mediate between the two theoretical approaches; as we shall see, wayfinding is an even more complex process than this description suggests.

22. Kent C. Bloomer and Charles W. Moore, *Body, Memory, and Architecture* (New Haven: Yale University Press, 1978), 78.

23. Reginald G. Golledge, "Environmental Cognition," in *Handbook of Environmental Psychology*, ed. Daniel Stokols and Irwin Altman (New York: John Wiley and Sons, 1987), 140.

24. Ibid., 142. Thus you first have spaces, then construct ways (paths) to get from one to another, in Golledge's view. It is arguable, however, that we may find certain paths interesting for quite idiosyncratic reasons, only then constructing landmarks (or, more likely, nodes) along it.

25. Malcolm Quantrill, *The Environmental Memory* (New York: Schocken Books, 1987), 50.

26. Stephen Kaplan and Rachel Kaplan, *Cognition and Environment: Functioning in an Uncertain World* (New York: Praeger Publishers, 1982), 9.

27. Ibid., 41. Accordingly, they state: "It thus may be that a cognitive map intuitively feels continuous even though it is actually made up of connected, but discrete, representations."

28. The authors note two studies by Weisman (1981) in this regard: first, the one alluded to, that the single most effective predictor of disorientation was the *structure* of the building; and second, that the buildings with the most confusing structures were the ones with the most signage. No surprise here.

29. Kevin Lynch, *The Image of the City* (Cambridge: Technology Press, 1960), 8.

30. Ibid., 9. "Vividly identified" and "powerfully structured" imply both sensory response and cognition.

31. Jon Lang, *Creating Architectural Theory* (New York: Van Nostrand Reinhold, 1987), 137.

32. Kaplan and Kaplan, *Cognition and Environment*, 60.

33. Ibid., 61.

34. Thiis-Evensen, *Archetypes in Architecture*, 297.

35. J. R. R. Tolkien, *The Fellowship of the Ring* (1954; London: Unwin Books, 1974), 43. Everyone will likely recall that Bilbo Baggins was the unlikely hero of *The Hobbit;* in the trilogy, he plays a far lesser, though still important, part.

36. Ibid.

37. Quantrill, *The Environmental Memory,* 177.

38. Rudolf Arnheim, "Buildings as Percepts," *Via: Architecture and Visual Perception* 6 (1983), 13.

39. Ibid., 14. Here one is reminded of the disquieting feeling that results from discovering that a building's intended use does not accord with the perceptual evaluation we have already made of it.

40. Thiis-Evensen, *Archetypes in Architecture,* 29.

41. Romedi Passini, *Wayfinding in Architecture* (New York: Van Nostrand Reinhold, 1992), 17.

42. Ibid., 21.

43. Gary W. Evans, Mary Anne Skorpanich, Tommy Gärling, Kendall J. Bryant, and Brian Bresolin, "The Effects of Pathway Configuration, Landmarks, and Stress on Environmental Cognition," *Journal of Environmental Psychology* 4 (1984): 325. Simply put, crowded shoppers drew less accurate maps than noncrowded shoppers.

44. Passini, *Wayfinding in Architecture,* 21.

45. Edward T. Hall, *The Hidden Dimension* (Garden City, N.Y.: Anchor Books, 1969), 115.

46. David Van Zanten, "Architectural Composition at the Ecole des Beaux-Arts from Charles Percier to Charles Garnier," in *The Architecture of the Ecole des Beaux-Arts* (New York: Museum of Modern Art, 1977), 118.

47. Le Corbusier, *Towards a New Architecture,* trans. Frederick Etchells (1927; New York: Holt, Rinehart and Winston, 1960), 173.

48. Paul Zucker, *Town and Square* (Cambridge: MIT Press, 1970), 25.

49. In fairness, we should also note the alternative theory concerning the design of such structures—that they have multiple astronomical functions requiring long, contained axes.

50. Lewis Mumford, *Culture of Cities* (1938; New York: Harcourt Brace Jovanovich, 1970), 434.

51. This is surely at the heart of the Kaplans' hesitancy to endorse that model.

52. Bernard Tschumi, *Sequences* (New York: Committee for the Visual Arts, 1981), 1.

53. Tschumi, *Sequences,* 2.

54. Passini, *Wayfinding in Architecture,* 35.

55. Ibid., 43. Passini bases his conclusion, in large measure, on the uncanny ability evinced by the "dead reckoning" navigational techniques of groups such as the Polynesians.

56. Ibid., 46. He assumes that the second two abilities are conditioned by the first.

57. John Peponis, Craig Zimring, and Yoon Kyung Choi, "Finding the Building in Wayfinding," *Environment and Behavior* 22, no. 5 (September 1990): 555.

58. Passini, *Wayfinding in Architecture,* 39.

59. Janet Reizenstein Carpman, Myron A. Grant, and Deborah A. Simmons, "No More Mazes," *Progressive Architecture* 66 (January 1985): 156.

60. Ibid., 157.

61. Edward R. Tufte, *Envisioning Information* (Cheshire, Conn.: Graphics Press, 1990), 37.

62. Ibid., 12.

63. Carol S. Holding, "Clusters and Reference Points in Cognitive Representations of the Environment," *Journal of Environmental Psychology* (1992): 45. The two results specifically were (1) due to their strong ties with numerous locations, reference points entered the subjects' hierarchies late; and (2) subjects made more accurate building placements when given reference anchors. Thus certain buildings in the larger complex (reference points) acted as keys to organization and identification.

64. Ibid.

65. Carol A. Lawton, "Gender Differences in Way-Finding Strategies: Relationship to Spatial Ability and Spatial Anxiety," *Sex Roles* 30, nos. 11–12 (1994): 765.

66. Evans et al., "The Effects of Pathway Configuration," 331. This may raise an interesting question as to the role of noise (or perhaps music) in "processing" human cognitive efficiency.

67. Ibid., 332.

7. Sensory Cues

1. Yi-Fu Tuan, *Space and Place: The Perspective of Experience* (Minneapolis: University of Minnesota Press, 1977), 6.

2. Chu Shu-chên, "Plum Blossoms," in *Women Poets of China,* trans. and ed. Kenneth Rexroth and Ling Chung (New York: McGraw-Hill, 1972), 47.

3. We will, for the sake of our argument, assume that Chu Shu-chên is reporting a personally experienced situation in poetic form.

4. Robert A. Baron and Jill Thomley, "A Whiff of Reality: Positive Affect as a Potential Mediator of the Effects of Pleasant Fragrances on Task Performance and Helping," *Environment and Behavior* 26, no. 6 (1994): 766.

5. In particular they cite the work of Baron and Warm, Dember, and Parasuraman. See R. A. Baron, "Environmentally-Induced Positive Affect: Its Impact on Self-Efficacy, Task Performance, Negotiation, and Conflict," *Journal of Applied Social Psychology* 26, no. 6 (1990): 766–84; Joel S. Warm, William N. Dember, and Raja Parasuraman, "Effects of Olfactory Stimulation on Performance and Stress in a Visual Sustained Attention Task," *Journal of the Society of Cosmetic Chemists* 12 (1991): 1–12.

6. Baron and Thomley, "A Whiff of Reality," 768. H. Ehrlichman and J. N. Halpern, "Affect and Memory: Effects of Pleasant and Unpleasant Odors on Retrieval of Happy and Unhappy Memories," *Journal of Personality and Social Psychology* 55 (1988): 769–79; Robert A. Baron and Marna I. Bronfen, "A Whiff of Reality: Empirical Evidence concerning the Effects of Pleasant Fragrances on Work-Related Behavior," *Journal of Applied Social Psychology* 24 (1994): 1179–1203.

7. Baron and Thomley, "A Whiff of Reality," 769. One interesting study found that individuals exposed to pleasant fragrances tended to process information in persuasive messages in a manner similar to that of individuals put in a positive mood by the bestowal of a monetary gift. See K. G. De Bono, "Pleasant Scents and Persuasion: An Information Processing Approach," *Journal of Applied Social Psychology* 22, no. 11 (1992): 910–19.

8. Charlotte Mew, "Rooms," in *The Penguin Book of Women Poets,* ed. Carol Cosman, Joan Keefe, and Kathleen Weaver (New York: Penguin Books, 1978), 364.

9. Michael Southworth, "The Sonic Environment of Cities," *Environment and Behavior,* June 1969, 59. While these are general conclusions, they were shared by both auditory and (to a lesser degree) visual-auditory subjects in his study.

10. Joseph Conrad, "Heart of Darkness," in *Tales of Land and Sea* (Garden City, N.Y.: Hanover House, 1953), 62.

11. Ibid., 64.

12. Tuan, *Space and Place,* 18.

13. Rainer Maria Rilke, *The Notebooks of Malte Laurids Brigge,* trans. M. D. Herter Norton (1949; New York: Capricorn Books, 1958), 13.

14. Thus have architects been amazed when their designs met with public disapproval not because of their appearance but because the processes that occurred within the structures were inherently noxious in sound or smell.

15. Piet Vroon with Anton van Amerongen and Hans de Vries, *Smell: The Secret Seducer,* trans. Paul Vincent (New York: Farrar, Straus and Giroux, 1994), 4.

16. Ibid. Also worth noting is the essential agreement between this statement and the position taken by Henry James (in chapter 3).

17. S. Van Toller, "Emotion and the Brain," in *Perfumery: The Psychology and Biology of Fragrance* (London: Chapman and Hall, 1988), 126.

18. J. R. King, "Anxiety Reduction Using Fragrances," in *Perfumery: The Psychology and Biology of Fragrance* (London: Chapman and Hall, 1988), 155.

19. Ibid., 156. See E. Gellhorn and G. N. Loofbourrow, *Emotions and Emotional Disorders* (New York: Harper and Row, 1963).

20. Trygg Engen, *Odor Sensation and Memory* (New York: Praeger Publishers, 1991), 10. The author notes that there is no innate avoidance response even to ethylmercaptan, the repellent substance that is added to natural gas as a warning agent. (Indeed, it should perhaps be a point of concern that, according to a National Geographic smell survey [October 1987], the number of readers rating mercaptans as "unpleasant" dropped with their age.) All that is required is a *distinctive* odor (and a learned association) to arouse us. Other researchers (Robert Tisserand, *Aromatherapy: To Heal and Tend the Body* [New Mexico: Lotus Press, 1988]) do, however, describe a "repulsion reaction" in humans to disease, decay, rot, and dampness that warn them of danger. Thus humans find the odors that indicate such states inherently repugnant.

21. Arthur I. Rubin and Jacqueline Elder, *Building for People: Behavioral Research Approaches and Directions,* Special Publication 474 (Washington, D.C.: National Bureau of Standards, 1980), 198.

22. Forrest Wilson, *A Graphic Survey of Perception and Behavior for the Design Professions* (New York: Van Nostrand Reinhold, 1984), 191.

23. Ibid.

24. Heidi A. Walk and Elizabeth E. Johns, "Interference and Facilitation in Short-Term Memory for Odors," *Perception and Psychophysics* 36, no. 6 (1984): 508.

25. Trygg Engen and Bruce M. Ross, "Long-Term Memory of Odors with and without Verbal Descriptions," *Journal of Experimental Psychology* 100, no. 2 (1973): 225. Engen and Ross hypothesize that odors have little attribute redundancy, leading to poor immediate retention but great resistance subsequently to the distortion of immediately retained odors.

26. Frank F. Schab, "Odor Memory: Taking Stock," *Psychological Bulletin* 109, no. 2 (1991): 242–51.

27. Michael D. Rabin and William S. Cain, "Odor Recognition: Familiarity, Identifiability, and Encoding Consistency," *Journal of Experimental Psychology: Learning, Memory, and Cognition* 10, no. 2 (1984): 325.

28. Engen and Ross, "Long-Term Memory of Odors," 226. Although other studies undertaken since this seminal investigation have questioned the degree to which smell is a unique sense modality, the enduring quality of odors seems clear.

29. Ibid.

30. Trygg Engen, "Remembering Odors and Their Names," *American Scientist,* September–October 1987, 498. Thus the superiority of déjà sentir over déjà vu.

31. Ibid.

32. Vroon, *Smell,* 103. Vroon describes this mechanism as "state-dependent retrieval"; what a person has learned in a certain physiological or mental state—or even place—can be remembered under the same circumstances.

33. Ibid., 105.

34. Engen, "Remembering Odors and Their Names," 497.

35. Charles Baudelaire, "A Phantom: The Perfume," trans. Lewis Piaget Shanks, in *The Flowers of Evil,* ed. Marthiel and Jackson Mathews (New York: New Directions, 1955), 48.

36. Juhani Pallasmaa, "Architecture of the Seven Senses," in *Questions of Perception: Phenomenology of Architecture,* ed. Steven Holl, Juhani Pallasmaa, and Alberto Pérez-Gómez (Tokyo: a + u Publishing, 1994), 32.

37. Ibid.

38. Alan Hirsch, "Scenting a Generation Gap," *Children's Environments* 9, no. 1 (1992): 13. While the list in the article is approximately twice as long as what we present here, our list is entirely representative of odor type.

39. Ibid.

40. Kenneth Grahame, *The Wind in the Willows* (1908; New York: Bantam Books, 1982), 70.

41. M. D. Kirk-Smith, C. Van Toller, and G. H. Dodd, "Unconscious Odour Conditioning in Human Subjects," *Biological Psychology* 17 (1983): 221–31.

42. David Meyers, "Nobody's First Home Is Perfect," *Chicago Tribune,* Home Guide, 1 April 1995, sec. 4, p. 2. The author says that many sales agents swear that cookies and pies baking in the kitchen can trigger potential buyers' memories of the homes they grew up in. Assuming they are fond memories, this tends to make the seller's home more pleasant.

43. Trygg Engen would likely argue that it is not the smell of coffee per se that matters but that an unfamiliar place—whose odors therefore tend to be viewed with suspicion—is made familiar with a common masking odor.

44. Baron and Thomley, "A Whiff of Reality," 767.

45. M. Iwahashi, "Scents and Science," *Vogue,* April 1992, 212–14.

46. Robert A. Baron and Marna I. Bronfen, "A Whiff of Reality: Empirical Evidence concerning the Effects of Pleasant Fragrances on Work-Related Behavior," *Journal of Applied Social Psychology* 24, no. 13 (1994): 1179.

47. Baron and Thomley, "A Whiff of Reality," 781. The authors point out that the rapid sensory adaptation to specific fragrances that would seem to militate against their use could be countered by alternating scents, and by normal employee mobility. Thus they conclude that there may in fact be some potential for the employment of scent in work settings.

48. Ibid.

49. C. Clifford, "New Scent Waves," *Self,* December 1985, 115–17.

50. Margaret Schleidt, Peter Neumann, and Harumi Morishita, "Pleasure and Disgust: Memories and Associations of Pleasant and Unpleasant Odours in Germany and Japan," *Chemical Senses* 13, no. 2 (1988): 287.

51. Ibid., 292.

52. J. Douglas Porteous, *Landscapes of the Mind: Worlds of Sense and Metaphor* (Toronto: University of Toronto Press, 1990), 25.

53. Ibid., 45.

54. Thomas Wolfe, *You Can't Go Home Again* (1934; New York: Harper and Row, 1973), 123. As one of the present authors is from New York, he can attest to the description's accuracy.

55. Rilke, *The Notebooks of Malte Laurids Brigge,* 14.

56. Southworth, "The Sonic Environment of Cities," 49.

57. Ibid., 52. He does point out that high information transfer accompanies a congruence of visual and auditory information; when attention-demanding sounds are incongruous with visual information, less total information is transmitted.

58. Douglas Pocock, "Sound and the Geographer," *The Geographical Association,* June 1989, 194.

59. Southworth, "The Sonic Environment of Cities," 70.

60. R. Murray Schafer, "Acoustic Space," in *Dwelling, Place, and Environment: Towards a Phenomenology of Person and World,* ed. David Seamon and Robert Mugerauer (New York: Columbia University Press, 1994), 87.

61. Paul Devereux and Robert G. Jahn, "Preliminary Investigations and Cognitive Considerations of the Acoustical Resonances of Selected Archaeological Sites," *Antiquity* 70 (July 1996): 666. Schafer similarly discusses the Neolithic cave of Hypogeum on Malta dating to circa 2400 B.C., which was likely a shrine or oracular chamber with remarkable acoustic properties. Specifically, its resonance frequency is about 90 Hz and thus has the capacity to dramatically amplify the male voice.

62. Aaron Watson and David Keating, "Architecture and Sound: An Acoustic Analysis of Megalithic Monuments in Prehistoric Britain," *Antiquity* 73 (February 1999): 326.

63. Ibid., 335.

64. Pocock, "Sound and the Geographer," 193.

65. Ibid., 194.

66. Rilke, *The Notebooks of Malte Laurids Brigge*, 14.

67. In fact, in Southworth's study the visual subjects (without hearing) had the worst impression of the city, finding much more imperfection in its form than did the other subjects.

68. Carl Sandburg, *Chicago Poems* (Urbana: University of Illinois Press, 1992), 17.

69. Keith Waldrop, "A Door Opening," *Poetry and the Problem of Beauty*, ed. Lisa Samuels, *Modern Language Studies* 27, no. 2 (spring 1997): 23.

70. Porteous, *Landscapes of the Mind*, 48.

71. Lee E. Farr, "Medical Consequences of Environmental Home Noises," in *People and Buildings*, ed. Robert Gutman (New York: Basic Books, 1972), 206.

72. Porteous, *Landscapes of the Mind*, 48. Even the extensive studies generated by audio engineers have been primarily concerned with *soundfields* (the environment of sound sources) rather than *soundscapes* (the environment of the receiver of the sound).

73. Ibid., 63. Schafer found, for example, that the isobel maps that were prepared for three Viennese parks—which are now located alongside busy streets—revealed minimum ambient sound levels of 48 dBA, and an average of 55 dBA. To put this in context, it should be noted that 52 dBA is the established Speech Interference Level for normal conversation at four meters.

74. R. Murray Schafer, *The Tuning of the World* (New York: Alfred A. Knopf, 1977), 9.

75. Indeed, Schafer has much to say about Muzak, which he refers to as Moozak, none of it complimentary. He points out that quite aside from the effective destruction of the music it purports to be playing, there is an even more insidious program at work; the conscious effort to control the psychological and physiological reactions of its victims to specific behavioral ends.

76. Schafer, *The Tuning of the World*, 96. The result, he maintains, is an extraordinary isolation and disengagement, whether experienced through the continual presence of the radio for the teenager, television for the housewife, and Moozak for everyone.

77. Ibid., 220. While we cannot attest to the truth of this observation, we can state—having actually experienced it—that a comment sotto voce from a parent to his errant child carried clearly from the stage to the top tier of seats.

78. Ibid. Curiously, a similar auditory experience can be had in the main entrance vestibule of the Beckman Institute on the University of Illinois at Urbana-Champaign campus. People react with delighted surprise upon hearing the echo of their voice.

79. Vitruvius, *The Ten Books on Architecture*, trans. by Morris Hicky Morgan (New York: Dover Publications, 1960), 143. Oddly enough, our evidence for the existence of these vessels is based on written description and some later illustrations; to the best of our knowledge, none have been found.

80. We make this organizational distinction while recognizing that the division of Vitruvius's text into "books" did not take place until the fifteenth century.

81. Vitruvius, *The Ten Books on Architecture,* 138.

82. Steen Eiler Rasmussen, *Experiencing Architecture* (Cambridge: MIT Press, 1962), 228.

83. Schafer, *The Tuning of the World,* 222.

84. Ibid. Actually, Schafer remains something of an optimist, as he assumes that the noise pollution that characterizes many structures is the simple result of ignorance.

85. Hall, *The Hidden Dimension,* 62. By this, Hall means that surface texture is merely the relatively uncalculated happenstance of the material—usually chosen for appearance, utility, and cost—being used.

86. Ibid., 66.

87. Thus our analysis in chapter 5 of the gardens at Katsura Imperial Villa, as well as the rather more modest tea garden in Kyoto.

88. Rasmussen, *Experiencing Architecture,* 177.

89. Pallasmaa, "Architecture of the Seven Senses," 33.

90. Ibid.

91. Susan J. Lederman and Susan G. Abbott, "Texture Perception: Studies of Inter-sensory Organization Using a Discrepancy Paradigm, and Visual Versus Tactual Psychophysics," *Journal of Experimental Psychology: Human Perception and Performance* 7, no. 4 (1981): 911.

92. Ibid., 914.

93. Ibid.

94. M. O. Ernst, M. S. Banks, and H. H. Bulthof, "Haptic Feedback Affects Visual Perception of Surfaces," *Perception* 28, supplement (1999): 106.

95. Sarah J. Rogers, *The Body and the Object: Ann Hamilton, 1984–1996* (Columbus, Ohio: Wexner Center for the Arts, Ohio State University, 1996), 15.

96. Ibid., 23.

97. Jonathan Miller, *Steps and Stairs* (Otis Elevator Company, a United Technologies Subsidary, England, n.d.), 8.

98. Ibid., 9.

99. John Templar, *The Staircase: History and Theories* (Cambridge: MIT Press, 1992), 23.

100. Ibid.

101. John Templar, *The Staircase: Studies of Hazards, Falls, and Safer Design* (Cambridge: MIT Press, 1992), 64.

102. Ibid. We have long known that sight and touch together enable us to better perceive spatial characteristics. J. J. Gibson notes the affinity of vision and touch and concludes that the flow of sense impressions is reinforced when the subject uses both senses.

103. Friedensreich Hundertwasser, *Hundertwasser Architecture: For a More Human Architecture in Harmony with Nature,* trans. Philip Mattson (New York: Taschen, 1997), 282.

104. Ibid. He does point out that the gradient should never exceed 10 percent, and tiles must be leveled to within 1 mm for obvious safety concerns.

105. Templar, *The Staircase: Studies of Hazards,* 66.

106. Hall, *The Hidden Dimension,* 1.

107. Ibid., 101. The last of these three concepts has tended to preoccupy the world of design, but the theory—notwithstanding—should be understood as a whole.

108. Robert Sommer, *Personal Space: The Behavioral Basis of Design* (Englewood Cliffs, N.J.: Prentice Hall, 1969), 86.

109. Hall, *The Hidden Dimension,* 116.

110. Ibid., 127.

111. Sommer, *Personal Space,* 26.

112. Ibid., 27.

113. W. H. Auden, "Prologue: The Birth of Architecture," in *About the House* (New York: Random House, 1959), 4.

114. Reginald G. Golledge and Robert J. Stimson, *Spatial Behavior: A Geographic Perspective* (New York: Guilford Press, 1997), 189. The authors postulate that the senses are viewed as functional systems designed to provide feedback and, more importantly, to seek out environmental information. This is in keeping with the theories of J. J. Gibson, whom they credit.

115. Helen Keller, *The World I Live In* (New York: Century, 1908), 80.

116. Ibid.

8. No Mere Ornament

1. J. R. R. Tolkien, *The Fellowship of the Ring* (1954; London: Unwin Books, 1974), 81.

2. H. G. Wells, "The Door in the Wall," in *The Door in the Wall and Other Stories* (1911; Boston: David R. Godine, 1980), 8.

3. Arthur Drexler, "Engineer's Architecture: Truth and Its Consequences," in *The Architecture of the Ecole Des Beaux-Arts,* ed. Arthur Drexler (New York: Museum of Modern Art, 1977), 38. This rests on the assumption that the viewer's eye is fully sensing the details of the architectural environment.

4. Robin Evans, "Figures, Doors, and Passages," *Architectural Design* 48, no. 4 (1978): 267.

5. Evans's proposition is an intriguing one. He believes that the combination of typical portrayals of human figures and residential plans from particular eras can together be taken as evidence of a way of life. He thus postulates there is a close connection between everyday conduct and the facts of architectural organization.

6. Evans, "Figures, Doors, and Passages," 270.

7. Ibid., 272.

8. John Bold, *John Webb: Architectural Theory and Practice in the Seventeenth Century* (Oxford: Clarendon Press, 1989), 95.

9. There is also an interesting suggestion here that the rise of the corridor enhances the development of axiality as a virtue in the nineteenth century.

10. Brodie Ann Bain, "Approaching Buildings: A Conceptual Model of the Entry Sequence," in *Coming of Age: Proceedings of the Twenty-First Annual Conference of the Environmental Design Research Association,* ed. Robert I. Selby, Kathryn H. Anthony, Jaepil Choi, and Brian Orland (Oklahoma City: EDRA, 1990), 205.

11. Ibid., 205–6. As the "mystery" element is taken from the same work of the Kaplans that we previously mentioned in regard to landscape, we may assume that it functions on the same level, and for the same reasons.

12. Ibid., 207. We might conclude that clear legibility of entry is more or less important to the degree that the entry is critical to our functioning.

13. Leon Battista Alberti, *The Ten Books of Architecture,* trans. Giacomo James Leoni (1485; New York: Dover Publications, 1986), 21.

14. Henri Focillon, *The Life of Forms in Art,* trans. Charles Beecher Hogan and George Kubler (1934; New York: Zone Books, 1989), 96. When Focillon refers to form he means *form-design,* a older and far more complex idea than the modern term *design* conveys.

15. Ibid., 97.

16. We discussed Rapoport's intriguing view of building types—primitive, vernacular, and high style—in an earlier chapter.

17. Juhani Pallasmaa, "An Architecture of the Seven Senses," in *Questions of Perception: Phenomenology of Architecture,* ed. Steven Holl, Juhani Pallasmaa, and Alberto Pérez-Gómez (Tokyo: a + u Publishing, 1994), 30.

18. Steven Holl, "Questions of Perception: Phenomenology of Architecture," in Holl, Pallasmaa, and Pérez-Gómez, *Questions of Perception,* 41.

19. Ibid., 91.

20. It should be noted that although Gehry was chosen (and largely funded) by the Pritzker Foundation—a private civic group—his project has been supported by the civic authorities, who surely recognize the economic significance of such design.

21. Blair Kamin, "Outsider Art Is Catalyst for Creativity," *Chicago Tribune,* 7 November 1999, sec. 2, p. 4.

22. Sir John Summerson, "What Is Ornament and What Is Not," *Via: Ornament,* ed. Stephen Kieran, 3 (1977): 7.

23. Ibid.

24. Marcus Vitruvius, *The Ten Books on Architecture,* trans. Morris Hicky Morgan (New York: Dover Publications, 1960), 16.

25. Ibid., 104. Nor does Vitruvius neglect the fascinating "history" of the Corinthian order. In fact, he relates a charming tale of a maiden of Corinth with all the conviction of an eyewitness.

26. E. H. Gombrich, *The Sense of Order: A Study in the Psychology of Decorative Art* (Ithaca, N.Y.: Cornell University Press, 1979), 171.

27. Ibid., 173.

28. Thomas Wolfe, *You Can't Go Home Again* (1934; New York: Harper and Row, 1973), 169

29. Joshua Meyrowitz, *No Sense of Place: The Impact of Electronic Media on Social Behavior* (New York: Oxford University Press, 1985), 115.

30. Ibid.

31. Data broadcast on commercial media, for example, are usually viewed with considerable skepticism, and telephone messages and e-mails seldom have the impact of personal, live conversation.

32. Meyrowitz, *No Sense of Place,* 116.

33. Of course, it is arguable that this has always been one of the key functions of doors and walls historically.

34. Robert Frost, "Mending Wall," in *The Poetry of Robert Frost,* ed. Edward Connery Lathem (New York: Holt, Rinehart and Winston, 1969), 34.

35. Ibid.

36. Bill Hillier and Julienne Hanson, *The Social Logic of Space* (1984; New York: Cambridge University Press, 1988), 26.

37. When fully considered, *party wall* is an odd name for this architectural device. It refers to the fact that it divides two parties from each other, but it also suggests (as Jill Stoner does) that it has the capacity for social formation.

38. Jill Stoner, "The Party Wall as the Architecture of Sharing," in *New Households, New Housing,* ed. Karen A. Franck and Sherry Ahrentzen (New York: Van Nostrand Reinhold, 1989), 127.

39. This also characterized the Berlin Wall, which divided two parties—once related—with equal claim, if not equal desire, to assert it.

40. Stoner, "The Party Wall as the Architecture of Sharing," 127.

41. Gordon H. Bower and Paul R. Cohen, "Emotional Influences in Memory and Thinking: Data and Theory," in *Affect and Cognition*, ed. Margaret Sydnor Clark and Susan T. Fiske (Hillsdale, N.J.: Lawrence Erlbaum, 1982), 291.

42. Philip Thiel, Ean Duane Harrison, and Richard S. Alden, "The Perception of Spatial Enclosure as a Function of the Position of Architectural Surfaces," *Environment and Behavior* 18 (March 1986): 227.

43. Ibid., 241.

44. Darhl M. Pedersen and Teri L. Topham, "Perception of Enclosure Effects of Architectural Surfaces in a Large Scale Interior Space," *Perceptual and Motor Skills* 70 (February 1990): 303.

45. Thiel, Harrison, and Alden, "The Perception of Spatial Enclosure," 242.

46. Ibid. We agree, as will become clear in our discussion of the CAVE immersive virtual reality in chapter 12.

47. Elwood L. Shafer Jr. and Thomas A. Richards, "A Comparison of Viewer Reactions to Outdoor Scenes and Photographs of Those Scenes," in *Psychology and the Built Environment*, ed. David Canter and Terence Lee (New York: John Wiley and Sons, 1974), 79. We realize that we accepted, in a previous chapter dealing with response to landscape characteristics, the validity of photographs. We do not, however, believe their reliability to be unqualified, or as dependable when applied to architectural enclosures.

48. Ibid., 71.

49. Indeed, one could argue that the sense of enclosure itself is primarily haptic in nature, and hence unavailable in a photographic representation.

50. Marco Frascari, "The Tell-the-Tale Detail," *Via: The Building of Architecture*, ed. Paula Behrens and Anthony Fisher, 7 (1984): 23.

51. Guy Thomas Buswell, *How People Look at Pictures: A Study of the Psychology of Perception in Art* (Chicago: University of Chicago Press, 1935), 7. The reader will doubtless note that these are two-dimensional works of art—not reality—that are being investigated. Pictures were also used in some of the previous studies. We are putting a similar, albeit more tentative, faith in the use of pictures in examining patterns of perception.

52. Ibid., 92.

53. A. Risso and A. Macia, "Eye Fixation Points and Landscape Choice," *Perception* 28, supplement (1999): 110.

54. Ibid.

55. Buswell, *How People Look at Pictures*, 98.

56. Gombrich, *The Sense of Order*, 122.

57. Alfred L. Yarbus, *Eye Movements and Vision* (New York: Plenum Press, 1967), 3.

58. Ibid., 211. Thus a new understanding of the comment that someone "just doesn't see things my way."

59. Herbert James Clark, "Recognition Memory for Random Shapes as a Function of Complexity, Association Value, and Delay," *Journal of Experimental Psychology* 69 (1965): 590–95.

60. Alvin G. Goldstein and June E. Chance, "Visual Recognition Memory for Complex Configurations," *Perception and Psychophysics* 9 (1970): 240.

61. Michael D. Rabin and William S. Cain, "Odor Recognition: Familiarity, Identifiability, and Encoding Consistency," *Journal of Experimental Psychology: Learning, Memory, and Cognition* 10, no. 2 (1984): 316.

62. Harry T. Lawless, "Recognition of Common Odors, Pictures, and Simple Shapes," *Perception and Psychophysics* 24 (1978): 493–95.

63. Ibid., 494. We take this to reflect the difference noted earlier, that of comparing abstract shapes to readily identifiable shapes.

64. G. W. Cermak, "Short-Term Recognition Memory for Complex Free-Form Figures," *Psychonomic Science* 25 (1971): 209–11.

65. David Van Zanten, "Architectural Composition at the Ecole Des Beaux-Arts from Charles Percier to Charles Garnier," in *The Architecture of the Ecole des Beaus-Arts,* ed. Arthur Drexler (New York: Museum of Modern Art, 1977), 268.

66. Drexler, "Engineer's Architecture," 38.

67. Paul Goldberger, "Chicago Unveils a Proud New Temple of Books," *New York Times,* 1 March 1992, sec. 2, p. 33.

68. Blair Kamin, "Old St. Patrick's Church Renovation, Chicago," *Architectural Record,* January 2001, 92.

69. Ibid., 89.

9. Objects of Our Lives

1. *Compact Edition of the Oxford English Dictionary,* 27th printing, s.v. "object." Indeed, rather more than a full page is devoted to this intriguing and inclusive word.

2. Russell W. Belk, "The Ineluctable Mysteries of Possessions," in *To Have Possessions: A Handbook on Ownership and Property,* ed. Floyd W. Rudmin (Corte Madera, Calif.: Select Press, 1991), 17.

3. Ibid., 18. It might be noted that many, perhaps most, of the anthropologists who have studied the function of artifacts in nonliterate cultures would agree with this conclusion.

4. That people have in their possession objects for which there can exist no acceptable substitute and which they accordingly will not discard, and whose presence causes feelings of elation and self-enlargement, persuasively argues for circumspection on the part of the designer.

5. Werner Muensterberger, *Collecting: An Unruly Passion* (Princeton: Princeton University Press, 1994), 10.

6. Eugene Rochberg-Halton, *Meaning and Modernity: Social Theory in the Pragmatic Attitude* (Chicago: University of Chicago Press, 1986), 184.

7. Ibid., 185. Animism refers to the belief that animals, plants, and various ritual objects have within them a spiritual energy and even persona. On the island of New Guinea this is referred to as mana, a significant force to be propitiated at appropriate ceremonies.

8. Ibid. He points out that the animist view is antithetical to people raised in the West, but this conclusion is somewhat less than convincing as seen in practice. That is, it is our observation that people do ascribe personal characteristics to objects and refer to them in anthropomorphized terms.

9. W. Jeffrey Burroughs, David R. Drews, and William K. Hallman, "Predicting Personality from Personal Possessions: A Self-Presentational Analysis," in *To Have Possessions: A Handbook on Ownership and Property,* ed. Floyd W. Rudmin (Corte Madera, Calif.: Select Press, 1991), 147.

10. Ibid., 148.

11. Melanie Wallendorf and Eric J. Arnould, "'My Favorite Things': A Cross-Cultural Inquiry into Object Attachment, Possessiveness, and Social Linkage," *Journal of Consumer Research* 14 (March 1988): 531.

12. This includes studies that indicate that others see our homes as expressions of

their owner's identities. R. W. Belk, K. D. Bahn, and R. N. Mayer, "Developmental Recognition of Consumption Symbolism," *Journal of Consumer Research* 9 (1982): 4–17.

13. E. K. Sadalla, B. Vershure, and W. J. Burroughs, "Identity Symbolism in Housing," *Environment and Behavior* 19 (1987): 569–87.

14. Burroughs, Drews, and Hallman, "Predicting Personality from Personal Possessions," 160.

15. E. L. Landon, "Self Concept and Consumer Purchase Intentions," *Journal of Consumer Research* 1 (1974): 44–51.

16. C. Cooper, "The House as Symbol of the Self," in *Designing for Human Behavior,* ed. J. Lang et al. (Stroudsburg, Pa.: Dowden, Hutchinson, and Ross, 1974), 130–46; B. Vershure, S. Magel, and E. K. Sadalla, "House Form and Social Identity," in *The Behavioral Basis of Design,* ed. P. Suedfeld et al. (Stroudsburg, Pa.: Dowden, Hutchinson, and Ross, 1977), 273–78; D. Canter, S. West, and R. Wools, "Judgments of People and Their Rooms," *British Journal of Social and Clinical Psychology* 13 (1974): 113–18; E. O. Laumann and J. S. House, "Living Room Styles and Social Attributes: The Patterning of Material Artifacts in a Modern Urban Community," *Sociology and Social Research* 54 (1970): 321–42.

17. Helga Dittmar, "Meanings of Material Possessions as Reflections of Identity: Gender and Social-Material Position in Society," in *To Have Possessions: A Handbook on Ownership and Property,* ed. Floyd W. Rudmin (Corte Madera, Calif.: Select Press, 1991), 167. Dittmar points out that the relationship of possessions to our sense of identity appears to be a particularly important one, as borne out by her 1989 studies. This, she suggests, is in part a reflection of people in an industrial mass-consumer culture tending to define themselves through what they own; this, in turn, is likely the result of an individual's achieving identity on his or her own through earned wealth and possessions (rather than inheritance).

18. Ibid., 180.

19. N. Laura Kamptner, "Personal Possessions and Their Meanings: A Life-Span Perspective," in *To Have Possessions: A Handbook on Ownership and Property,* ed. Floyd W. Rudmin (Corte Madera, Calif.: Select Press, 1991), 225. Kamptner goes on to note the many studies (Csikszentmihali and Rochberg-Halton in 1981; Dittmar in 1989; Parker in 1980; Rudmin in 1990; Sherman and Newman in 1977–1978) that support her comments.

20. Dittmar, "Meanings of Material Possessions as Reflections of Identity," 181.

21. Ibid., 183.

22. Belk, "The Ineluctable Mysteries of Possessions," 24.

23. Cooper, "The House as Symbol of the Self," 131.

24. The authors bear sole responsibility for this observation.

25. Belk, "The Ineluctable Mysteries of Possessions," 25.

26. Ibid., 41.

27. Muensterberger, *Collecting: An Unruly Passion,* 14.

28. Mihaly Csikszentmihalyi and Eugene Rochberg-Halton, *The Meaning of Things: Domestic Symbols and the Self* (New York: Cambridge University Press, 1981), ix.

29. Ananda K. Coomaraswamy, *Figures of Speech or Figures of Thought: Collected Essays on the Traditional or "Normal" View of Art* (London: Luzac, 1946), 89.

30. Csikszentmihalyi and Rochberg-Halton, *The Meaning of Things,* 17.

31. In the foreword of the conference proceedings of the Research Workshop on Materialism and Other Consumption Orientations (Kingston, Ontario, 25–28 June 1992), Floyd Rudmin and Marsha Richins make a similar point when they comment that "the 'natural' need to acquire, accumulate and consume objects, people, ideas, experiences,

and possessions of all types is reaching some very real limits. The normal materialistic lifestyle is now facing local and global environmental pressures to desist."

32. Thomas Hardy, *The Return of the Native* (1878; New York: New American Library of World Literature, 1959), 142.

33. Ibid., 136.

34. Kenneth Grahame, *The Wind in the Willows* (New York: Bantam Books, 1982), 51.

35. Carl Jung, letter of 26 July 1934, in *C. G. Jung: Word and Image,* ed. Aniela Jaffé (Princeton: Princeton University Press, 1979), 196.

36. Jung, *Memories, Dreams, Reflections,* 226.

37. E. V. Walter, *Placeways: A Theory of the Human Environment* (Chapel Hill: University of North Carolina Press, 1988), 143.

38. Belk, "The Ineluctable Mysteries of Possessions," 32.

39. Helen Dudar, "The Artful Addiction of Sigmund Freud," *Smithsonian,* August 1990, 104.

40. Muensterberger, *Collecting: An Unruly Passion,* 137.

41. Helga Dittmar, *The Social Psychology of Material Possessions: To Have Is to Be* (New York: St. Martin's Press, 1992), 10.

42. Ibid., 89. Dittmar persuasively makes the case that most objects, while serving an obvious function (e.g., an automobile or stereo), simultaneously signify symbolic elements (our freedom of movement or taste in music). This is especially true in regard to the contents of the house, such as furniture, which can convey social standing, wealth, and status.

43. Csikszentmihalyi and Rochberg-Halton, *The Meaning of Things,* 144.

44. Ibid., 145. This having been said, it is instructive to examine the response of a sixty-two-year-old grandmother in regard to her special objects: "Well, they represent my hard-earned final composite identity." For most of us, as for the families in the study, this is likely the reality.

45. Charles Moore, Gerald Allen, and Donlyn Lyndon, *The Place of Houses* (New York: Holt, Rinehart and Winston, 1974), 99. The fireplace mantel often plays a similar role.

46. Ibid., 226.

47. Philippa Tristram, *Living Space in Fact and Fiction* (New York: Routledge, 1989), 1.

48. Moore, Allen, and Lyndon, *The Place of Houses,* 231.

49. Frank Russel, ed. *John Soane* (London: Academy Editions, 1983), 34.

50. Stefan Buzas, *Sir John Soane's Museum* (Berlin: Ernst Wasmuth Verlag, 1994), 15.

51. Martin Pawley, "The Time House," in *Meaning in Architecture,* ed. Charles Jencks and George Baird (New York: George Braziller, 1970), 123.

52. Pawley, "The Time House," 143. The five axioms referred to here were discussed in detail in chapter 3.

53. Thomas Hardy, "On an Invitation to the United States," in *Poems of the Past and the Present* (New York: Harper and Brothers, 1901), 66.

54. Florence Emily Hardy, *The Life of Thomas Hardy, 1840–1928* (1962; London, 1975), 254.

55. Alas, to no avail. When the well was sunk for the house, extensive human remains were found, as were Roman-British shards of pottery.

56. Grahame, *The Wind in the Willows,* 85.

57. Kamptner, "Personal Possessions and Their Meanings," 224.

58. Dittmar, *The Social Psychology of Material Possessions,* 108.

59. Ibid., 109. This position is echoed in G. Carp's study of Victoria Plaza, *A Future*

for the Aged: Victoria Plaza and Its Residents (Austin: University of Texas Press, 1966), where the relocation of the elderly resulted in their surrender of furniture and other personal possessions. The study concludes that such objects were very much missed, for their own sake and as reminders of family events, but also because the substitution of less-refined items for them served as confirmation and reminder of the individual's loss of status in society.

60. Edmund Sherman and Evelyn S. Newman, "The Meaning of Cherished Personal Possessions for the Elderly," *International Journal of Aging and Human Development* 8, no. 2 (1977–1978): 182.

61. Ibid., 191.

62. Dittmar, *The Social Psychology of Material Possessions,* 109.

63. R. Butler and M. Lewis, *Aging and Mental Health: Positive Psychosocial Approaches,* 3d ed. (St. Louis: C. V. Mosby, 1982), 37.

64. Ibid. Of course, this book was first published in 1973, and such enlightened procedures are still little in evidence; indeed, even the third edition of this book has less than a page devoted to the vital importance of people's possessions in maintaining self-identity.

65. Simone de Beauvoir, *The Coming of Age* (New York: G. P. Putnam's Sons, 1972), 469.

66. Virginia Woolf, "Street Haunting: A London Adventure," in *Collected Essays,* vol. 4 (London: Hogarth Press, 1967), 166.

67. Csikszentmihalyi and Rochberg-Halton, *The Meaning of Things,* 138. One is reminded of Winston Churchill's comment "We shape our buildings; thereafter they shape us" ("Schools of Tomorrow," *Time,* 12 September 1960, 74).

68. Peter K. Lunt and Sonia M. Livingstone, *Mass Consumption and Personal Identity* (Buckingham, England: Open University Press, 1992), 20.

69. Ibid., 21.

70. Jean Baudrillard, "Consumer Society," in *Jean Baudrillard: Selected Writings,* ed. M. Poster (Cambridge: Polity, 1988), 31.

71. Ibid., 33. During the nineteenth century, many small markets gathered together into what became the prototype for the modern department store. The new entrepreneurs were aware from the start of the primary social role of the department store. Thus stores such as the Bon Marché (1878) and the Magasin du Printemps (1881), both in Paris, were conceived as richly decorated and spacious light courts serving, in Emile Zola's words, as a "cathedral of modern commerce, solid and light, made for a congregation of clients."

72. Wallendorf and Arnould, "My Favorite Things," 543.

73. Ibid.

74. Tristam, *Living Space in Fact and Fiction,* 260.

75. Ibid.

76. Dittmar, *The Social Psychology of Material Possessions,* 110.

77. Ibid. We see a real distinction between this reference to self-referential signs and the social-referential signs pointed to by Baudrillard.

78. Henry James, *The Portrait of a Lady* (1881; Cambridge: Houghton Mifflin, 1956), 172.

79. Stephen Barker, ed., *Excavations and Their Objects: Freud's Collection of Antiquity* (Albany: State University of New York Press, 1996), xi.

80. Lynn Gamwell, "A Collector Analyses Collecting: Sigmund Freud on the Passion to Possess," in *Excavations and Their Objects: Freud's Collection of Antiquity,* ed. Stephen Barker (Albany: State University of New York Press, 1996), 6.

81. Ibid.

10. The Light Fantastic

1. Mark Twain, *The Innocents Abroad, or The New Pilgrim's Progress* (1869; New York: Harper and Row, 1980), 248–50.

2. Henri Focillon, *The Life of Forms in Art,* trans. Charles Beecher Hogan and George Kubler (1934; New York: Zone Books, 1989), 75.

3. Henry Adams, *Mont-Saint-Michel and Chartres* (1905; Boston: Houghton Mifflin, 1963), 137.

4. Henry Plummer, *Poetics of Light* (Tokyo: a + u Publishing, 1987), 24.

5. Paul Scheerbart, *Glass Architecture,* ed. Dennis Sharp, trans. James Palmes (1914; New York: Praeger, 1972), 71. So convinced was Taut of the redeeming qualities of light and color that he designed a brilliantly colored set of children's building blocks he called Dandanah, the Fairy Palace.

6. Although designed in 1929, the Madonna della Strada was not actually built until 1938.

7. Plummer, *The Poetics of Light,* 139.

8. Ibid., 13. It is worth noting that H. G. Wells took care to describe the light in the enchanted garden as "perfectly and subtly luminous," and again as a "warm and mellow light."

9. Marietta S. Millet, *Light Revealing Architecture* (New York: Van Nostrand Reinhold, 1996), 1.

10. Judith H. Heerwagen, "Affective Functioning, 'Light Hunger,' and Room Brightness Preferences," *Environment and Behavior* 22 (September 1990): 610.

11. Ibid., 614.

12. Frank H. Mahnke and Rudolf H. Mahnke, *Color and Light in Man-Made Environments* (New York: Van Nostrand Reinhold, 1987), 40.

13. Ibid., 53.

14. J. B. Maas, J. K. Jayson, and D. A. Kleiber, "Effects of Spectral Differences in Illumination on Fatigue," *Journal of Applied Psychology* 59 (1974): 524–26.

15. Fritz Hollwich, *The Influence of Ocular Light Perception on Metabolism in Man and in Animal,* trans. Hunter and Hildegarde Hannum (New York: Springer-Verlag, 1979), 90.

16. Ibid.

17. L. W. Mayron, J. N. Ott, R. Nations, and E. L. Mayron, "Light, Radiation, and Academic Behaviour: Initial Studies on the Effects of Full-Spectrum Lighting and Radiation Shielding on Behaviour and Academic Performance of School Children," *Academic Therapy* 10 (1974): 44.

18. Hollwich, *The Influence of Ocular Light Perception,* 91.

19. Rikard Küller and Carin Lindsten, "Health and Behavior of Children in Classrooms with and without Windows," *Journal of Environmental Psychology* 12 (1992): 316.

20. Heerwagen, "Affective Functioning, 'Light Hunger,' and Room Brightness Preferences," 631.

21. Deborah T. Sharpe, *The Psychology of Color and Design* (Totowa, N.J.: Littlefield, Adams, 1981), 86.

22. Hazel Rossotti, *Colour: Why the World Isn't Grey* (Princeton: Princeton University Press, 1983), 209.

23. Igor Knez, "Effects of Indoor Lighting on Mood and Cognition," *Journal of Environmental Psychology* 15 (1995): 39.

24. Ibid., 46.

25. Ibid., 47.

26. Millet, *Light Revealing Architecture,* 2.

27. Ettore Sottsass, "Travel Notes," *Terrazzo,* spring 1989, 38.

28. Ibid. The term *illumination,* as already noted, is equally capable of profound overtones; perhaps another term is in order for the sort of prosaic lighting paradigm that Sottsass scorns. We prefer *illumined,* but many others are possible.

29. Maxim Gorky, in Richard Snow, *Coney Island: A Postcard Journey to the City of Fire* (New York: Brightwaters Press, 1984), 18.

30. Ibid., 19. Come daylight, and a tour of a papier-mâché underworld, Gorky returned to his senses, proclaiming that "hell is very badly done."

31. James Huneker, in Snow, *Coney Island,* 19. This observation turned out to be prescient, as fire in fact swept Dreamland in 1911.

32. Plummer, *The Poetics of Light,* 11.

33. Millet, *Light Revealing Architecture,* 2.

34. Sigrid Asmus, "Introductory Essay," in *James Turrell: Four Light Installations,* ed. Laura J. Millin (Seattle: Real Comet Press, 1982), 7.

35. Richard Andrews, "Interview," in *James Turrell: Four Light Installations,* 10.

36. Ibid.

37. Pamela Hammond, "Interview," in *James Turrell: Four Light Installations,* 19.

38. Millet, *Light Revealing Architecture,* 94.

39. Asmus, "Introductory Essay," 7.

40. Andrews, "Interview," 11.

41. Richard Andrews and Chris Bruce, *James Turrell: Sensing Space* (Seattle: Henry Gallery Association, 1992), 50.

42. Jeffrey Hogrefe, "In Pursuit of God's Light," *Metropolis,* August–September 2000, 82.

43. Junichirō Tanizaki, *In Praise of Shadows,* trans. Thomas J. Harper and Edward G. Seidensticker (New Haven: Leete's Island Books, 1977), 17, 18, 20.

44. It is surely no exaggeration to say that shadow has been a staple of pictorial representation, from film to comic strips, and always to the ends of fear. Eisenberg's famous comic strip *The Shadow* took the device to its expressionist extreme pictorially, and the script took it to its psychological limits.

45. Zinaida Hippius, "L'Imprévisibilité," trans. Temira Pachmuss, in *The Penguin Book of Women Poets,* ed. Carol Cosman, Joan Keefe, and Kathleen Weaver (New York: Penguin Books, 1978), 187.

46. Plummer, *The Poetics of Light,* 155.

47. Frank Lloyd Wright, *The Natural House* (1954), in *Frank Lloyd Wright: Collected Writings, 1949–1959,* ed. Bruce Brooks Pfeiffer, vol. 5 (New York: Rizzoli, 1995), 115.

48. Tadao Ando, *Japan Architect,* no. 1 (1991): 126.

49. Ibid. One might also note Ando's remarkable sensitivity to materials, whose textures he exploits to the end of understanding architecture "through the body."

50. Zeynep Çelik, "Cultural Intersections: Re-visioning Architecture and the City in the Twentieth Century," in *At the End of the Century: One Hundred Years of Architecture,* ed. Richard Koshalek and Elizabeth A. T. Smith (New York: Harry N. Abrams, 1998), 226.

51. Todd Williams, "The House That Turns to the Sun," *House and Garden,* February 1987, 198.

52. Emil Nolde, "Primitive Art," in *Voices of German Expressionism,* ed. Victor H. Miese (Englewood Cliffs, N.J.: Prentice-Hall 1970), 36.

53. Frances Anderton, "Architecture for All Senses," *Architectural Review,* October 1991, 27.

54. Ibid.

55. Rossotti, *Colour: Why the World Isn't Grey,* 16.

56. Anders Hård, "The Natural Colour System and Its Universal Application in the Study of Environmental Design," in *Colour for Architecture,* ed. Tom Porter and Byron Mikellides (London: Studio Vista, 1976), 119.

57. Johannes Itten, *The Elements of Color: A Treatise on the Color System of Johannes Itten Based on His Book "The Art of Color,"* ed. Faber Birren, trans. Ernst Van Hagen (New York: Van Nostrand Reinhold, 1970), 12.

58. Sharpe, *The Psychology of Color and Design,* 9.

59. Ibid.

60. Rose H. Alschuler and La Berta Weiss Hattwick, *Painting and Personality: A Study of Young Children* (Chicago: University of Chicago Press, 1947), 15.

61. Ibid., 18.

62. Ibid., 104. They found that interest in green tended to parallel, although not as emphatically, interest in blue.

63. Sharpe, *The Psychology of Color and Design,* 18.

64. John C. Garrett and Charles I. Brooks, "Effect of Ballot Color, Sex of Candidate, and Sex of College Students of Voting Age on Their Voting Behavior," *Psychological Reports* 60 (1987): 39. When names were gender specific, men tended to vote for men, and women for women.

65. N. Clayton Silver and Rozana Ferrante, "Sex Differences in Color Preferences among an Elderly Sample," *Perceptual and Motor Skills* 80 (1995): 921. It is perhaps of interest that one would have to combine the female preference for blue, red, and pink (56.36) to equal the male preference for blue alone (56.63).

66. Sharpe, *The Psychology of Color and Design,* 136.

67. Ibid., 131. Thus the relative success of pink for bakery boxes.

68. Andrew D. Lyons, "Synaesthesia—a Cognitive Model of Cross Modal Association," Sydney Conservatorium of Music, University of Sydney. http://www.vislab.usyd.edu.au/user/alyons. Accessed 24 May 2001.

69. Ibid., 2.

70. Avery N. Gilbert, Robyn Martin, and Sarah E. Kemp, "Cross-Modal Correspondence between Vision and Olfaction: The Color of Smells," *American Journal of Psychology* 109, no. 3 (fall 1996): 336.

71. Ibid., 349.

72. Sarah E. Kemp and Avery N. Gilbert, "Odor Intensity and Color Lightness Are Correlated Sensory Dimensions," *American Journal of Psychology* 110, no. 1 (spring 1997): 45.

73. Tom Porter and Byron Mikellides, *Colour for Architecture* (London: Studio Vista, 1976), 14.

74. Ibid., 13.

75. Mahnke and Mahnke, *Color and Light in Man-Made Environments,* 18.

76. Jennifer L. Etnier and Charles J. Hardy, "The Effects of Environmental Color," *Journal of Sport Behavior,* August 1997, 299.

77. Ibid., 310.

78. Pamela J. Profusek and David W. Rainey, "Effects of Baker-Miller Pink and Red on Anxiety State, Grip Strength, and Motor Precision," *Perceptual and Motor Skills* 65 (1987): 941. Thus it has been used in the schizophrenic wards of mental hospitals and police holding cells for calming purposes.

79. Leonard Weller and Randy Livingston, "Effect of Color of Questionnaire on Emotional Responses," *Journal of General Psychology* 115, no. 4 (1988): 438.

80. Patricia Valdez and Albert Mehrabian, "Effects of Color on Emotion," *Journal of Experimental Psychology* 123, no. 4 (1994): 394.

81. Ibid., 406. Thus bismuth pink scores low for arousal and dominance, tending to confirm its effectiveness as a sedative.

82. Ibid., 407. Variations in hue tended to have little or no effect, however.

83. Sharpe, *The Psychology of Color and Design*, 41.

84. Ibid., 149.

85. Robert E. MacLaury, "From Brightness to Hue: An Explanatory Model of Color-Category Evolution," *Current Anthropology* 33, no. 2 (April 1992): 137.

86. Israel Abramov and James Gordon, "Color Appearance: On Seeing Red—or Yellow, or Green, or Blue," *Annual Review of Psychology* (1994): 466.

87. Marilyn A. Read, Alan I. Sugawara, and Jeanette A. Brandt, "Impact of Space and Color in the Physical Environment on Preschool Children's Cooperative Behavior," *Environment and Behavior* 31, no. 3 (May 1999): 413.

88. Ibid., 423.

89. Michael Lancaster, *Colourscape* (London: Academy Editions, 1996), 23.

90. Lois Swirnoff, *Dimensional Color* (New York: Van Nostrand Reinhold, 1992), 5.

91. Ibid., 15. A far cry, she comments, from the surfaces of early twentieth-century architecture, which "appear mute or sterile."

92. Lancaster, *Colourscape*, 61. Such a process would, at the least, help new buildings become better neighbors to those already in place, a courtesy that seems in short supply of late.

93. Jean-Philippe Lenclos, in Lancaster, *Colourscape*, 72.

94. Michael Webb, *House Design: Regina Pizzinini and Leon Luxemburg* (Mulgrave, Australia: Images Publishing Group, 1998), 12.

95. Kevin P. Keim, *An Architectural Life: Memoirs and Memories of Charles W. Moore* (Boston: Bullfinch Press, 1996), 197.

96. Charles W. Moore, *An Architectural Life*, 199.

97. Friedensreich Hundertwasser, *Hundertwasser Architecture: For a More Human Architecture in Harmony with Nature* (New York: Taschen, 1997), 253.

98. We heartily recommend that the reader examine the series of models, as they are both informative and intriguing. They appear on pages 253–55 of Hundertwasser's book.

99. Hundertwasser, *Hundertwasser Architecture*, 258. We might remember here our comment relative to the inhabitants of Pessac about giving license to a building's inhabitants to alter that building.

11. Sensory Schematics

1. Russell W. Belk, "The Ineluctable Mysteries of Possessions," in *To Have Possessions: A Handbook on Ownership and Property*, ed. Floyd W. Rudmin (Corte Madera, Calif.: Select Press, 1991), 35–36.

2. Werner Muensterberger, *Collecting: An Unruly Passion* (Princeton: Princeton University Press, 1994), 10.

3. Eugene Rochberg-Halton, *Meaning and Modernity: Social Theory in the Pragmatic Attitude* (Chicago: University of Chicago Press, 1986), 185.

4. David Seamon, "Phenomenology and Environment-Behavior Research," in

Advances in Environment, Behavior, and Design, ed. Ervin H. Zube and Gary T. Moore, vol. 1 (New York: Plenum Press, 1987), 4.

5. Ibid., 6.

6. David Seamon, "The Phenomenological Contribution to Environmental Psychology," *Journal of Environmental Psychology* 2 (1982): 123.

7. Maurice Sauzet, "Sensory Phenomena as a Reference for the Architectural Project," *Architecture and Behavior* 5, no. 2 (1989): 153.

8. Maurice Sauzet, "The Space of the Senses," *Techniques and Architecture,* July 1990, 99.

9. Anna Jackson and Chris Johnson, *Australian Architecture Now* (London: Thames and Hudson, 2000), 206.

10. Ibid.

11. Rachel Kaplan and Stephen Kaplan, *The Experience of Nature: A Psychological Perspective* (Cambridge: Cambridge University Press, 1989), 52–55. For a fuller explication of their theory, the reader might return to chapter 5. Of real interest is the correlation of the Kaplans' inventory of characteristics with that of Brodie Ann Bain's model of the "successful entry," which are sense of place, legibility, and mystery.

12. Charles W. Rusch, "On Understanding Awareness," *Journal of Aesthetic Education* 4, no. 4 (October 1970): 58.

13. Rusch points out that these defined levels, fairly discrete in childhood, are more continuous in adults.

14. Kaplan and Kaplan, *The Experience of Nature,* 11.

15. For a fuller explication of these ethnic and cultural factors, refer to David Howes's position discussed in the middle of chapter 3; a complete discussion of context codes (as defined by E. T. Hall) can be found in chapter 4.

16. A. Richard Williams, *The Urban Stage: A Reflexion of Architecture and Urban Design* (San Francisco: San Francisco Center for Architecture and Urban Studies, 1980), xviii.

17. Helen Keller, "Three Days to See," *Atlantic Monthly,* January 1933, 36, 42.

18. Kristi Cameron, "3-D Tufte," *Metropolis,* February 2001, 18.

19. Accordingly, we have omitted any photograph of the sculpture.

20. Marcel Joray and Jesús Rafael Soto, *Soto* (Neuchâtel-Suisse: Editions du Griffon, 1984), 174.

21. The welded-bronze musical sculptures of Harry Bertoia immediately come to mind.

22. Bernhard Leitner, *Sound:Space* (New York: New York University Press, 1978), 13.

23. Anyone who has attended a blues or rock concert will have some notion of the visceral qualities of sound.

24. Saul Anton, "An Egg for All Seasons," *Metropolis,* November 1999, 130.

25. Ibid.

26. James Corner, "Time, Material, and Event: The Work of Michael Van Valkenburgh," in *Design with the Land: Landscape Architecture of Michael Van Valkenburgh,* ed. Brooke Hodge (New York: Princeton Architectural Press, 1994), 6.

27. Jean Piaget, *The Mechanisms of Perception,* trans. G. N. Seagrim (1961; New York: Basic Books, 1969), 70.

28. There are, of course, exceptions to this observation, although they do not fall within the usual definition of architectural spaces. Conditions of overload, for example, are common in amusement parks, and deprivation is the defining quality of specialized

isolation facilities. We observe that not only are these cases exceptional, but they are characterized by user control and/or knowledge of outcomes.

29. We think it possible for the Slider to have a mnemonic function as well. The symbols for figure/ground (■) and icon (●) might be shaded—or color coded—to indicate mnemonic potency. It will likely fall to the cultural anthropologists to decide what spatial memories can be considered cultural, and not simply personal, which is surely necessary for wider practical use.

30. Jim Murphy, "Cornering the Loop," *Progressive Architecture,* October 1983, 78.

31. David A. Greenspan, "333 Wacker Drive," *Inland Architect,* 27, no. 3 (1983): 13. The author points out that there may be almost too much of a good thing, in that the rich, detailed materials draw unflattering attention to the place where base and shaft meet.

32. Gerald T. Cobb, in Steven Holl, *The Chapel of St. Ignatius* (New York: Princeton Architectural Press, 1999), 9.

33. Ibid.

34. Sheri Olson, "What Is Sacred Space? Steven Holl's Chapel of St. Ignatius Answers with Texture, Light, and Color," *Architectural Record* 185, no. 7 (July 1997): 47.

35. Gerald T. Cobb, in Holl, *The Chapel of St. Ignatius,* 9.

36. Olson, "What Is Sacred Space,"48.

37. Holl, *The Chapel of St. Ignatius,* 82.

38. Ibid., 92.

39. Joseph Glicksohn, "Subjective Time Estimation in Altered Sensory Environments," *Environment and Behavior* 24 (September 1992): 634.

40. D. Zakay, D. Nitzan, and J. Glocksohn, "The Influence of Task Difficulty and External Tempo on Subjective Time Estimation," *Perception and Psychophysics* 34 (1983): 451–56.

41. David Leiser, Eliahu Stern, and Joachim Meyer, "Mean Velocity and Total Time Estimation Effects of Order and Proportions," *Journal of Environmental Psychology* 11 (1991): 355.

42. Williams, *The Urban Stage,* 35.

43. Ibid.

44. The Fibonacci sequence, in which each number is the sum of the previous two, was first remarked upon by Leonardo of Pisa (derisively called Fibonacci) in the early thirteenth century. This extraordinary mathematician, who was the author of the *Liber Abaci* that introduced Arabic numerals to Europe, found in this sequence a mathematical analogy to the geometric method of developing the golden mean. The Fibonacci sequence also provides the basis for the logarithmic spiral that underlies gnomic growth patterns in many life-forms. Thus Pallasmaa chose a significant metaphor for the entry to an educational institution.

45. Dan Hoffman, "Driveway Square," *Arkkitehti—Finnish Architectural Review* nos. 5–6 (1996); translation found at http://www.uiah.fi/esittely/historia/square.htm.

46. Peter MacKeith, "Juhani Pallasmaa," *World Architecture,* no. 25 (1993): 42.

47. Ibid.

48. Joseph Giovannini, "Nordic Tracks: A Museum by Juhani Pallasmaa Interprets Lapland's Lost Vernacular," *Architecture,* October 1998, 109.

49. Ibid., 110.

50. Peter Zumthor, *Peter Zumthor Works: Buildings and Projects, 1979–1997* (Baden, Switzerland: Lars Müller Publishers, 1998), 156.

51. Raymund Ryan, "Primal Therapy," *Architectural Review* 202, no. 1206 (1997): 44.

12. Getting Somewhere

1. John Summerson, *Heavenly Mansions* (New York: W. W. Norton, 1963), 112.

2. Philippa Tristram, *Living Space in Fact and Fiction* (New York: Routledge, 1989), 267.

3. Joel Meyrowitz, *No Sense of Place: The Impact of Electronic Media on Social Behavior* (New York: Oxford University Press, 1985), 117.

4. David Pearson, "Making Sense of Architecture," *Architecture Review 10: Sensuality and Architecture* (October 1991): 68.

5. A. Richard Williams, *The Urban Stage: A Reflexion of Architecture and Urban Design* (San Francisco: San Francisco Center for Architecture and Urban Studies, 1980), 309.

6. Ibid.

7. Arthur I. Rubin and Jacqueline Elder, *Building for People: Behavioral Research Approaches and Directions,* Special Publication 474, (Washington, D.C.: National Bureau of Standards, 1980), 146.

8. "Eyetracking Facility." Beckman Institute for Advanced Science and Technology Web site. http://www.beckman.uiuc.edu/research/eyetracking.html (13 April 2001).

9. Ibid.

10. Richard Sexton, *Parallel Utopias* (San Francisco: Chronicle Books, 1995), 104.

11. Ibid. Clearly, these codes will produce a fair amount of consistency, notwithstanding their nonspecific character.

12. Environmental Simulation Laboratory, Center for Environmental Design Research, and University of California, Berkeley, "Sun, Wind, and Comfort in Toronto," *Progressive Architecture* 73, no. 1 (January 1992): 97.

13. Edward Arens and Peter Bosselmann, "Wind, Sun, and Temperature—Predicting the Thermal Comfort of People in Outdoor Spaces," in *Proceedings of American Society of Civil Engineers* (Berkeley, Calif.: Center for Environmental Design Research, 1986), 1.

14. Ibid., 5.

15. Ulla Westerberg, "Climatic Planning: Physics or Symbolism?" *Architecture and Behaviour* 10 (1994): 49.

16. Ibid., 60. Westerberg points out that while his data are valid for virtually all parts of Sweden, a different series of base calculations would be needed for different geographic locations.

17. Forrest Wilson, *A Graphic Survey of Perception and Behavior for the Design Professions* (New York: Van Nostrand Reinhold, 1984), 198.

18. F. J. Langdon, "Human Sciences and the Environment in Buildings," *Build International* 6 (January–February 1973): 106.

19. L. H. Hawkins, "The Influence of Air Ions, Temperature, and Humidity of Subjective Wellbeing and Comfort," *Journal of Environmental Psychology* 1 (1981): 279.

20. Michael Southworth, "The Sonic Environment of Cities," *Environment and Behavior* 1 (June 1969): 67.

21. R. Murray Schafer, *The Soundscape: Our Sonic Environment and the Tuning of the World* (1977; Rochester, Vt.: Destiny Books, 1994), 131.

22. Rubin and Elder, *Building for People,* 128.

23. Ibid., 130. Designing a building plan on the sonic or olfactory characteristics of the events that are to take place in the various spaces would mark a real change from current methodology—which centers on the events in isolation.

24. The scentometer is a commercially available machine for measuring odor intensities at sites where a problem is perceived by air pollution control inspectors.

25. Charles Platt, "You've Got Smell," *Wired* 7 (November 1999): 258.

26. Ibid., 261. One of the biggest problems with incorporating odor concerns is not its generation but its evacuation once generated.

27. Platt reports that the Illinois Institute of Technology in Chicago has a patent pending on a peripheral device that releases odors, and that a company in Massachusetts (MicroChips) announced a chip containing compartments whose odoriferous contents can be selectively released. And there are still others.

28. Forrest Wilson, *A Graphic Survey of Perception and Behavior for the Design Professions* (New York: Van Nostrand Reinhold, 1984), 3.

29. Ibid., 274.

30. This sharply contrasts to the practices, for example, of the medieval architects who designed in situ, relying for direction on a traditional mental image shared by the community.

31. Indeed, beaux-arts architectural drawings, notable for their fine use of line, shade, and color, often addressed artistic issues more than actual design considerations.

32. Juhani Pallasmaa, "An Architecture of the Seven Senses," in *Questions of Perception: Phenomenology of Architecture,* ed. Steven Holl, Juhani Pallasmaa, and Alberto Pérez-Gómez (Tokyo: a + u Publishing, 1994), 29.

33. Edmund N. Bacon, "Bringing Us Back to Our Senses: The New Paradigm for Teaching Design," *Ekistics* 55, nos. 328–30 (1988): 113.

34. CATIA was developed by the Dassault Corporation of France for the design of Mirage jet fighters and has been used in the design of Chrysler's Viper automobile and Boeing's 777 civilian aircraft.

35. "CATIA at Frank O. Gehry and AMP Associates, Inc." http://www-3.ibm.com/solutions/engineering/esindus.nsf/Public/sufran, 2.

36. Gordon Wright, "Compounding the Curves," *Building Design and Construction,* May 2000, 2. http://www.findarticles.com/cf_0/m3024/5_41/62215535?print.jhtml.

37. Ibid., 3.

38. Paul Goldberger, "Digital Dreams: What If Howard Roark Had Used a Mac?" *New Yorker,* 12 March 2001, 97.

39. The exhibition was organized by Joseph Rosa, curator of the Heinz Architectural Center at the Carnegie Museum of Art in Pittsburgh, and held there in March 2001. It included the work of Greg Lynn, Peter Eisenman, Peter Stamberg, Jesse Reise, and Nanako Umemoto, and others. Surprisingly, it also had a project by Gehry.

40. Goldberger, "Digital Dreams," 96.

41. Greg Lynn, "Embryologic Houses©™," *Domus* 822 (January 2000): 12.

42. Ibid.

43. Greg Lynn FORM, http://www.basilisk.com/G/GREG_LYNN_FORM_760.html, 2 June 2001, 1.

44. Greg Lynn, *Animate Form* (New York: Princeton Architectural Press, 1999), 9.

45. Ibid., 10.

46. For example, the NCSA/UIUC 2001–2002 Faculty Fellowship was awarded to Joy Monice Malnar, AIA, School of Architecture, and Eric Loth, Ph.D., Department of Aeronautical and Astronautical Engineering, to conduct a study, "CAVE Visualization of the Massing of Large Urban Multi-purpose Buildings and Their Unsteady Air Flowfields." The object of the study is the design of a building with consideration of wind patterns at plaza level.

47. Karen E. Lange, "Djénné: West Africa's Eternal City," *National Geographic* 199, no. 6 (June 2001): 104.

48. For more information on this city see www.nationalgeographic.com/ngm/0106.

49. The CAVE is a trademark of the Board of Trustees of the University of Illinois.

50. The Infinity Wall, a large-screen multiprojection display, is in process of development.

51. In some applications, users interact with the CAVE through speech commands.

52. William R. Sherman and Alan B. Craig, "Literacy in Virtual Reality: A New Medium," *Computer Graphic* 29, no. 4 (November 1995).

53. Richard Powers, *Plowing the Dark* (New York: Farrar, Straus and Giroux, 2000), 3.

54. CRUMBS was created by John Pixton, Rachael Brady, George Baxter, Patrick Moran, Clinton Potter, Bridget Carragher, and Andrew Belmont of the National Center for Supercomputing Applications (NCSA) Biological Imaging Group. It is an IrisGL CAVE application that was presented for the first time at SIGGraph '94. It is used to study complex phenomena such as the human spine, development of a chicken embryo, and star formations.

55. The program allows designers who are not computer specialists to create sketches with the basic elements of line, plane, and rectangular volume. A grid system, color palette, and scaling device are also included on the menu.

56. Bacon, "Bringing Us Back to Our Senses," 113.

57. Karen A. Franck, "When I Enter Virtual Reality, What Body Will I Leave Behind," *Architectural Design* 65 (November–December 1995): 20.

58. In September 1998, COSMOS, the first six-sided version of the CAVE, was built at Gifu Prefectural Science and Technology Promotional Center in Japan. This was followed by the creation of the VR-CUBE at the Center for Parallel Computers, Royal Institute of Technology, in Stockholm, Sweden. This was in turn followed by six-sided environments at the VR-Center in Nord at Aalborg University, Denmark, and the C6 at the Virtual Reality Application Center at Iowa State University. In November 2001 a six-sided immersive virtual reality environment (called ALICE) was completed for the Beckman Institute at the University of Illinois Urbana-Champaign.

59. Geoffrey Scott, *The Architecture of Humanism* (New York: W. W. Norton, 1969), 159.

60. Robert Ousterhout, "Drawing the Line and Knowing the Ropes: On the Origins of Architectural Drawings in the Medieval Mediterranean," Center for Advanced Study, University of Illinois at Urbana-Champaign, 17 October 2000.

61. Marina Panos was a senior architecture student in the first architectural design studio at UIUC taught in the NCSA CAVE during the spring 2001 semester.

62. It is noteworthy that one of the authors teaches architectural design in the CAVE, as well as a seminar in sensory design that examines both scientific studies and their phenomenological implications. Obviously, we see no necessary contradiction.

63. Wilfried Wang, *Herzog and de Meuron*, trans. Katja Steiner, Bruce Almberg, and Ehingen Catherine Schelbert (Basel, Switzerland: Birkhäuser Verlag, 1998), 191.

64. Ibid., 164.

65. Catherine Slessor, "Hanging Gardens," *Architectural Review* 205, no. 1224 (February 1999): 38.

66. James Weirick, "Straight Arrow," *Architecture Australia* 87, no. 5 (September–October 1998): 2. http://pandora.nla.gov.au/nph-arch/2000/S2000-Sep-25/http://www.archmedia.com.au/aa/1998/vol87no5/arrow.htm.

67. James Weirick, "Straight Arrow," 4.

68. "Waikato Bay of Plenty: 2001 NZIA-RESENE Local Awards for Architecture," *New Zealand Architecture,* January–February 2002, 64.

69. Mohsen Mostafavi, "Enriching Identities: The Architecture of Laurie Baker," *a + u* 363 (December 2000): 17.

70. Ibid., 22.

71. Carl G. Jung, *Memories, Dreams, Reflections,* recorded and edited by Aniela Jaffe, trans. Richard and Clara Winston (1961; New York: Vintage Books, 1973), 223.

72. Lewis Carroll, *Alice in Wonderland* (1865; New York: Book-of-the-Month Club, 1994), 85.

Permissions

Lines from "Rooms," by Charlotte Mew, are from Charlotte Mew, *Collected Poems and Selected Prose,* edited by Val Warner (Manchester: Carcanet Books, 1981). Reprinted with permission from Carcanet Press Limited, United Kingdom.

Selections from "The Door in the Wall," by H. G. Wells, are from H. G. Wells, *"The Door in the Wall" and Other Stories* (Boston: David R. Godine, 1996). Copyright 1911, 1939 by H. G. Wells. Reprinted by permission of David R. Godine, Publisher.

Lines from poetry by Tiberianus are from *Minor Latin Poets, Volume II,* Loeb Classical Library L434, translated by J. W. Duff and A. M. Duff (Cambridge: Harvard University Press, 1954 [1934]). Reprinted by permission of the publishers and the Trustees of the Loeb Classical Library. The Loeb Classical Library is a registered trademark of the President and Fellows of Harvard College.

Lines from "A Phantom: The Perfume," by Charles Baudelaire, are from Charles Baudelaire, *The Flowers of Evil,* translated by Lewis Piaget Shanks (New York: Henry Holt and Co., 1926). Reprinted by permission of Henry Holt and Co., LLC.

Quotations from "The Road Goes Ever On and On" and "Still round the Corner" from *The Fellowship of the Ring,* by J. R. R. Tolkien. Copyright 1954, 1965, 1966 by J. R. R. Tolkien. Copyright renewed 1982 by Christopher R. Tolkien, Michael H. R. Tolkien, John F. R. Tolkien, and Priscilla M. A. R. Tolkien. Copyright renewed 1993, 1994 by Christopher R. Tolkien, John F. R. Tolkien, and Priscilla M. A. R. Tolkien. Reprinted by permission of Houghton Mifflin Company. All rights reserved.

Index

Abram, David, 24, 25
absolute space vs. object space, 122–23
abstraction in the arts: embrace of, 31–32
acoustics, 143–44; designing acoustic environments, 140, 270–72
Acropolis, Athenian, 199–200
active touch, 144–46
Adams, Henry, 200
Adena peoples: largest ritual object of, 93–94, 95, 306n.43
aerial sonography, 269
aesthetic response, 26; as sign of environment favorable to effective human functioning, 97
aesthetics: common desire for aesthetic expression, 294n.55; formal, x
affordances: notion of, 98–99, 100, 236
Albers, Josef, 28
Alberti, Leon Battista, 159
Alden, Richard S., 165
Alexander, Christopher, 25
ALICE, 331n.58
Allen, Gerald, 60–61, 68, 77, 187
Alpine Architecture (Taut), 200
Alsayyad, Nezar, 72
Alschuler, Rose H., 220
Amba (Turrell), 209, Plate 6
Ambasz, Emilio, 94, Plate 2

ambient odors, 133–34
ambient sound levels, 142, 314n.73
American garden design, 92–94, 95
American Institute of Architects, 37
Amesbury Abbey, 156, 157
Anderton, Frances, 217
Ando, Tadao, 214–16, 256, 258
Andresen, Brit, 231–33
Animate Form (Lynn), 276
animism, 319n.7; critical, 180, 229
anomie: state of, 263
anthropology of the senses, 53–55
Antigone (Sophocles), 83–84
Anton, Saul, 242
anxiety, navigation, 128
Apollo: temple of, 80
Appleton, 100
archetypal form, 287
archetype: biological foundation of, 13; primordial, 12–14; type as symbolic form of, 14–15
architect: engineer's role entwined with, 294n.46
Architect's Small House Bureau, 37
architectural classification by type, ix–x; earliest forms of, 8–9; general meaning of architectural types, 5–6
architectural color, 224–27

Joy Monice Malnar, AIA, is associate professor of architecture at the University of Illinois at Urbana-Champaign. She has been a faculty fellow of the National Center for Supercomputing/University of Illinois at Urbana-Champaign, engaging in collaborative research with CAVE technology. She has participated in conferences on sensory design in Singapore, Sydney, and Seoul, and, with Frank Vodvarka, she coauthored *The Interior Dimension: A Theoretical Approach to Enclosed Space.*

Frank Vodvarka is associate professor of fine arts at Loyola University Chicago, where he teaches design, color theory, photography, and the history of architecture. He coauthored *The Interior Dimension: A Theoretical Approach to Enclosed Space* with Joy Monice Malnar. His exhibition record includes more than twenty-five shows of drawings, photographs, and constructions, and he is currently represented by the Fine Arts Building Gallery in Chicago.